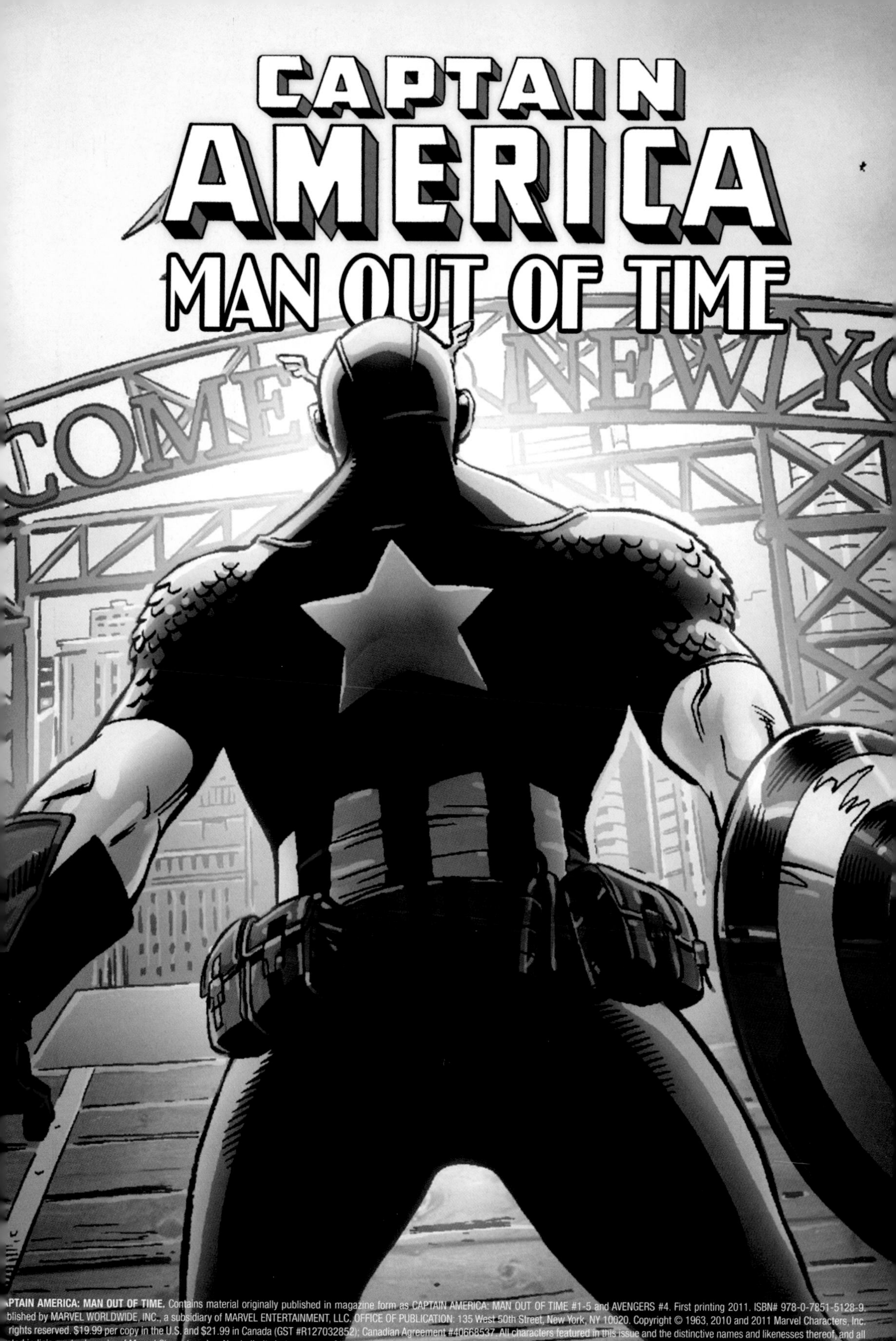

CAPTAIN AMERICA
MAN OUT OF TIME

APTAIN AMERICA: MAN OUT OF TIME. Contains material originally published in magazine form as CAPTAIN AMERICA: MAN OUT OF TIME #1-5 and AVENGERS #4. First printing 2011. ISBN# 978-0-7851-5128-9.
blished by MARVEL WORLDWIDE, INC., a subsidiary of MARVEL ENTERTAINMENT, LLC. OFFICE OF PUBLICATION: 135 West 50th Street, New York, NY 10020. Copyright © 1963, 2010 and 2011 Marvel Characters, Inc.
 rights reserved. $19.99 per copy in the U.S. and $21.99 in Canada (GST #R127032852); Canadian Agreement #40668537. All characters featured in this issue and the distinctive names and likenesses thereof, and all
ated indicia are trademarks of Marvel Characters, Inc. No similarity between any of the names, characters, persons, and/or institutions in this magazine with those of any living or dead person or institution is intended,
d any such similarity which may exist is purely coincidental. **Printed in the U.S.A.** ALAN FINE, EVP - Office of the President, Marvel Worldwide, Inc. and EVP & CMO Marvel Characters B.V.; DAN BUCKLEY, Publisher &
esident - Print, Animation & Digital Divisions; JOE QUESADA, Chief Creative Officer; JIM SOKOLOWSKI, Chief Operating Officer; DAVID BOGART, SVP of Business Affairs & Talent Management; TOM BREVOORT, SVP of
blishing; C.B. CEBULSKI, SVP of Creator & Content Development; DAVID GABRIEL, SVP of Publishing Sales & Circulation; MICHAEL PASCIULLO, SVP of Brand Planning & Communications; JIM O'KEEFE, VP of Operations
 ogistics; DAN CARR, Executive Director of Publishing Technology; JUSTIN F. GABRIE, Director of Publishing & Editorial Operations; SUSAN CRESPI, Editorial Operations Manager; ALEX MORALES, Publishing Operations
 nager; STAN LEE, Chairman Emeritus. For information regarding advertising in Marvel Comics or on Marvel.com, please contact John Dokes, SVP Integrated Sales and Marketing, at jdokes@marvel.com. For Marvel
scription inquiries, please call 800-217-9158. **Manufactured between 4/11/2011 and 5/9/2011 by R.R. DONNELLEY, INC., SALEM, VA, USA.**

987654321

CAPTAIN AMERICA
MAN OUT OF TIME

Writer: **MARK WAID**

Pencils & Breakdowns: **JORGE MOLINA**

Inks & Finishes: **KARL KESEL** with **SCOTT HANNA** (Issue #3)

Colorist: **FRANK D'ARMATA**

Letterer: **VC'S JOE SABINO**

Cover Art: **BRYAN HITCH, PAUL NEARY & PAUL MOUNTS**

Associate Editor: **LAUREN SANKOVITCH**

Editor: **TOM BREVOORT**

CAPTAIN AMERICA CREATED BY
JOE SIMON & JACK KIRBY

Collection Editor: **JEFF YOUNGQUIST**

Editorial Assistants: **JAMES EMMETT & JOE HOCHSTEIN**

Assistant Editors: **ALEX STARBUCK & NELSON RIBEIRO**

Editors, Special Projects: **JENNIFER GRÜNWALD & MARK D. BEAZLEY**

Senior Vice President of Sales: **DAVID GABRIEL**

SVP of Brand Planning & Communications: **MICHAEL PASCIULLO**

Design: **SPRING HOTELING**

Editor in Chief: **AXEL ALONSO**

Chief Creative Officer: **JOE QUESADA**

Publisher: **DAN BUCKLEY**

Executive Producer: **ALAN FINE**

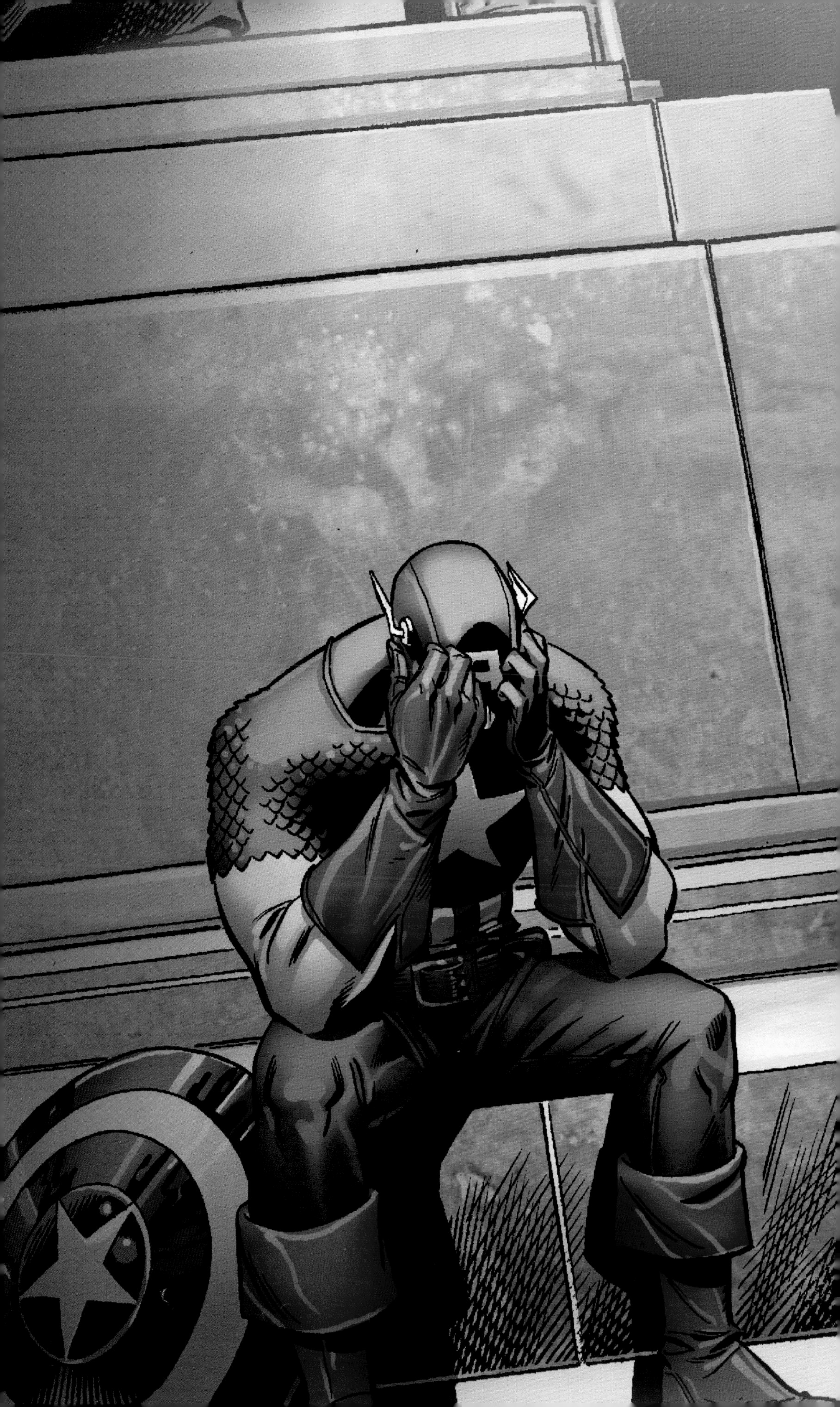

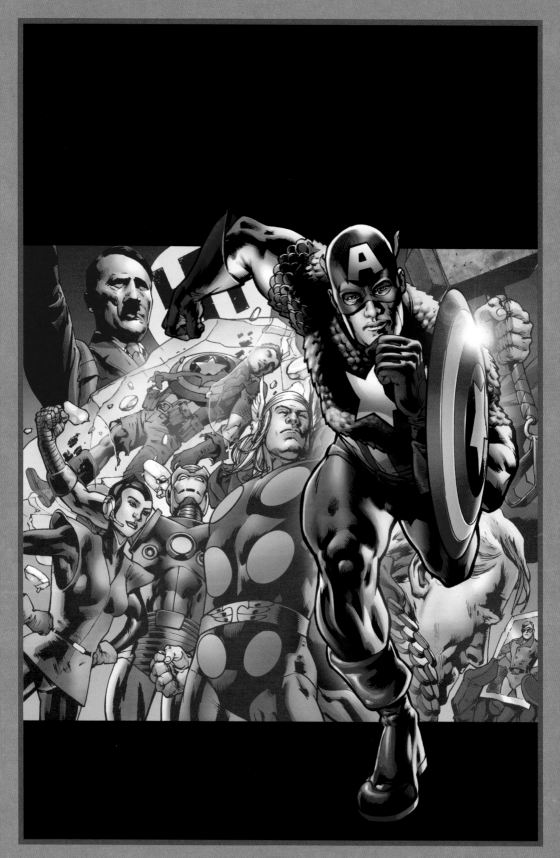

[1]

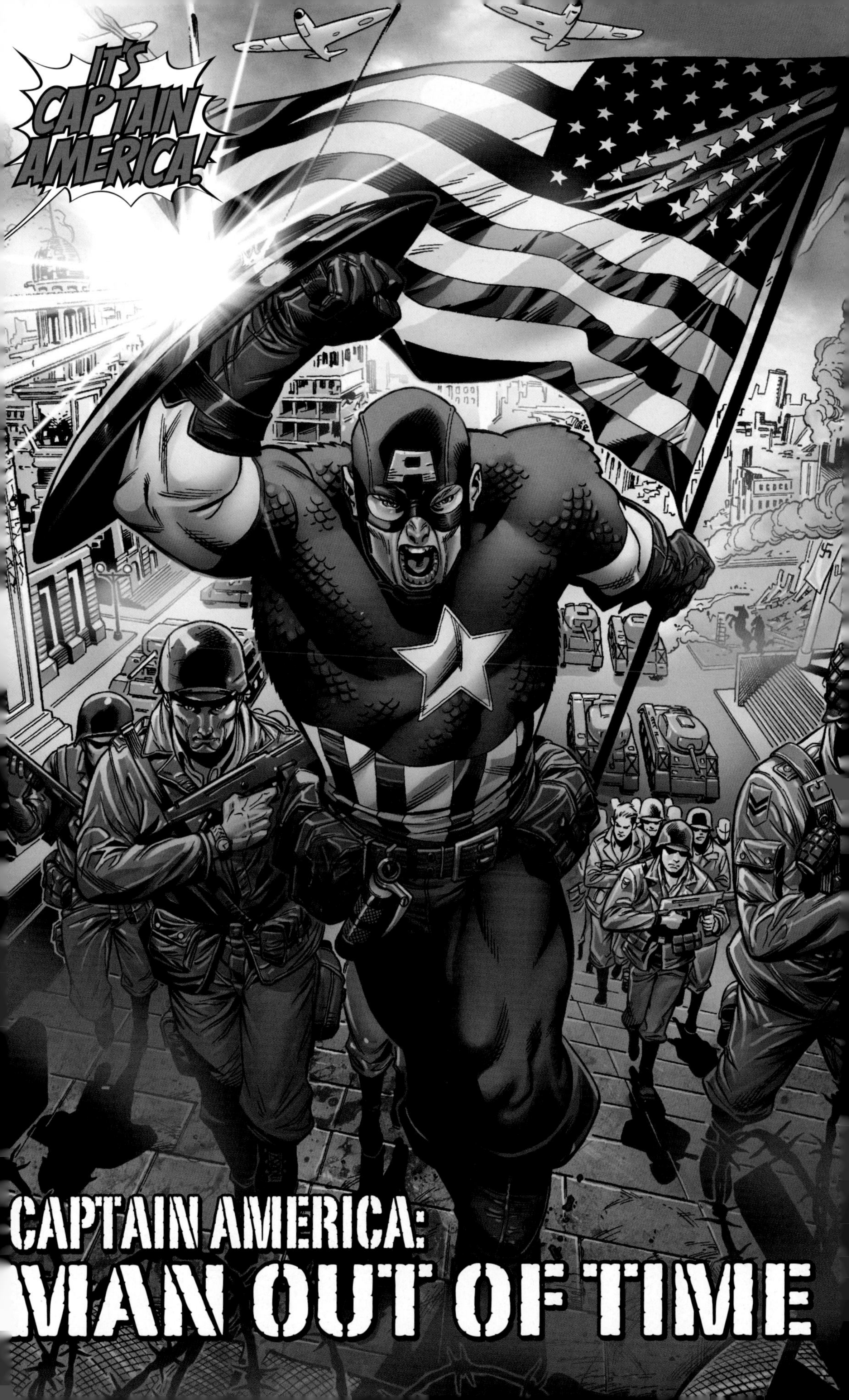
IT'S CAPTAIN AMERICA!
CAPTAIN AMERICA:
MAN OUT OF TIME

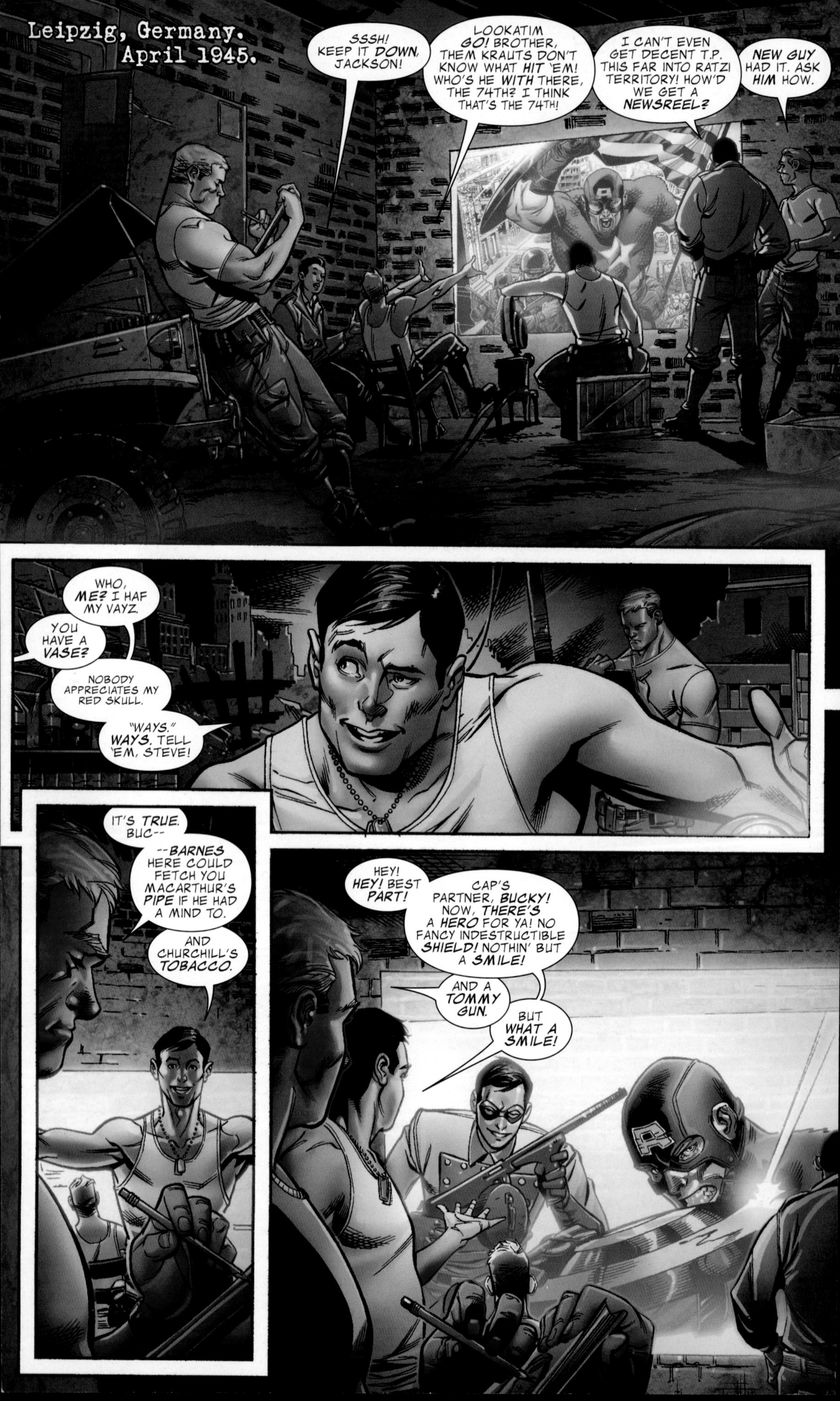

Leipzig, Germany. April 1945.
SSSH! KEEP IT DOWN, JACKSON!
LOOKATIM GO! BROTHER, THEM KRAUTS DON'T KNOW WHAT HIT 'EM! WHO'S HE WITH THERE, THE 74TH? I THINK THAT'S THE 74TH!
I CAN'T EVEN GET DECENT T.P. THIS FAR INTO RATZI TERRITORY! HOW'D WE GET A NEWSREEL?
NEW GUY HAD IT. ASK HIM HOW.
WHO, ME? I HAF MY VAYZ.
YOU HAVE A VASE?
NOBODY APPRECIATES MY RED SKULL.
"WAYS." WAYS. TELL 'EM, STEVE!
IT'S TRUE. BUC--
--BARNES HERE COULD FETCH YOU MACARTHUR'S PIPE IF HE HAD A MIND TO.
AND CHURCHILL'S TOBACCO.
HEY! HEY! BEST PART!
CAP'S PARTNER, BUCKY! NOW, THERE'S A HERO FOR YA! NO FANCY INDESTRUCTIBLE SHIELD! NOTHIN' BUT A SMILE!
AND A TOMMY GUN.
BUT WHAT A SMILE!

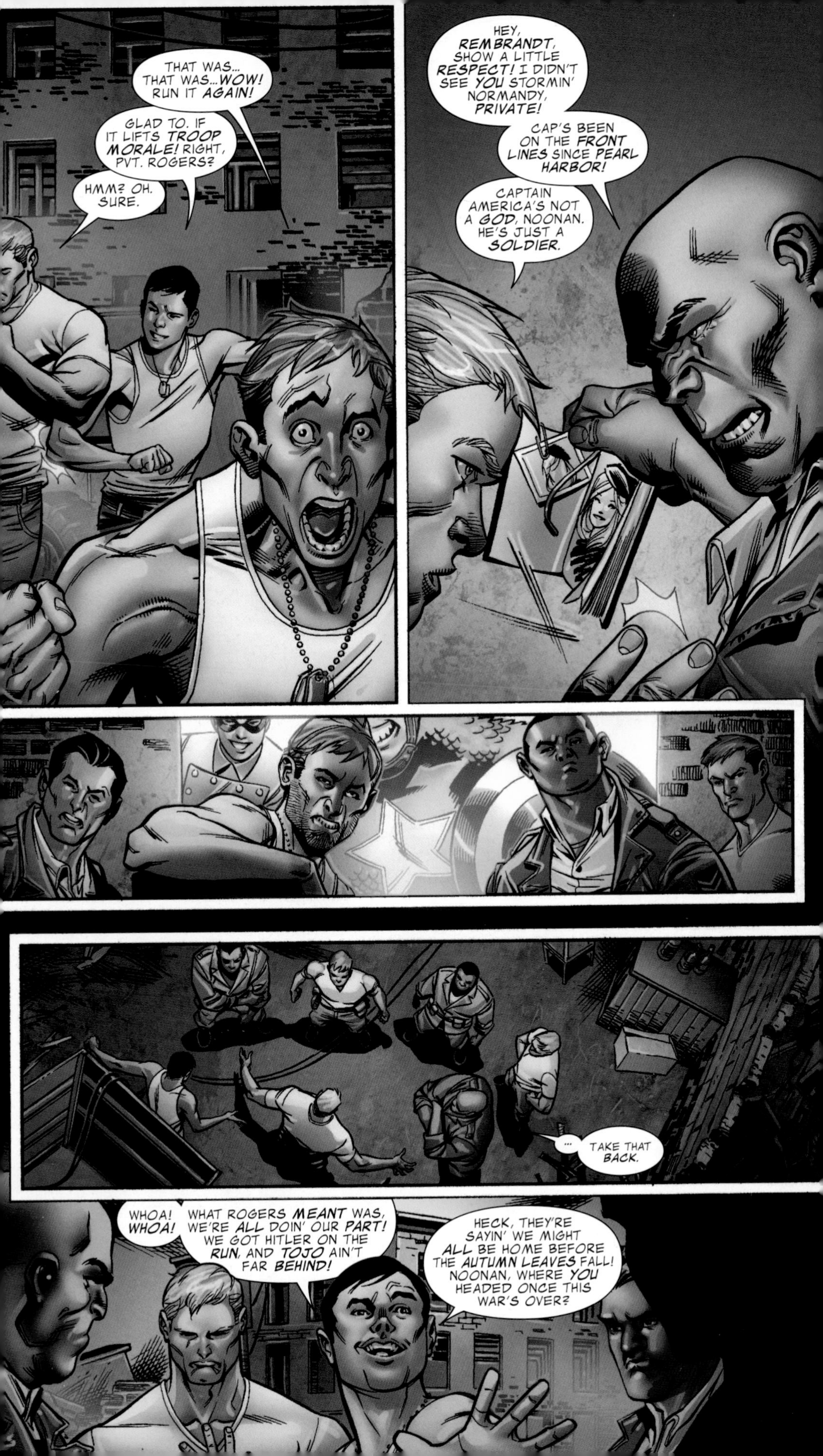

THAT WAS... THAT WAS...WOW! RUN IT AGAIN!
GLAD TO. IF IT LIFTS TROOP MORALE! RIGHT, PVT. ROGERS?
HMM? OH. SURE.
HEY, REMBRANDT, SHOW A LITTLE RESPECT! I DIDN'T SEE YOU STORMIN' NORMANDY, PRIVATE!
CAP'S BEEN ON THE FRONT LINES SINCE PEARL HARBOR!
CAPTAIN AMERICA'S NOT A GOD, NOONAN. HE'S JUST A SOLDIER.
...
TAKE THAT BACK.
WHOA! WHOA!
WHAT ROGERS MEANT WAS, WE'RE ALL DOIN' OUR PART! WE GOT HITLER ON THE RUN, AND TOJO AIN'T FAR BEHIND!
HECK, THEY'RE SAYIN' WE MIGHT ALL BE HOME BEFORE THE AUTUMN LEAVES FALL! NOONAN, WHERE YOU HEADED ONCE THIS WAR'S OVER?

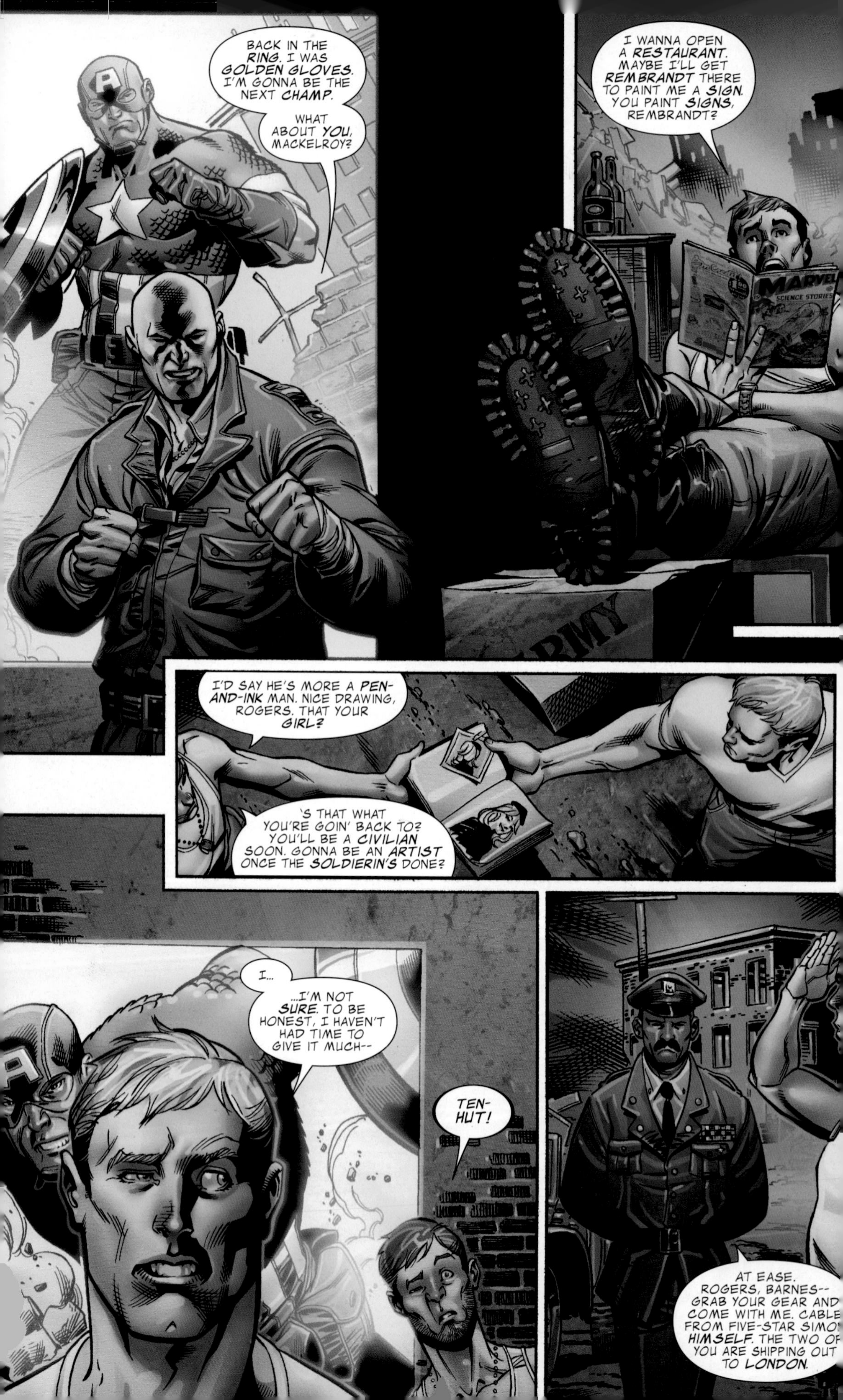
BACK IN THE RING. I WAS GOLDEN GLOVES. I'M GONNA BE THE NEXT CHAMP.
WHAT ABOUT YOU, MACKELROY?
I WANNA OPEN A RESTAURANT. MAYBE I'LL GET REMBRANDT THERE TO PAINT ME A SIGN. YOU PAINT SIGNS, REMBRANDT?
MARVEL SCIENCE STORIES
ARMY
I'D SAY HE'S MORE A PEN-AND-INK MAN. NICE DRAWING, ROGERS. THAT YOUR GIRL?
'S THAT WHAT YOU'RE GOIN' BACK TO? YOU'LL BE A CIVILIAN SOON. GONNA BE AN ARTIST ONCE THE SOLDIERIN'S DONE?
I...
...I'M NOT SURE. TO BE HONEST, I HAVEN'T HAD TIME TO GIVE IT MUCH--
TEN-HUT!
AT EASE. ROGERS, BARNES--GRAB YOUR GEAR AND COME WITH ME. CABLE FROM FIVE-STAR SIMO HIMSELF. THE TWO OF YOU ARE SHIPPING OUT TO LONDON.

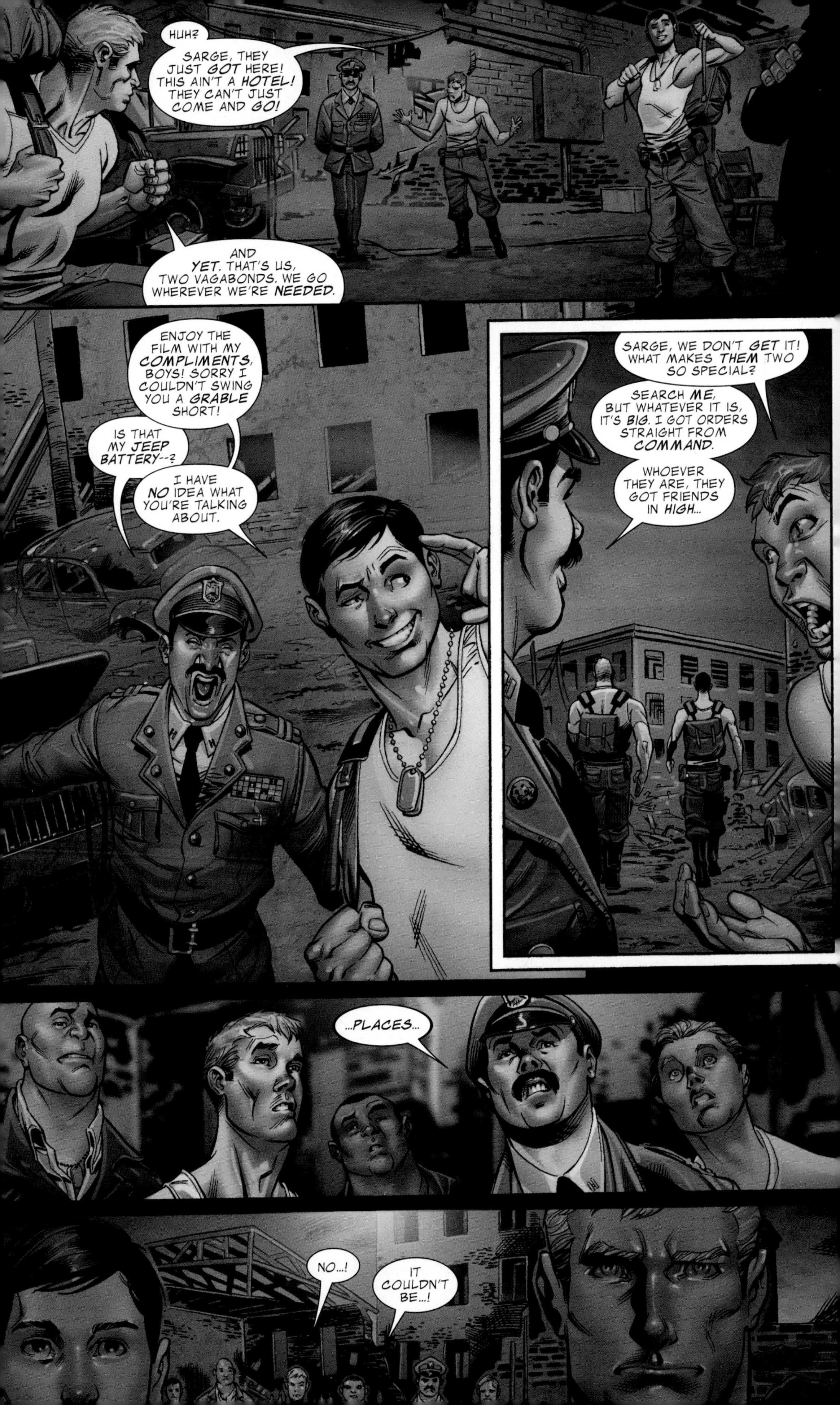
HUH?
SARGE, THEY JUST GOT HERE! THIS AIN'T A HOTEL! THEY CAN'T JUST COME AND GO!
AND YET. THAT'S US, TWO VAGABONDS. WE GO WHEREVER WE'RE NEEDED.
ENJOY THE FILM WITH MY COMPLIMENTS, BOYS! SORRY I COULDN'T SWING YOU A GRABLE SHORT!
IS THAT MY JEEP BATTERY--?
I HAVE NO IDEA WHAT YOU'RE TALKING ABOUT.
SARGE, WE DON'T GET IT! WHAT MAKES THEM TWO SO SPECIAL?
SEARCH ME, BUT WHATEVER IT IS, IT'S BIG. I GOT ORDERS STRAIGHT FROM COMMAND.
WHOEVER THEY ARE, THEY GOT FRIENDS IN HIGH...
...PLACES...
NO...!
IT COULDN'T BE...!

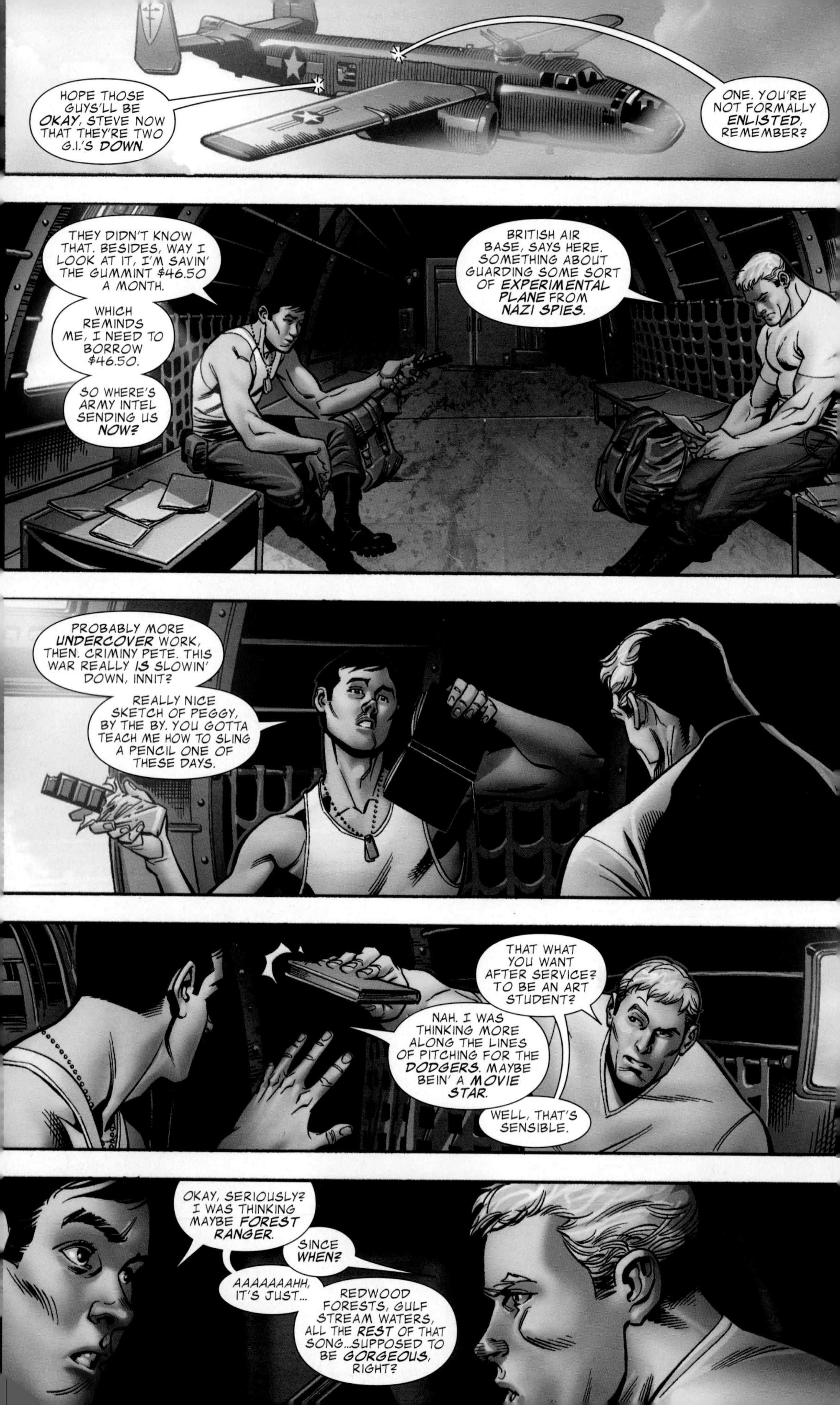
HOPE THOSE GUYS'LL BE OKAY, STEVE NOW THAT THEY'RE TWO G.I.'S DOWN.
ONE. YOU'RE NOT FORMALLY ENLISTED, REMEMBER?
THEY DIDN'T KNOW THAT. BESIDES, WAY I LOOK AT IT, I'M SAVIN' THE GUMMINT $46.50 A MONTH.
WHICH REMINDS ME, I NEED TO BORROW $46.50.
SO WHERE'S ARMY INTEL SENDING US NOW?
BRITISH AIR BASE, SAYS HERE. SOMETHING ABOUT GUARDING SOME SORT OF EXPERIMENTAL PLANE FROM NAZI SPIES.
PROBABLY MORE UNDERCOVER WORK, THEN. CRIMINY PETE. THIS WAR REALLY IS SLOWIN' DOWN, INNIT?
REALLY NICE SKETCH OF PEGGY, BY THE BY. YOU GOTTA TEACH ME HOW TO SLING A PENCIL ONE OF THESE DAYS.
THAT WHAT YOU WANT AFTER SERVICE? TO BE AN ART STUDENT?
NAH. I WAS THINKING MORE ALONG THE LINES OF PITCHING FOR THE DODGERS. MAYBE BEIN' A MOVIE STAR.
WELL, THAT'S SENSIBLE.
OKAY, SERIOUSLY? I WAS THINKING MAYBE FOREST RANGER.
SINCE WHEN?
AAAAAAAHH, IT'S JUST...
REDWOOD FORESTS, GULF STREAM WATERS, ALL THE REST OF THAT SONG...SUPPOSED TO BE GORGEOUS, RIGHT?

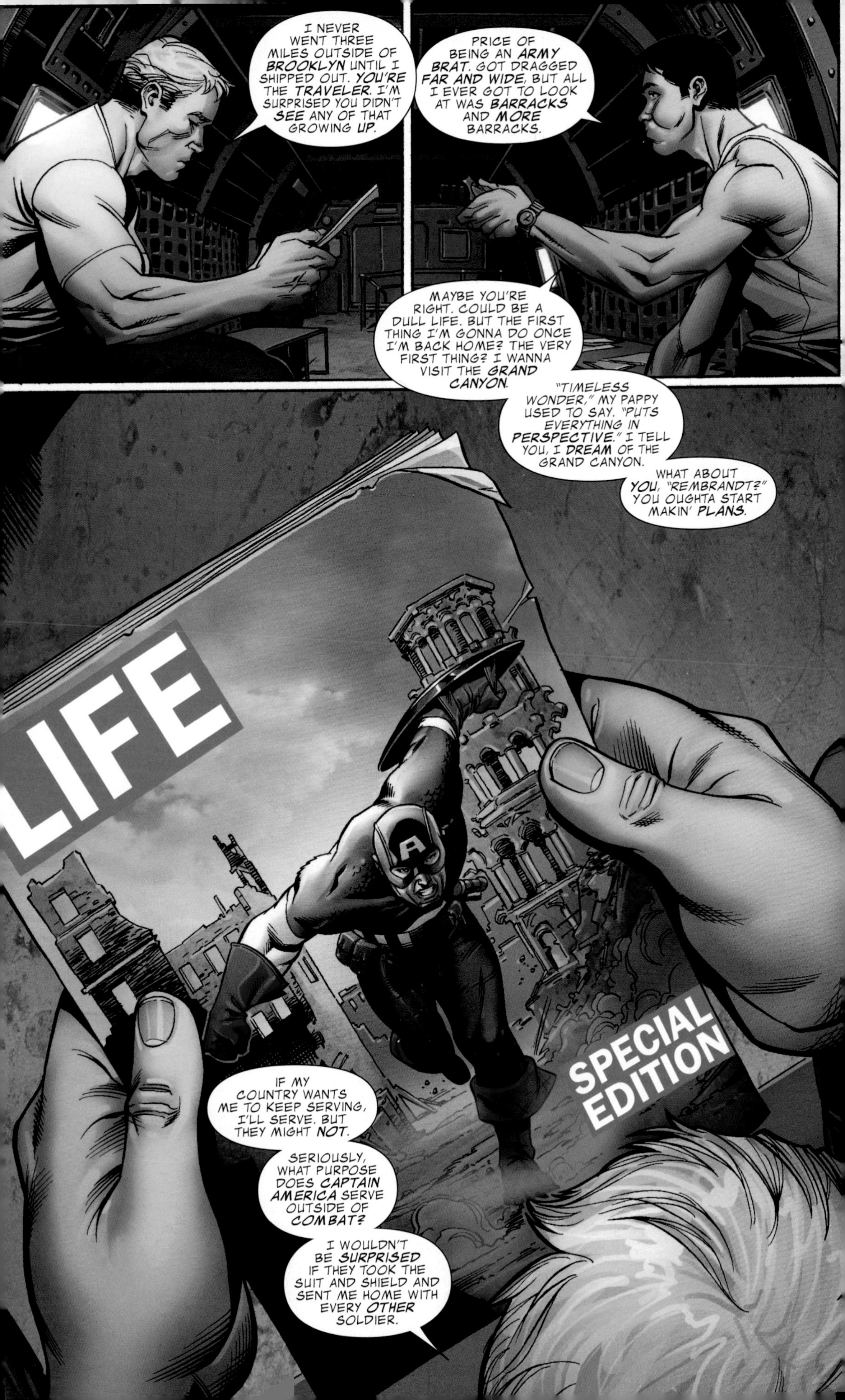
I NEVER WENT THREE MILES OUTSIDE OF BROOKLYN UNTIL I SHIPPED OUT. YOU'RE THE TRAVELER. I'M SURPRISED YOU DIDN'T SEE ANY OF THAT GROWING UP.
PRICE OF BEING AN ARMY BRAT. GOT DRAGGED FAR AND WIDE, BUT ALL I EVER GOT TO LOOK AT WAS BARRACKS AND MORE BARRACKS.
MAYBE YOU'RE RIGHT. COULD BE A DULL LIFE. BUT THE FIRST THING I'M GONNA DO ONCE I'M BACK HOME? THE VERY FIRST THING? I WANNA VISIT THE GRAND CANYON.
"TIMELESS WONDER," MY PAPPY USED TO SAY. "PUTS EVERYTHING IN PERSPECTIVE." I TELL YOU, I DREAM OF THE GRAND CANYON.
WHAT ABOUT YOU, "REMBRANDT?" YOU OUGHTA START MAKIN' PLANS.
LIFE
SPECIAL EDITION
IF MY COUNTRY WANTS ME TO KEEP SERVING, I'LL SERVE. BUT THEY MIGHT NOT.
SERIOUSLY, WHAT PURPOSE DOES CAPTAIN AMERICA SERVE OUTSIDE OF COMBAT?
I WOULDN'T BE SURPRISED IF THEY TOOK THE SUIT AND SHIELD AND SENT ME HOME WITH EVERY OTHER SOLDIER.

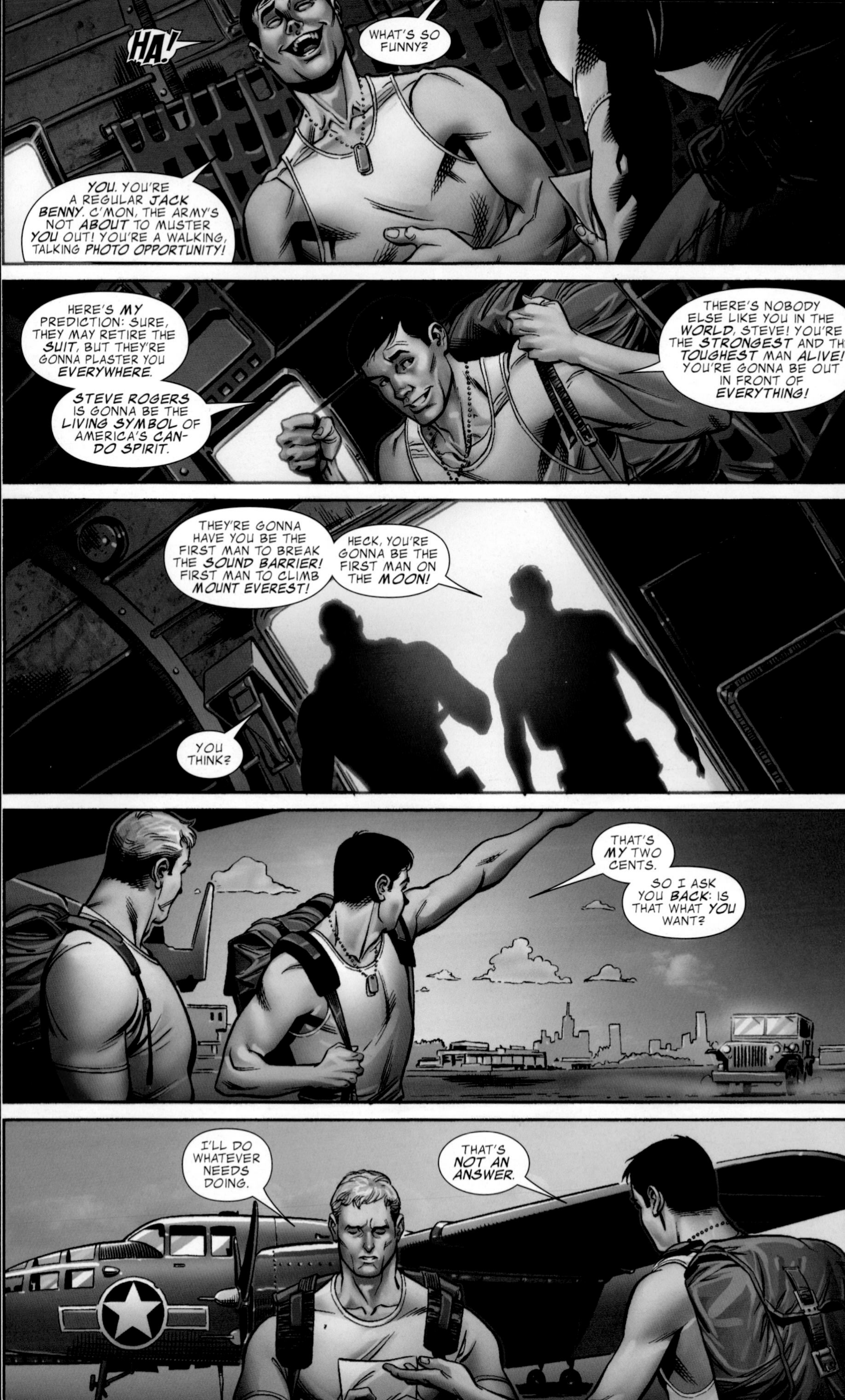
HA!
WHAT'S SO FUNNY?
YOU. YOU'RE A REGULAR JACK BENNY. C'MON, THE ARMY'S NOT ABOUT TO MUSTER YOU OUT! YOU'RE A WALKING, TALKING PHOTO OPPORTUNITY!
HERE'S MY PREDICTION: SURE, THEY MAY RETIRE THE SUIT, BUT THEY'RE GONNA PLASTER YOU EVERYWHERE.
STEVE ROGERS IS GONNA BE THE LIVING SYMBOL OF AMERICA'S CAN-DO SPIRIT.
THERE'S NOBODY ELSE LIKE YOU IN THE WORLD, STEVE! YOU'RE THE STRONGEST AND THE TOUGHEST MAN ALIVE! YOU'RE GONNA BE OUT IN FRONT OF EVERYTHING!
THEY'RE GONNA HAVE YOU BE THE FIRST MAN TO BREAK THE SOUND BARRIER! FIRST MAN TO CLIMB MOUNT EVEREST!
HECK, YOU'RE GONNA BE THE FIRST MAN ON THE MOON!
YOU THINK?
THAT'S MY TWO CENTS.
SO I ASK YOU BACK: IS THAT WHAT YOU WANT?
I'LL DO WHATEVER NEEDS DOING.
THAT'S NOT AN ANSWER.

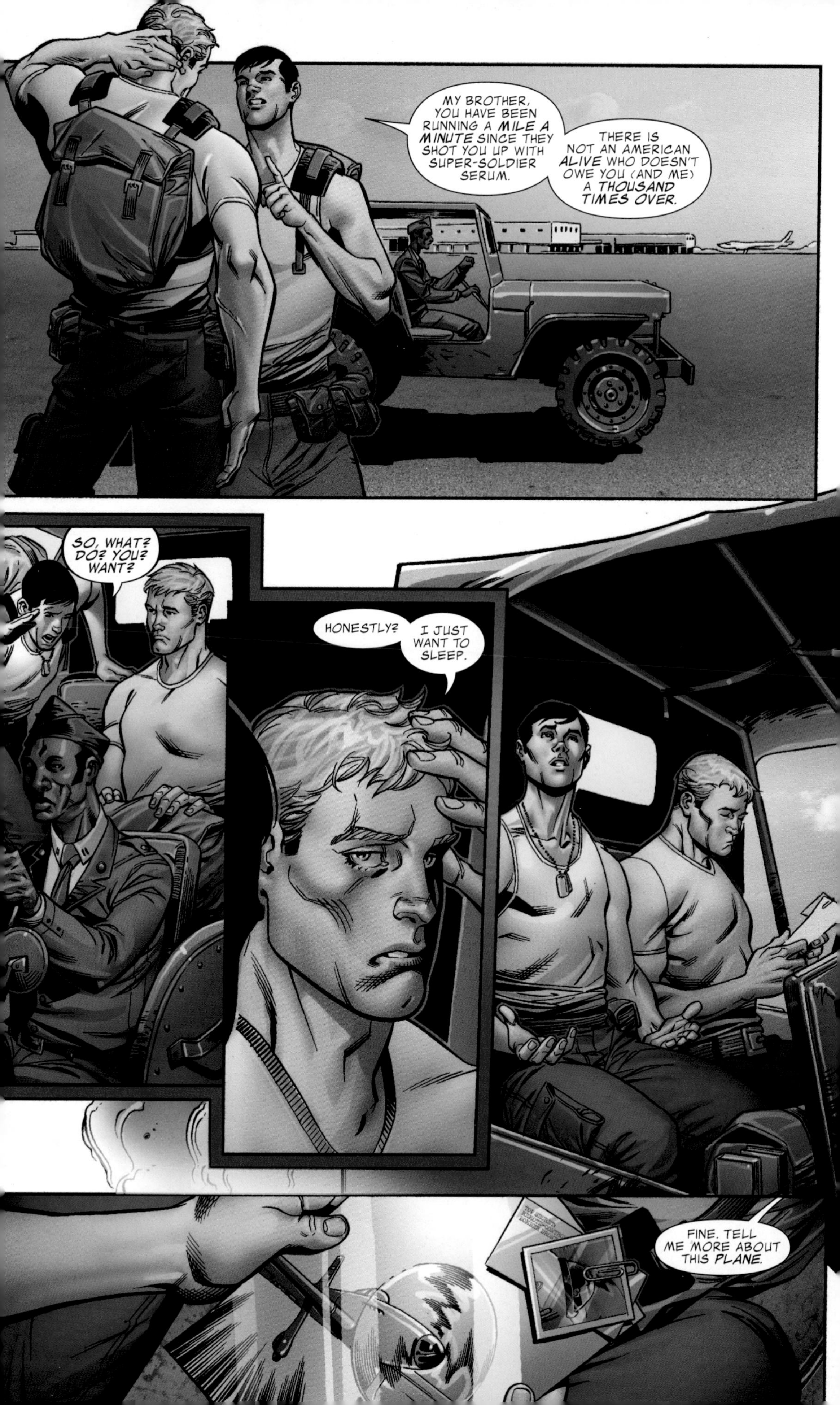
MY BROTHER, YOU HAVE BEEN RUNNING A MILE A MINUTE SINCE THEY SHOT YOU UP WITH SUPER-SOLDIER SERUM.
THERE IS NOT AN AMERICAN ALIVE WHO DOESN'T OWE YOU (AND ME) A THOUSAND TIMES OVER.
SO, WHAT? DO? YOU? WANT?
HONESTLY?
I JUST WANT TO SLEEP.
FINE. TELL ME MORE ABOUT THIS PLANE.

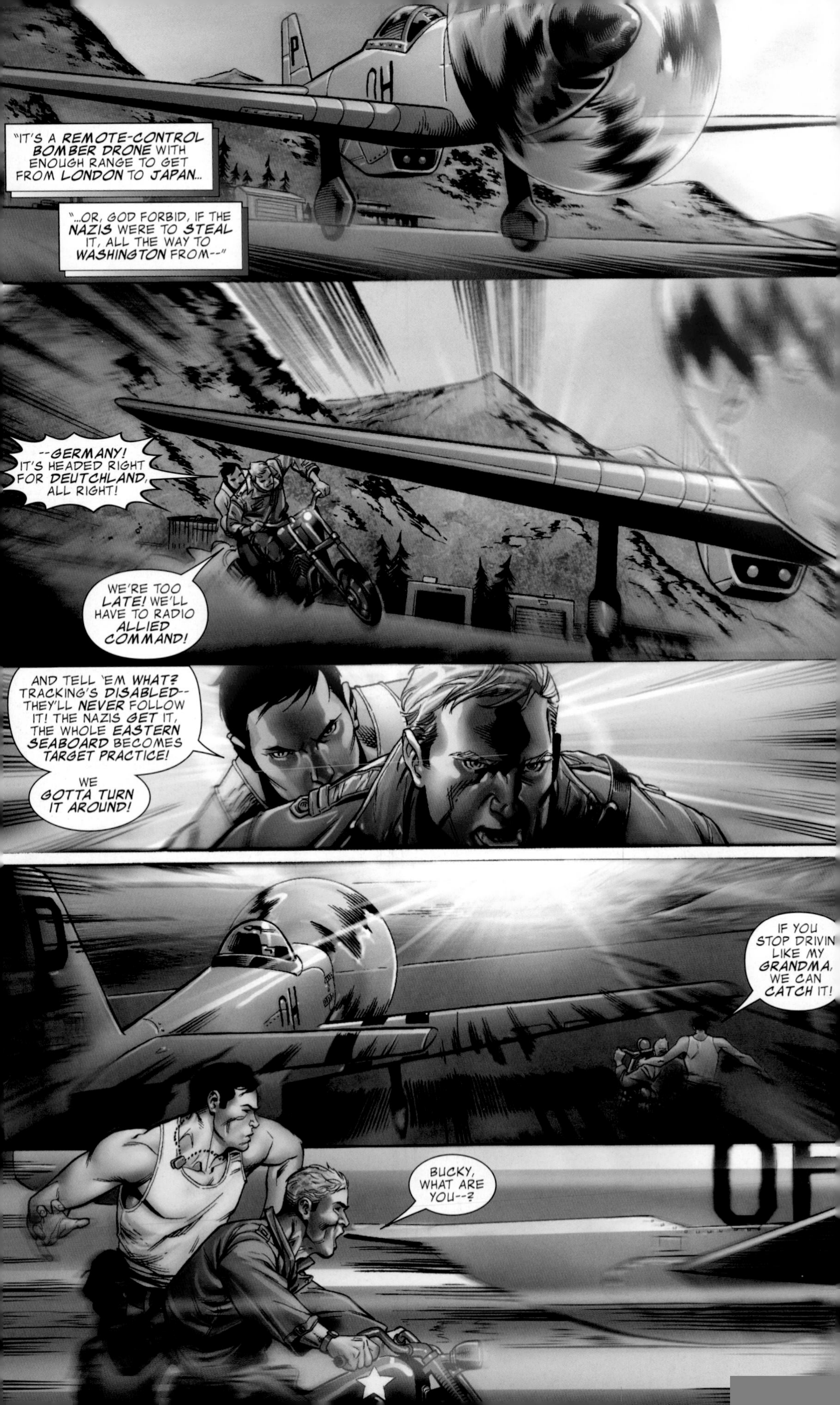
"IT'S A REMOTE-CONTROL BOMBER DRONE WITH ENOUGH RANGE TO GET FROM LONDON TO JAPAN...
"...OR, GOD FORBID, IF THE NAZIS WERE TO STEAL IT, ALL THE WAY TO WASHINGTON FROM--"
--GERMANY! IT'S HEADED RIGHT FOR DEUTCHLAND, ALL RIGHT!
WE'RE TOO LATE! WE'LL HAVE TO RADIO ALLIED COMMAND!
AND TELL 'EM WHAT? TRACKING'S DISABLED-- THEY'LL NEVER FOLLOW IT! THE NAZIS GET IT, THE WHOLE EASTERN SEABOARD BECOMES TARGET PRACTICE!
WE GOTTA TURN IT AROUND!
IF YOU STOP DRIVIN' LIKE MY GRANDMA, WE CAN CATCH IT!
BUCKY, WHAT ARE YOU--?

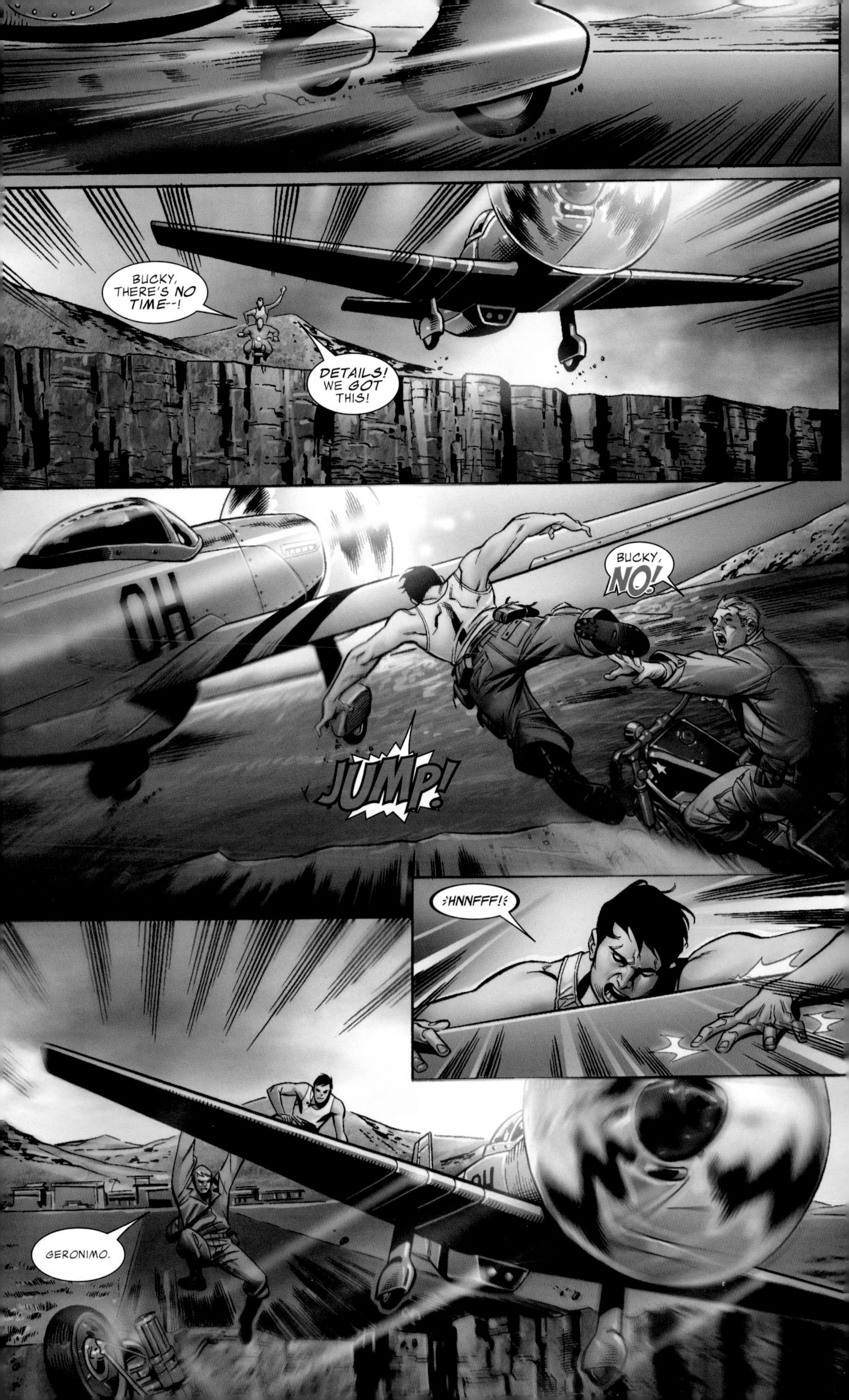
BUCKY, THERE'S NO TIME--!
DETAILS! WE GOT THIS!
BUCKY, NO!
JUMP!
HNNFFF!
GERONIMO.

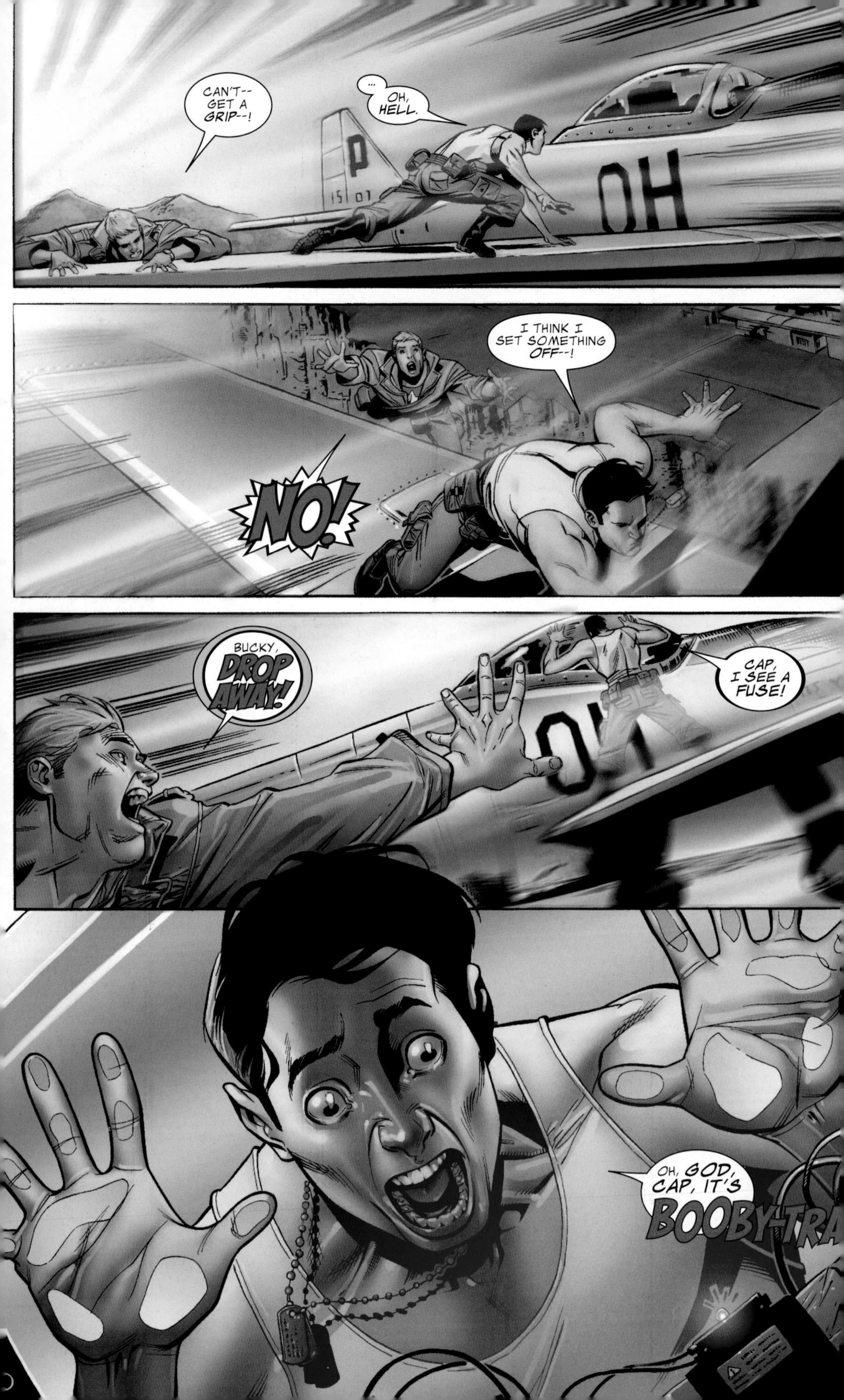
CAN'T-- GET A GRIP--!
... OH, HELL.
P
15 07
OH
I THINK I SET SOMETHING OFF--!
NO!
BUCKY, DROP AWAY!
CAP, I SEE A FUSE!
OH, GOD, CAP, IT'S BOOBY-TRA

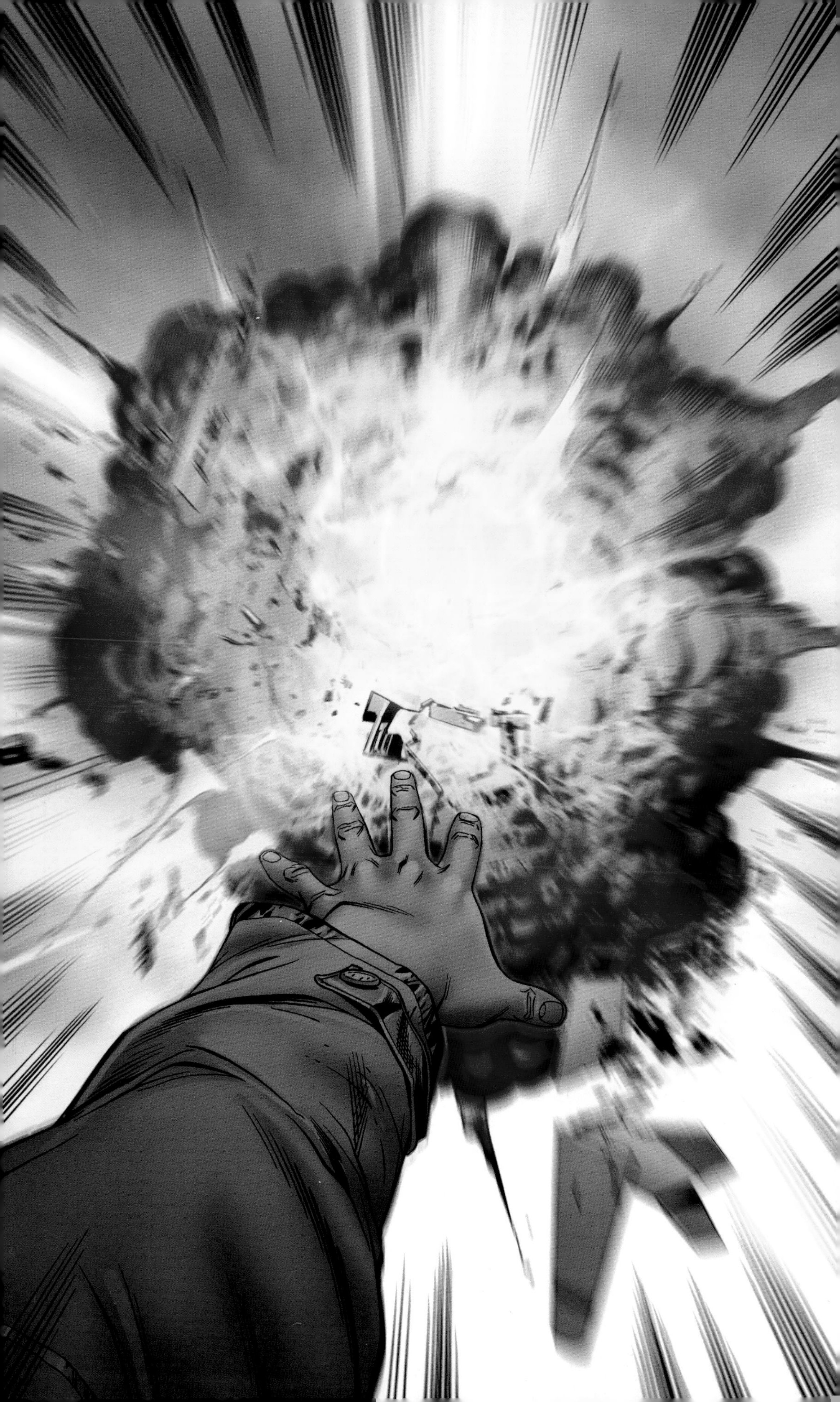

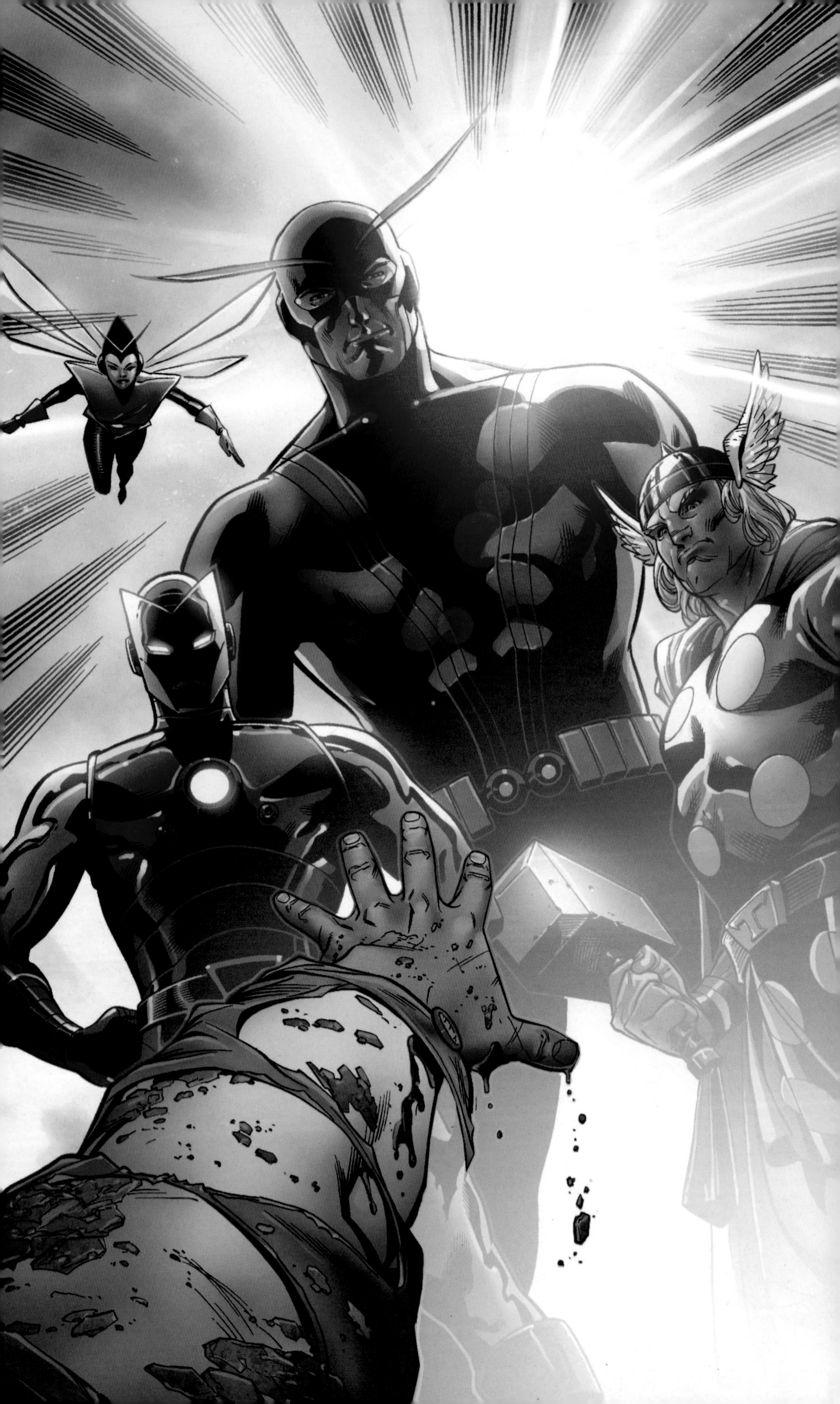

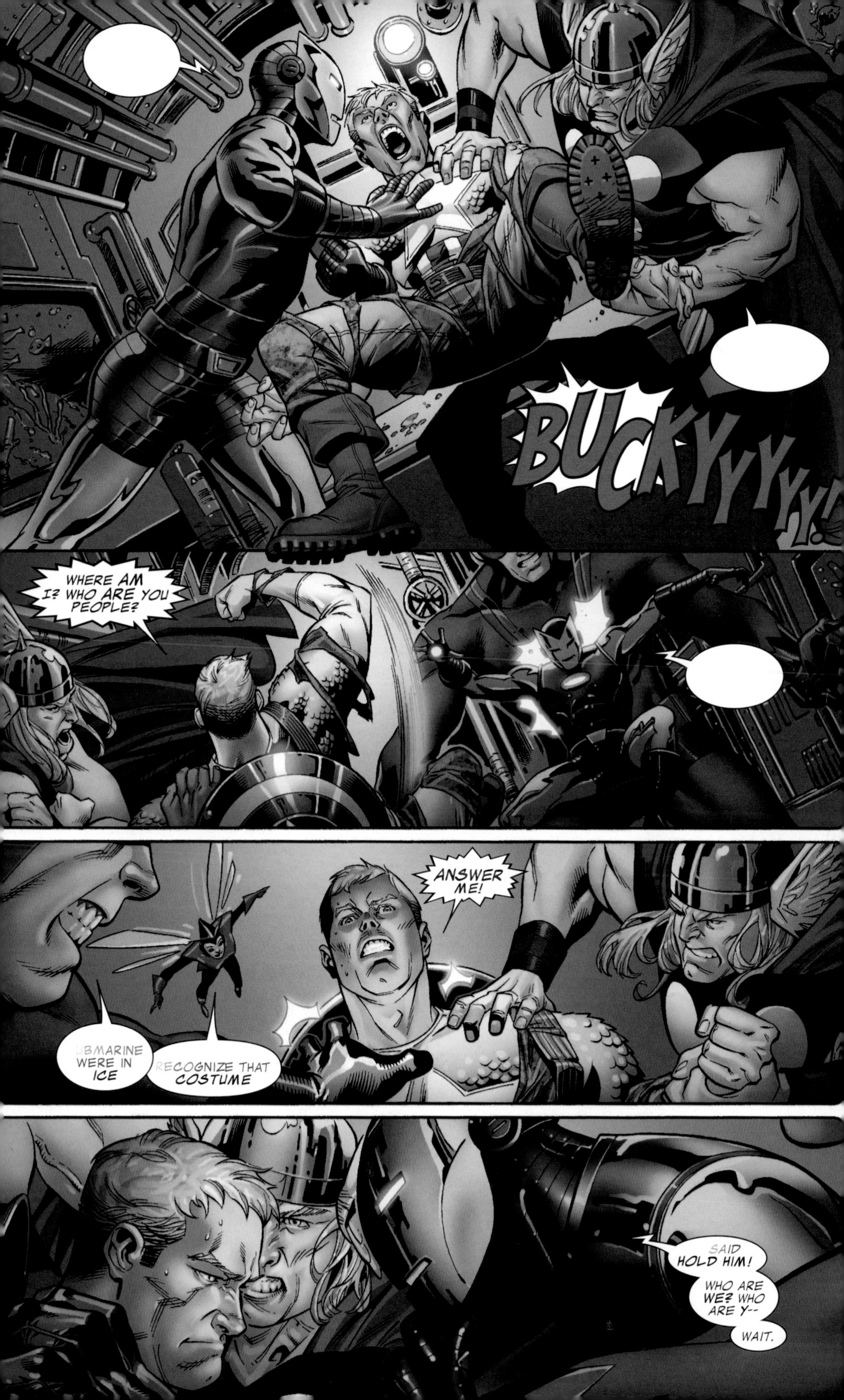
BUCKYYYYY!
WHERE AM I? WHO ARE YOU PEOPLE?
ANSWER ME!
UBMARINE WERE IN ICE
RECOGNIZE THAT COSTUME
SAID HOLD HIM!
WHO ARE WE? WHO ARE Y--
WAIT.

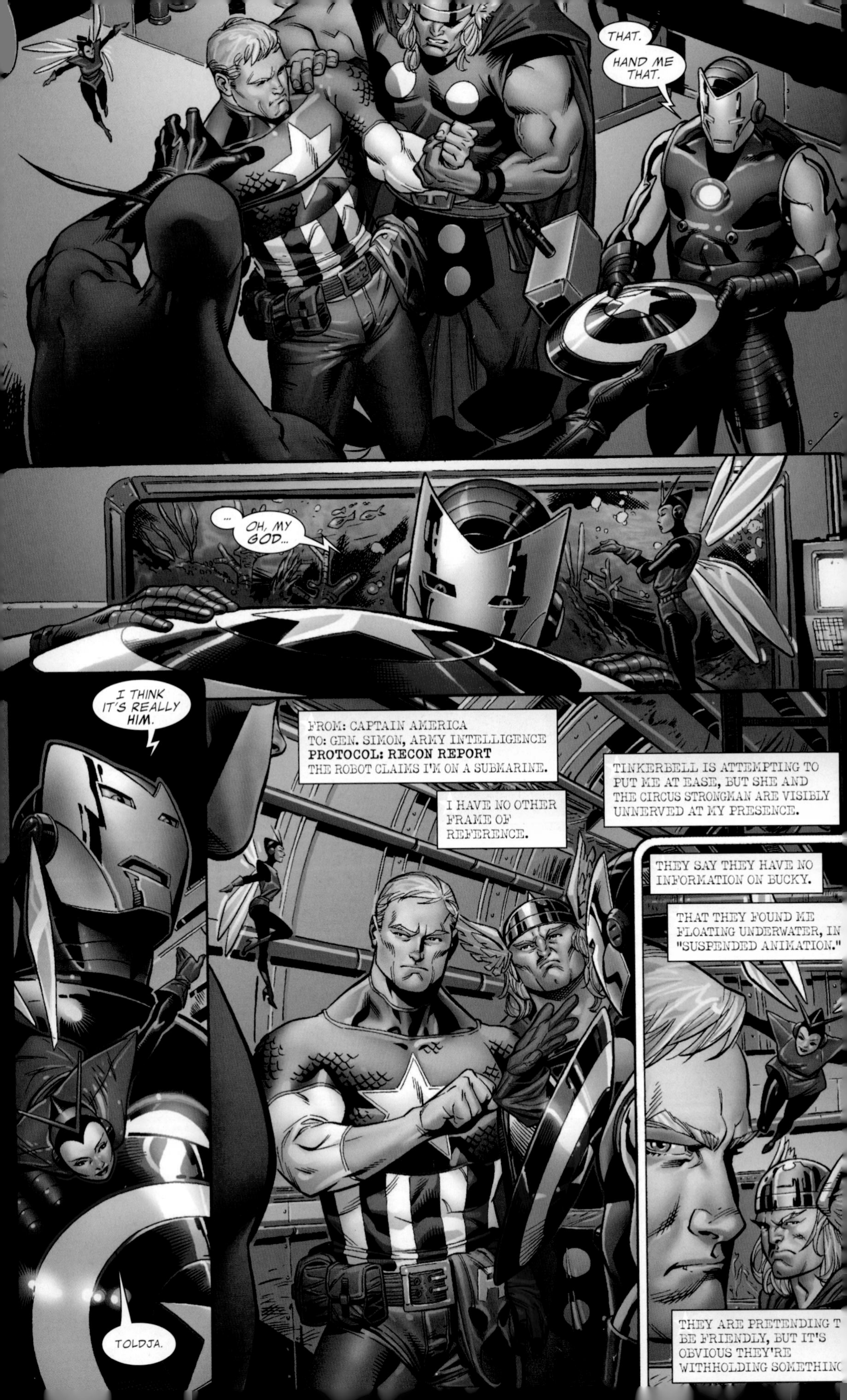

THAT.
HAND ME THAT.
... OH, MY GOD...
I THINK IT'S REALLY HIM.
FROM: CAPTAIN AMERICA
TO: GEN. SIMON, ARMY INTELLIGENCE
PROTOCOL: RECON REPORT
THE ROBOT CLAIMS I'M ON A SUBMARINE.
I HAVE NO OTHER FRAME OF REFERENCE.
TINKERBELL IS ATTEMPTING TO PUT ME AT EASE, BUT SHE AND THE CIRCUS STRONGMAN ARE VISIBLY UNNERVED AT MY PRESENCE.
THEY SAY THEY HAVE NO INFORMATION ON BUCKY.
THAT THEY FOUND ME FLOATING UNDERWATER, IN "SUSPENDED ANIMATION."
TOLDJA.
THEY ARE PRETENDING T BE FRIENDLY, BUT IT'S OBVIOUS THEY'RE WITHHOLDING SOMETHINC

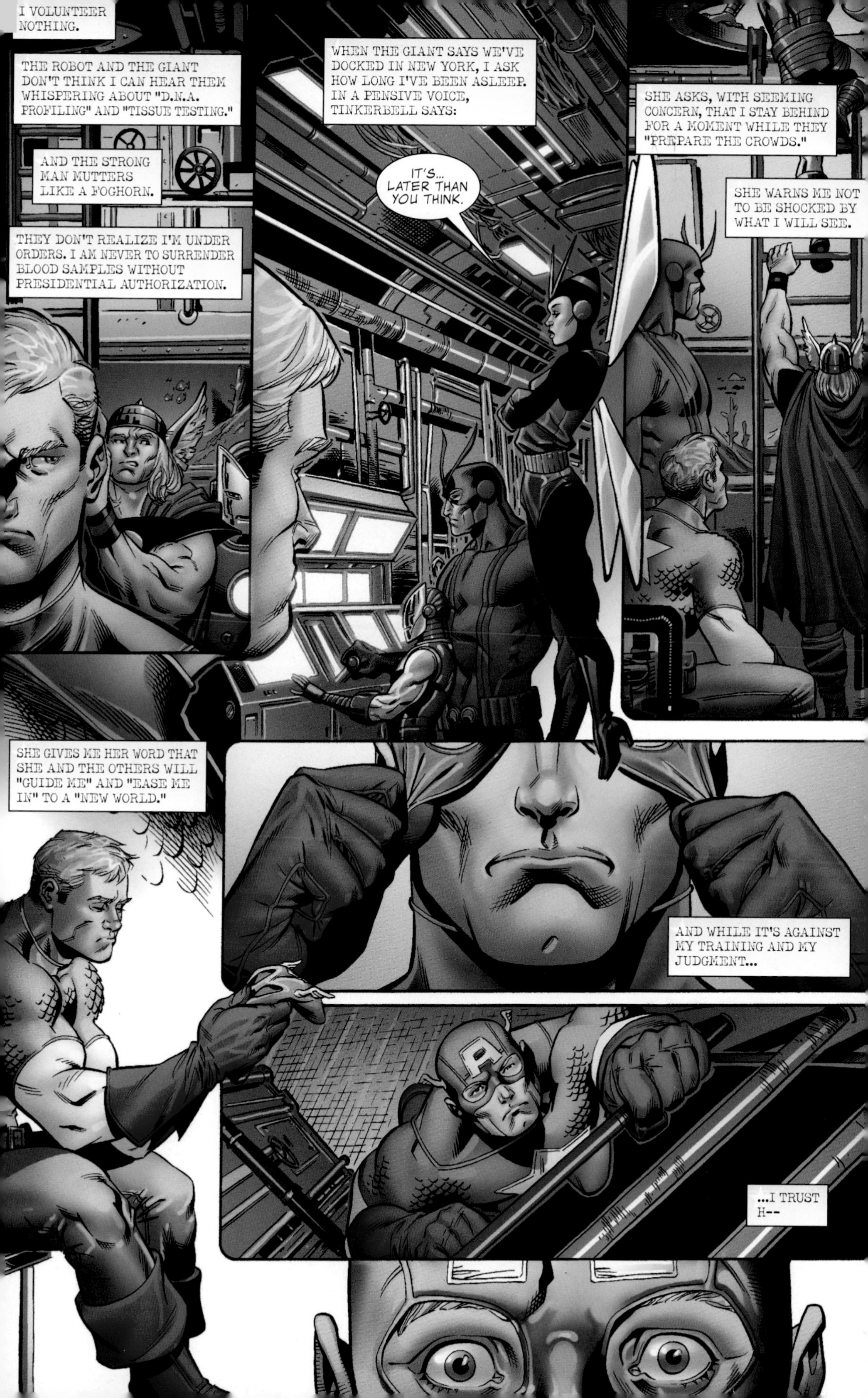
I VOLUNTEER NOTHING.
THE ROBOT AND THE GIANT DON'T THINK I CAN HEAR THEM WHISPERING ABOUT "D.N.A. PROFILING" AND "TISSUE TESTING."
AND THE STRONG MAN MUTTERS LIKE A FOGHORN.
THEY DON'T REALIZE I'M UNDER ORDERS. I AM NEVER TO SURRENDER BLOOD SAMPLES WITHOUT PRESIDENTIAL AUTHORIZATION.
WHEN THE GIANT SAYS WE'VE DOCKED IN NEW YORK, I ASK HOW LONG I'VE BEEN ASLEEP. IN A PENSIVE VOICE, TINKERBELL SAYS:
IT'S... LATER THAN YOU THINK.
SHE ASKS, WITH SEEMING CONCERN, THAT I STAY BEHIND FOR A MOMENT WHILE THEY "PREPARE THE CROWDS."
SHE WARNS ME NOT TO BE SHOCKED BY WHAT I WILL SEE.
SHE GIVES ME HER WORD THAT SHE AND THE OTHERS WILL "GUIDE ME" AND "EASE ME IN" TO A "NEW WORLD."
AND WHILE IT'S AGAINST MY TRAINING AND MY JUDGMENT...
...I TRUST H--

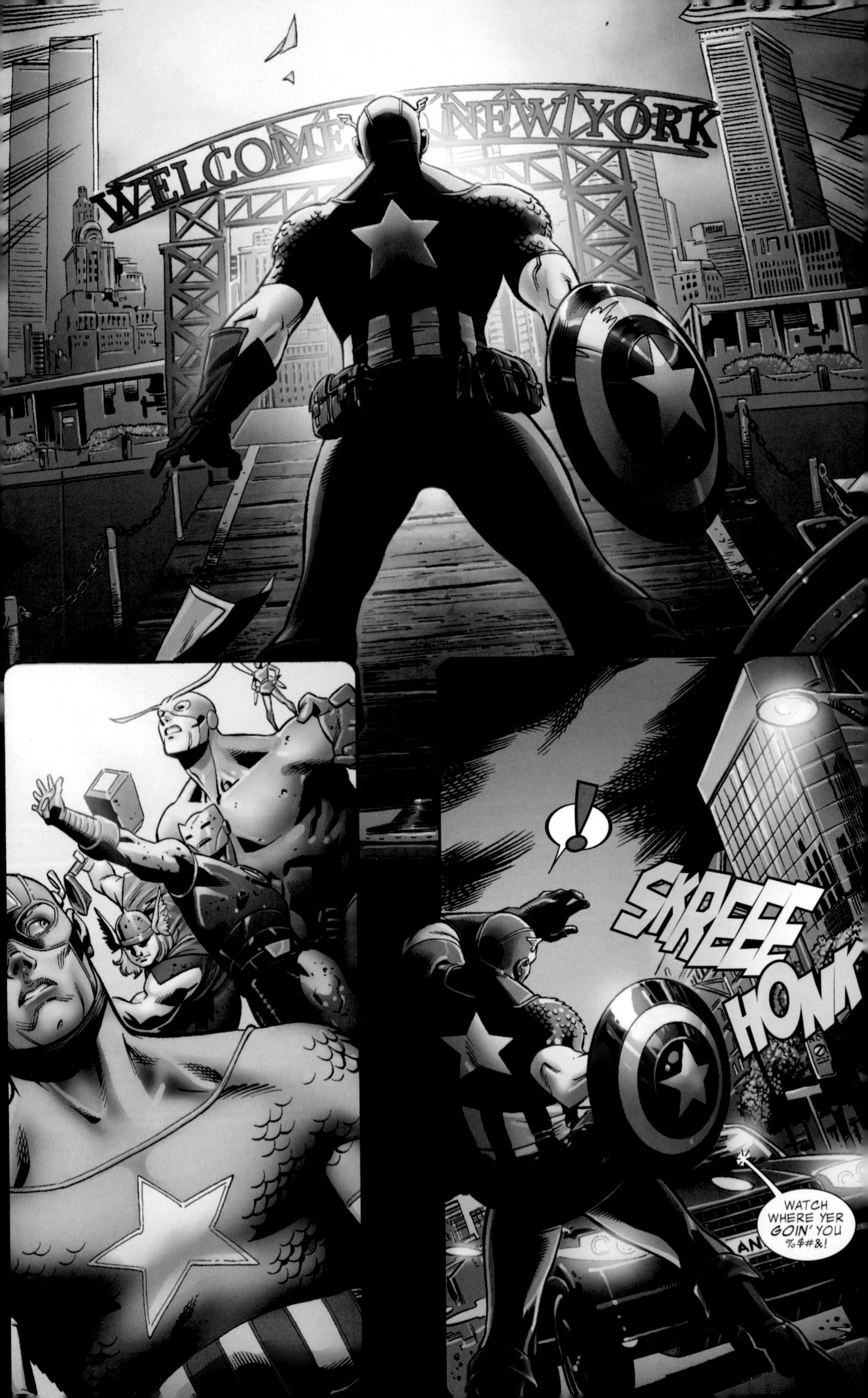
WELCOME TO NEW YORK
!
SKREEE
HONK
WATCH WHERE YER GOIN' YOU %$#&!

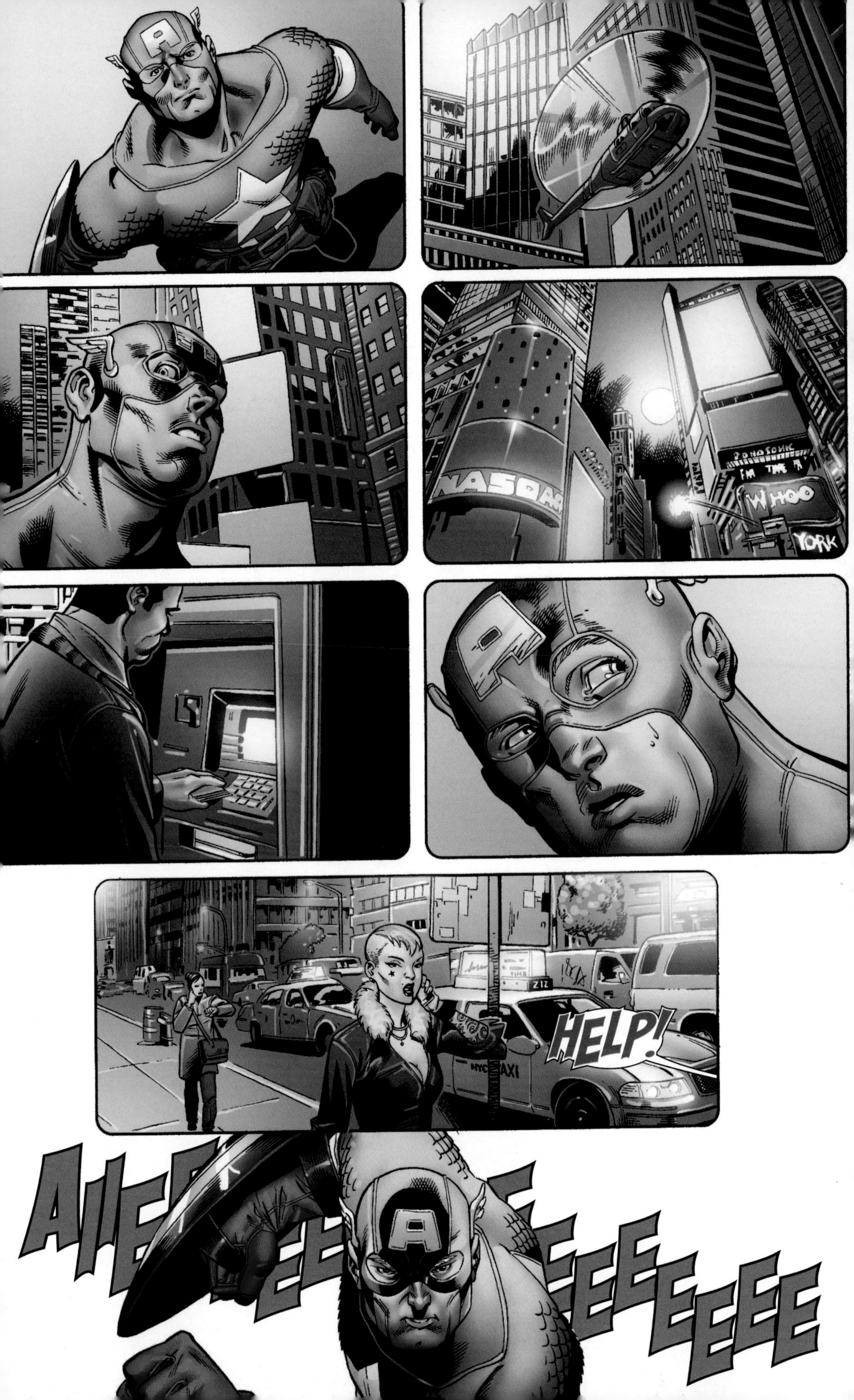
YORK
HELP!
AIEEEEEEEEEEEEEE

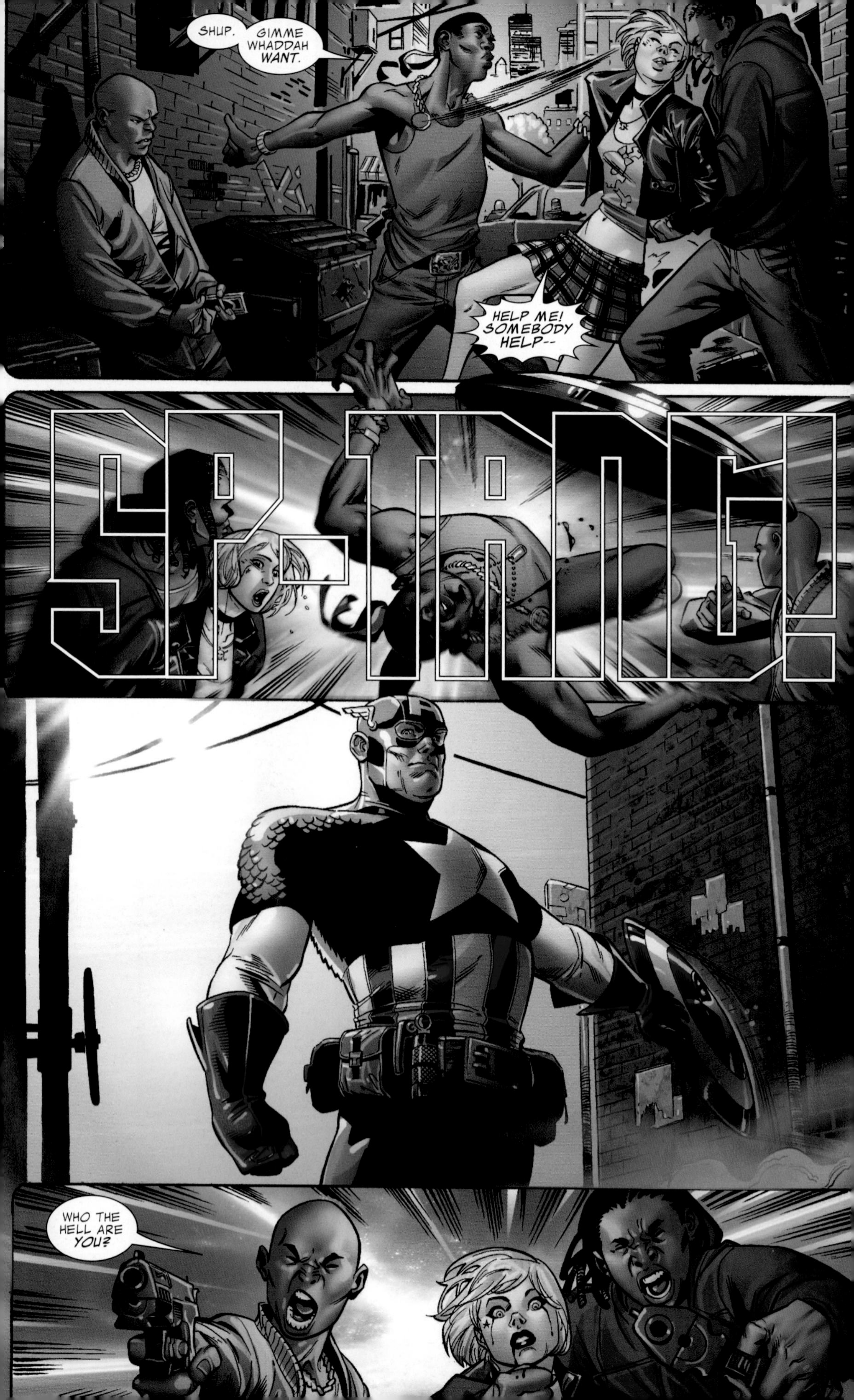
SHUP.
GIMME WHADDAH WANT.
HELP ME! SOMEBODY HELP--
SP-TANG!
WHO THE HELL ARE YOU?

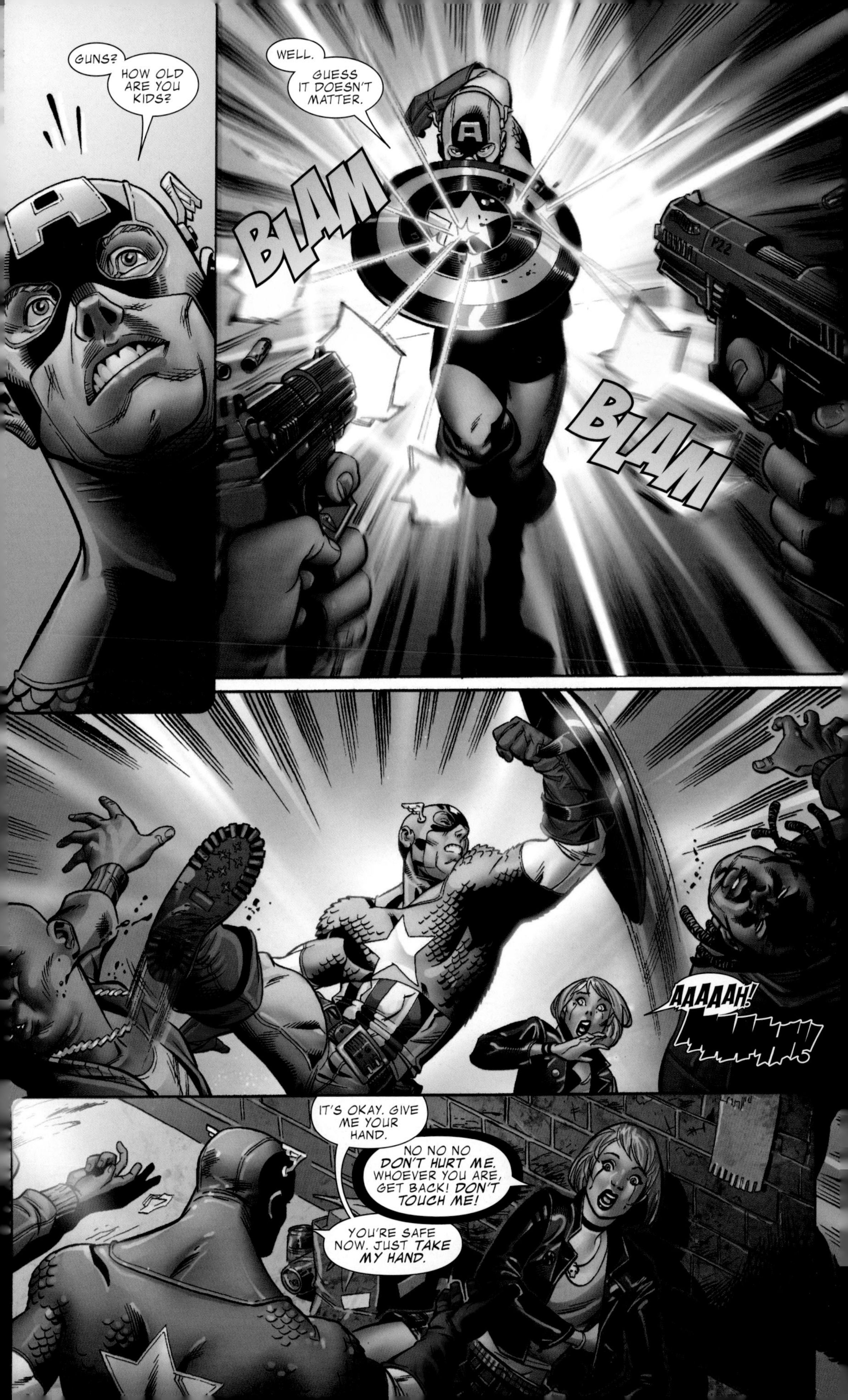
GUNS? HOW OLD ARE YOU KIDS?
WELL. GUESS IT DOESN'T MATTER.
BLAM
BLAM
AAAAAH!
IT'S OKAY. GIVE ME YOUR HAND.
NO NO NO DON'T HURT ME. WHOEVER YOU ARE, GET BACK! DON'T TOUCH ME!
YOU'RE SAFE NOW. JUST TAKE MY HAND.

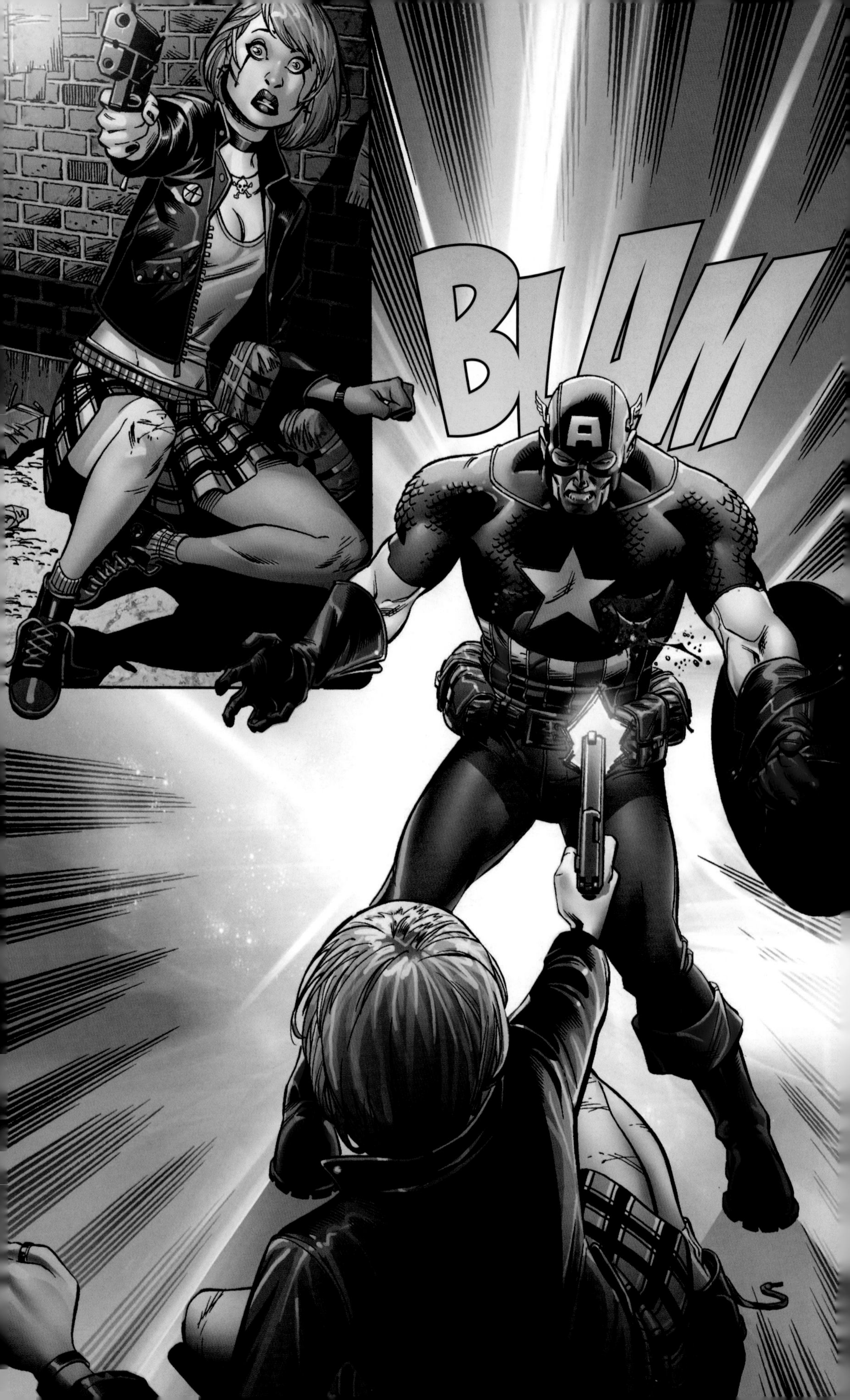
BLAM

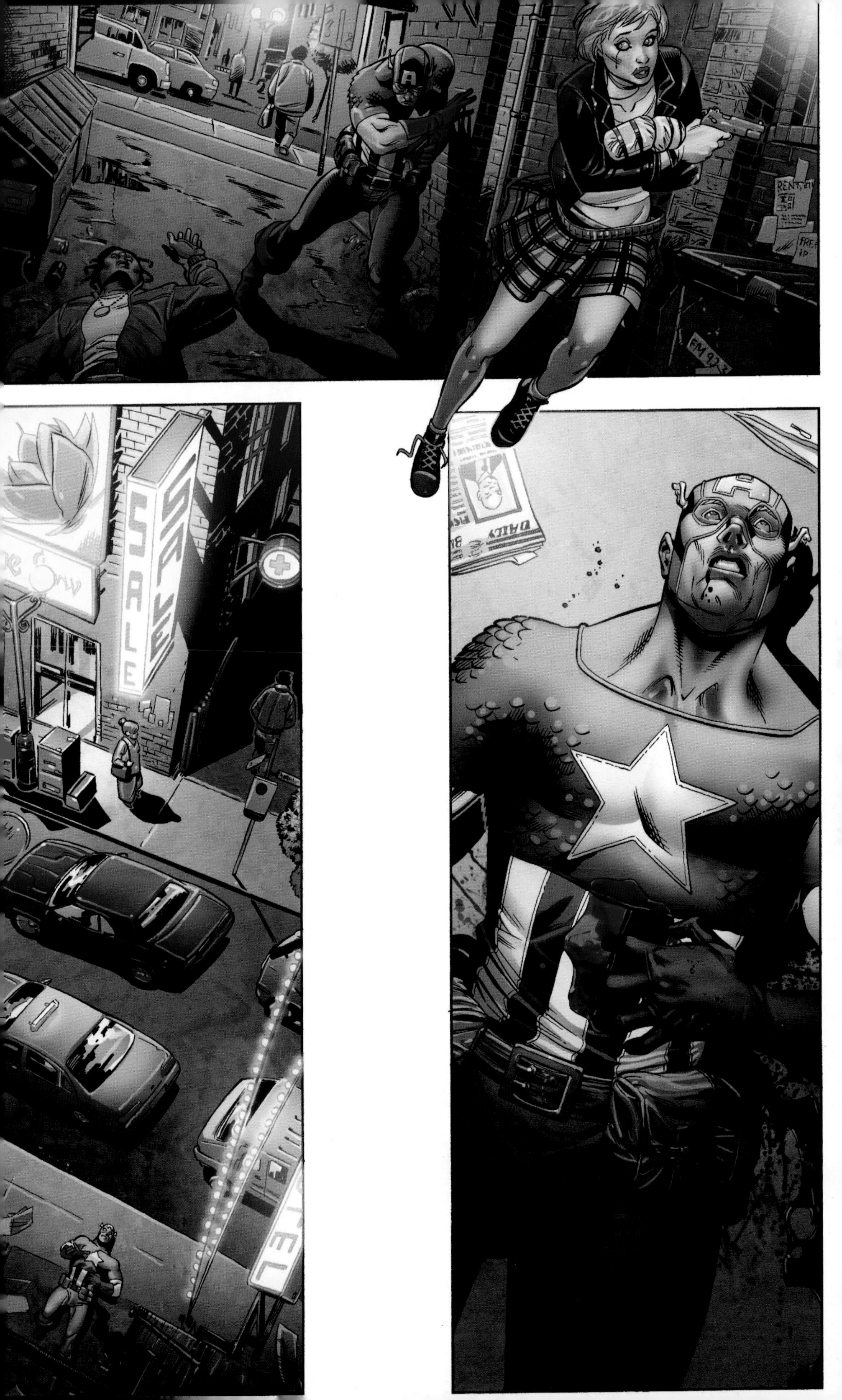
SALE
SALE
RENT
FM 92.3

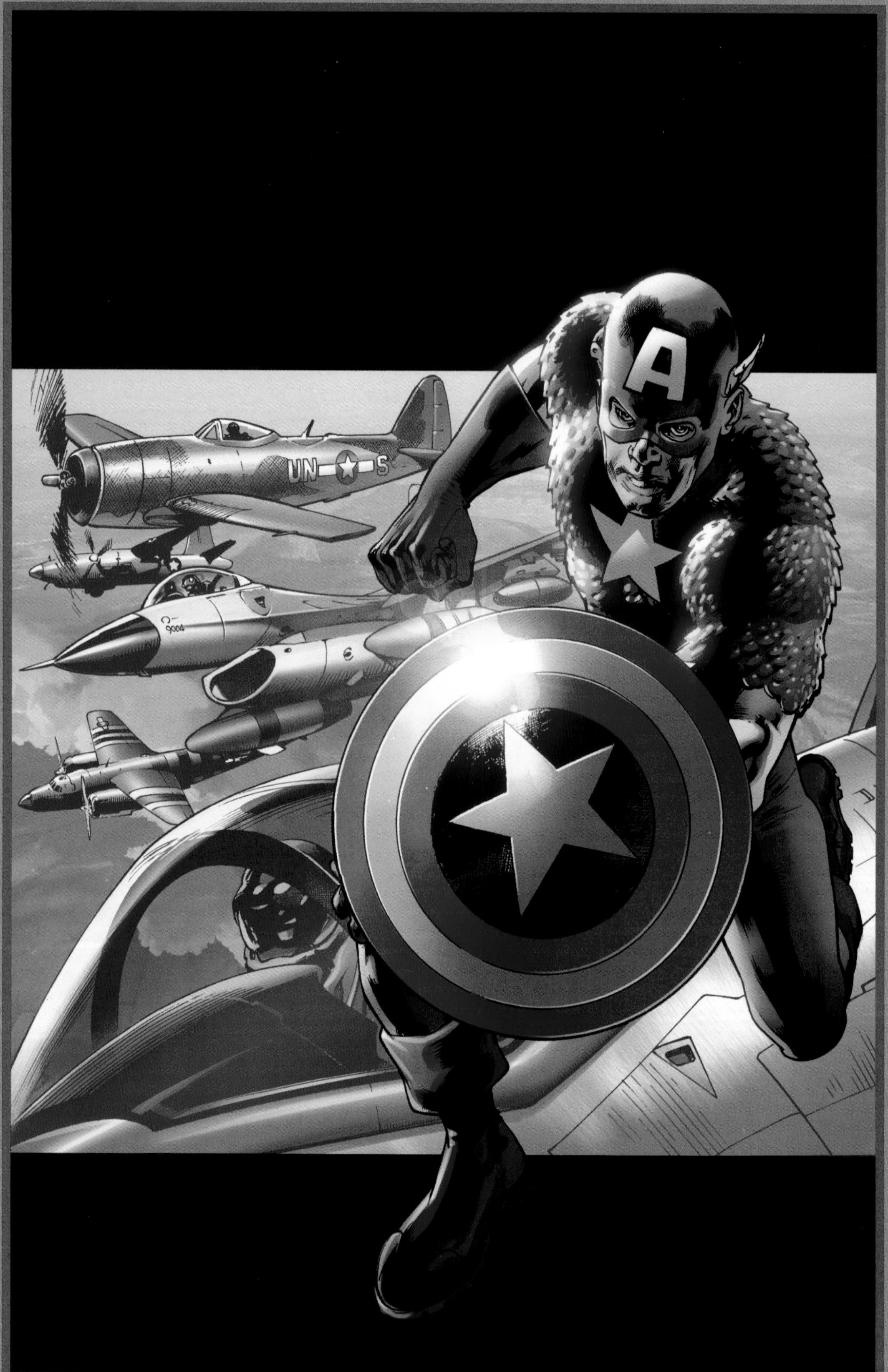
UN S

[2]

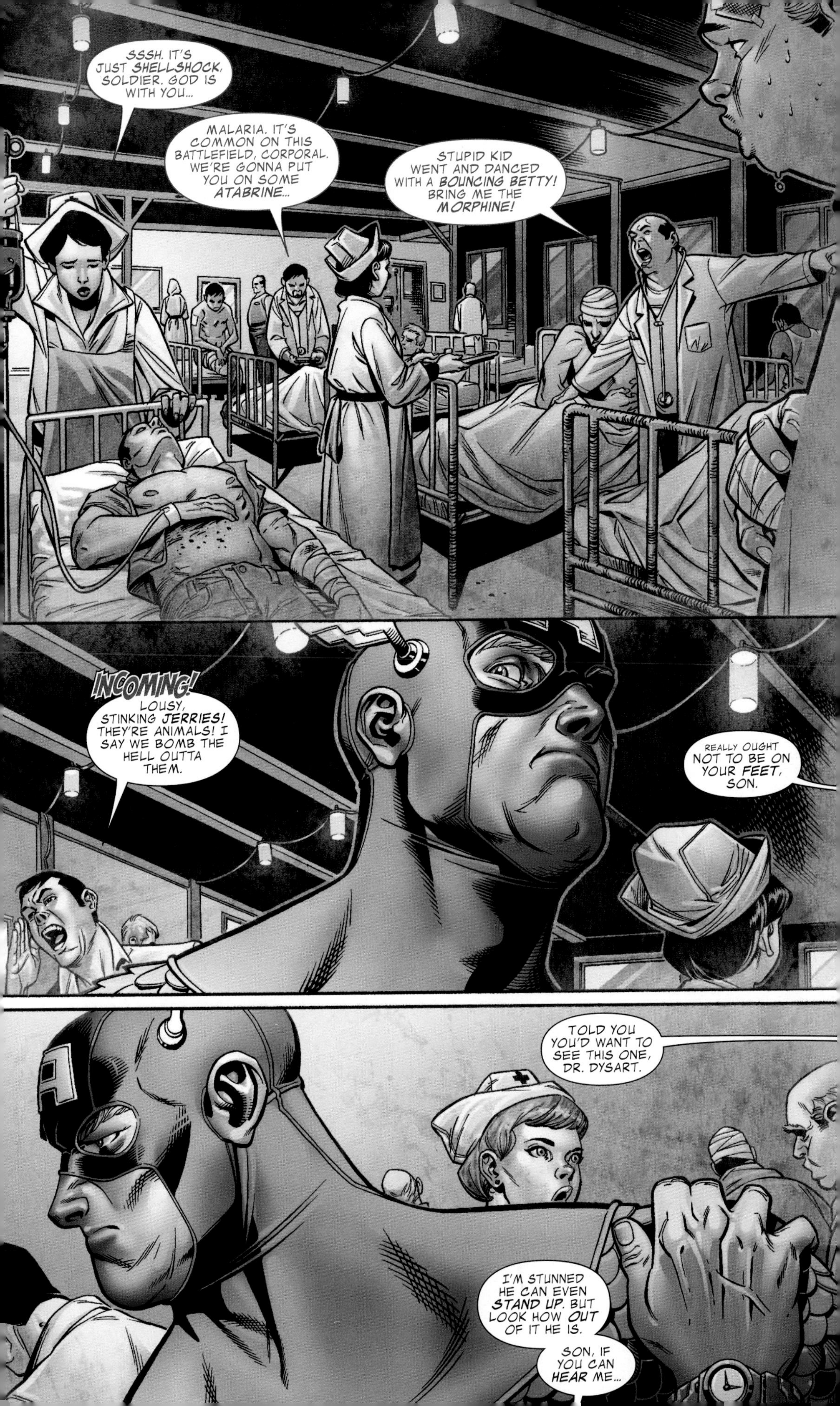

SSSH. IT'S JUST SHELLSHOCK, SOLDIER. GOD IS WITH YOU...
MALARIA. IT'S COMMON ON THIS BATTLEFIELD, CORPORAL. WE'RE GONNA PUT YOU ON SOME ATABRINE...
STUPID KID WENT AND DANCED WITH A BOUNCING BETTY! BRING ME THE MORPHINE!
INCOMING!
LOUSY, STINKING JERRIES! THEY'RE ANIMALS! I SAY WE BOMB THE HELL OUTTA THEM.
REALLY OUGHT NOT TO BE ON YOUR FEET, SON.
TOLD YOU YOU'D WANT TO SEE THIS ONE, DR. DYSART.
I'M STUNNED HE CAN EVEN STAND UP. BUT LOOK HOW OUT OF IT HE IS.
SON, IF YOU CAN HEAR ME...

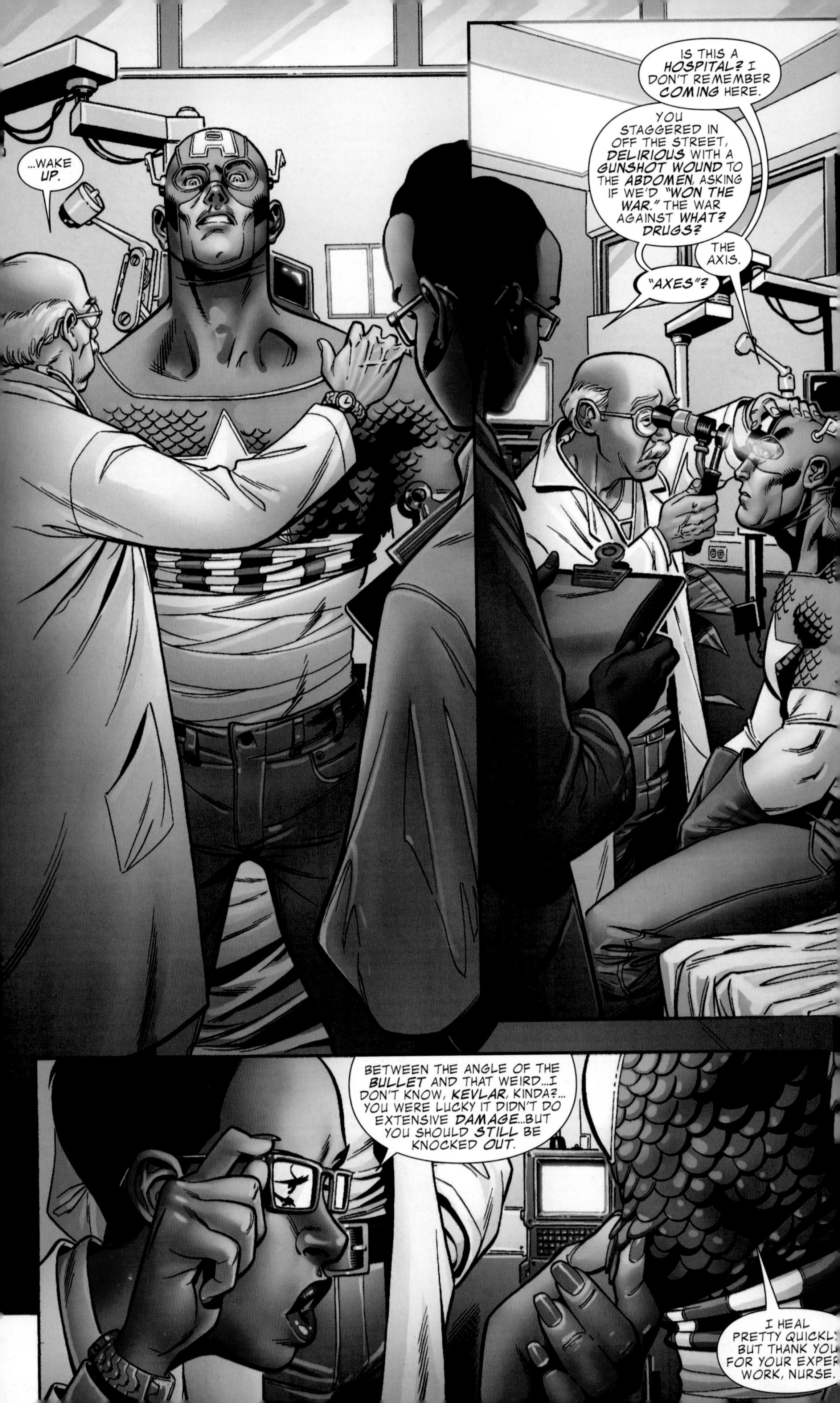
...WAKE UP.
IS THIS A HOSPITAL? I DON'T REMEMBER COMING HERE.
YOU STAGGERED IN OFF THE STREET, DELIRIOUS WITH A GUNSHOT WOUND TO THE ABDOMEN, ASKING IF WE'D "WON THE WAR." THE WAR AGAINST WHAT? DRUGS?
THE AXIS.
"AXES"?
BETWEEN THE ANGLE OF THE BULLET AND THAT WEIRD...I DON'T KNOW, KEVLAR, KINDA?... YOU WERE LUCKY IT DIDN'T DO EXTENSIVE DAMAGE...BUT YOU SHOULD STILL BE KNOCKED OUT.
I HEAL PRETTY QUICKL BUT THANK YOU FOR YOUR EXPER WORK, NURSE.

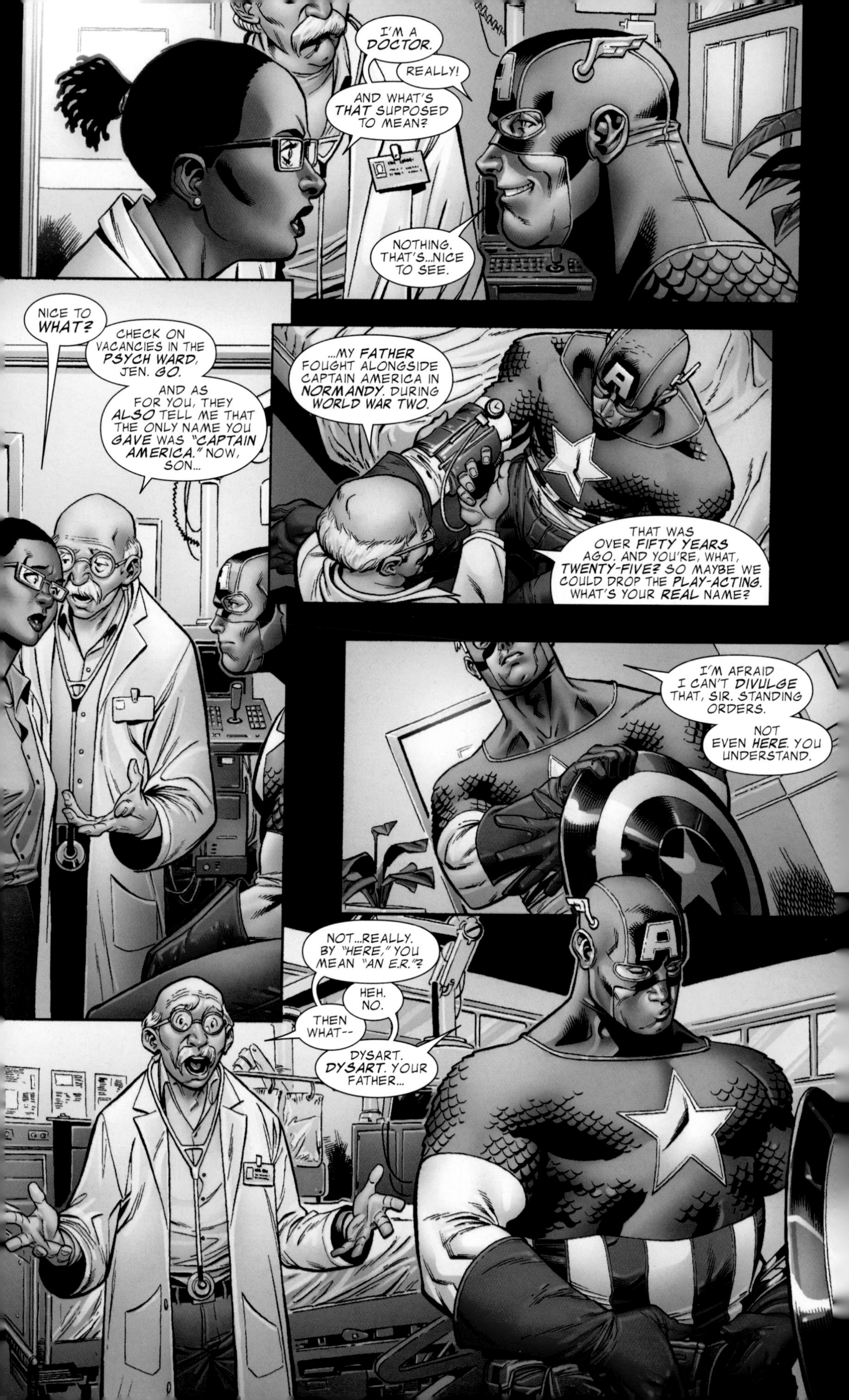
I'M A DOCTOR.
REALLY!
AND WHAT'S THAT SUPPOSED TO MEAN?
NOTHING. THAT'S...NICE TO SEE.
NICE TO WHAT?
CHECK ON VACANCIES IN THE PSYCH WARD, JEN. GO.
AND AS FOR YOU, THEY ALSO TELL ME THAT THE ONLY NAME YOU GAVE WAS "CAPTAIN AMERICA." NOW, SON...
...MY FATHER FOUGHT ALONGSIDE CAPTAIN AMERICA IN NORMANDY. DURING WORLD WAR TWO.
THAT WAS OVER FIFTY YEARS AGO. AND YOU'RE, WHAT, TWENTY-FIVE? SO MAYBE WE COULD DROP THE PLAY-ACTING. WHAT'S YOUR REAL NAME?
I'M AFRAID I CAN'T DIVULGE THAT, SIR. STANDING ORDERS.
NOT EVEN HERE. YOU UNDERSTAND.
NOT...REALLY. BY "HERE," YOU MEAN "AN E.R."?
HEH. NO.
THEN WHAT--
DYSART. DYSART. YOUR FATHER...

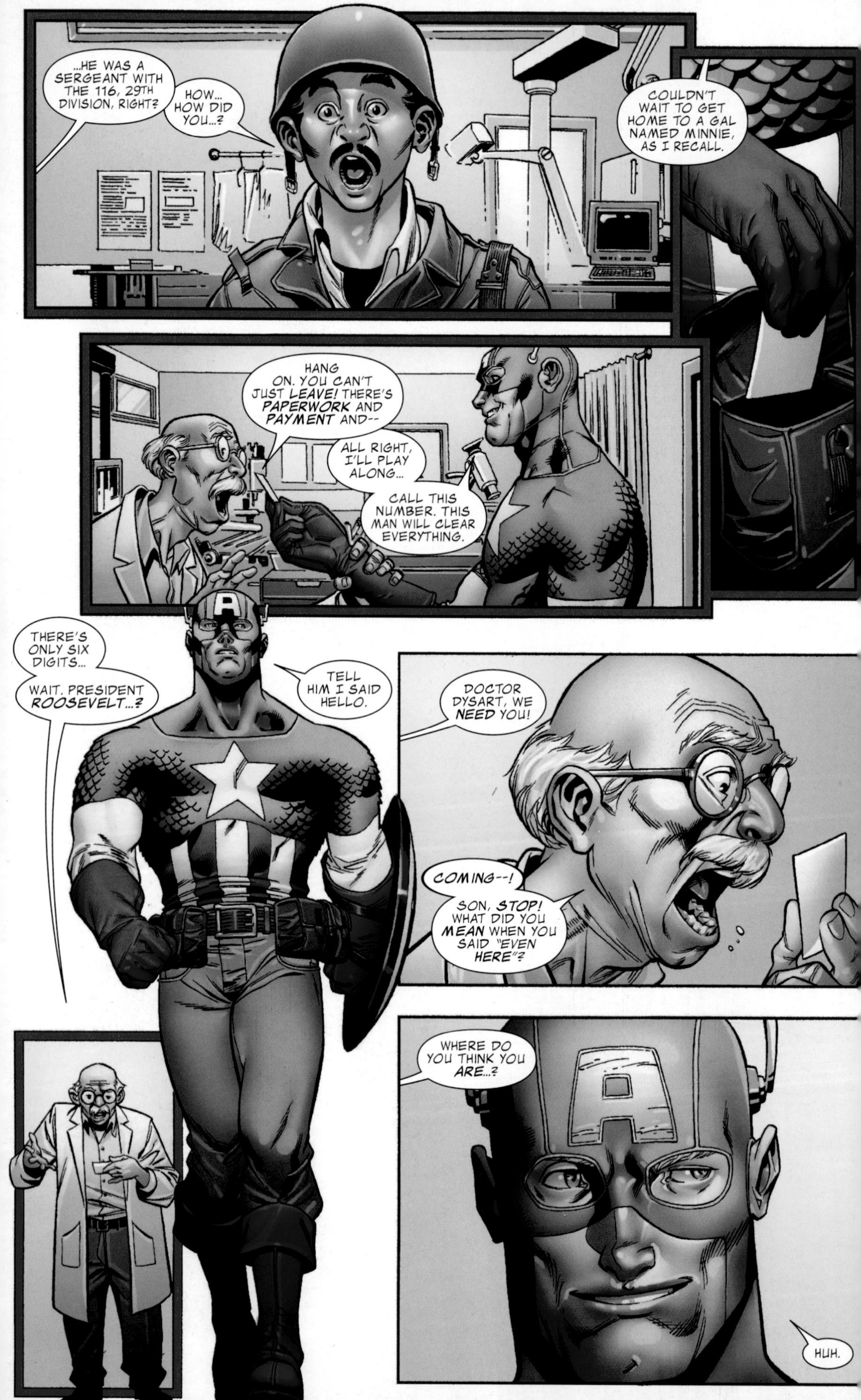
...HE WAS A SERGEANT WITH THE 116, 29TH DIVISION, RIGHT?
HOW... HOW DID YOU...?
COULDN'T WAIT TO GET HOME TO A GAL NAMED MINNIE, AS I RECALL.
HANG ON. YOU CAN'T JUST LEAVE! THERE'S PAPERWORK AND PAYMENT AND--
ALL RIGHT, I'LL PLAY ALONG...
CALL THIS NUMBER. THIS MAN WILL CLEAR EVERYTHING.
THERE'S ONLY SIX DIGITS...
WAIT. PRESIDENT ROOSEVELT...?
TELL HIM I SAID HELLO.
DOCTOR DYSART, WE NEED YOU!
COMING--!
SON, STOP! WHAT DID YOU MEAN WHEN YOU SAID "EVEN HERE"?
WHERE DO YOU THINK YOU ARE...?
HUH.

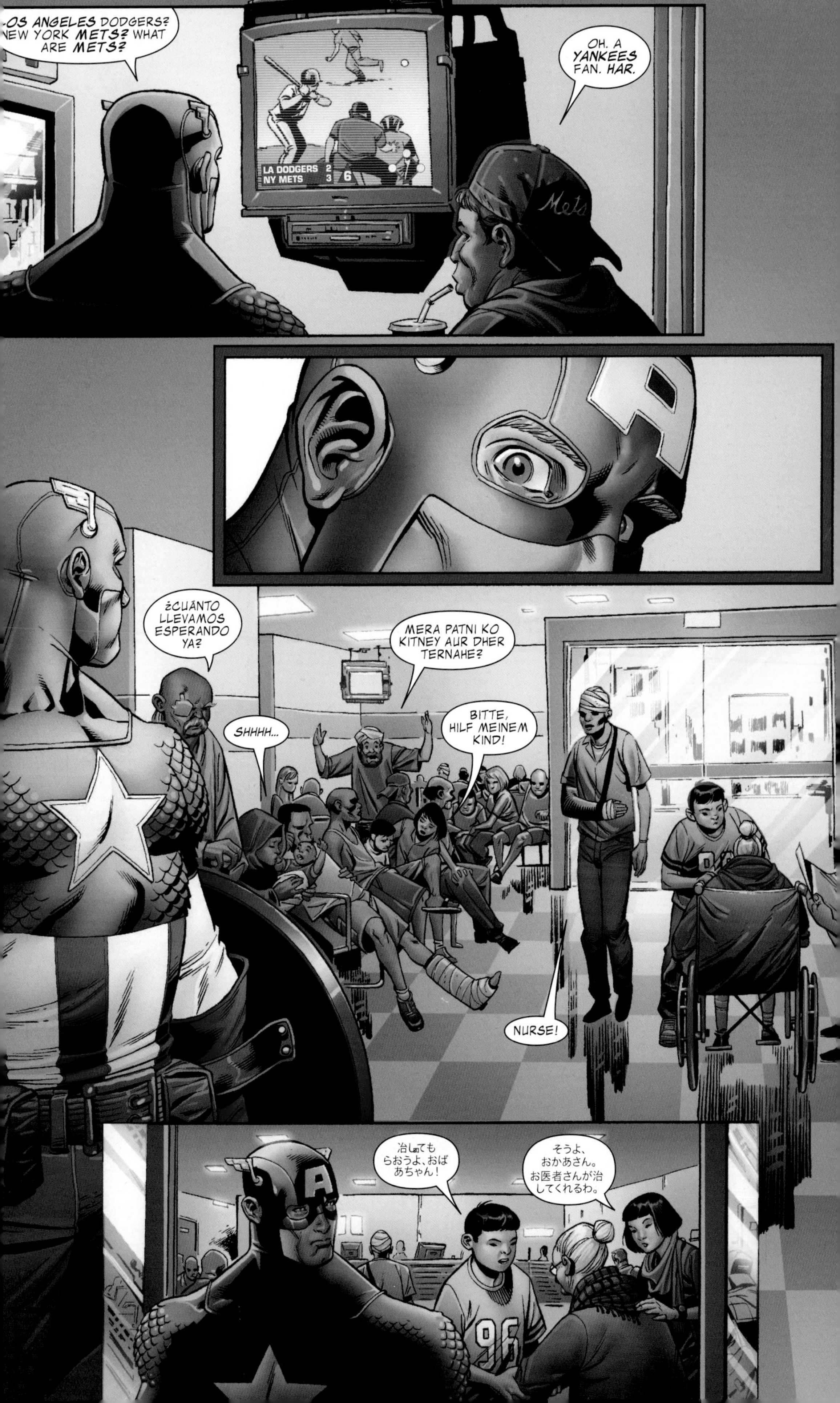

-OS ANGELES DODGERS? NEW YORK METS? WHAT ARE METS?
LA DODGERS 2
NY METS 3 6
OH. A YANKEES FAN. HAR.
¿CUÁNTO LLEVAMOS ESPERANDO YA?
MERA PATNI KO KITNEY AUR DHER TERNAHE?
SHHHH...
BITTE, HILF MEINEM KIND!
NURSE!
治しゎても らおうよ、おば あちゃん！
そうよ、 おかあさん。 お医者さんが治 してくれるわ。

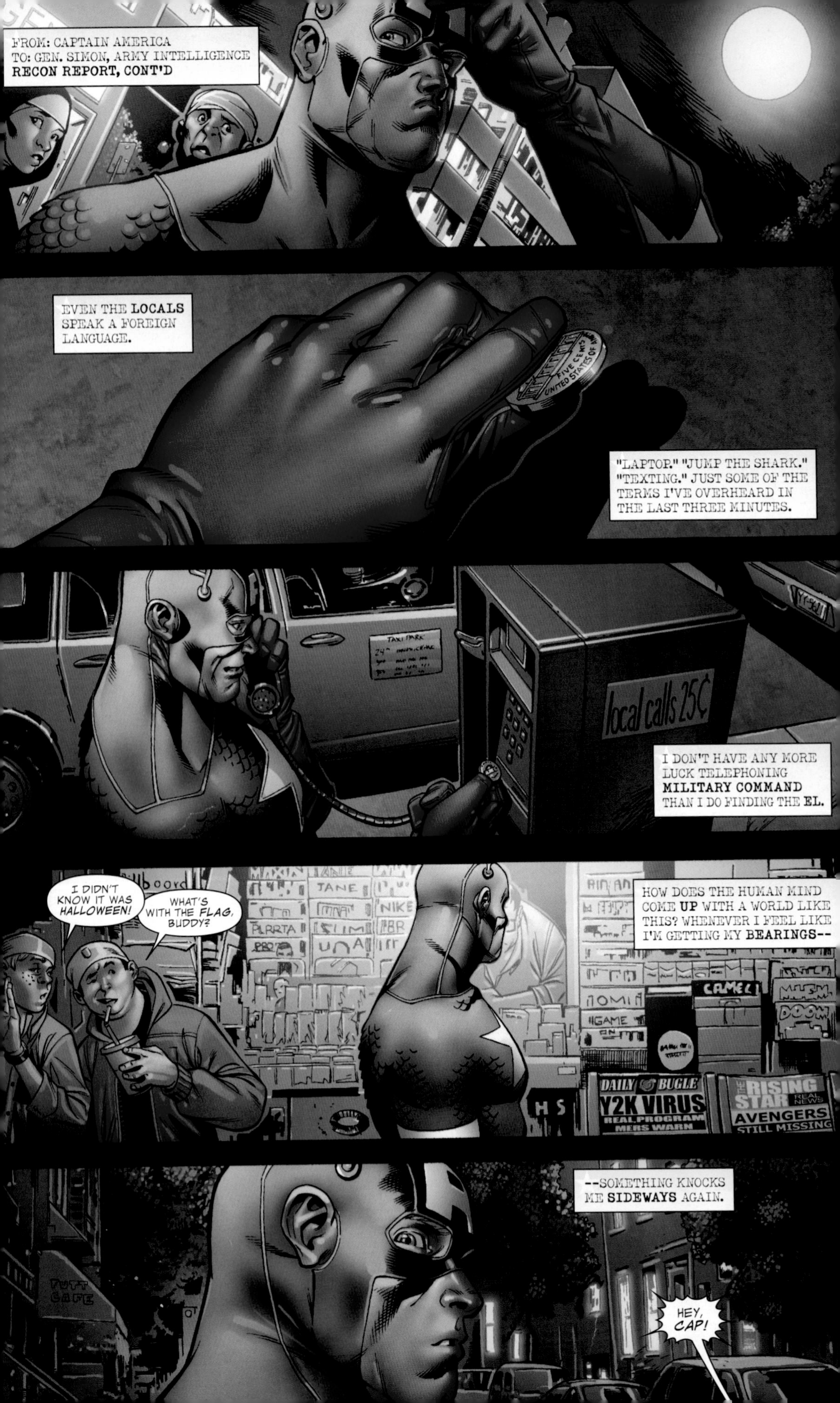
FROM: CAPTAIN AMERICA
TO: GEN. SIMON, ARMY INTELLIGENCE
RECON REPORT, CONT'D
EVEN THE LOCALS SPEAK A FOREIGN LANGUAGE.
FIVE CENTS UNITED STATES OF A
"LAPTOP." "JUMP THE SHARK." "TEXTING." JUST SOME OF THE TERMS I'VE OVERHEARD IN THE LAST THREE MINUTES.
TAXI PARK
local calls 25¢
I DON'T HAVE ANY MORE LUCK TELEPHONING MILITARY COMMAND THAN I DO FINDING THE EL.
I DIDN'T KNOW IT WAS HALLOWEEN!
WHAT'S WITH THE FLAG, BUDDY?
HOW DOES THE HUMAN MIND COME UP WITH A WORLD LIKE THIS? WHENEVER I FEEL LIKE I'M GETTING MY BEARINGS--
JANE
NIKE
CAMEL
DOOM
GAME
DAILY BUGLE
Y2K VIRUS
REAL PROGRAMMERS WARN
THE RISING STAR REAL NEWS
AVENGERS STILL MISSING
--SOMETHING KNOCKS ME SIDEWAYS AGAIN.
HEY, CAP!

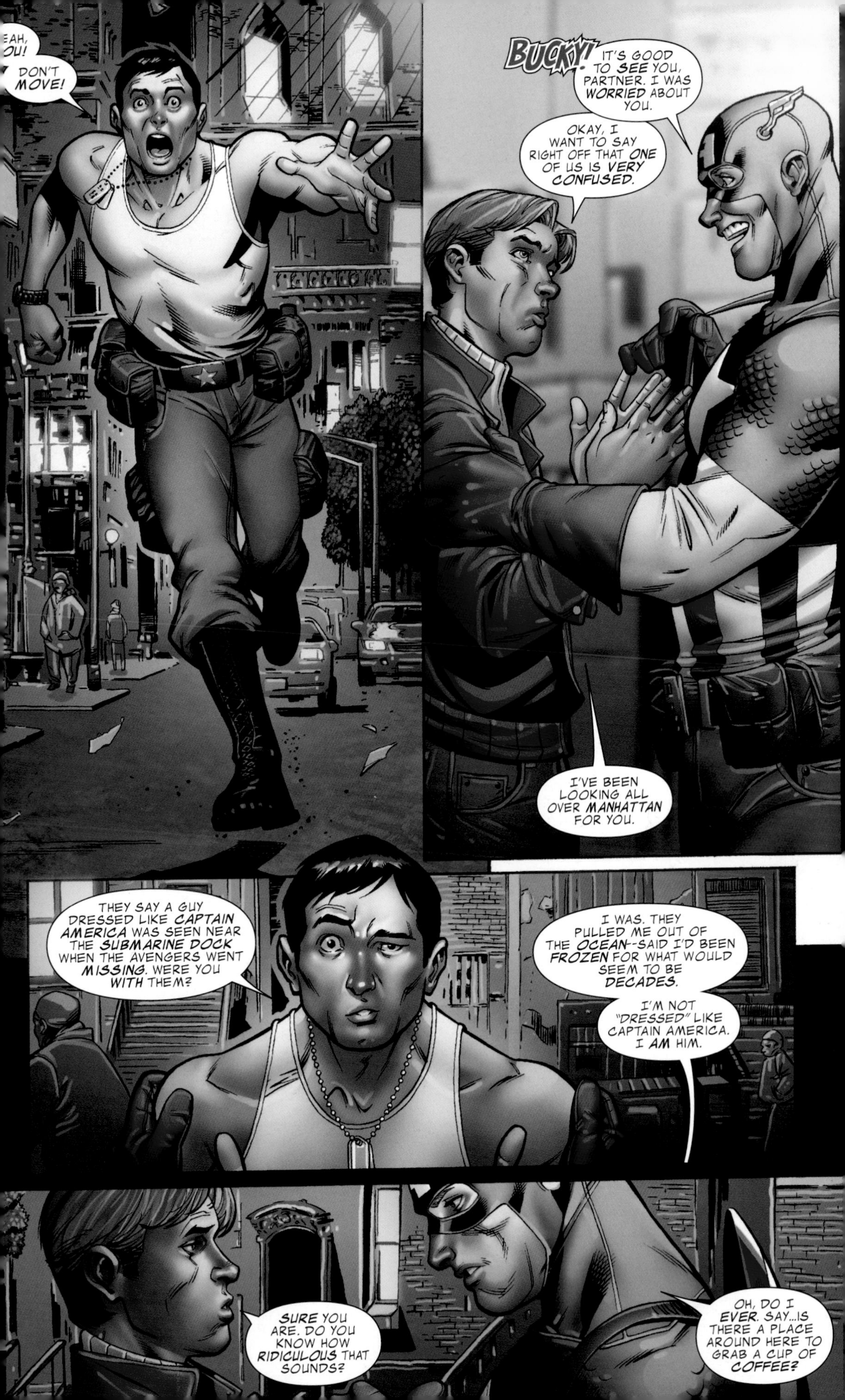

EAH, OU! DON'T MOVE!
BUCKY!
IT'S GOOD TO SEE YOU, PARTNER. I WAS WORRIED ABOUT YOU.
OKAY, I WANT TO SAY RIGHT OFF THAT ONE OF US IS VERY CONFUSED.
I'VE BEEN LOOKING ALL OVER MANHATTAN FOR YOU.
THEY SAY A GUY DRESSED LIKE CAPTAIN AMERICA WAS SEEN NEAR THE SUBMARINE DOCK WHEN THE AVENGERS WENT MISSING. WERE YOU WITH THEM?
I WAS. THEY PULLED ME OUT OF THE OCEAN--SAID I'D BEEN FROZEN FOR WHAT WOULD SEEM TO BE DECADES.
I'M NOT "DRESSED" LIKE CAPTAIN AMERICA. I AM HIM.
SURE YOU ARE. DO YOU KNOW HOW RIDICULOUS THAT SOUNDS?
OH, DO I EVER. SAY...IS THERE A PLACE AROUND HERE TO GRAB A CUP OF COFFEE?

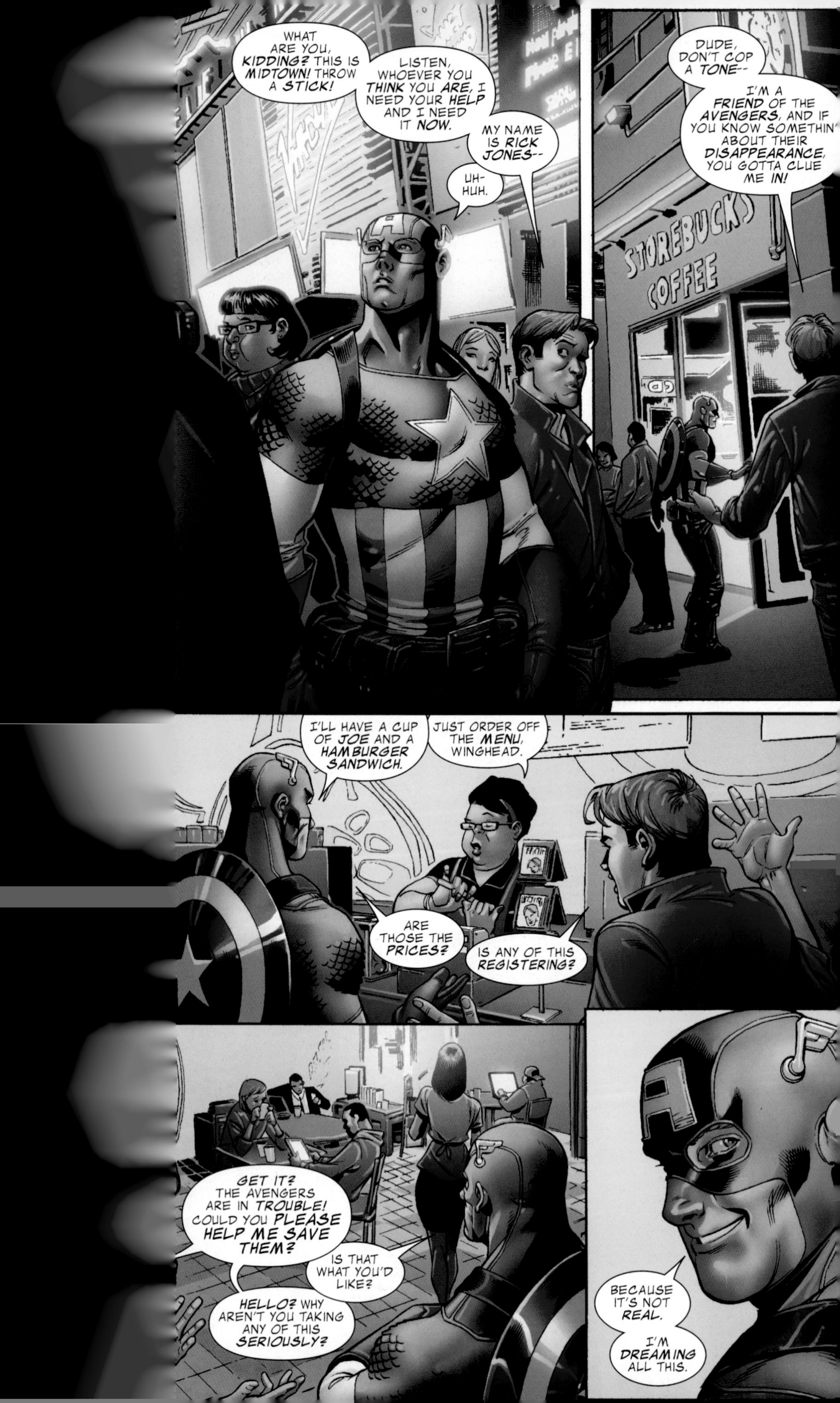
WHAT ARE YOU, KIDDING? THIS IS MIDTOWN! THROW A STICK!
LISTEN, WHOEVER YOU THINK YOU ARE, I NEED YOUR HELP AND I NEED IT NOW.
MY NAME IS RICK JONES--
UH-HUH.
DUDE, DON'T COP A TONE--
I'M A FRIEND OF THE AVENGERS, AND IF YOU KNOW SOMETHIN' ABOUT THEIR DISAPPEARANCE, YOU GOTTA CLUE ME IN!
STOREBUCKS COFFEE
I'LL HAVE A CUP OF JOE AND A HAMBURGER SANDWICH.
JUST ORDER OFF THE MENU, WINGHEAD.
ARE THOSE THE PRICES?
IS ANY OF THIS REGISTERING?
GET IT? THE AVENGERS ARE IN TROUBLE! COULD YOU PLEASE HELP ME SAVE THEM?
IS THAT WHAT YOU'D LIKE?
HELLO? WHY AREN'T YOU TAKING ANY OF THIS SERIOUSLY?
BECAUSE IT'S NOT REAL.
I'M DREAMING ALL THIS.

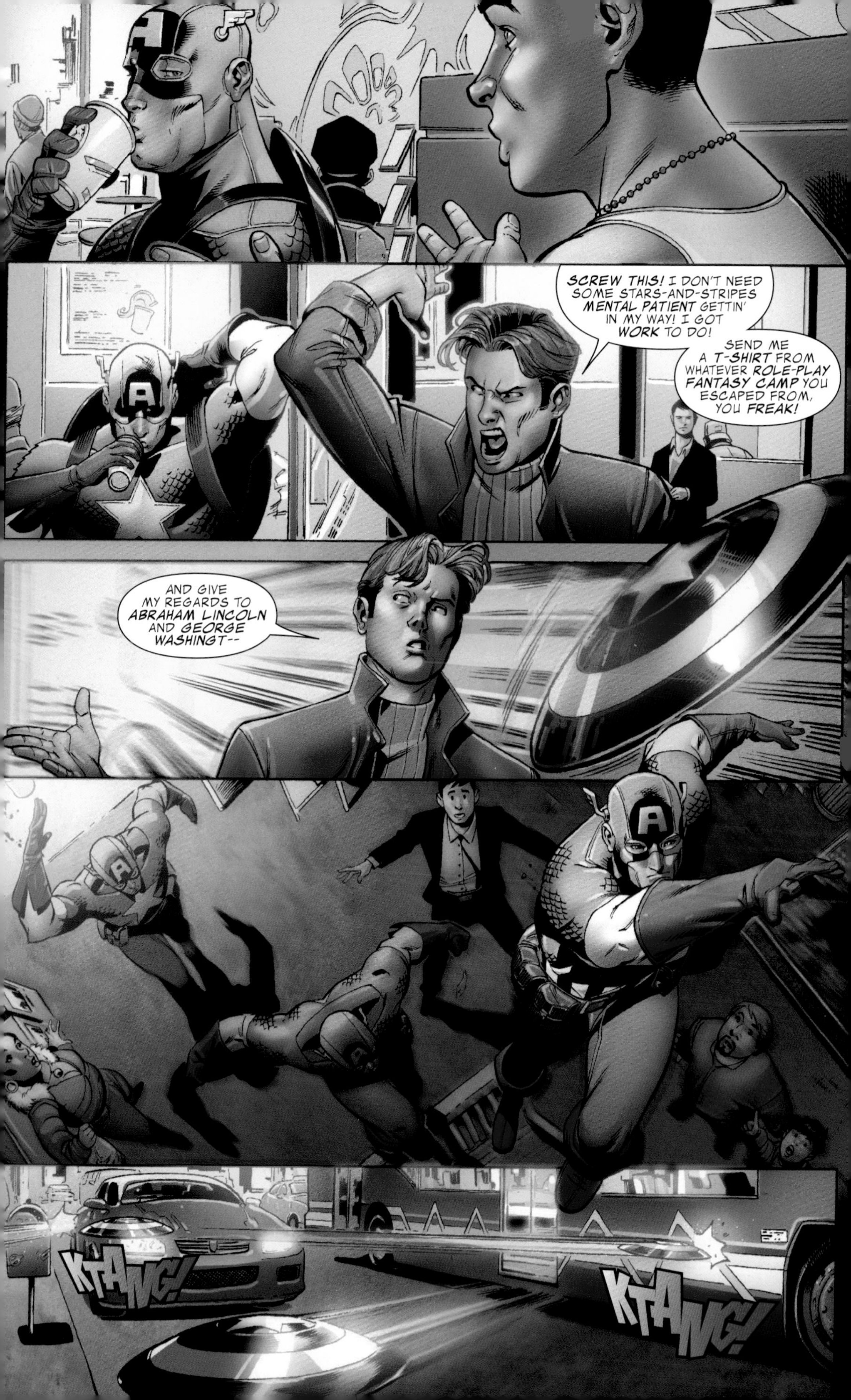
SCREW THIS! I DON'T NEED SOME STARS-AND-STRIPES MENTAL PATIENT GETTIN' IN MY WAY! I GOT WORK TO DO!
SEND ME A T-SHIRT FROM WHATEVER ROLE-PLAY FANTASY CAMP YOU ESCAPED FROM, YOU FREAK!
AND GIVE MY REGARDS TO ABRAHAM LINCOLN AND GEORGE WASHINGT--
KTANG!
KTANG!

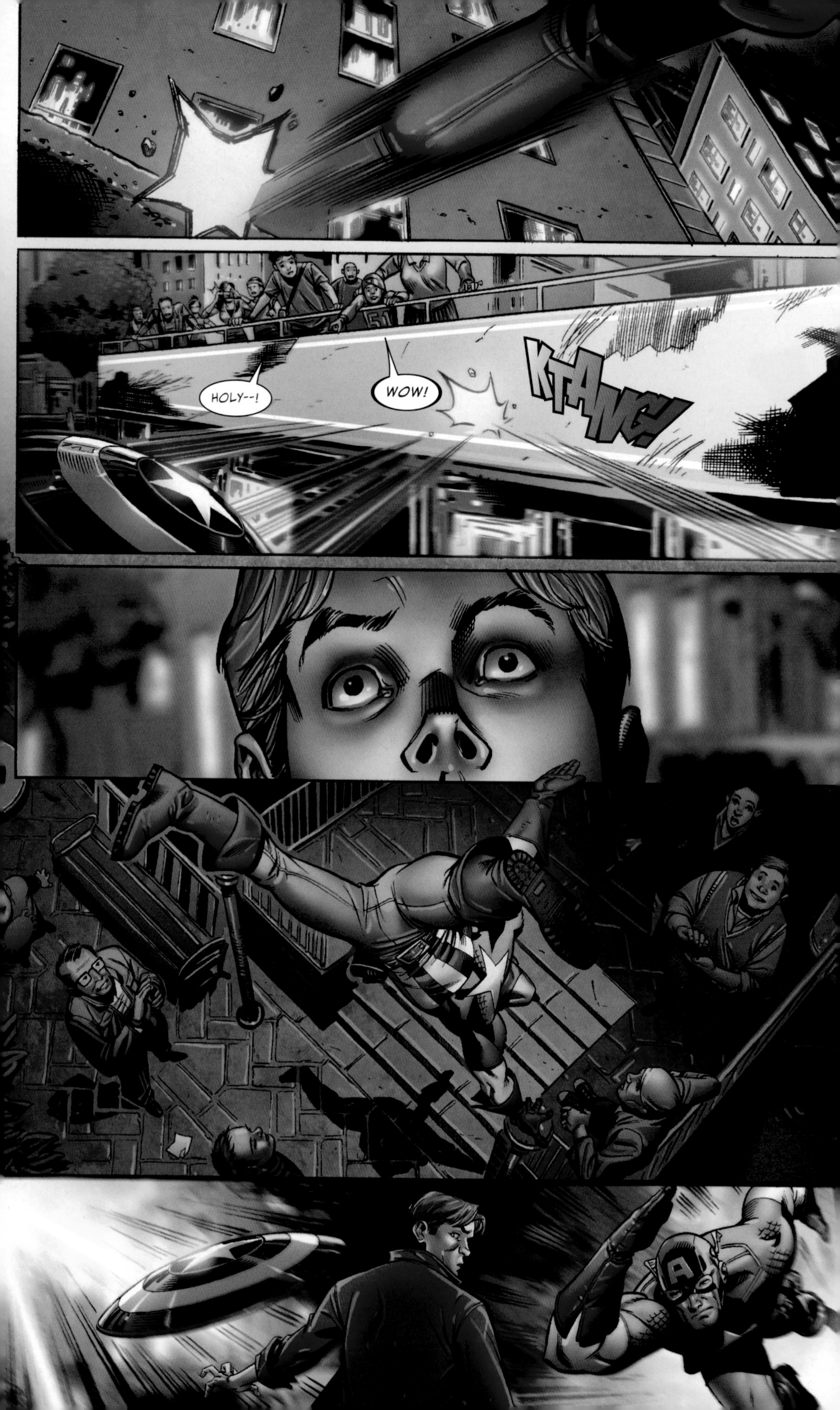
HOLY--!
WOW!
KTANG!

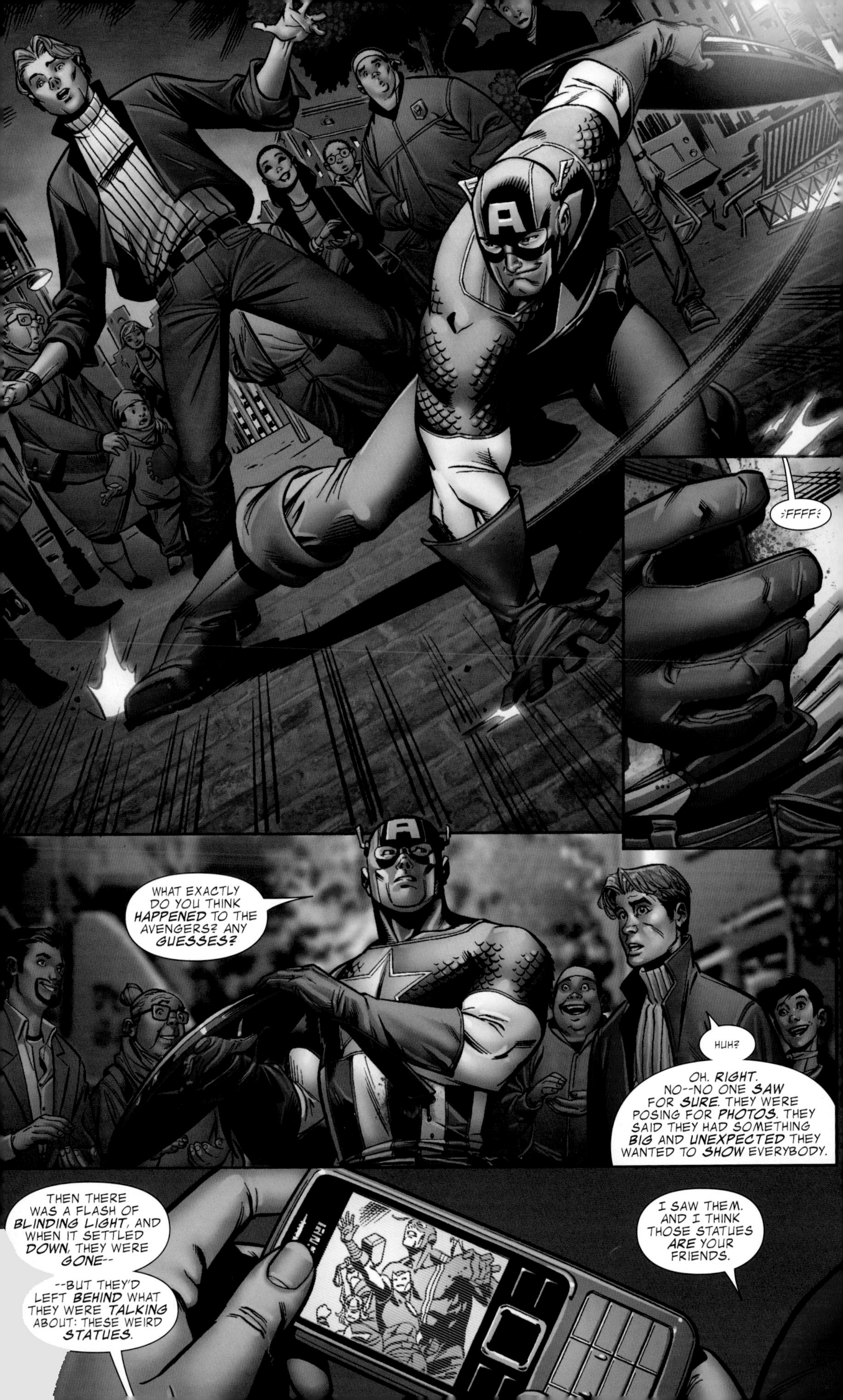

:FFFF:
WHAT EXACTLY DO YOU THINK HAPPENED TO THE AVENGERS? ANY GUESSES?
HUH?
OH. RIGHT. NO--NO ONE SAW FOR SURE. THEY WERE POSING FOR PHOTOS. THEY SAID THEY HAD SOMETHING BIG AND UNEXPECTED THEY WANTED TO SHOW EVERYBODY.
THEN THERE WAS A FLASH OF BLINDING LIGHT, AND WHEN IT SETTLED DOWN, THEY WERE GONE--
--BUT THEY'D LEFT BEHIND WHAT THEY WERE TALKING ABOUT: THESE WEIRD STATUES.
I SAW THEM. AND I THINK THOSE STATUES ARE YOUR FRIENDS.

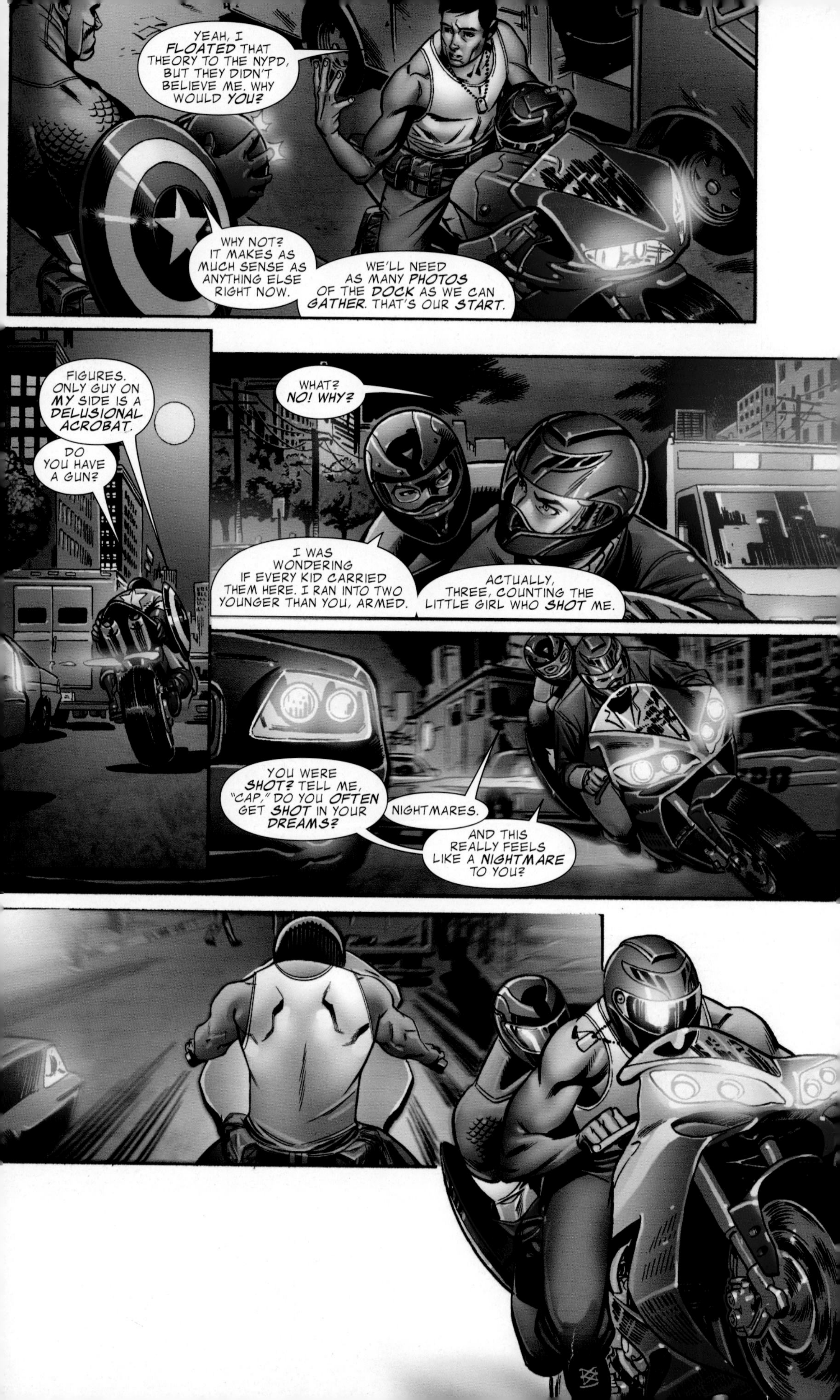

YEAH, I FLOATED THAT THEORY TO THE NYPD, BUT THEY DIDN'T BELIEVE ME. WHY WOULD YOU?
WHY NOT? IT MAKES AS MUCH SENSE AS ANYTHING ELSE RIGHT NOW.
WE'LL NEED AS MANY PHOTOS OF THE DOCK AS WE CAN GATHER. THAT'S OUR START.
FIGURES. ONLY GUY ON MY SIDE IS A DELUSIONAL ACROBAT.
DO YOU HAVE A GUN?
WHAT? NO! WHY?
I WAS WONDERING IF EVERY KID CARRIED THEM HERE. I RAN INTO TWO YOUNGER THAN YOU, ARMED.
ACTUALLY, THREE, COUNTING THE LITTLE GIRL WHO SHOT ME.
YOU WERE SHOT? TELL ME, "CAP," DO YOU OFTEN GET SHOT IN YOUR DREAMS?
NIGHTMARES.
AND THIS REALLY FEELS LIKE A NIGHTMARE TO YOU?

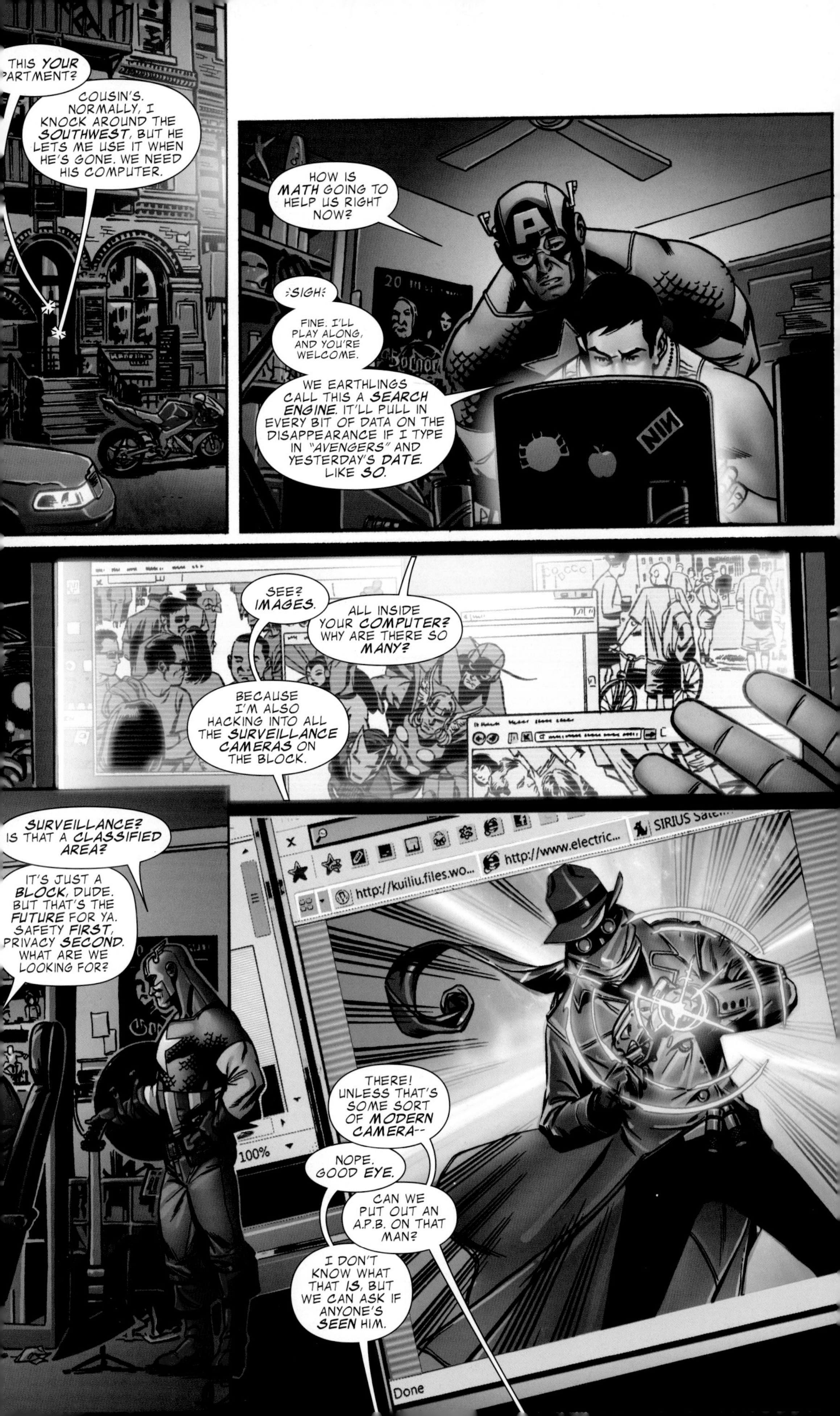
THIS YOUR
PARTMENT?
COUSIN'S. NORMALLY, I KNOCK AROUND THE SOUTHWEST, BUT HE LETS ME USE IT WHEN HE'S GONE. WE NEED HIS COMPUTER.
HOW IS MATH GOING TO HELP US RIGHT NOW?
SIGH
FINE. I'LL PLAY ALONG, AND YOU'RE WELCOME.
WE EARTHLINGS CALL THIS A SEARCH ENGINE. IT'LL PULL IN EVERY BIT OF DATA ON THE DISAPPEARANCE IF I TYPE IN "AVENGERS" AND YESTERDAY'S DATE. LIKE SO.
SEE? IMAGES.
ALL INSIDE YOUR COMPUTER? WHY ARE THERE SO MANY?
BECAUSE I'M ALSO HACKING INTO ALL THE SURVEILLANCE CAMERAS ON THE BLOCK.
SURVEILLANCE? IS THAT A CLASSIFIED AREA?
IT'S JUST A BLOCK, DUDE. BUT THAT'S THE FUTURE FOR YA. SAFETY FIRST, PRIVACY SECOND. WHAT ARE WE LOOKING FOR?
SIRIUS Sate...
http://www.electric...
http://kuiliu.files.wo...
100%
Done
THERE! UNLESS THAT'S SOME SORT OF MODERN CAMERA--
NOPE. GOOD EYE.
CAN WE PUT OUT AN A.P.B. ON THAT MAN?
I DON'T KNOW WHAT THAT IS, BUT WE CAN ASK IF ANYONE'S SEEN HIM.

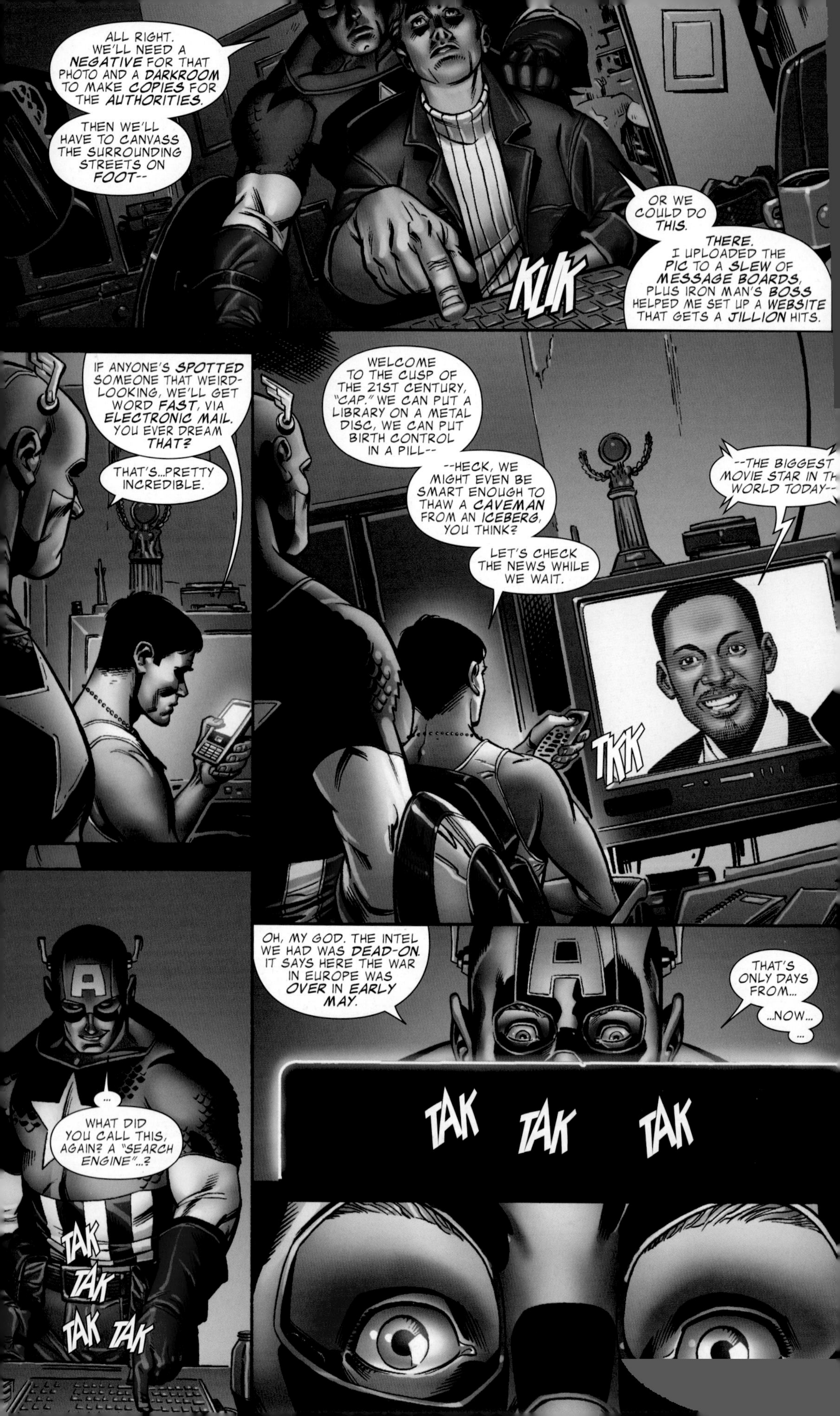

ALL RIGHT. WE'LL NEED A NEGATIVE FOR THAT PHOTO AND A DARKROOM TO MAKE COPIES FOR THE AUTHORITIES.
THEN WE'LL HAVE TO CANVASS THE SURROUNDING STREETS ON FOOT--
OR WE COULD DO THIS.
KLIK
THERE. I UPLOADED THE PIC TO A SLEW OF MESSAGE BOARDS, PLUS IRON MAN'S BOSS HELPED ME SET UP A WEBSITE THAT GETS A JILLION HITS.
IF ANYONE'S SPOTTED SOMEONE THAT WEIRD-LOOKING, WE'LL GET WORD FAST, VIA ELECTRONIC MAIL. YOU EVER DREAM THAT?
THAT'S...PRETTY INCREDIBLE.
WELCOME TO THE CUSP OF THE 21ST CENTURY, "CAP." WE CAN PUT A LIBRARY ON A METAL DISC, WE CAN PUT BIRTH CONTROL IN A PILL--
--HECK, WE MIGHT EVEN BE SMART ENOUGH TO THAW A CAVEMAN FROM AN ICEBERG, YOU THINK?
LET'S CHECK THE NEWS WHILE WE WAIT.
--THE BIGGEST MOVIE STAR IN TH WORLD TODAY--
TKK
...
WHAT DID YOU CALL THIS, AGAIN? A "SEARCH ENGINE"...?
TAK
TAK
TAK TAK
OH, MY GOD. THE INTEL WE HAD WAS DEAD-ON. IT SAYS HERE THE WAR IN EUROPE WAS OVER IN EARLY MAY.
THAT'S ONLY DAYS FROM...
...NOW...
...
TAK TAK TAK

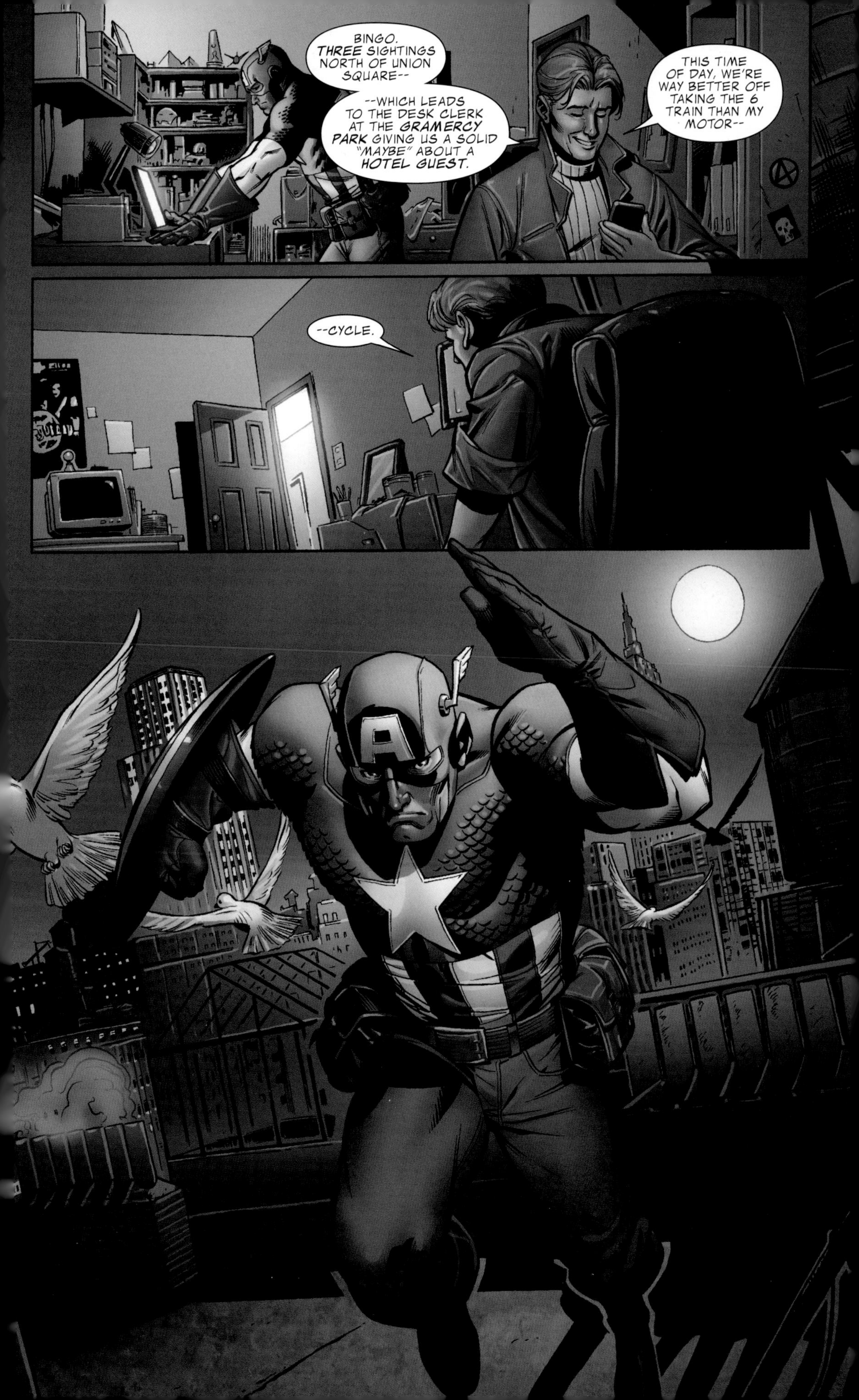
BINGO. THREE SIGHTINGS NORTH OF UNION SQUARE--
--WHICH LEADS TO THE DESK CLERK AT THE GRAMERCY PARK GIVING US A SOLID "MAYBE" ABOUT A HOTEL GUEST.
THIS TIME OF DAY, WE'RE WAY BETTER OFF TAKING THE 6 TRAIN THAN MY MOTOR--
--CYCLE.

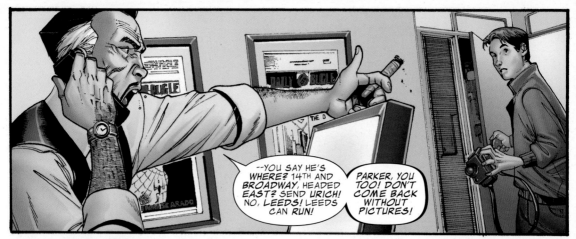

--YOU SAY HE'S WHERE? 14TH AND BROADWAY, HEADED EAST? SEND URICH! NO, LEEDS! LEEDS CAN RUN!

PARKER, YOU TOO! DON'T COME BACK WITHOUT PICTURES!

--WHERE, JUST HOURS AGO, LOCAL ACTIVISTS PROTESTED--

--WAIT! FORGET ME, GET HIM! GET THE SHOT! LADIES AND GENTLEMEN--

--YOU'RE SEEING LIVE FOOTAGE OF THE MYSTERY MAN WHO JUST HOURS AGO BROUGHT MIDTOWN TO A STANDSTILL WITH A SUPERHUMAN DISPLAY OF ACROBATICS!

IS HE AN ACTOR? IS THIS A PUBLICITY STUNT OF SOME KIND? OR IS THERE A NEW HERO ON THE SCENE?

NO ONE AUTHORIZED THIS, MR. PRESIDENT. WHOEVER HE IS, HE'S A WILD CARD, BUT OUR BEST MEN ARE ALREADY ON IT. WE WILL GET ANSWERS.

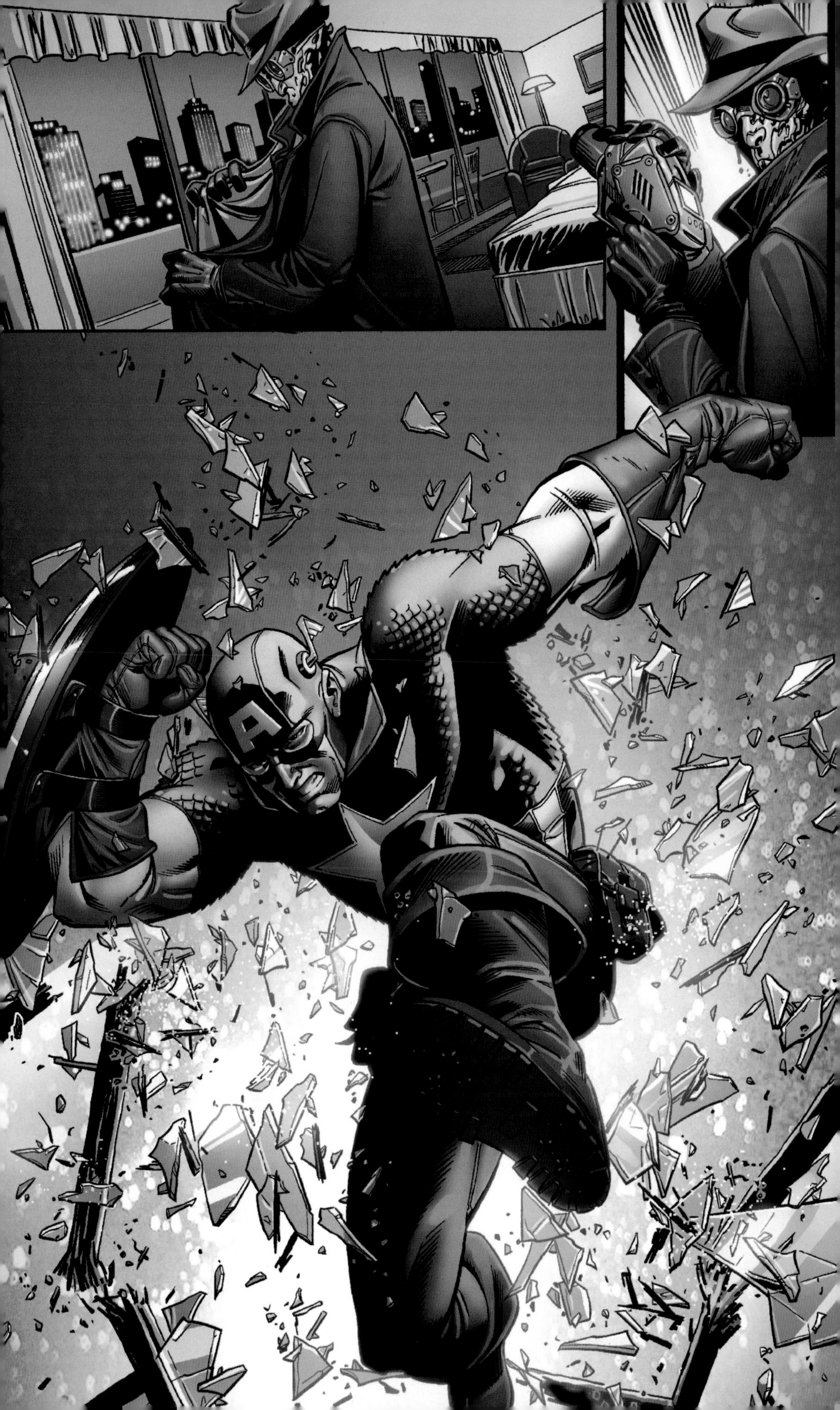

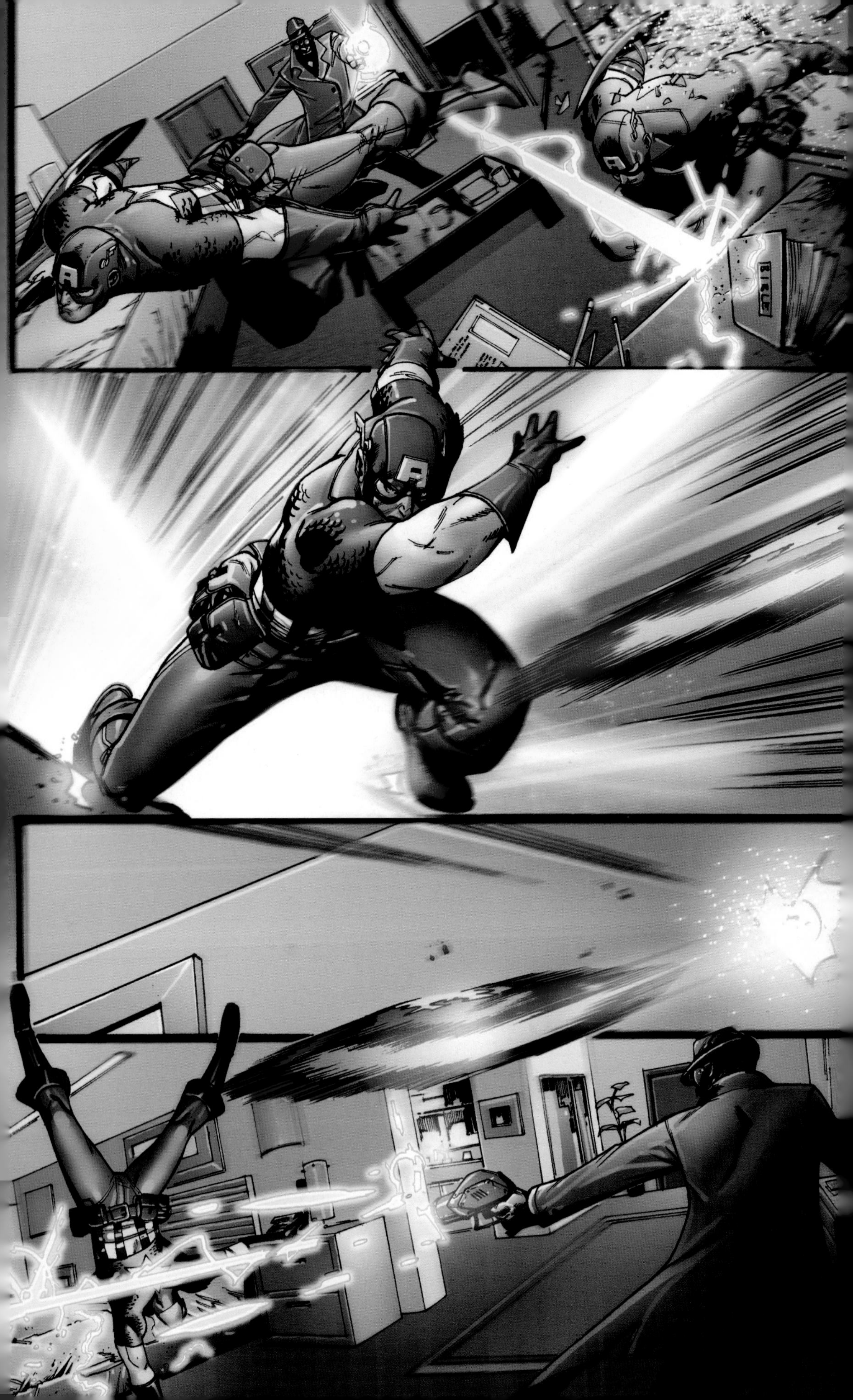

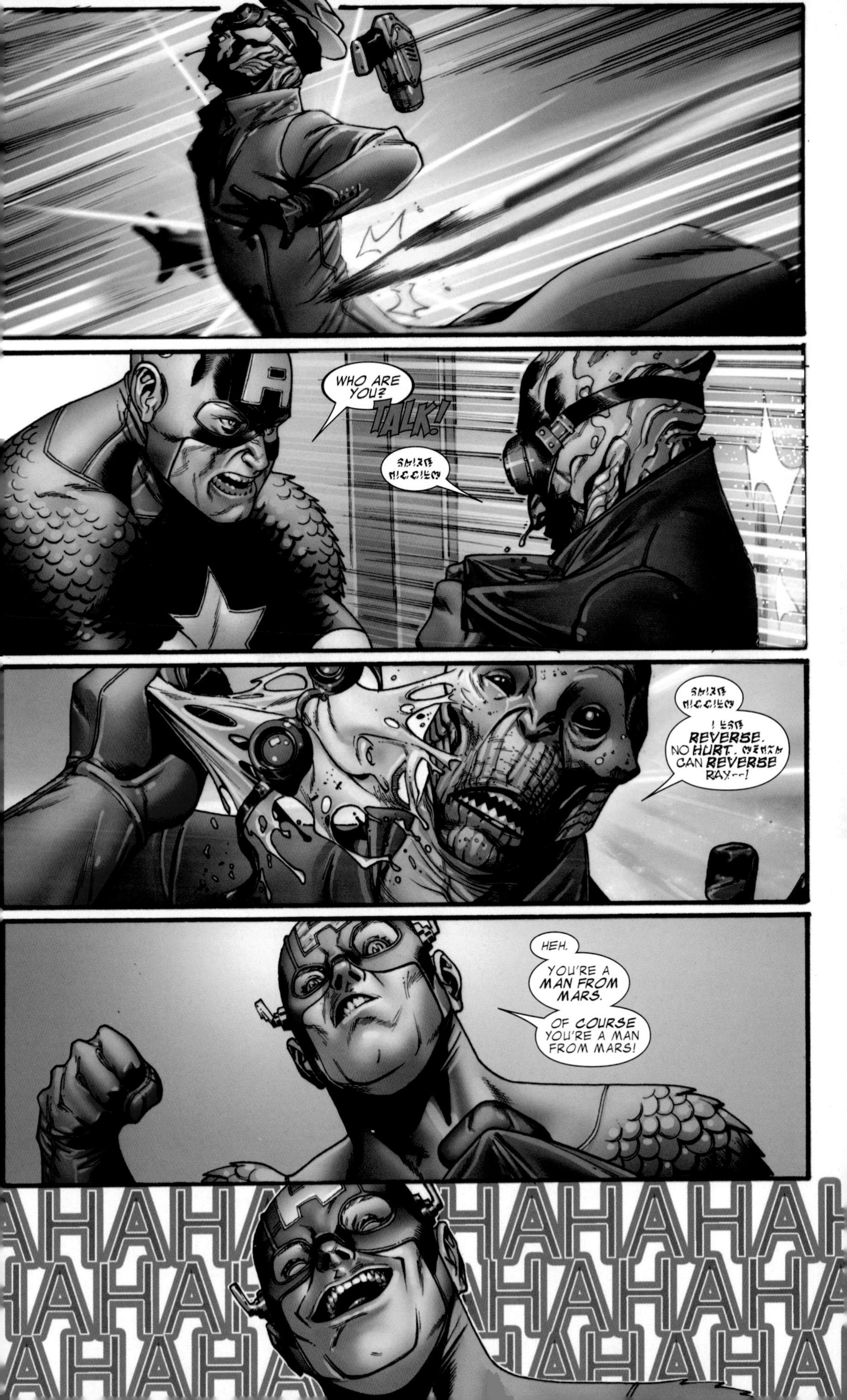
WHO ARE YOU? TALK!
REVERSE. NO HURT. CAN REVERSE RAY--!
HEH.
YOU'RE A MAN FROM MARS.
OF COURSE YOU'RE A MAN FROM MARS!
HAHAHAHAHAHAHAHAHAHAHAHAHAHAHAHAHA

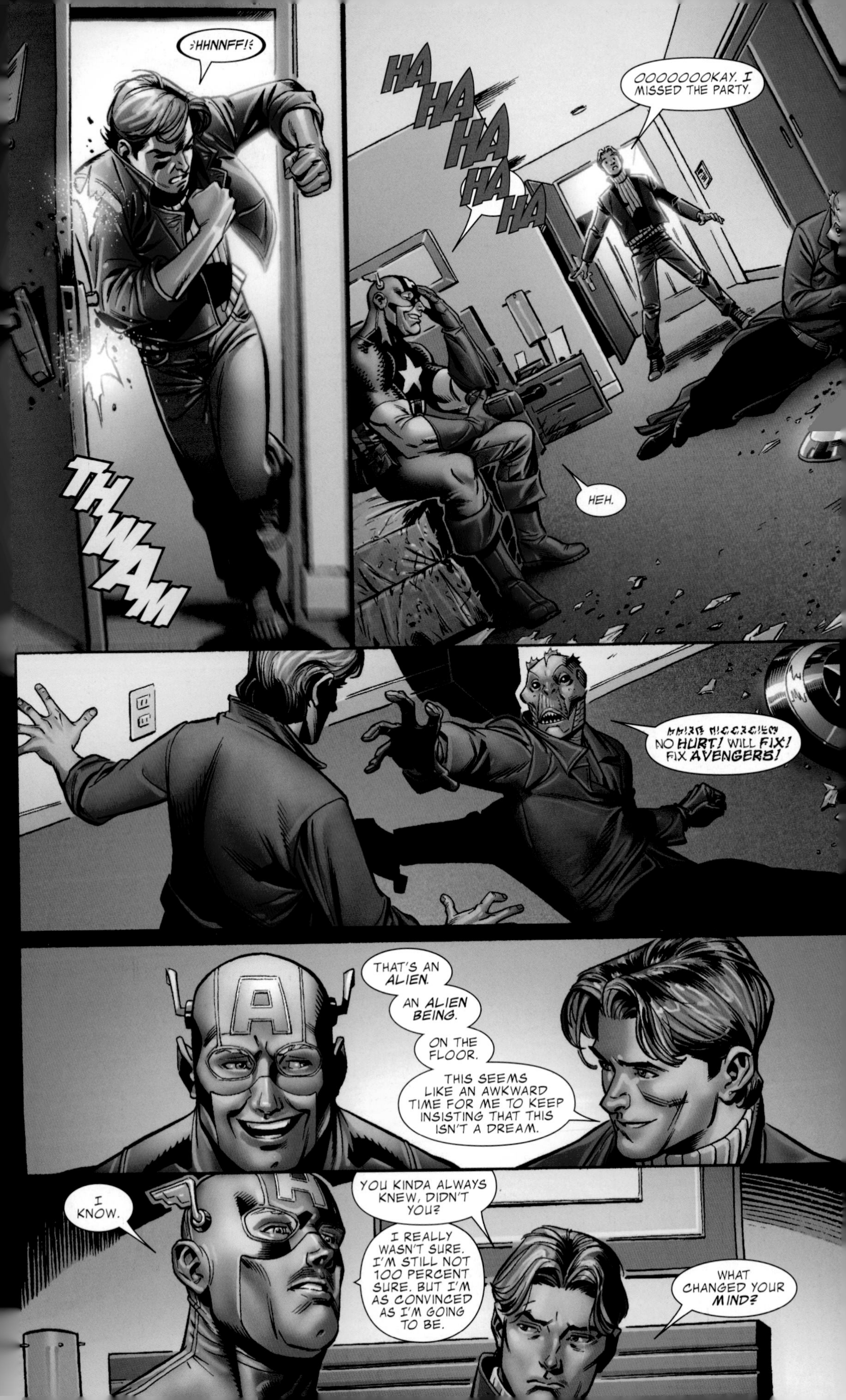
HHNNFF!
THWAM
HA HA HA HA HA HA
OOOOOOOKAY. I MISSED THE PARTY.
HEH.
NO HURT! WILL FIX! FIX AVENGERS!
THAT'S AN ALIEN.
AN ALIEN BEING.
ON THE FLOOR.
THIS SEEMS LIKE AN AWKWARD TIME FOR ME TO KEEP INSISTING THAT THIS ISN'T A DREAM.
I KNOW.
YOU KINDA ALWAYS KNEW, DIDN'T YOU?
I REALLY WASN'T SURE. I'M STILL NOT 100 PERCENT SURE. BUT I'M AS CONVINCED AS I'M GOING TO BE.
WHAT CHANGED YOUR MIND?

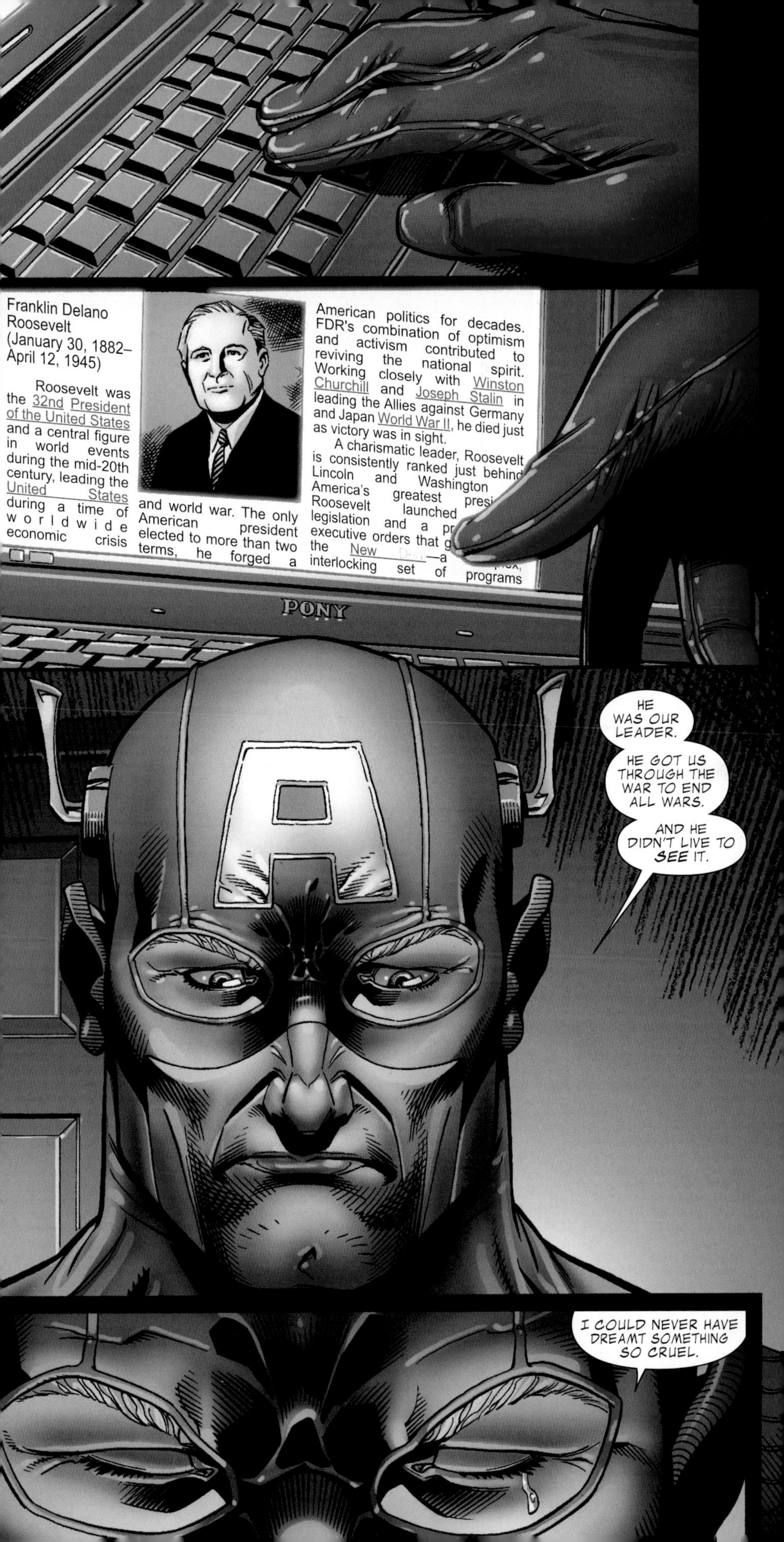
Franklin Delano Roosevelt (January 30, 1882–April 12, 1945)
Roosevelt was the 32nd President of the United States and a central figure in world events during the mid-20th century, leading the United States during a time of worldwide economic crisis
and world war. The only American president elected to more than two terms, he forged a
American politics for decades. FDR's combination of optimism and activism contributed to reviving the national spirit. Working closely with Winston Churchill and Joseph Stalin in leading the Allies against Germany and Japan World War II, he died just as victory was in sight.
A charismatic leader, Roosevelt is consistently ranked just behind Lincoln and Washington America's greatest presi
Roosevelt launched legislation and a pr executive orders that g the New D —a interlocking set of programs
PONY
HE WAS OUR LEADER.
HE GOT US THROUGH THE WAR TO END ALL WARS.
AND HE DIDN'T LIVE TO *SEE* IT.
I COULD NEVER HAVE DREAMT SOMETHING SO CRUEL.

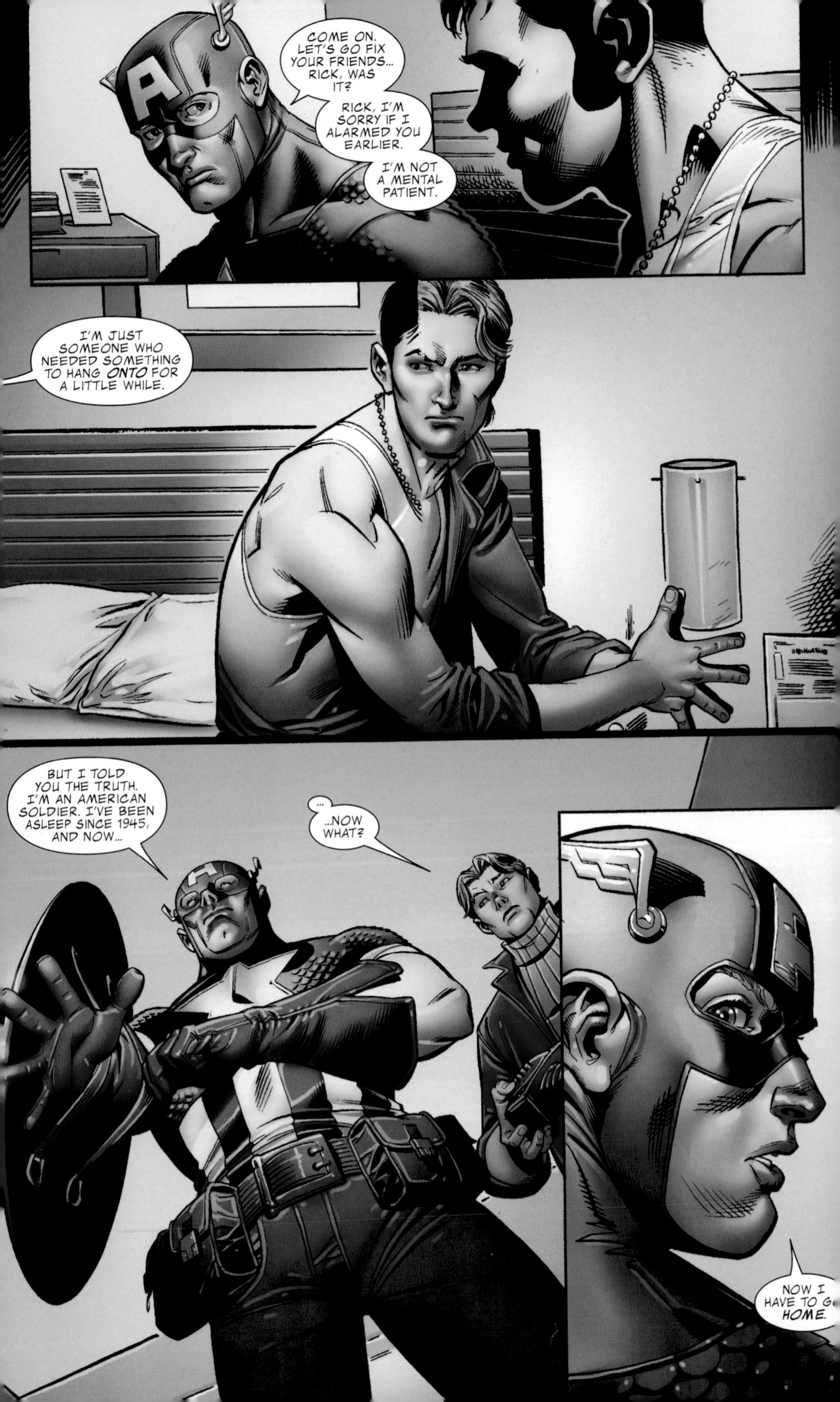
COME ON. LET'S GO FIX YOUR FRIENDS... RICK, WAS IT?
RICK, I'M SORRY IF I ALARMED YOU EARLIER.
I'M NOT A MENTAL PATIENT.
I'M JUST SOMEONE WHO NEEDED SOMETHING TO HANG *ONTO* FOR A LITTLE WHILE.
BUT I TOLD YOU THE TRUTH. I'M AN AMERICAN SOLDIER. I'VE BEEN ASLEEP SINCE 1945, AND NOW...
...
...NOW WHAT?
NOW I HAVE TO G *HOME*.

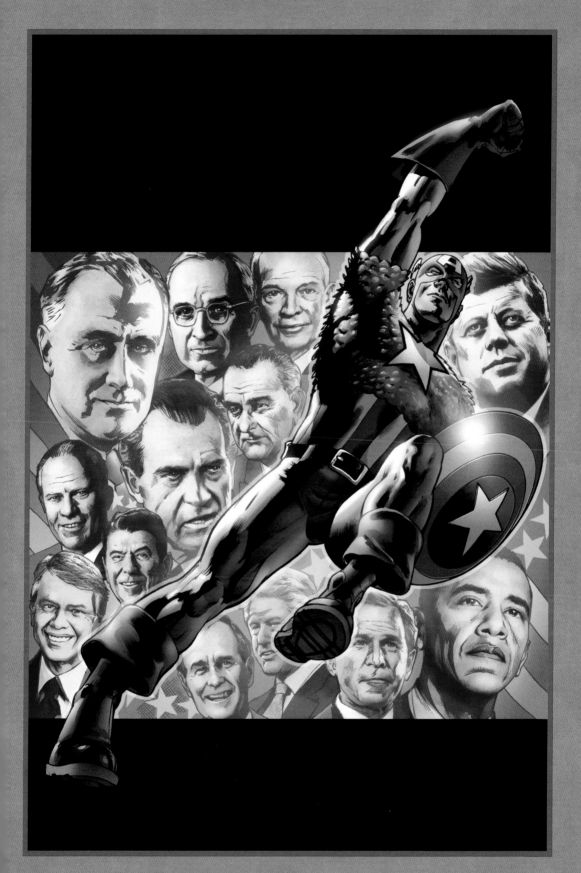

[3]

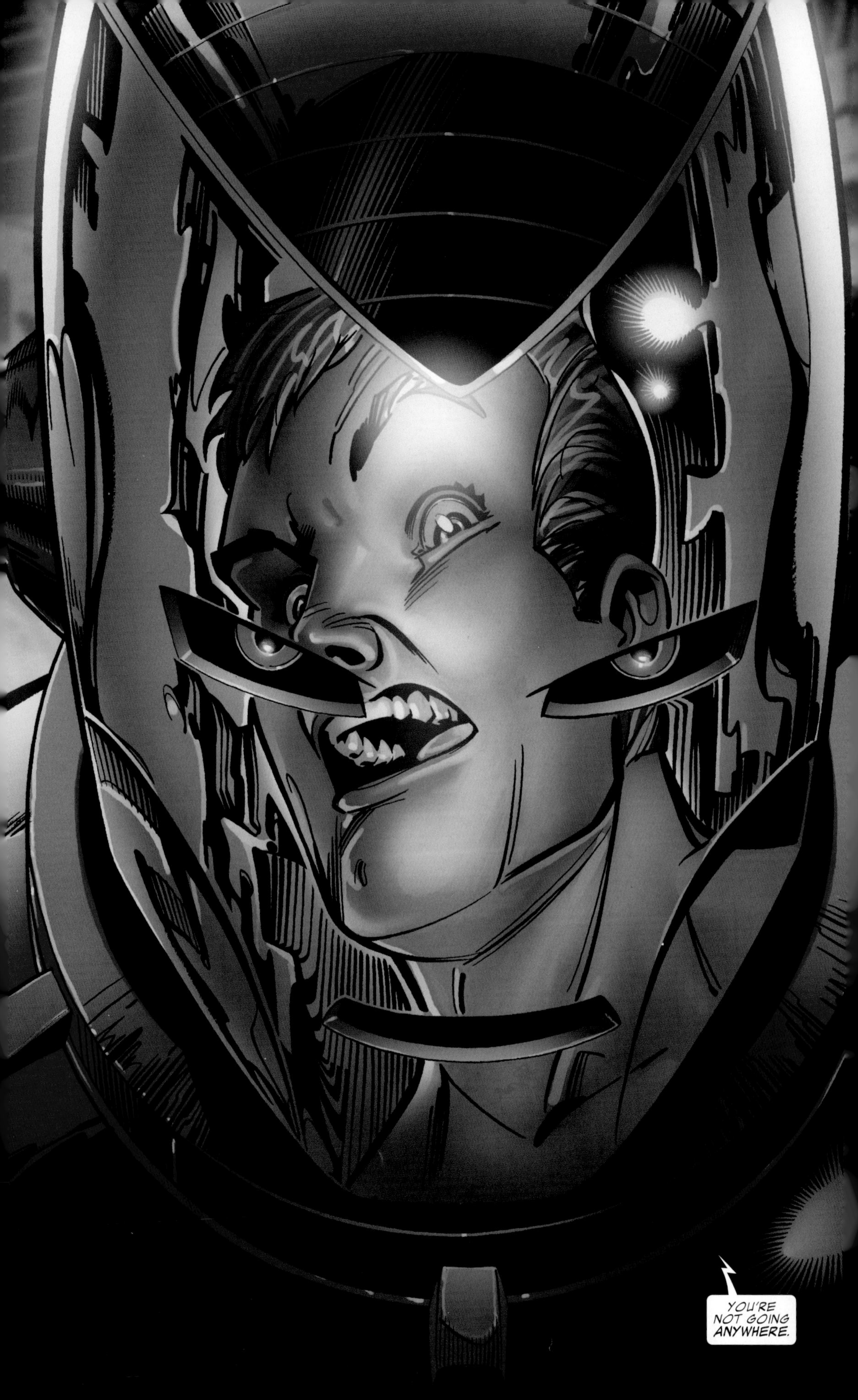
YOU'RE NOT GOING ANYWHERE.

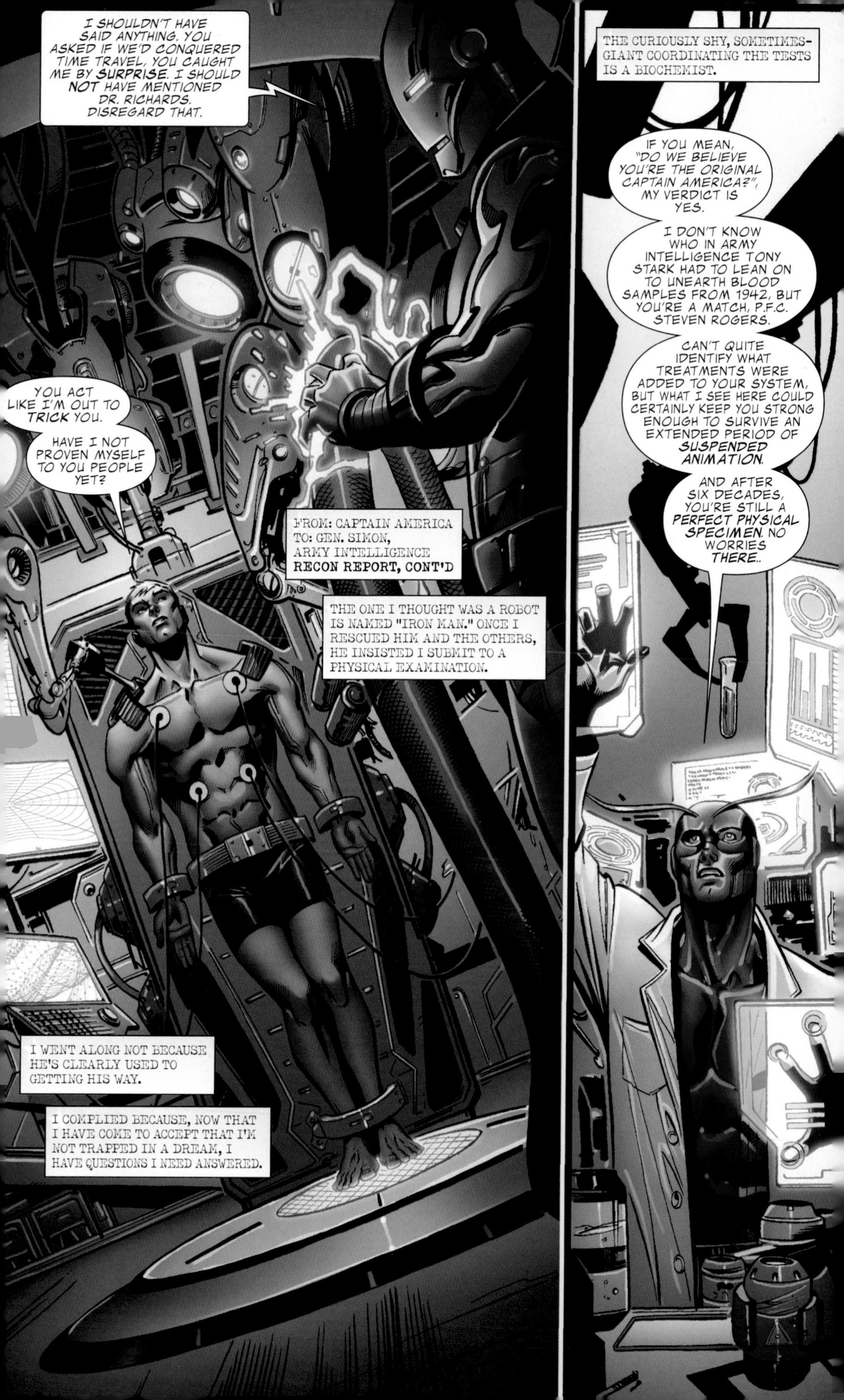

I SHOULDN'T HAVE SAID ANYTHING. YOU ASKED IF WE'D CONQUERED TIME TRAVEL, YOU CAUGHT ME BY SURPRISE. I SHOULD NOT HAVE MENTIONED DR. RICHARDS. DISREGARD THAT.
YOU ACT LIKE I'M OUT TO TRICK YOU.
HAVE I NOT PROVEN MYSELF TO YOU PEOPLE YET?
FROM: CAPTAIN AMERICA
TO: GEN. SIMON, ARMY INTELLIGENCE
RECON REPORT, CONT'D
THE ONE I THOUGHT WAS A ROBOT IS NAMED "IRON MAN." ONCE I RESCUED HIM AND THE OTHERS, HE INSISTED I SUBMIT TO A PHYSICAL EXAMINATION.
I WENT ALONG NOT BECAUSE HE'S CLEARLY USED TO GETTING HIS WAY.
I COMPLIED BECAUSE, NOW THAT I HAVE COME TO ACCEPT THAT I'M NOT TRAPPED IN A DREAM, I HAVE QUESTIONS I NEED ANSWERED.
THE CURIOUSLY SHY, SOMETIMES-GIANT COORDINATING THE TESTS IS A BIOCHEMIST.
IF YOU MEAN, "DO WE BELIEVE YOU'RE THE ORIGINAL CAPTAIN AMERICA?", MY VERDICT IS YES.
I DON'T KNOW WHO IN ARMY INTELLIGENCE TONY STARK HAD TO LEAN ON TO UNEARTH BLOOD SAMPLES FROM 1942, BUT YOU'RE A MATCH, P.F.C. STEVEN ROGERS.
CAN'T QUITE IDENTIFY WHAT TREATMENTS WERE ADDED TO YOUR SYSTEM, BUT WHAT I SEE HERE COULD CERTAINLY KEEP YOU STRONG ENOUGH TO SURVIVE AN EXTENDED PERIOD OF SUSPENDED ANIMATION.
AND AFTER SIX DECADES, YOU'RE STILL A PERFECT PHYSICAL SPECIMEN. NO WORRIES THERE..

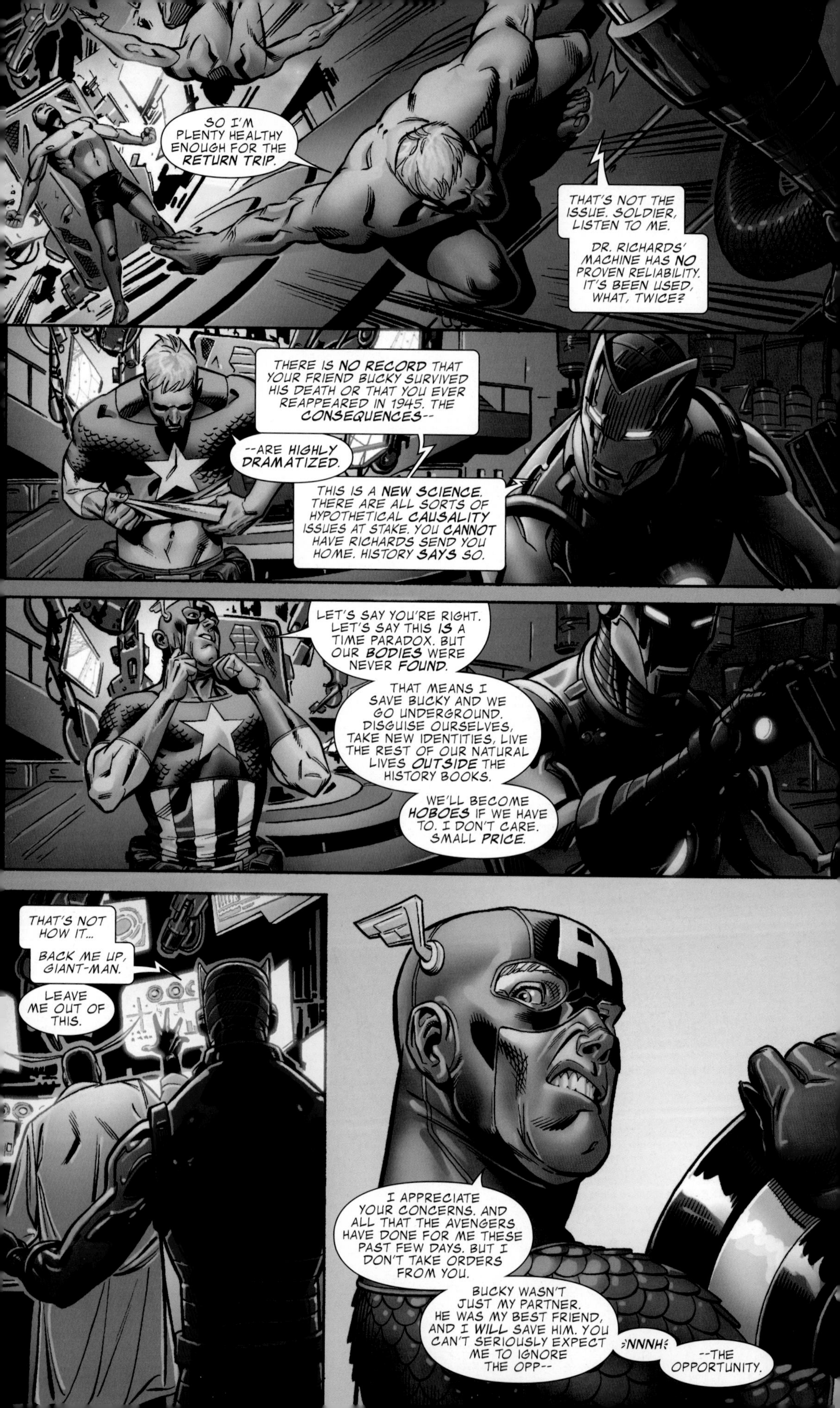
SO I'M PLENTY HEALTHY ENOUGH FOR THE RETURN TRIP.
THAT'S NOT THE ISSUE. SOLDIER, LISTEN TO ME.
DR. RICHARDS' MACHINE HAS NO PROVEN RELIABILITY. IT'S BEEN USED, WHAT, TWICE?
THERE IS NO RECORD THAT YOUR FRIEND BUCKY SURVIVED HIS DEATH OR THAT YOU EVER REAPPEARED IN 1945. THE CONSEQUENCES--
--ARE HIGHLY DRAMATIZED.
THIS IS A NEW SCIENCE. THERE ARE ALL SORTS OF HYPOTHETICAL CAUSALITY ISSUES AT STAKE. YOU CANNOT HAVE RICHARDS SEND YOU HOME. HISTORY SAYS SO.
LET'S SAY YOU'RE RIGHT. LET'S SAY THIS IS A TIME PARADOX. BUT OUR BODIES WERE NEVER FOUND.
THAT MEANS I SAVE BUCKY AND WE GO UNDERGROUND. DISGUISE OURSELVES, TAKE NEW IDENTITIES, LIVE THE REST OF OUR NATURAL LIVES OUTSIDE THE HISTORY BOOKS.
WE'LL BECOME HOBOES IF WE HAVE TO. I DON'T CARE. SMALL PRICE.
THAT'S NOT HOW IT...
BACK ME UP, GIANT-MAN.
LEAVE ME OUT OF THIS.
I APPRECIATE YOUR CONCERNS. AND ALL THAT THE AVENGERS HAVE DONE FOR ME THESE PAST FEW DAYS. BUT I DON'T TAKE ORDERS FROM YOU.
BUCKY WASN'T JUST MY PARTNER. HE WAS MY BEST FRIEND, AND I WILL SAVE HIM. YOU CAN'T SERIOUSLY EXPECT ME TO IGNORE THE OPP--
NNNH
--THE OPPORTUNITY.

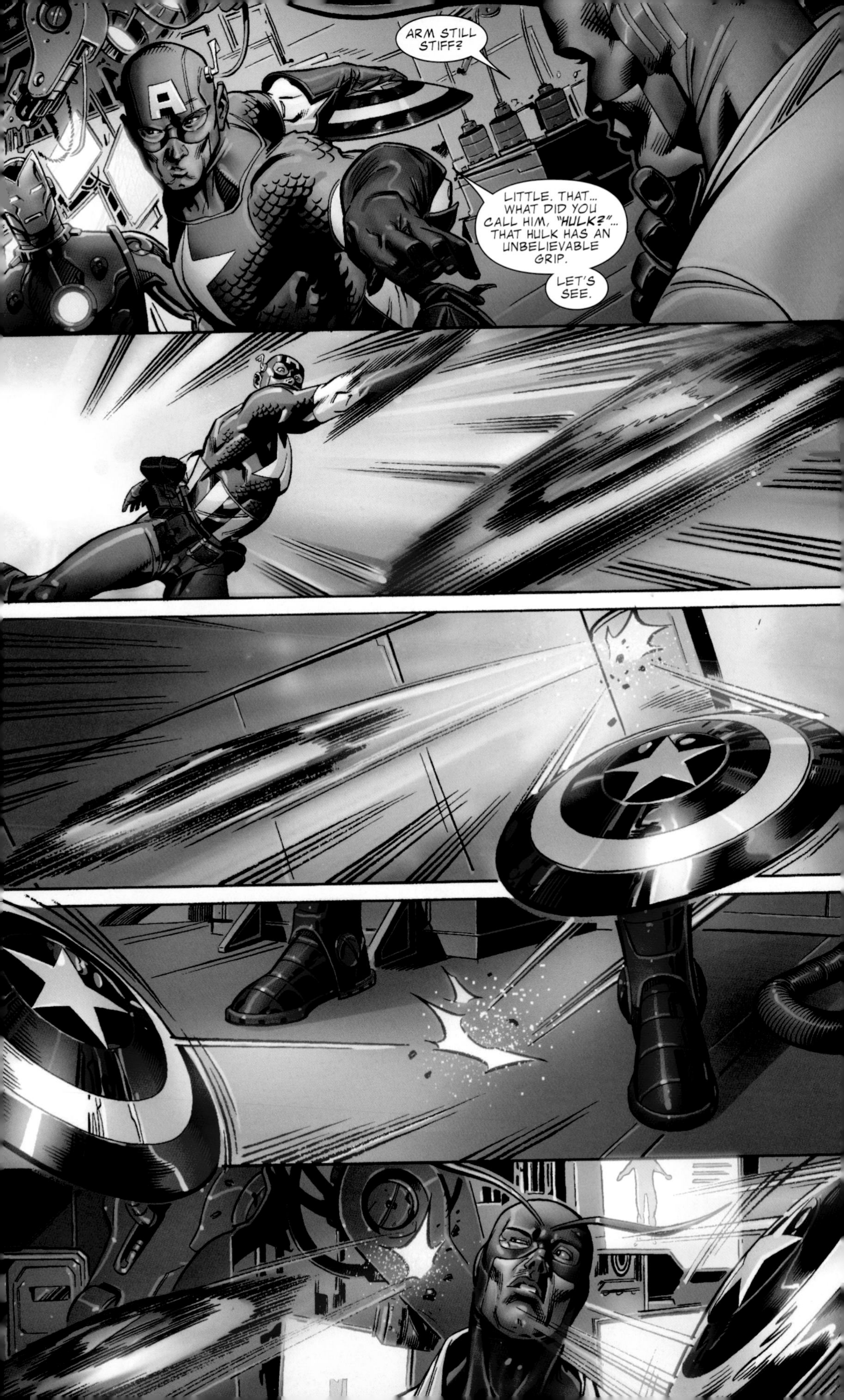
ARM STILL STIFF?
LITTLE. THAT... WHAT DID YOU CALL HIM, "HULK?"... THAT HULK HAS AN UNBELIEVABLE GRIP.
LET'S SEE.

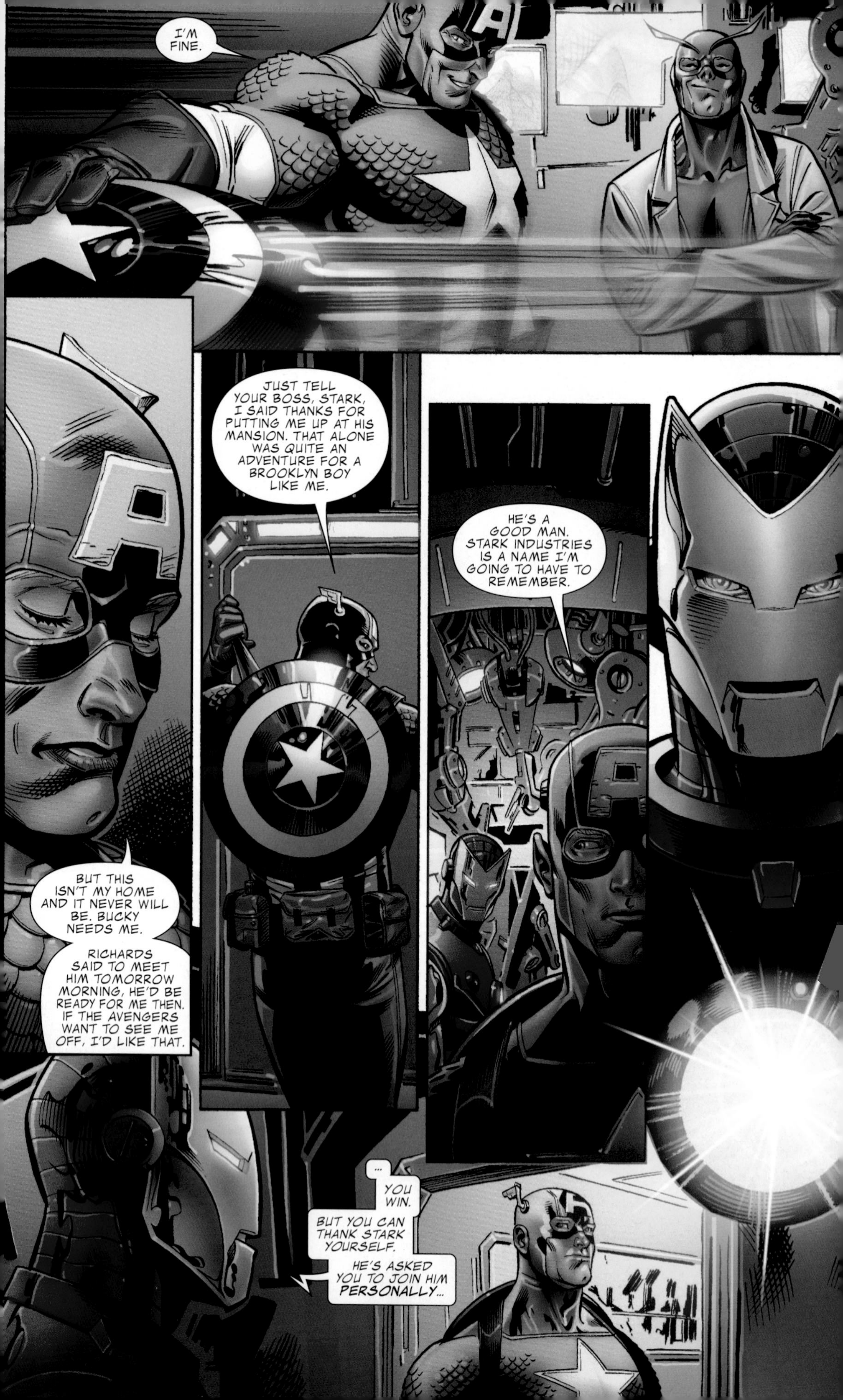
I'M FINE.
JUST TELL YOUR BOSS, STARK, I SAID THANKS FOR PUTTING ME UP AT HIS MANSION. THAT ALONE WAS QUITE AN ADVENTURE FOR A BROOKLYN BOY LIKE ME.
HE'S A GOOD MAN. STARK INDUSTRIES IS A NAME I'M GOING TO HAVE TO REMEMBER.
BUT THIS ISN'T MY HOME AND IT NEVER WILL BE. BUCKY NEEDS ME.
RICHARDS SAID TO MEET HIM TOMORROW MORNING, HE'D BE READY FOR ME THEN. IF THE AVENGERS WANT TO SEE ME OFF, I'D LIKE THAT.
...
YOU WIN.
BUT YOU CAN THANK STARK YOURSELF.
HE'S ASKED YOU TO JOIN HIM PERSONALLY...

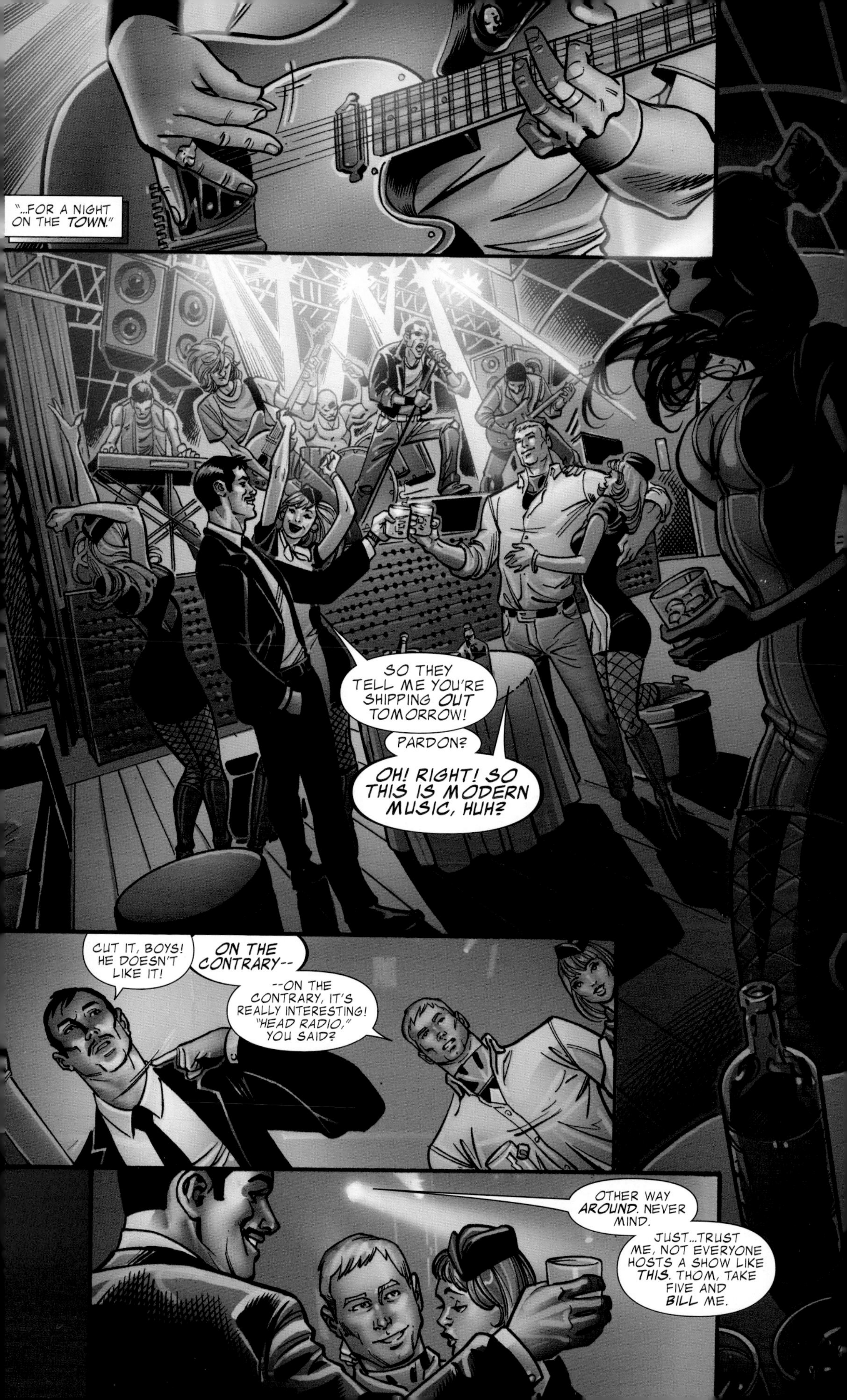

"...FOR A NIGHT ON THE TOWN."
SO THEY TELL ME YOU'RE SHIPPING OUT TOMORROW!
PARDON?
OH! RIGHT! SO THIS IS MODERN MUSIC, HUH?
CUT IT, BOYS! HE DOESN'T LIKE IT!
ON THE CONTRARY--
--ON THE CONTRARY, IT'S REALLY INTERESTING! "HEAD RADIO," YOU SAID?
OTHER WAY AROUND. NEVER MIND.
JUST...TRUST ME, NOT EVERYONE HOSTS A SHOW LIKE THIS. THOM, TAKE FIVE AND BILL ME.

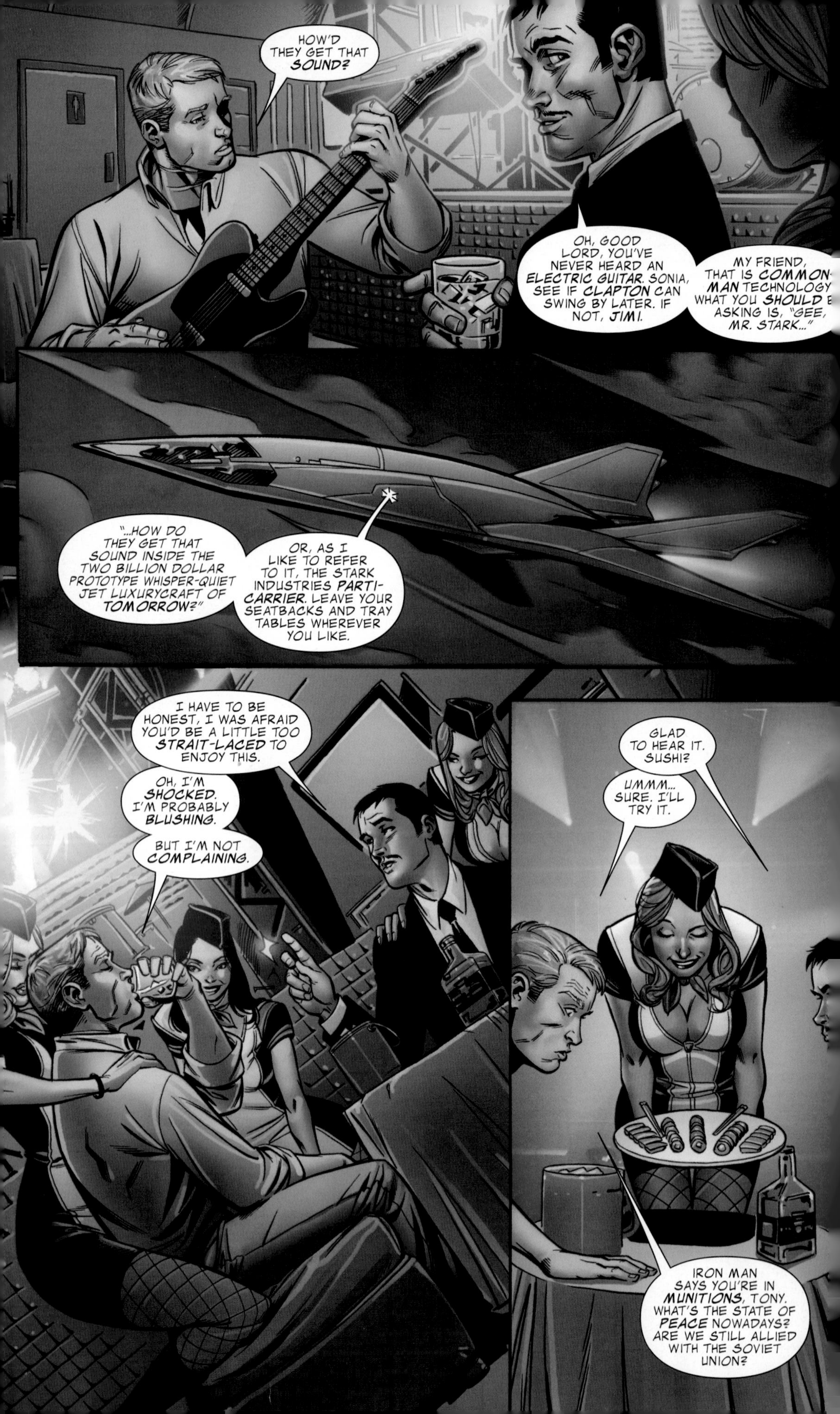
HOW'D THEY GET THAT SOUND?
OH, GOOD LORD, YOU'VE NEVER HEARD AN ELECTRIC GUITAR. SONIA, SEE IF CLAPTON CAN SWING BY LATER. IF NOT, JIMI.
MY FRIEND, THAT IS COMMON-MAN TECHNOLOGY. WHAT YOU SHOULD BE ASKING IS, "GEE, MR. STARK...
"...HOW DO THEY GET THAT SOUND INSIDE THE TWO BILLION DOLLAR PROTOTYPE WHISPER-QUIET JET LUXURYCRAFT OF TOMORROW?"
OR, AS I LIKE TO REFER TO IT, THE STARK INDUSTRIES PARTI-CARRIER. LEAVE YOUR SEATBACKS AND TRAY TABLES WHEREVER YOU LIKE.
I HAVE TO BE HONEST, I WAS AFRAID YOU'D BE A LITTLE TOO STRAIT-LACED TO ENJOY THIS.
OH, I'M SHOCKED. I'M PROBABLY BLUSHING.
BUT I'M NOT COMPLAINING.
GLAD TO HEAR IT. SUSHI?
UMMM... SURE. I'LL TRY IT.
IRON MAN SAYS YOU'RE IN MUNITIONS, TONY. WHAT'S THE STATE OF PEACE NOWADAYS? ARE WE STILL ALLIED WITH THE SOVIET UNION?

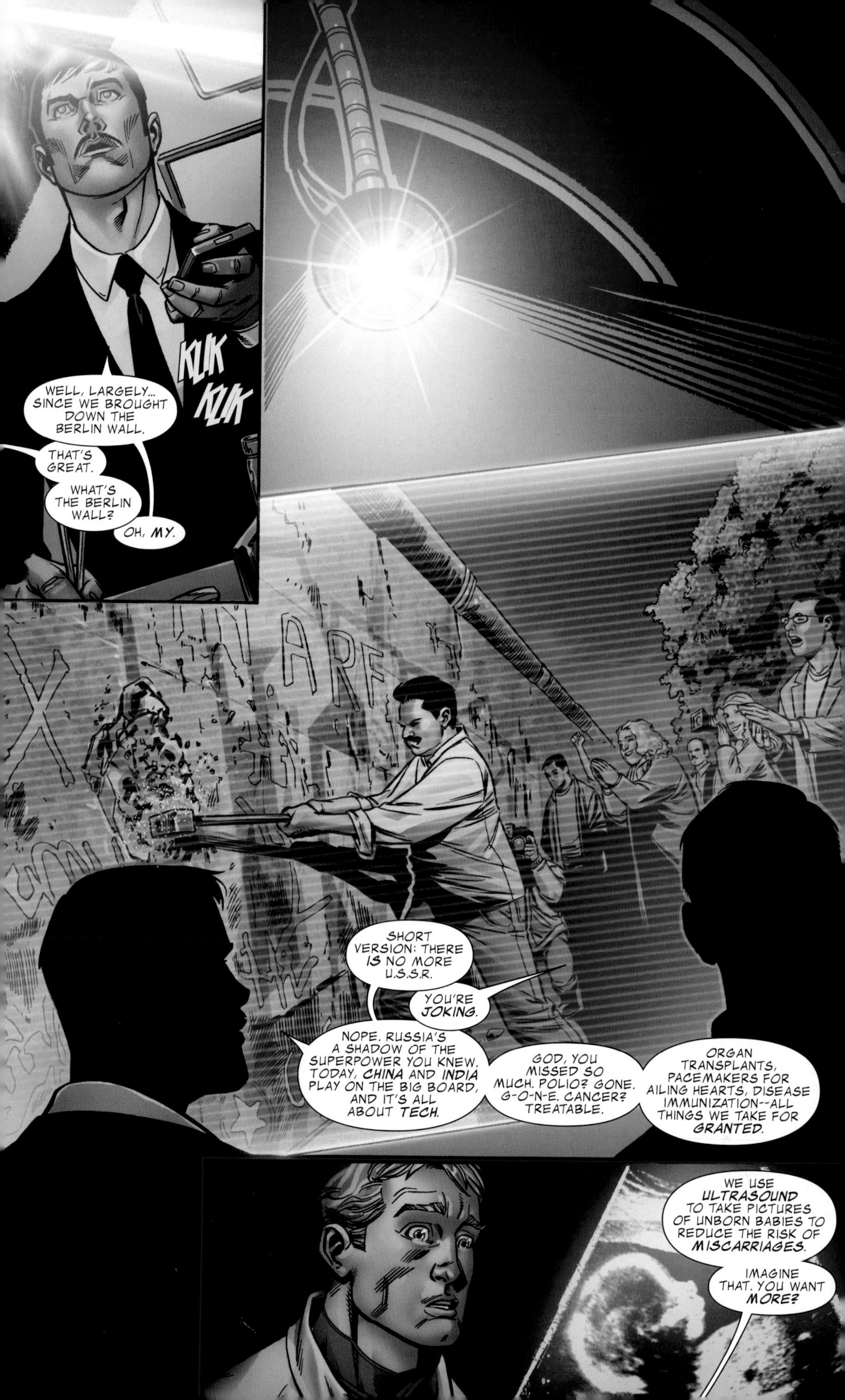
KLIK KLIK
WELL, LARGELY... SINCE WE BROUGHT DOWN THE BERLIN WALL.
THAT'S GREAT.
WHAT'S THE BERLIN WALL?
OH, MY.
SHORT VERSION: THERE IS NO MORE U.S.S.R.
YOU'RE JOKING.
NOPE. RUSSIA'S A SHADOW OF THE SUPERPOWER YOU KNEW. TODAY, CHINA AND INDIA PLAY ON THE BIG BOARD, AND IT'S ALL ABOUT TECH.
GOD, YOU MISSED SO MUCH. POLIO? GONE. G-O-N-E. CANCER? TREATABLE.
ORGAN TRANSPLANTS, PACEMAKERS FOR AILING HEARTS, DISEASE IMMUNIZATION--ALL THINGS WE TAKE FOR GRANTED.
WE USE ULTRASOUND TO TAKE PICTURES OF UNBORN BABIES TO REDUCE THE RISK OF MISCARRIAGES.
IMAGINE THAT. YOU WANT MORE?

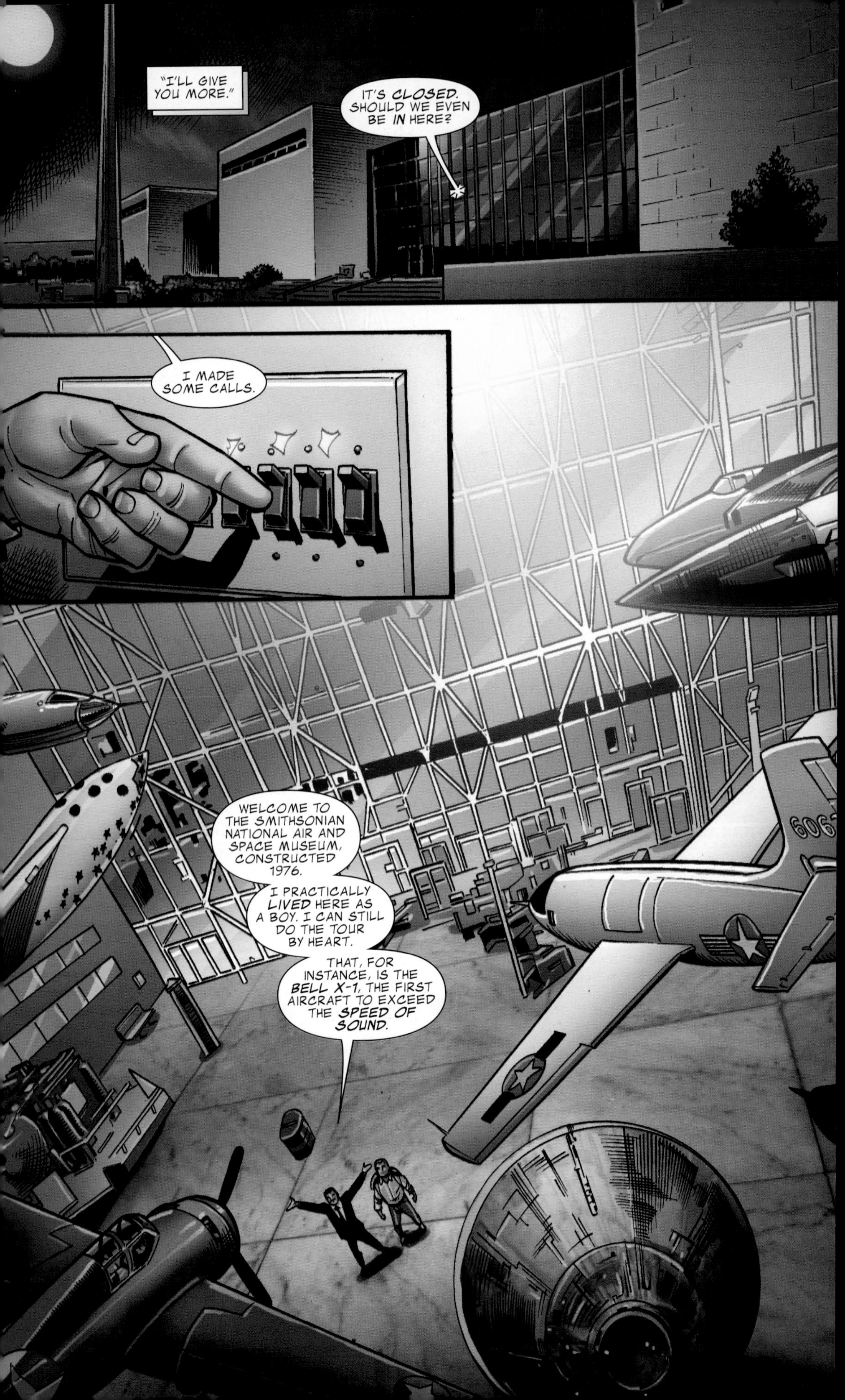
"I'LL GIVE YOU MORE."
IT'S CLOSED. SHOULD WE EVEN BE IN HERE?
I MADE SOME CALLS.
WELCOME TO THE SMITHSONIAN NATIONAL AIR AND SPACE MUSEUM, CONSTRUCTED 1976.
I PRACTICALLY LIVED HERE AS A BOY. I CAN STILL DO THE TOUR BY HEART.
THAT, FOR INSTANCE, IS THE BELL X-1, THE FIRST AIRCRAFT TO EXCEED THE SPEED OF SOUND.

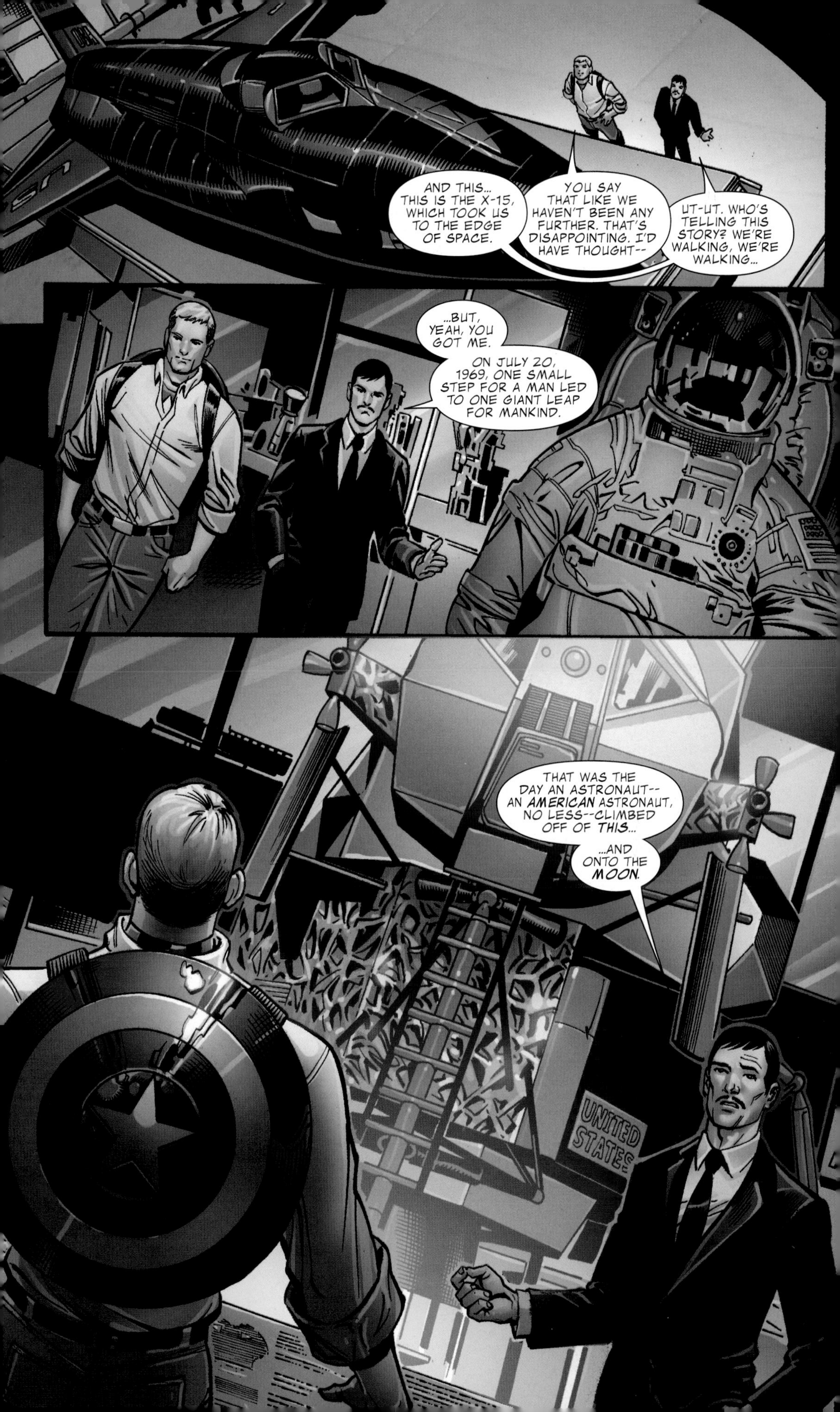
AND THIS... THIS IS THE X-15, WHICH TOOK US TO THE EDGE OF SPACE.
YOU SAY THAT LIKE WE HAVEN'T BEEN ANY FURTHER. THAT'S DISAPPOINTING. I'D HAVE THOUGHT--
UT-UT. WHO'S TELLING THIS STORY? WE'RE WALKING, WE'RE WALKING...
...BUT, YEAH, YOU GOT ME.
ON JULY 20, 1969, ONE SMALL STEP FOR A MAN LED TO ONE GIANT LEAP FOR MANKIND.
THAT WAS THE DAY AN ASTRONAUT-- AN *AMERICAN* ASTRONAUT, NO LESS--CLIMBED OFF OF *THIS*...
...AND ONTO THE *MOON*.
UNITED STATES

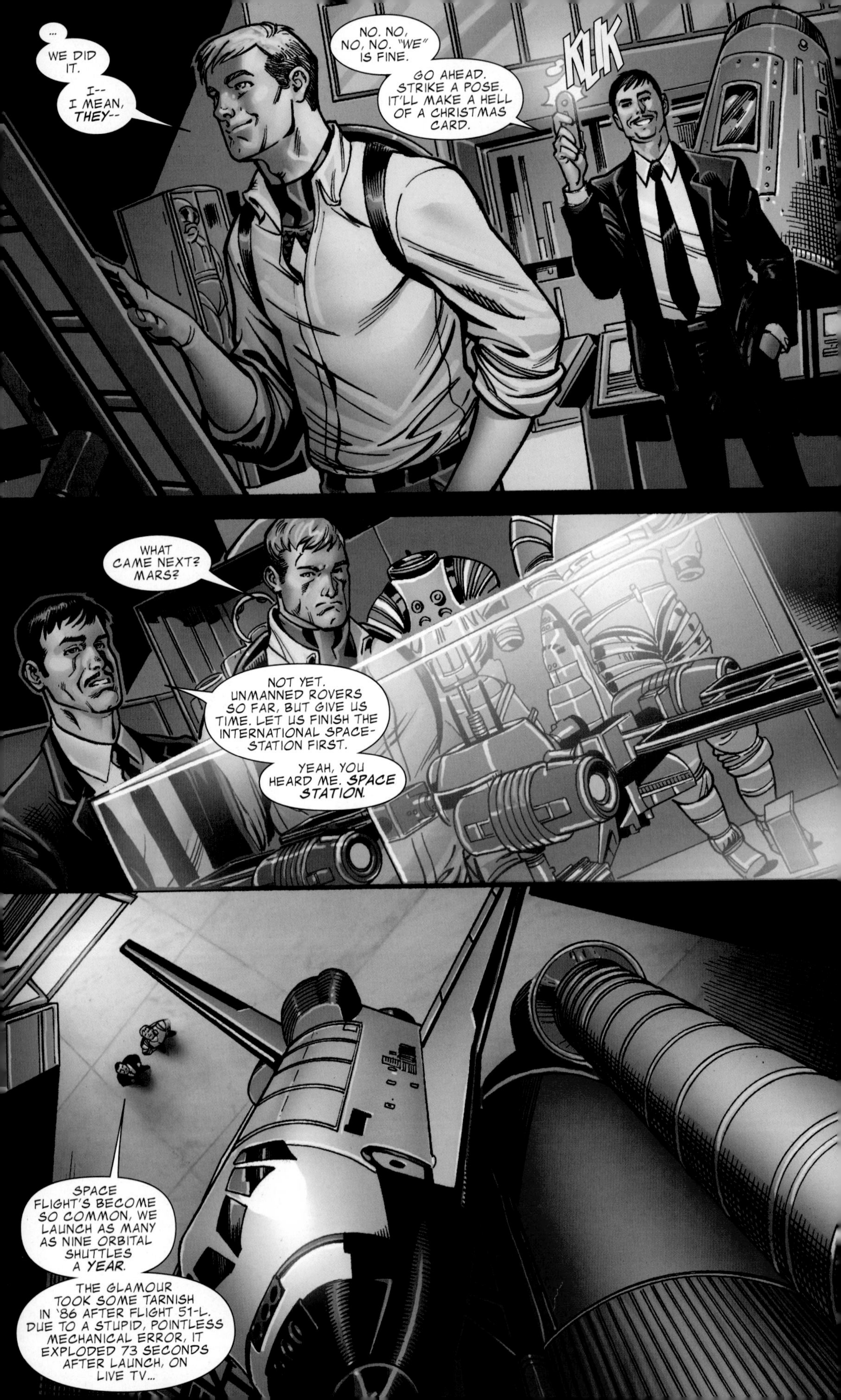
...
WE DID IT.
I-- I MEAN, THEY--
NO. NO, NO, NO. "WE" IS FINE.
GO AHEAD. STRIKE A POSE. IT'LL MAKE A HELL OF A CHRISTMAS CARD.
KLIK
WHAT CAME NEXT? MARS?
NOT YET. UNMANNED ROVERS SO FAR, BUT GIVE US TIME. LET US FINISH THE INTERNATIONAL SPACE-STATION FIRST.
YEAH, YOU HEARD ME. SPACE STATION.
SPACE FLIGHT'S BECOME SO COMMON, WE LAUNCH AS MANY AS NINE ORBITAL SHUTTLES A YEAR.
THE GLAMOUR TOOK SOME TARNISH IN '86 AFTER FLIGHT 51-L. DUE TO A STUPID, POINTLESS MECHANICAL ERROR, IT EXPLODED 73 SECONDS AFTER LAUNCH, ON LIVE TV...

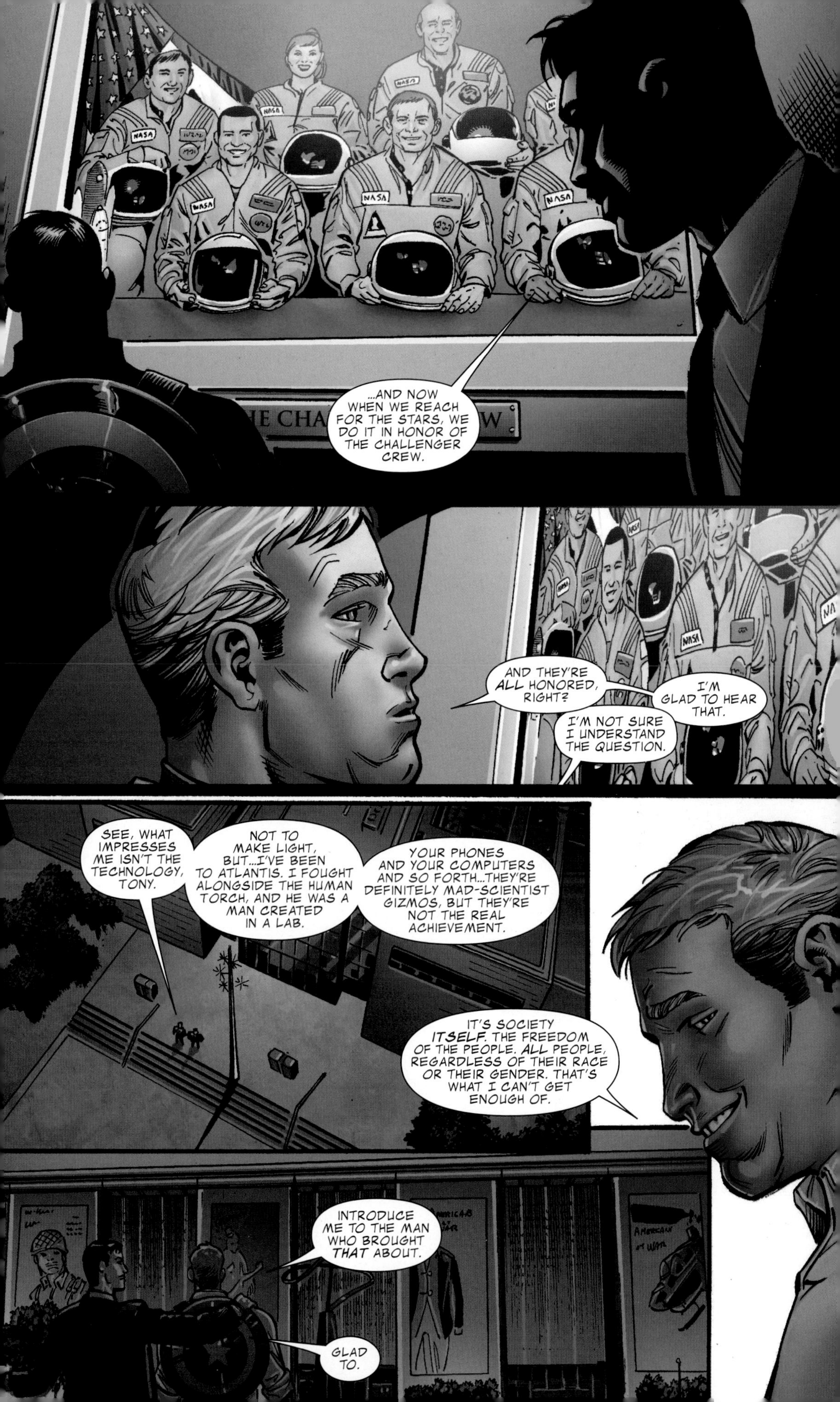
...AND NOW WHEN WE REACH FOR THE STARS, WE DO IT IN HONOR OF THE CHALLENGER CREW.
AND THEY'RE ALL HONORED, RIGHT?
I'M NOT SURE I UNDERSTAND THE QUESTION.
I'M GLAD TO HEAR THAT.
SEE, WHAT IMPRESSES ME ISN'T THE TECHNOLOGY, TONY.
NOT TO MAKE LIGHT, BUT...I'VE BEEN TO ATLANTIS. I FOUGHT ALONGSIDE THE HUMAN TORCH, AND HE WAS A MAN CREATED IN A LAB.
YOUR PHONES AND YOUR COMPUTERS AND SO FORTH...THEY'RE DEFINITELY MAD-SCIENTIST GIZMOS, BUT THEY'RE NOT THE REAL ACHIEVEMENT.
IT'S SOCIETY ITSELF. THE FREEDOM OF THE PEOPLE. ALL PEOPLE, REGARDLESS OF THEIR RACE OR THEIR GENDER. THAT'S WHAT I CAN'T GET ENOUGH OF.
INTRODUCE ME TO THE MAN WHO BROUGHT THAT ABOUT.
GLAD TO.

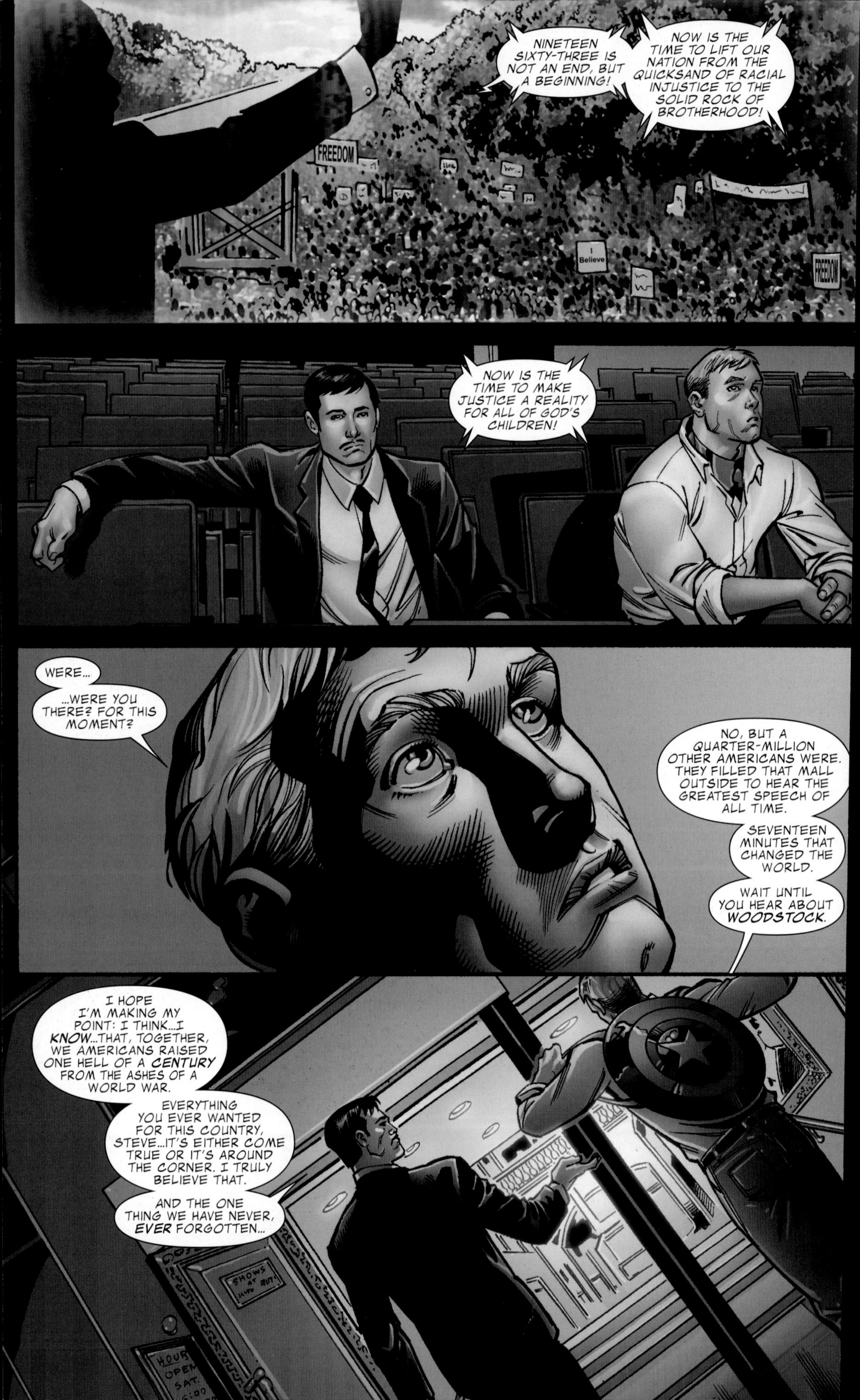
NINETEEN SIXTY-THREE IS NOT AN END, BUT A BEGINNING!
NOW IS THE TIME TO LIFT OUR NATION FROM THE QUICKSAND OF RACIAL INJUSTICE TO THE SOLID ROCK OF BROTHERHOOD!
FREEDOM
I Believe
FREEDOM
NOW IS THE TIME TO MAKE JUSTICE A REALITY FOR ALL OF GOD'S CHILDREN!
WERE...
...WERE YOU THERE? FOR THIS MOMENT?
NO, BUT A QUARTER-MILLION OTHER AMERICANS WERE. THEY FILLED THAT MALL OUTSIDE TO HEAR THE GREATEST SPEECH OF ALL TIME.
SEVENTEEN MINUTES THAT CHANGED THE WORLD.
WAIT UNTIL YOU HEAR ABOUT WOODSTOCK.
I HOPE I'M MAKING MY POINT: I THINK...I KNOW...THAT, TOGETHER, WE AMERICANS RAISED ONE HELL OF A CENTURY FROM THE ASHES OF A WORLD WAR.
EVERYTHING YOU EVER WANTED FOR THIS COUNTRY, STEVE...IT'S EITHER COME TRUE OR IT'S AROUND THE CORNER. I TRULY BELIEVE THAT.
AND THE ONE THING WE HAVE NEVER, EVER FORGOTTEN...
SHOWS

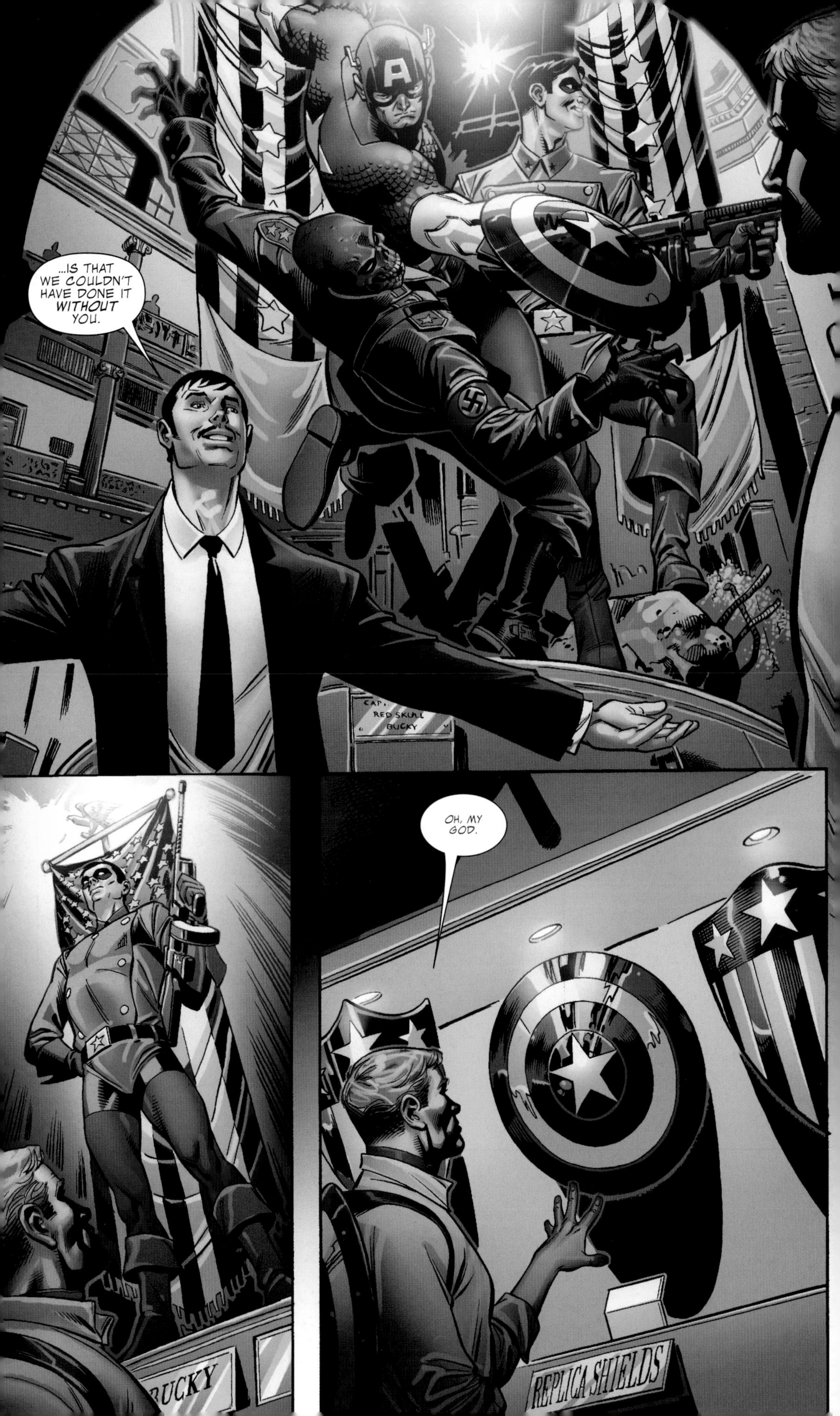
...IS THAT WE COULDN'T HAVE DONE IT WITHOUT YOU.
CAP.
RED SKULL
BUCKY
OH, MY GOD.
BUCKY
REPLICA SHIELDS

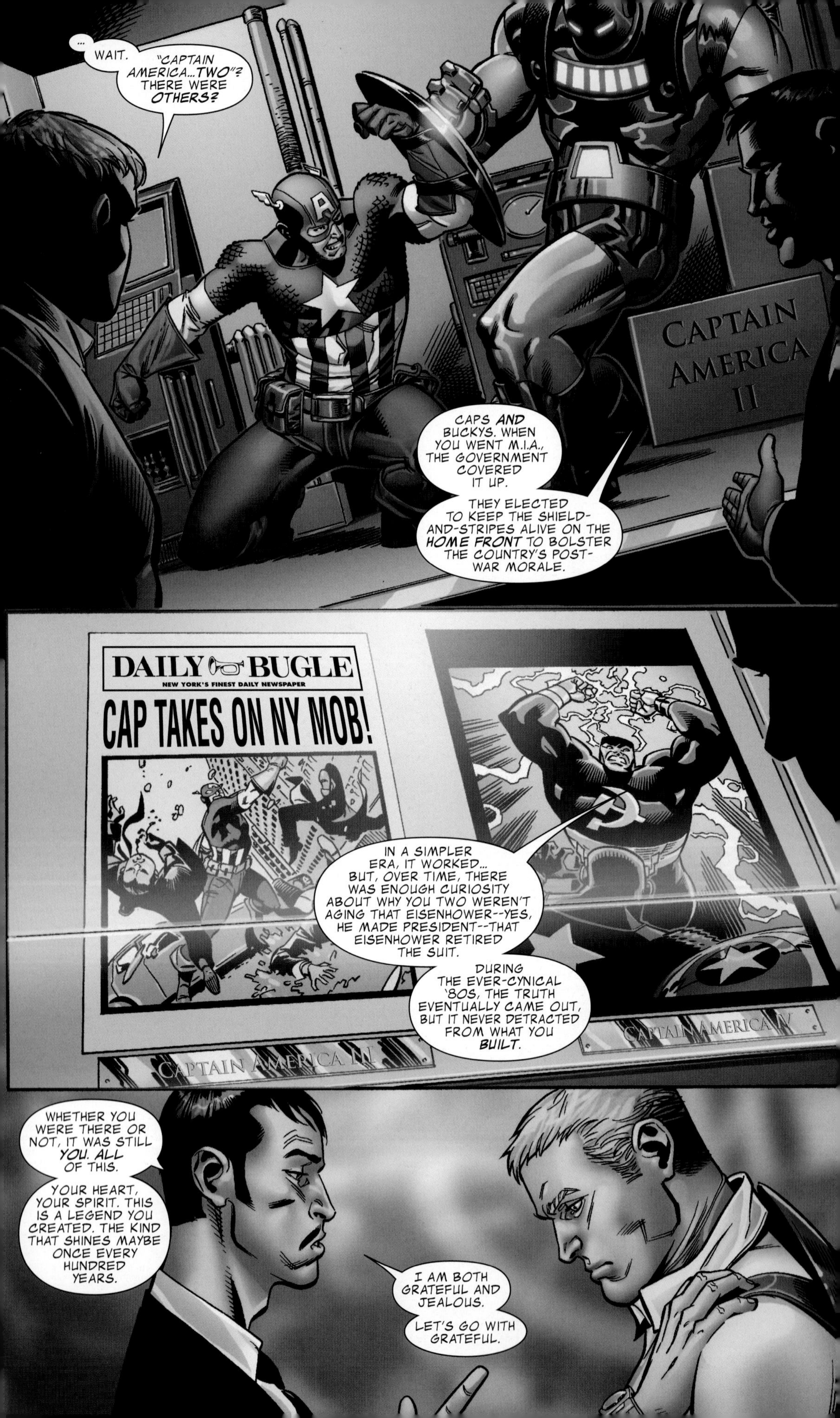

...WAIT. "CAPTAIN AMERICA...TWO"? THERE WERE OTHERS?
CAPTAIN AMERICA II
CAPS AND BUCKYS. WHEN YOU WENT M.I.A., THE GOVERNMENT COVERED IT UP.
THEY ELECTED TO KEEP THE SHIELD-AND-STRIPES ALIVE ON THE HOME FRONT TO BOLSTER THE COUNTRY'S POST-WAR MORALE.
DAILY BUGLE
NEW YORK'S FINEST DAILY NEWSPAPER
CAP TAKES ON NY MOB!
IN A SIMPLER ERA, IT WORKED... BUT, OVER TIME, THERE WAS ENOUGH CURIOSITY ABOUT WHY YOU TWO WEREN'T AGING THAT EISENHOWER--YES, HE MADE PRESIDENT--THAT EISENHOWER RETIRED THE SUIT.
DURING THE EVER-CYNICAL '80S, THE TRUTH EVENTUALLY CAME OUT, BUT IT NEVER DETRACTED FROM WHAT YOU BUILT.
CAPTAIN AMERICA III
CAPTAIN AMERICA IV
WHETHER YOU WERE THERE OR NOT, IT WAS STILL YOU. ALL OF THIS.
YOUR HEART, YOUR SPIRIT. THIS IS A LEGEND YOU CREATED. THE KIND THAT SHINES MAYBE ONCE EVERY HUNDRED YEARS.
I AM BOTH GRATEFUL AND JEALOUS.
LET'S GO WITH GRATEFUL.

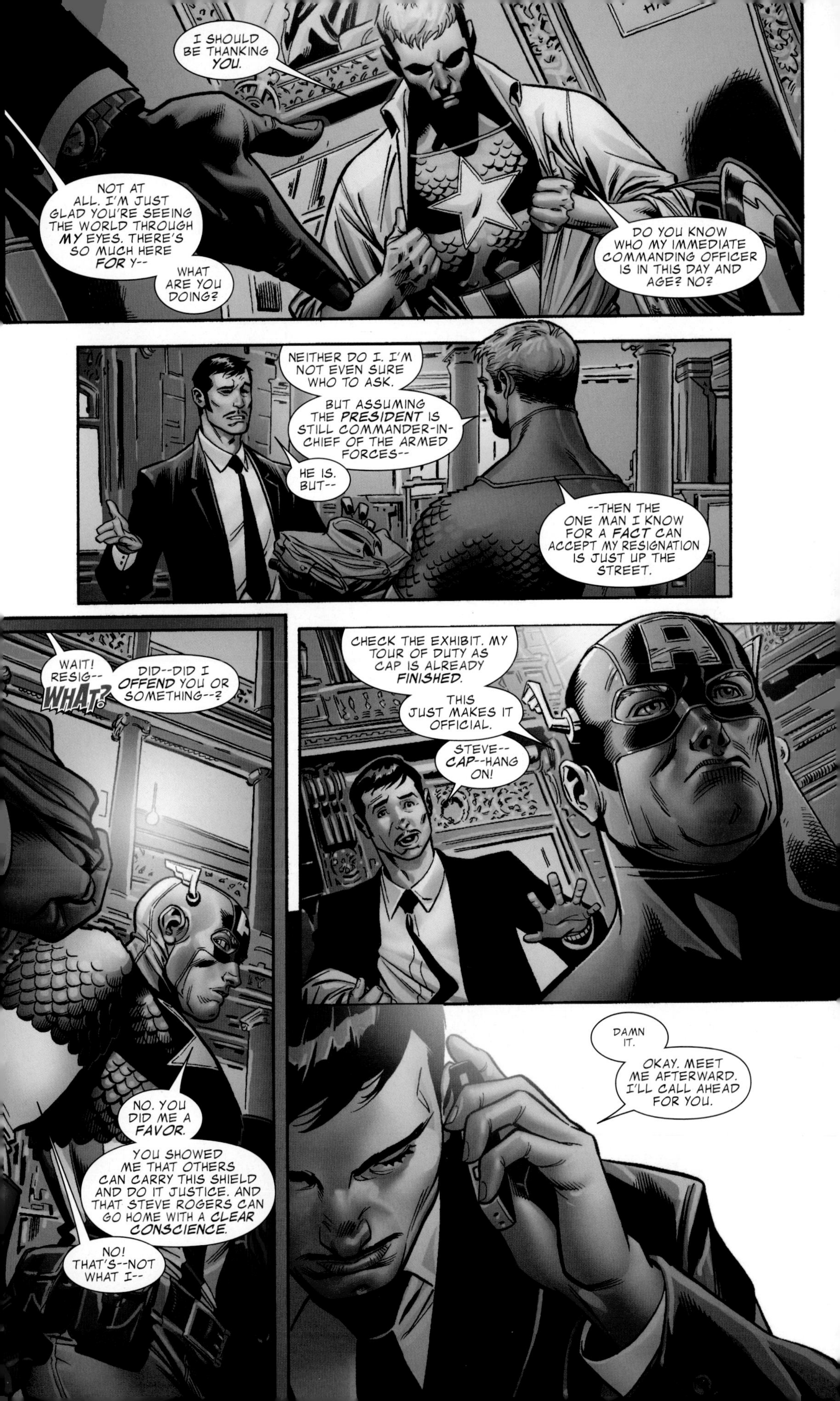
I SHOULD BE THANKING YOU.
NOT AT ALL. I'M JUST GLAD YOU'RE SEEING THE WORLD THROUGH MY EYES. THERE'S SO MUCH HERE FOR Y--
WHAT ARE YOU DOING?
DO YOU KNOW WHO MY IMMEDIATE COMMANDING OFFICER IS IN THIS DAY AND AGE? NO?
NEITHER DO I. I'M NOT EVEN SURE WHO TO ASK.
BUT ASSUMING THE PRESIDENT IS STILL COMMANDER-IN-CHIEF OF THE ARMED FORCES--
HE IS. BUT--
--THEN THE ONE MAN I KNOW FOR A FACT CAN ACCEPT MY RESIGNATION IS JUST UP THE STREET.
WAIT! RESIG-- WHAT?
DID--DID I OFFEND YOU OR SOMETHING--?
NO. YOU DID ME A FAVOR.
YOU SHOWED ME THAT OTHERS CAN CARRY THIS SHIELD AND DO IT JUSTICE. AND THAT STEVE ROGERS CAN GO HOME WITH A CLEAR CONSCIENCE.
NO! THAT'S--NOT WHAT I--
CHECK THE EXHIBIT. MY TOUR OF DUTY AS CAP IS ALREADY FINISHED.
THIS JUST MAKES IT OFFICIAL.
STEVE-- CAP--HANG ON!
DAMN IT.
OKAY. MEET ME AFTERWARD. I'LL CALL AHEAD FOR YOU.

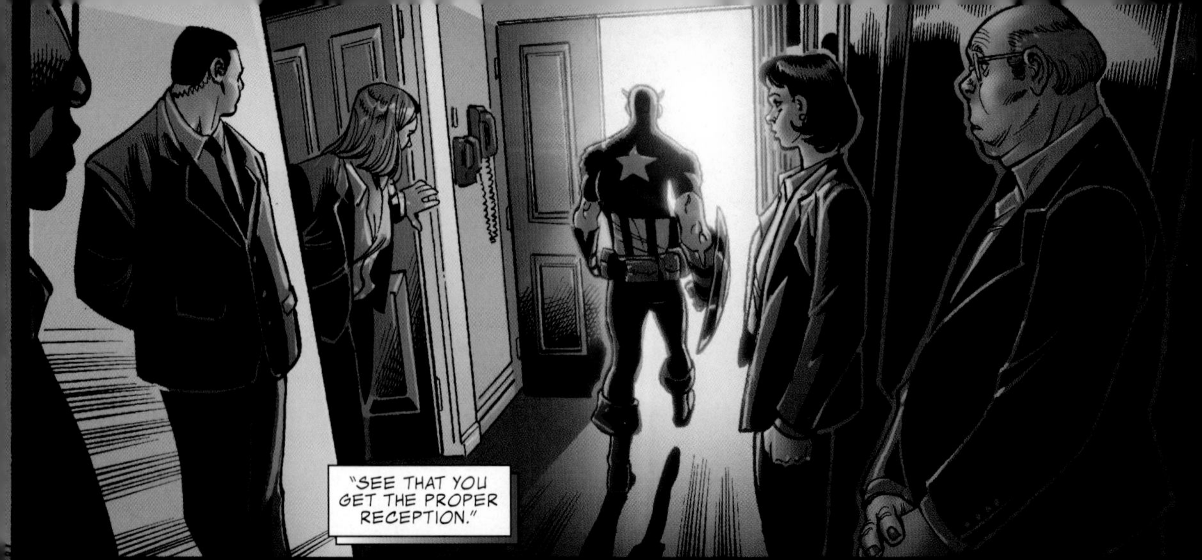
"SEE THAT YOU GET THE PROPER RECEPTION."

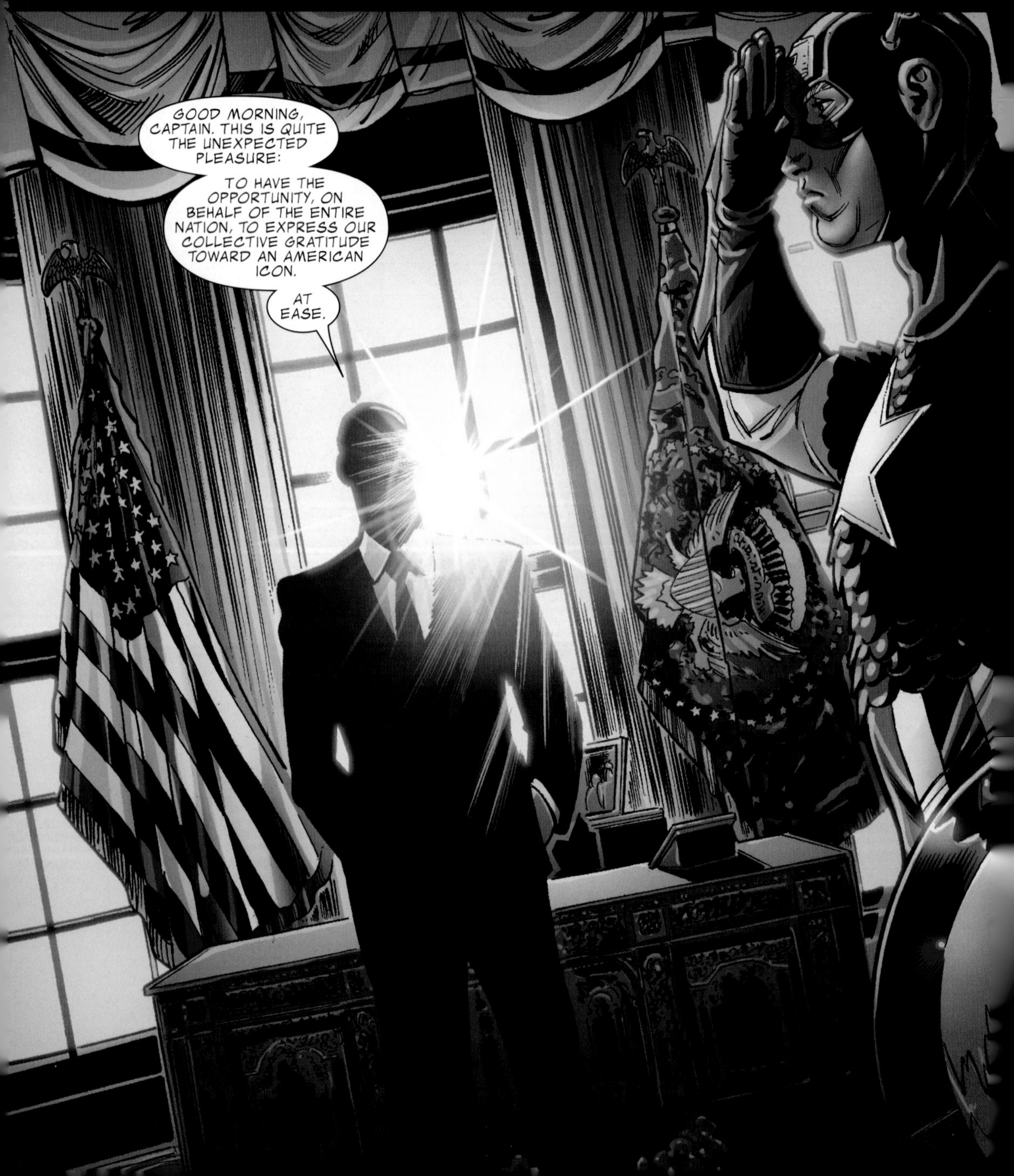
GOOD MORNING, CAPTAIN. THIS IS QUITE THE UNEXPECTED PLEASURE:
TO HAVE THE OPPORTUNITY, ON BEHALF OF THE ENTIRE NATION, TO EXPRESS OUR COLLECTIVE GRATITUDE TOWARD AN AMERICAN ICON.
AT EASE.

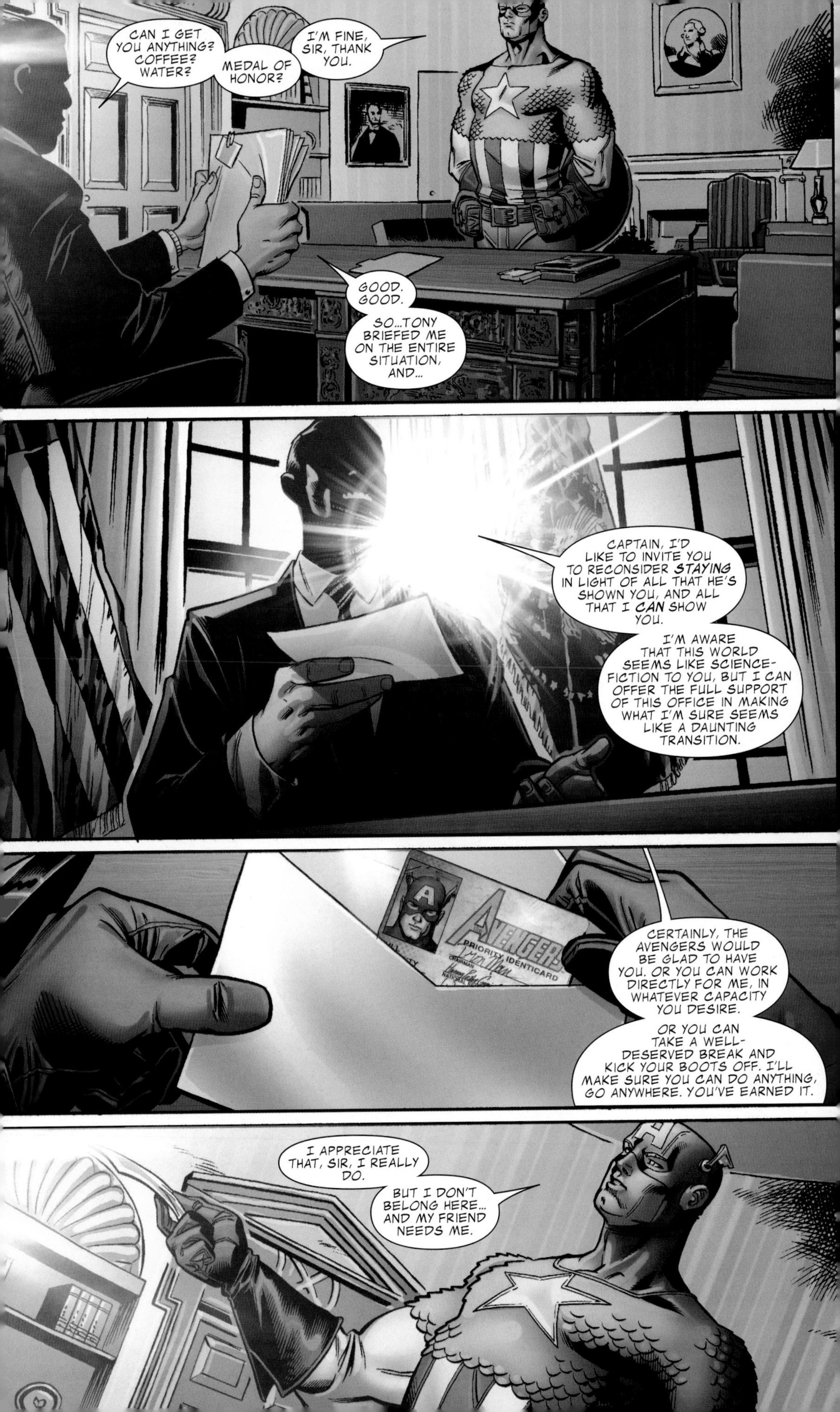
CAN I GET YOU ANYTHING? COFFEE? WATER?
MEDAL OF HONOR?
I'M FINE, SIR, THANK YOU.
GOOD. GOOD.
SO...TONY BRIEFED ME ON THE ENTIRE SITUATION, AND...
CAPTAIN, I'D LIKE TO INVITE YOU TO RECONSIDER STAYING IN LIGHT OF ALL THAT HE'S SHOWN YOU, AND ALL THAT I CAN SHOW YOU.
I'M AWARE THAT THIS WORLD SEEMS LIKE SCIENCE-FICTION TO YOU, BUT I CAN OFFER THE FULL SUPPORT OF THIS OFFICE IN MAKING WHAT I'M SURE SEEMS LIKE A DAUNTING TRANSITION.
AVENGERS
PRIORITY IDENTICARD
CERTAINLY, THE AVENGERS WOULD BE GLAD TO HAVE YOU. OR YOU CAN WORK DIRECTLY FOR ME, IN WHATEVER CAPACITY YOU DESIRE.
OR YOU CAN TAKE A WELL-DESERVED BREAK AND KICK YOUR BOOTS OFF. I'LL MAKE SURE YOU CAN DO ANYTHING, GO ANYWHERE. YOU'VE EARNED IT.
I APPRECIATE THAT, SIR, I REALLY DO.
BUT I DON'T BELONG HERE... AND MY FRIEND NEEDS ME.

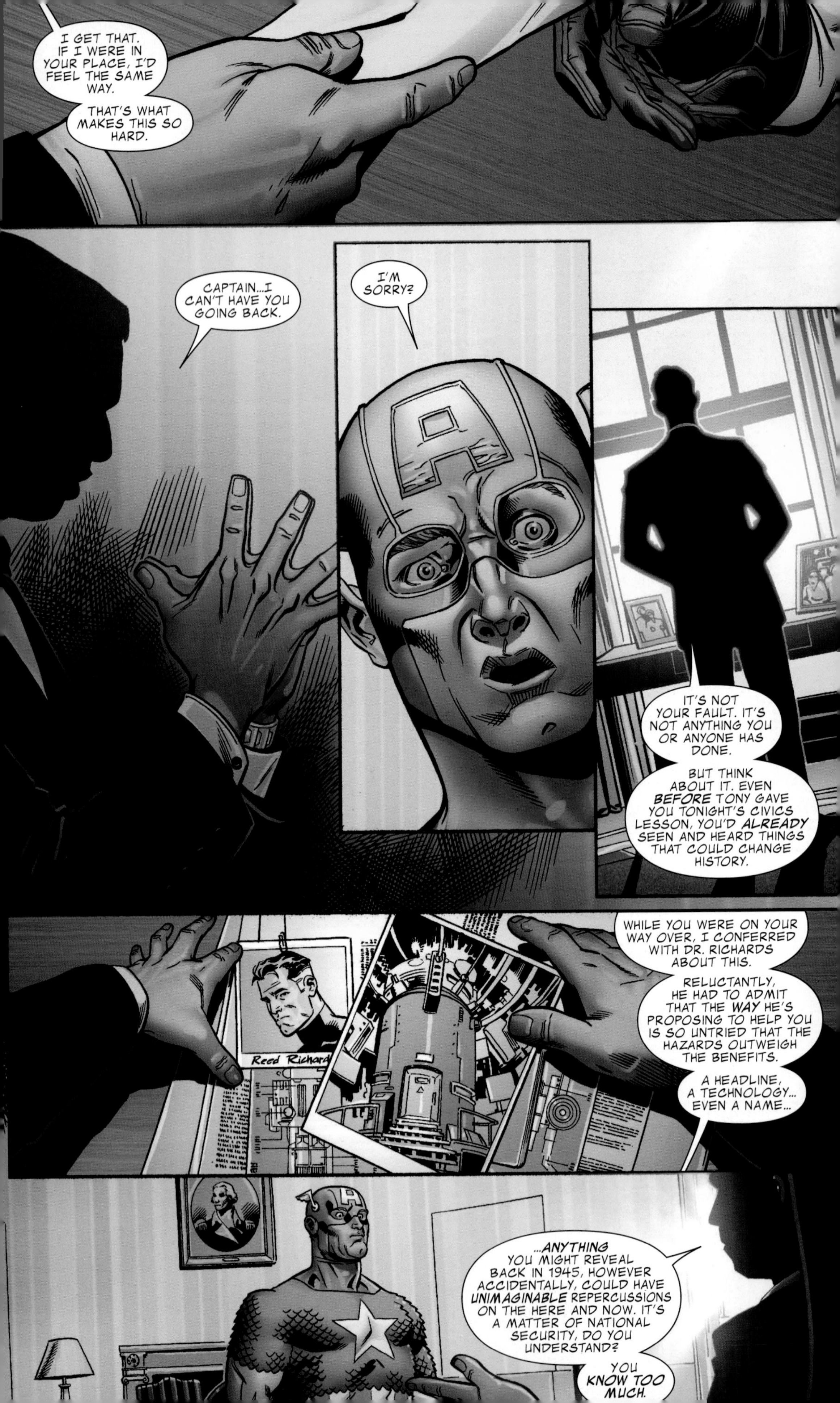
I GET THAT. IF I WERE IN YOUR PLACE, I'D FEEL THE SAME WAY.
THAT'S WHAT MAKES THIS SO HARD.
CAPTAIN...I CAN'T HAVE YOU GOING BACK.
I'M SORRY?
IT'S NOT YOUR FAULT. IT'S NOT ANYTHING YOU OR ANYONE HAS DONE.
BUT THINK ABOUT IT. EVEN *BEFORE* TONY GAVE YOU TONIGHT'S CIVICS LESSON, YOU'D *ALREADY* SEEN AND HEARD THINGS THAT COULD CHANGE HISTORY.
Reed Richard
WHILE YOU WERE ON YOUR WAY OVER, I CONFERRED WITH DR. RICHARDS ABOUT THIS.
RELUCTANTLY, HE HAD TO ADMIT THAT THE *WAY* HE'S PROPOSING TO HELP YOU IS SO UNTRIED THAT THE HAZARDS OUTWEIGH THE BENEFITS.
A HEADLINE, A TECHNOLOGY... EVEN A NAME...
...*ANYTHING* YOU MIGHT REVEAL BACK IN 1945, HOWEVER ACCIDENTALLY, COULD HAVE *UNIMAGINABLE* REPERCUSSIONS ON THE HERE AND NOW. IT'S A MATTER OF NATIONAL SECURITY, DO YOU UNDERSTAND?
YOU *KNOW TOO MUCH.*

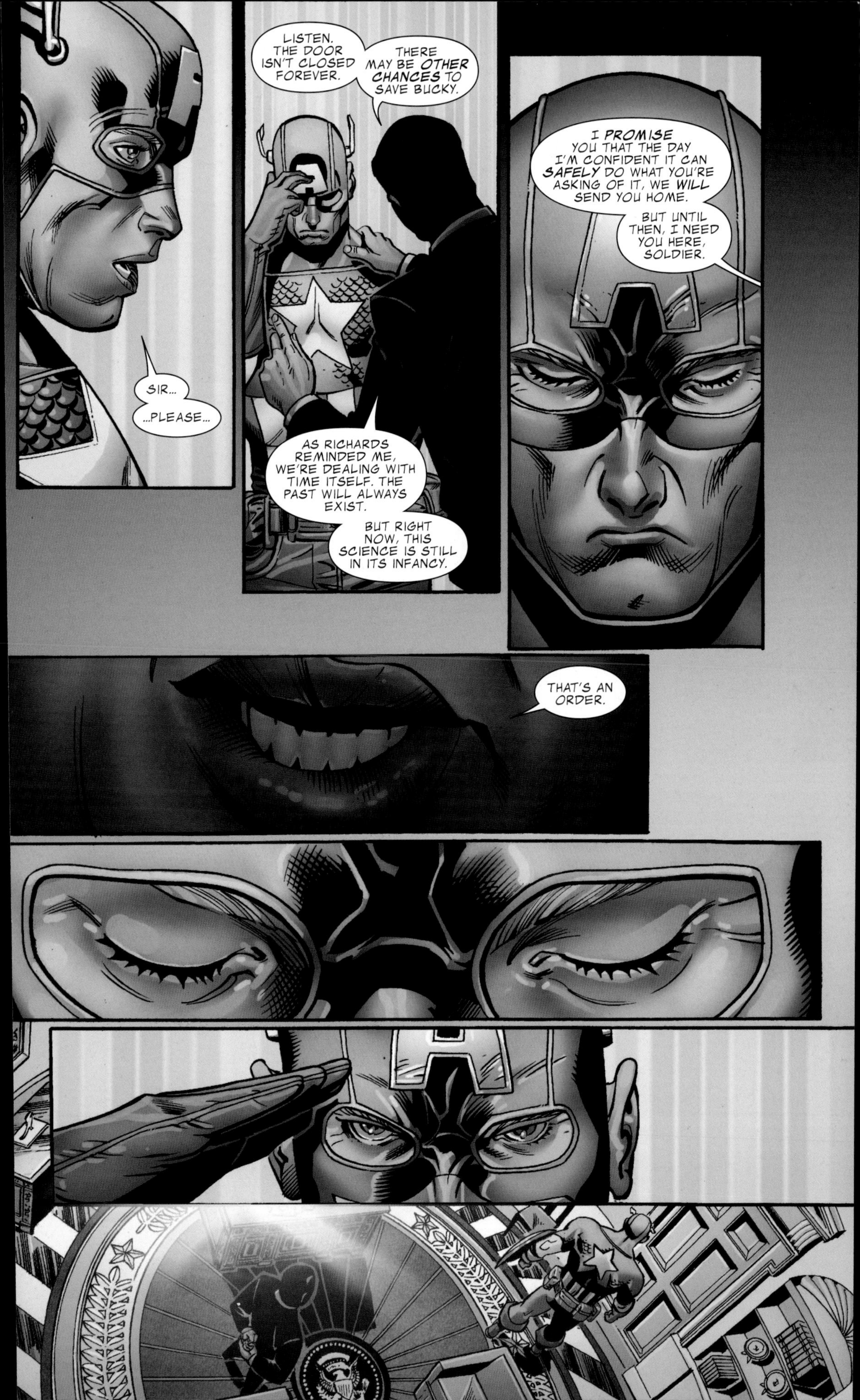

SIR...
...PLEASE...
LISTEN. THE DOOR ISN'T CLOSED FOREVER.
THERE MAY BE OTHER CHANCES TO SAVE BUCKY.
AS RICHARDS REMINDED ME, WE'RE DEALING WITH TIME ITSELF. THE PAST WILL ALWAYS EXIST.
BUT RIGHT NOW, THIS SCIENCE IS STILL IN ITS INFANCY.
I PROMISE YOU THAT THE DAY I'M CONFIDENT IT CAN SAFELY DO WHAT YOU'RE ASKING OF IT, WE WILL SEND YOU HOME.
BUT UNTIL THEN, I NEED YOU HERE, SOLDIER.
THAT'S AN ORDER.

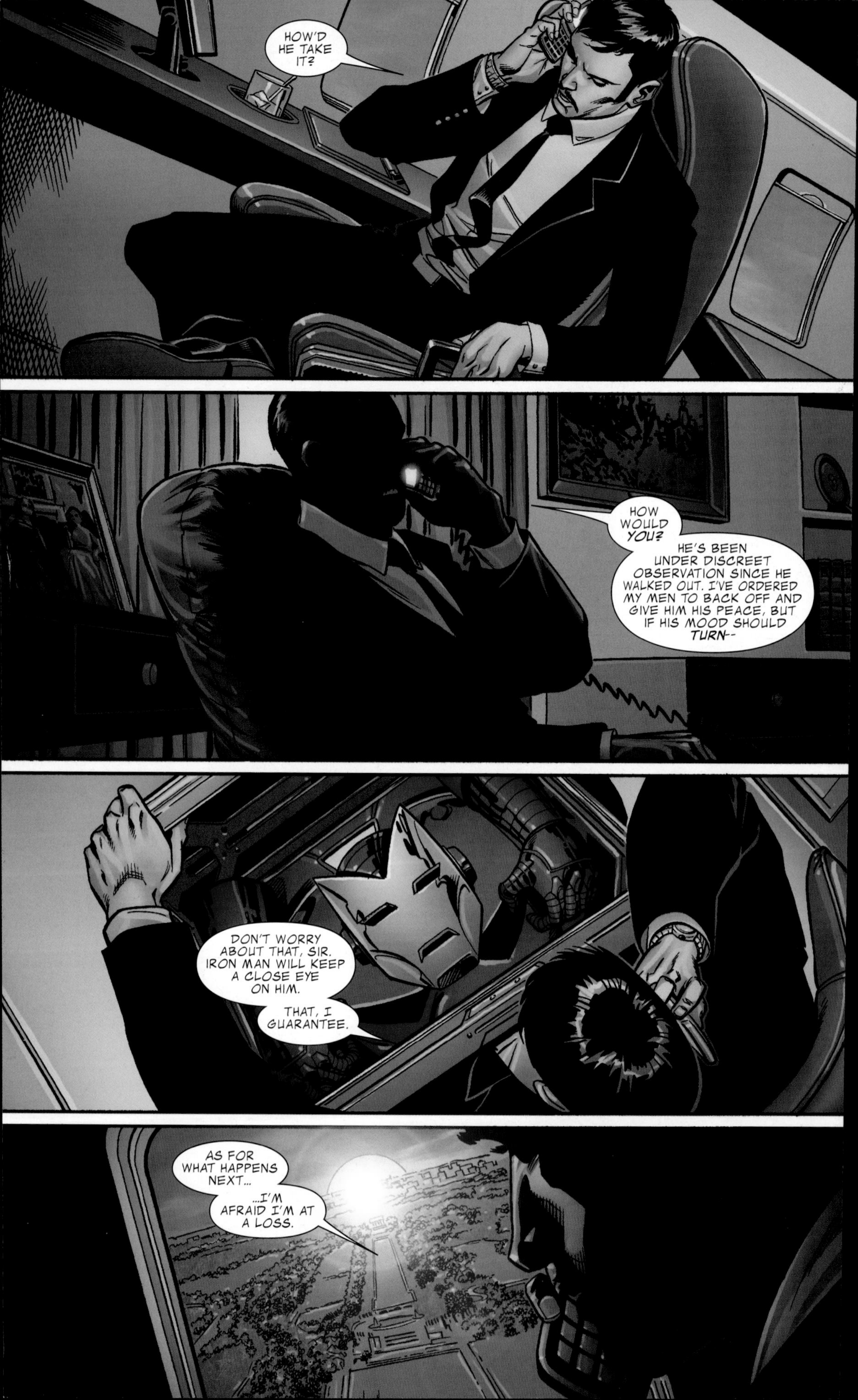

HOW'D HE TAKE IT?
HOW WOULD *YOU?*
HE'S BEEN UNDER DISCREET OBSERVATION SINCE HE WALKED OUT. I'VE ORDERED MY MEN TO BACK OFF AND GIVE HIM HIS PEACE, BUT IF HIS MOOD SHOULD *TURN*--
DON'T WORRY ABOUT THAT, SIR. IRON MAN WILL KEEP A CLOSE EYE ON HIM.
THAT, I GUARANTEE.
AS FOR WHAT HAPPENS NEXT...
...I'M AFRAID I'M AT A LOSS.

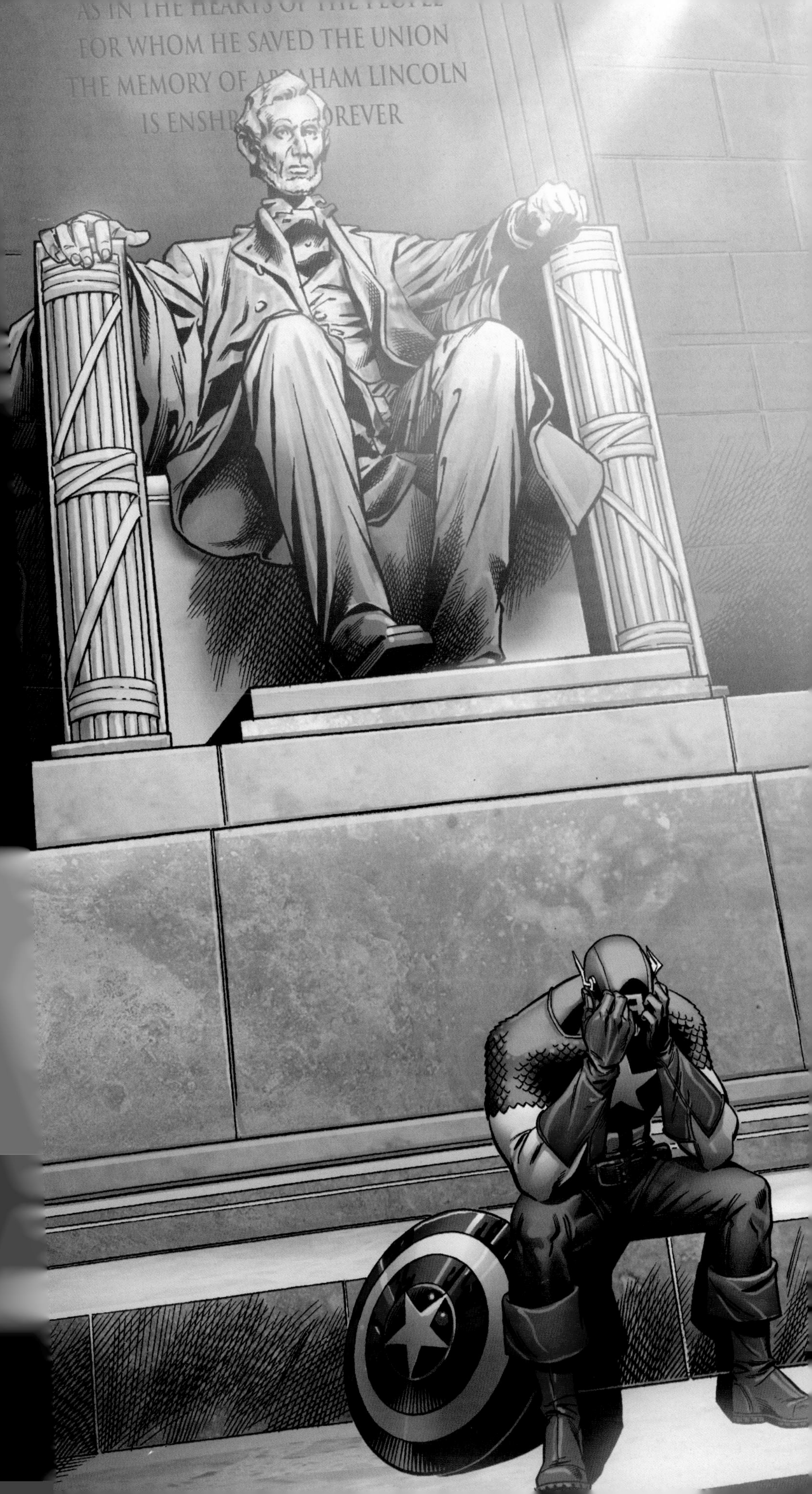
FOR WHOM HE SAVED THE UNION

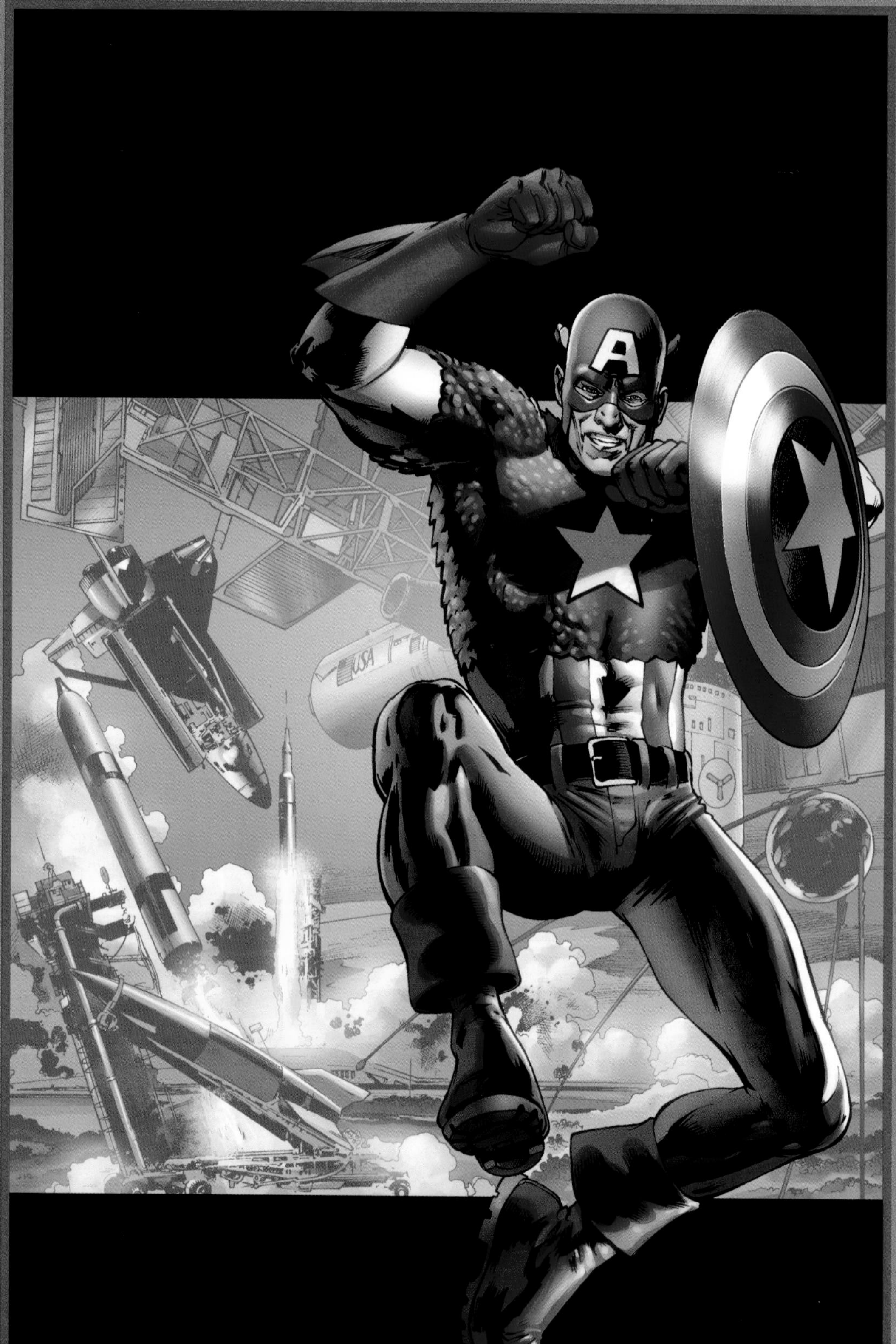
USA

[4]

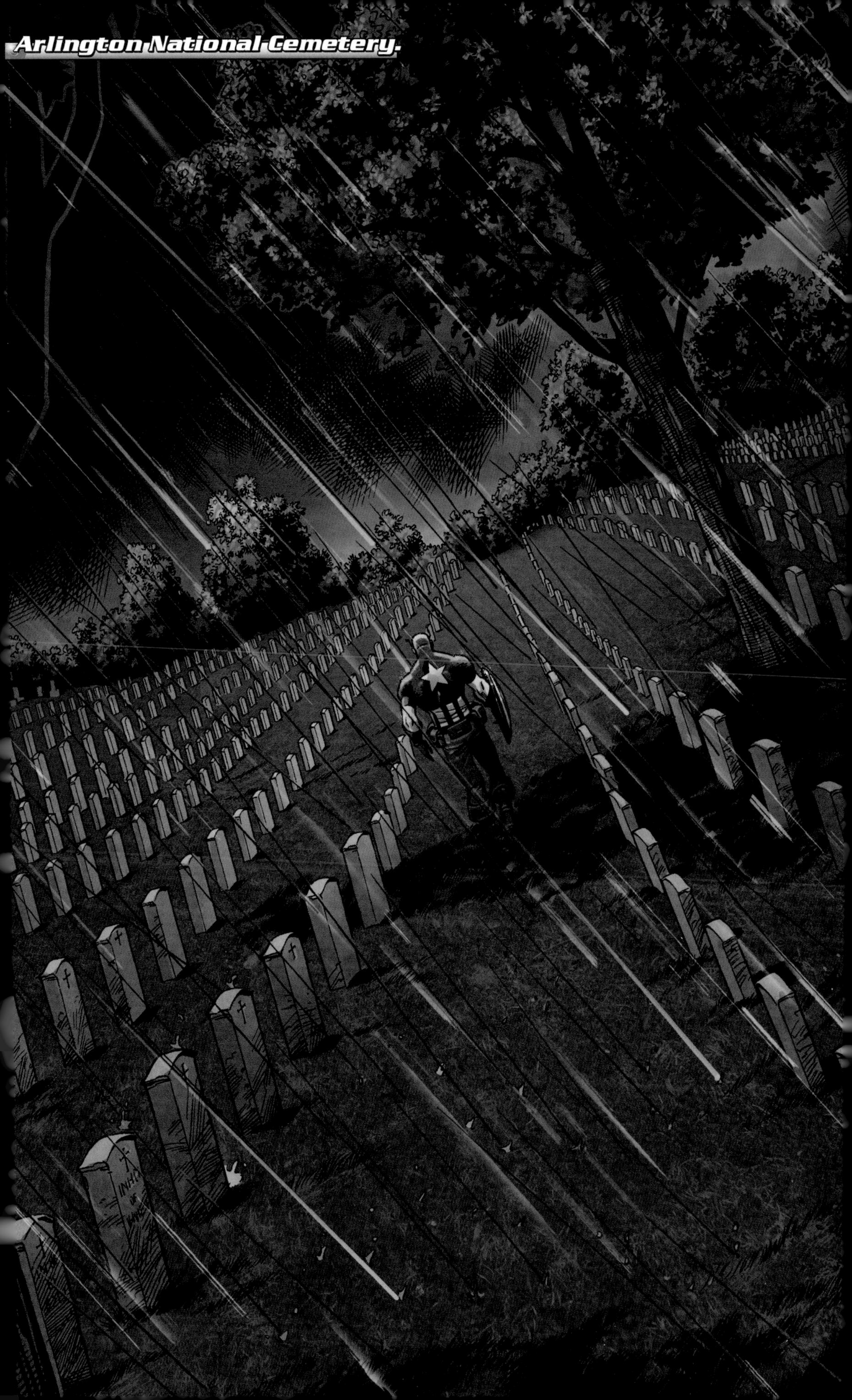
Arlington National Cemetery.

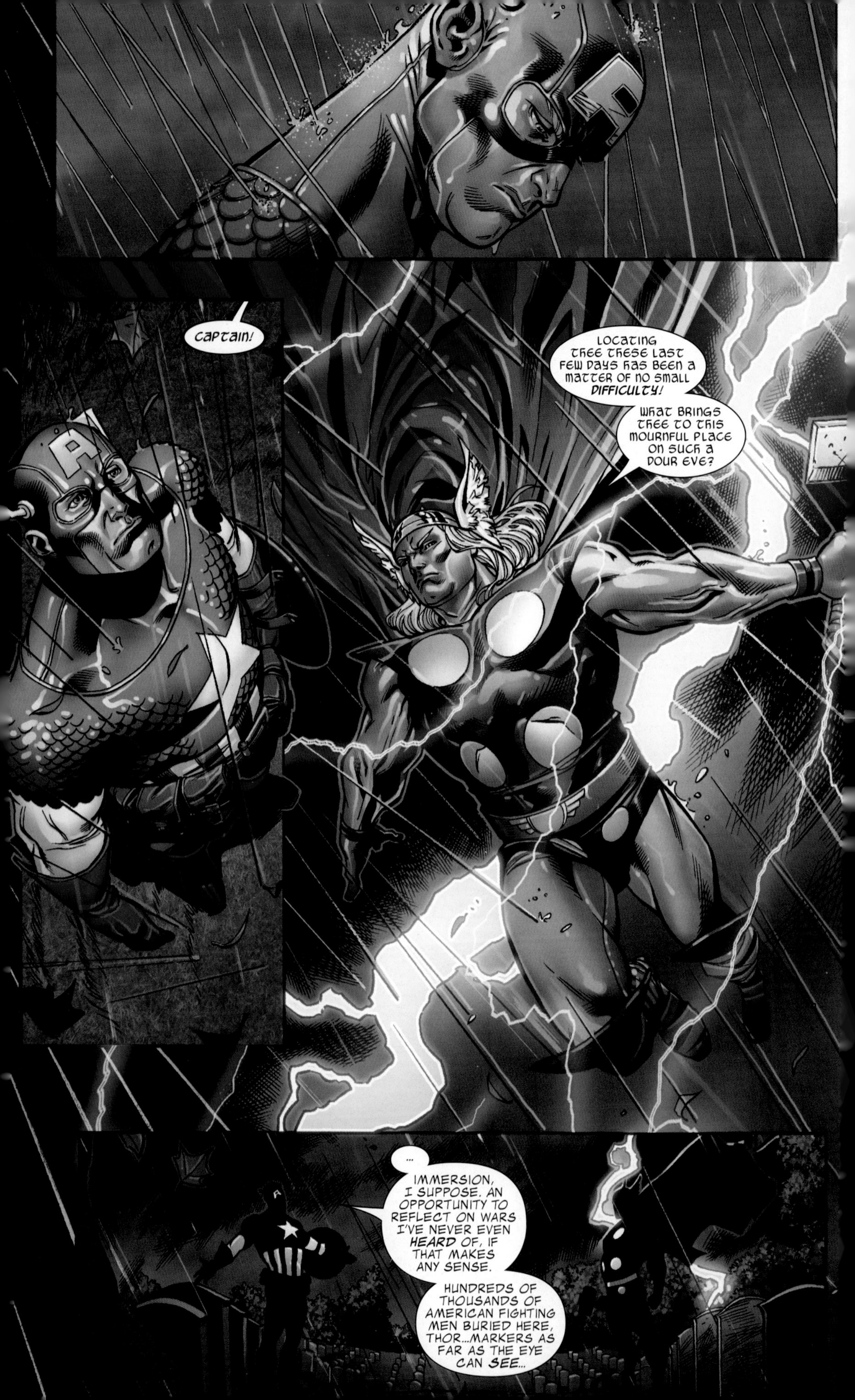

CAPTAIN!
LOCATING THEE THESE LAST FEW DAYS HAS BEEN A MATTER OF NO SMALL DIFFICULTY!
WHAT BRINGS THEE TO THIS MOURNFUL PLACE ON SUCH A DOUR EVE?
...
IMMERSION, I SUPPOSE. AN OPPORTUNITY TO REFLECT ON WARS I'VE NEVER EVEN HEARD OF, IF THAT MAKES ANY SENSE.
HUNDREDS OF THOUSANDS OF AMERICAN FIGHTING MEN BURIED HERE, THOR...MARKERS AS FAR AS THE EYE CAN SEE...

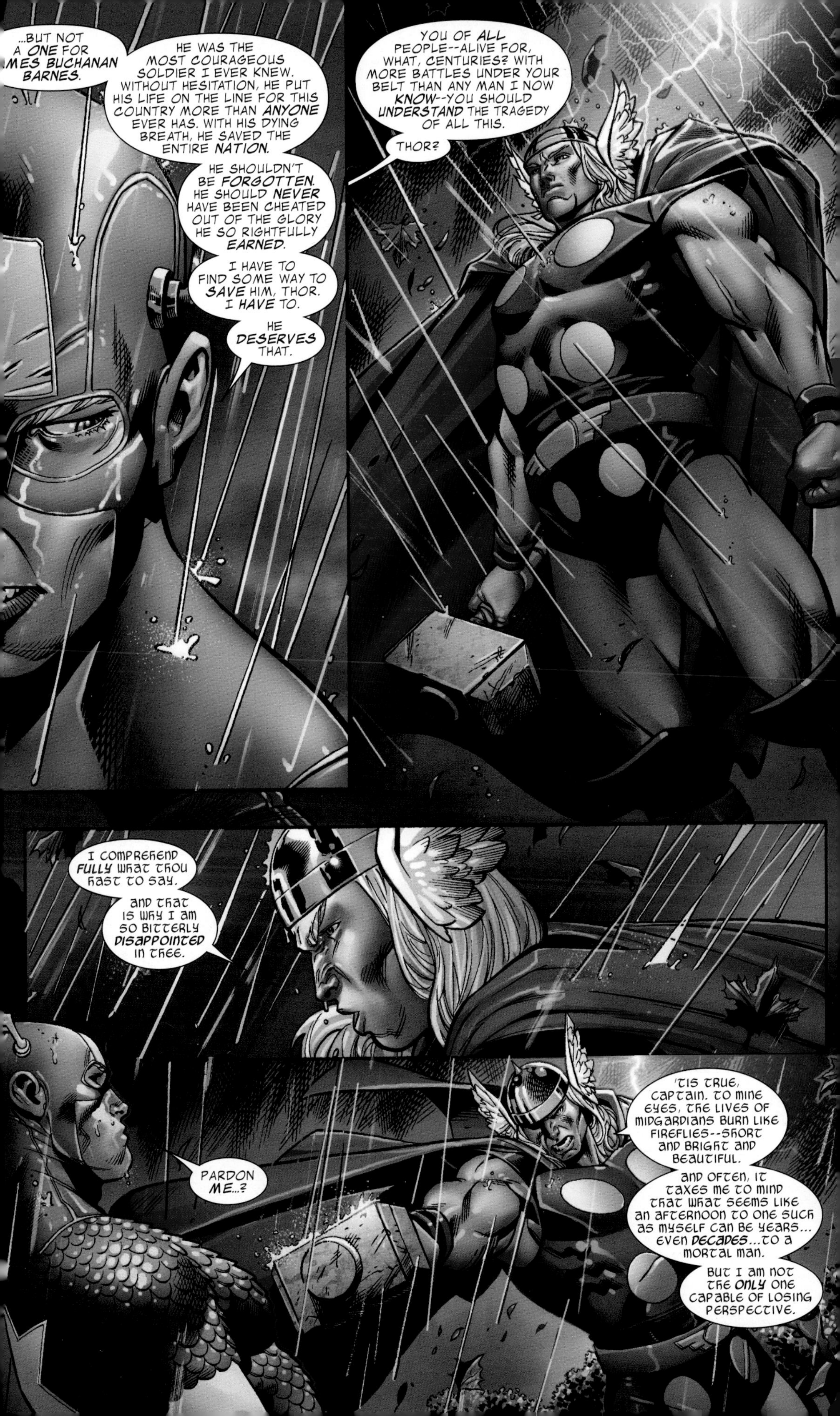

...BUT NOT A ONE FOR AMES BUCHANAN BARNES.
HE WAS THE MOST COURAGEOUS SOLDIER I EVER KNEW. WITHOUT HESITATION, HE PUT HIS LIFE ON THE LINE FOR THIS COUNTRY MORE THAN ANYONE EVER HAS. WITH HIS DYING BREATH, HE SAVED THE ENTIRE NATION.
HE SHOULDN'T BE FORGOTTEN. HE SHOULD NEVER HAVE BEEN CHEATED OUT OF THE GLORY HE SO RIGHTFULLY EARNED.
I HAVE TO FIND SOME WAY TO SAVE HIM, THOR. I HAVE TO.
HE DESERVES THAT.
YOU OF ALL PEOPLE--ALIVE FOR, WHAT, CENTURIES? WITH MORE BATTLES UNDER YOUR BELT THAN ANY MAN I NOW KNOW--YOU SHOULD UNDERSTAND THE TRAGEDY OF ALL THIS.
THOR?
I COMPREHEND FULLY WHAT THOU HAST TO SAY.
AND THAT IS WHY I AM SO BITTERLY DISAPPOINTED IN THEE.
PARDON ME...?
'TIS TRUE, CAPTAIN. TO MINE EYES, THE LIVES OF MIDGARDIANS BURN LIKE FIREFLIES--SHORT AND BRIGHT AND BEAUTIFUL.
AND OFTEN, IT TAXES ME TO MIND THAT WHAT SEEMS LIKE AN AFTERNOON TO ONE SUCH AS MYSELF CAN BE YEARS... EVEN DECADES...TO A MORTAL MAN.
BUT I AM NOT THE ONLY ONE CAPABLE OF LOSING PERSPECTIVE.

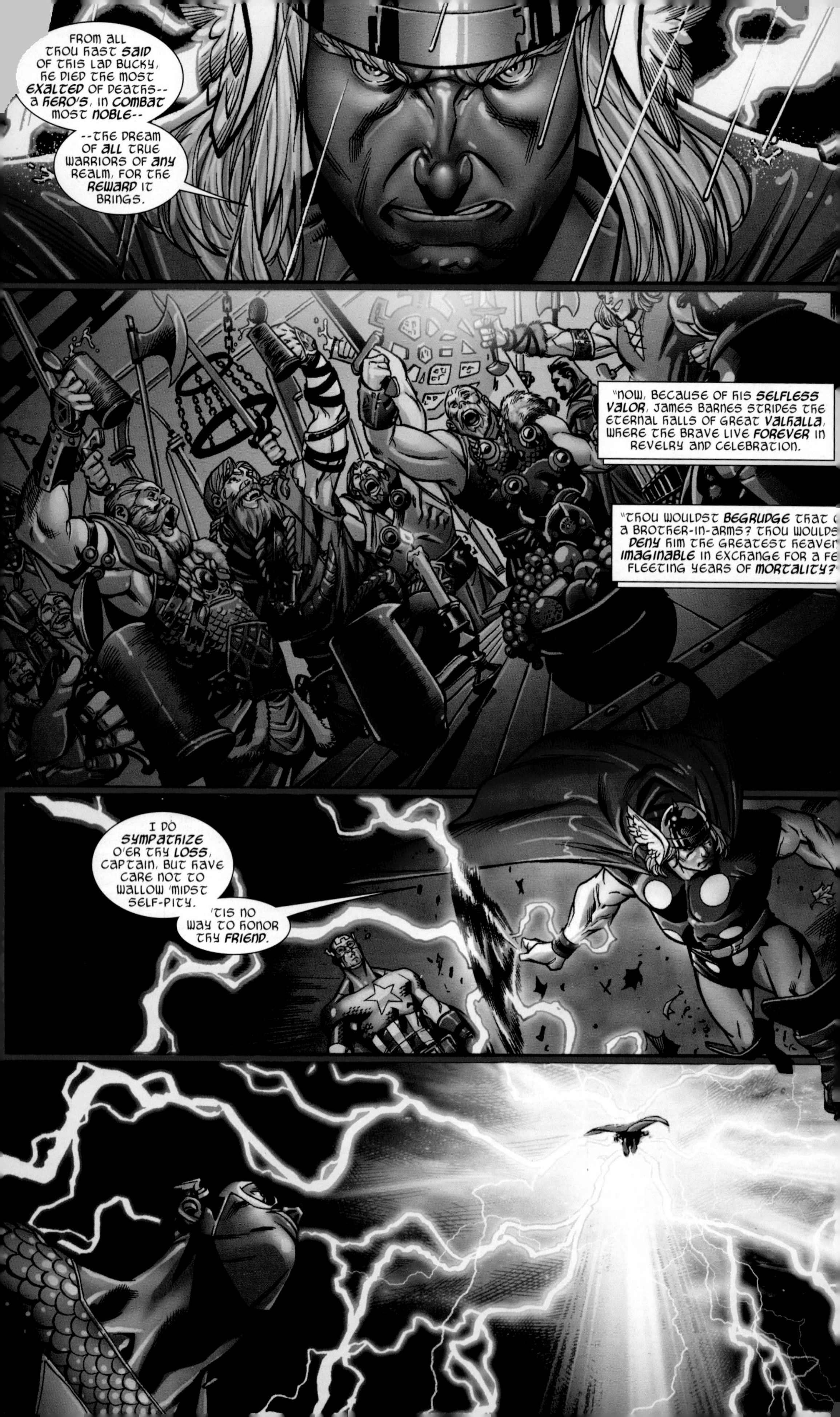
FROM ALL THOU HAST SAID OF THIS LAD BUCKY, HE DIED THE MOST EXALTED OF DEATHS-- A HERO'S, IN COMBAT MOST NOBLE--
--THE DREAM OF ALL TRUE WARRIORS OF ANY REALM, FOR THE REWARD IT BRINGS.
"NOW, BECAUSE OF HIS SELFLESS VALOR, JAMES BARNES STRIDES THE ETERNAL HALLS OF GREAT VALHALLA, WHERE THE BRAVE LIVE FOREVER IN REVELRY AND CELEBRATION.
"THOU WOULDST BEGRUDGE THAT A BROTHER-IN-ARMS? THOU WOULDS DENY HIM THE GREATEST HEAVE IMAGINABLE IN EXCHANGE FOR A FE FLEETING YEARS OF MORTALITY?
I DO SYMPATHIZE O'ER THY LOSS, CAPTAIN, BUT HAVE CARE NOT TO WALLOW 'MIDST SELF-PITY.
'TIS NO WAY TO HONOR THY FRIEND.

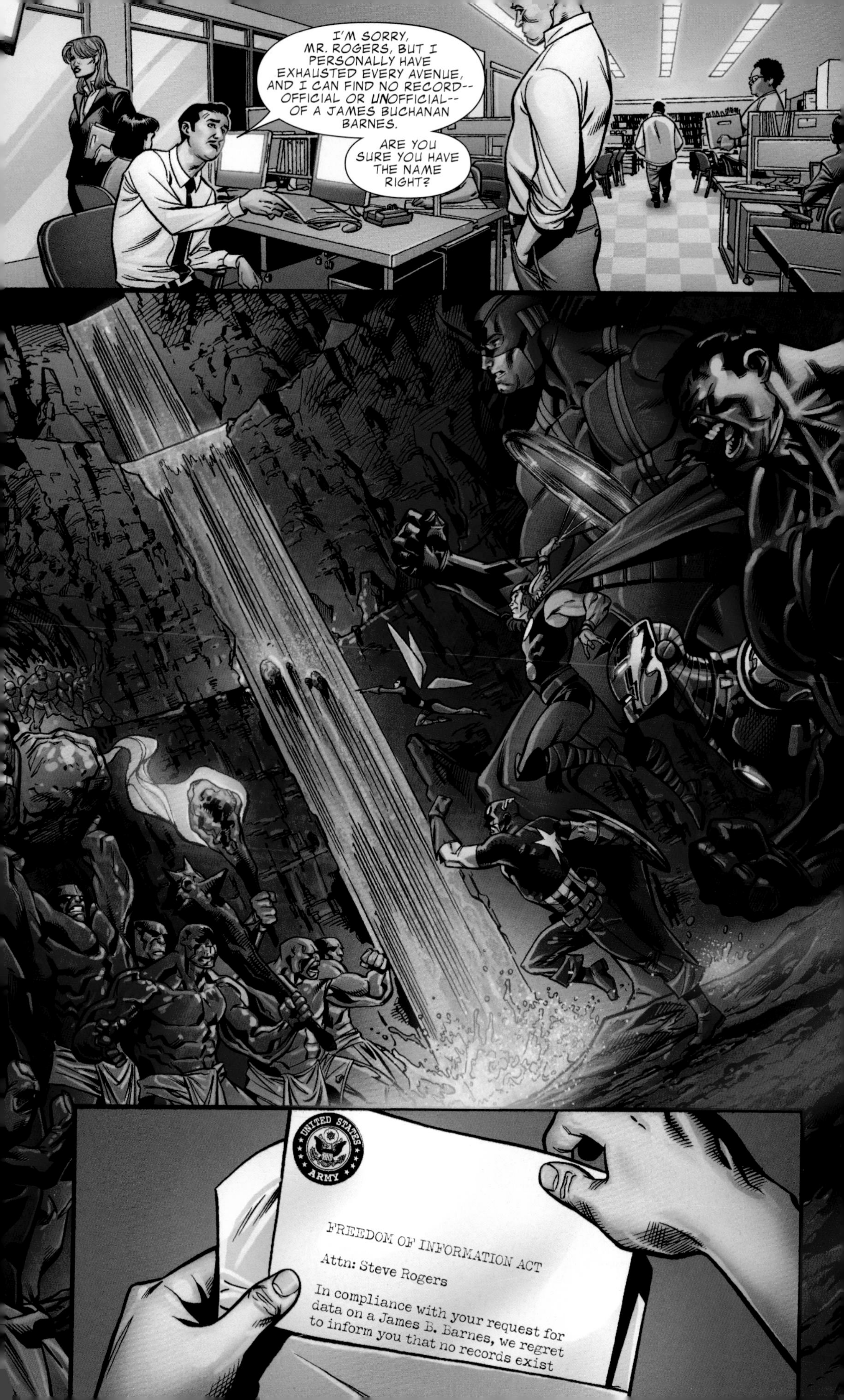
I'M SORRY, MR. ROGERS, BUT I PERSONALLY HAVE EXHAUSTED EVERY AVENUE, AND I CAN FIND NO RECORD-- OFFICIAL OR UNOFFICIAL-- OF A JAMES BUCHANAN BARNES.
ARE YOU SURE YOU HAVE THE NAME RIGHT?
UNITED STATES ARMY
FREEDOM OF INFORMATION ACT
Attn: Steve Rogers
In compliance with your request for data on a James B. Barnes, we regret to inform you that no records exist

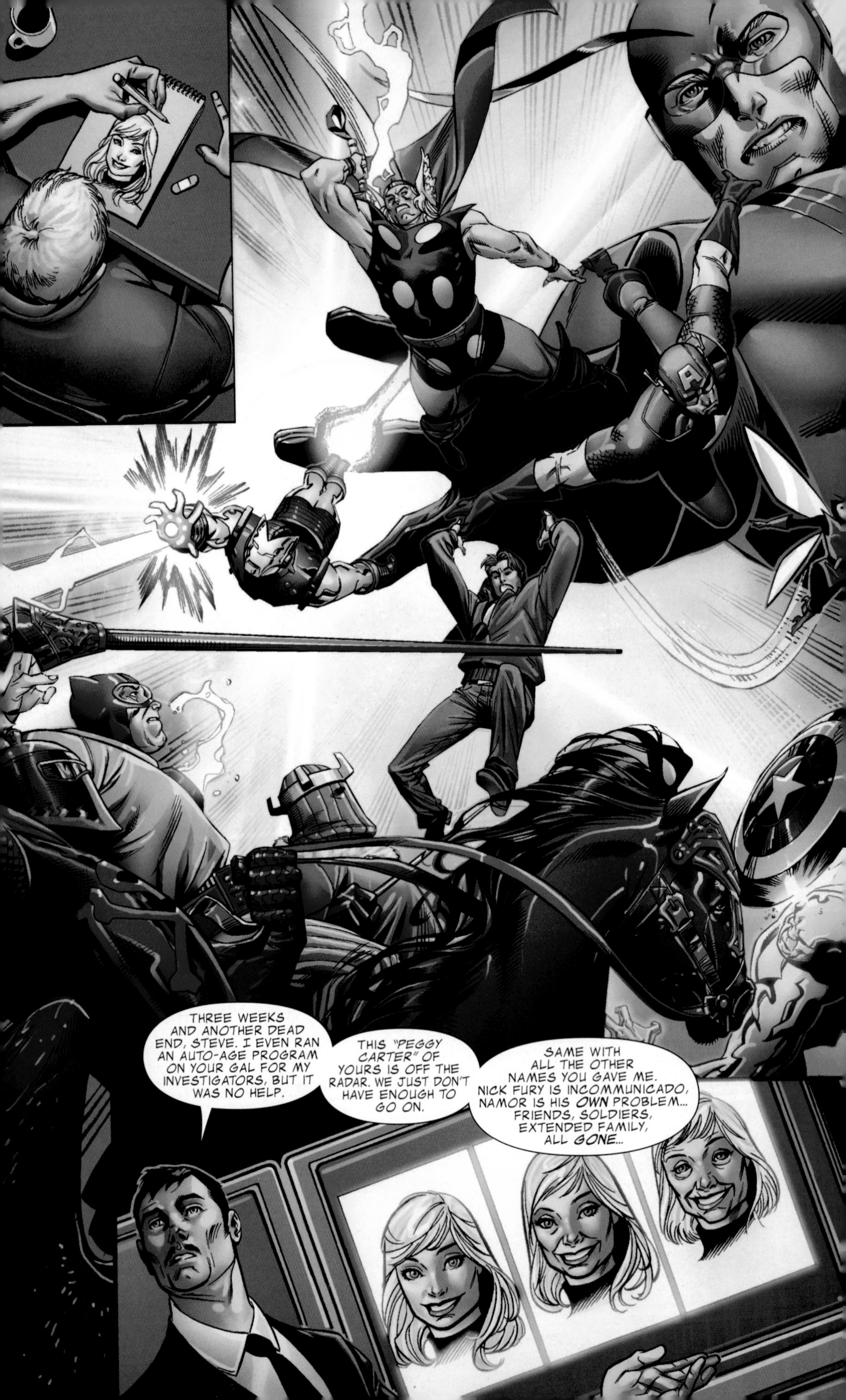
THREE WEEKS AND ANOTHER DEAD END, STEVE. I EVEN RAN AN AUTO-AGE PROGRAM ON YOUR GAL FOR MY INVESTIGATORS, BUT IT WAS NO HELP.
THIS "PEGGY CARTER" OF YOURS IS OFF THE RADAR. WE JUST DON'T HAVE ENOUGH TO GO ON.
SAME WITH ALL THE OTHER NAMES YOU GAVE ME. NICK FURY IS INCOMMUNICADO, NAMOR IS HIS OWN PROBLEM... FRIENDS, SOLDIERS, EXTENDED FAMILY, ALL GONE...

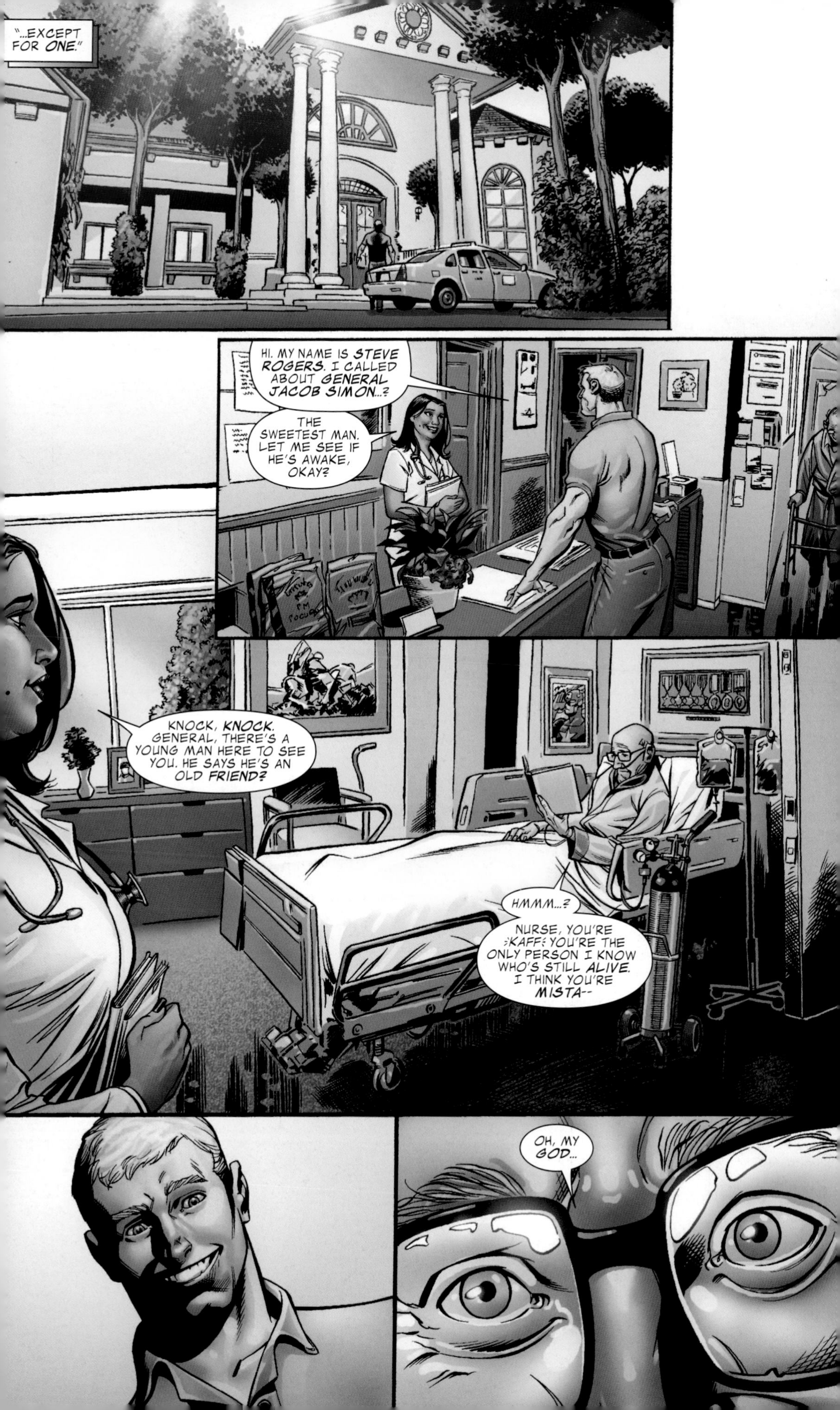
"...EXCEPT FOR ONE."
HI. MY NAME IS STEVE ROGERS. I CALLED ABOUT GENERAL JACOB SIMON...?
THE SWEETEST MAN. LET ME SEE IF HE'S AWAKE, OKAY?
KNOCK, KNOCK. GENERAL, THERE'S A YOUNG MAN HERE TO SEE YOU. HE SAYS HE'S AN OLD FRIEND?
HMMM...?
NURSE, YOU'RE *KAFF* YOU'RE THE ONLY PERSON I KNOW WHO'S STILL ALIVE. I THINK YOU'RE MISTA--
OH, MY GOD...

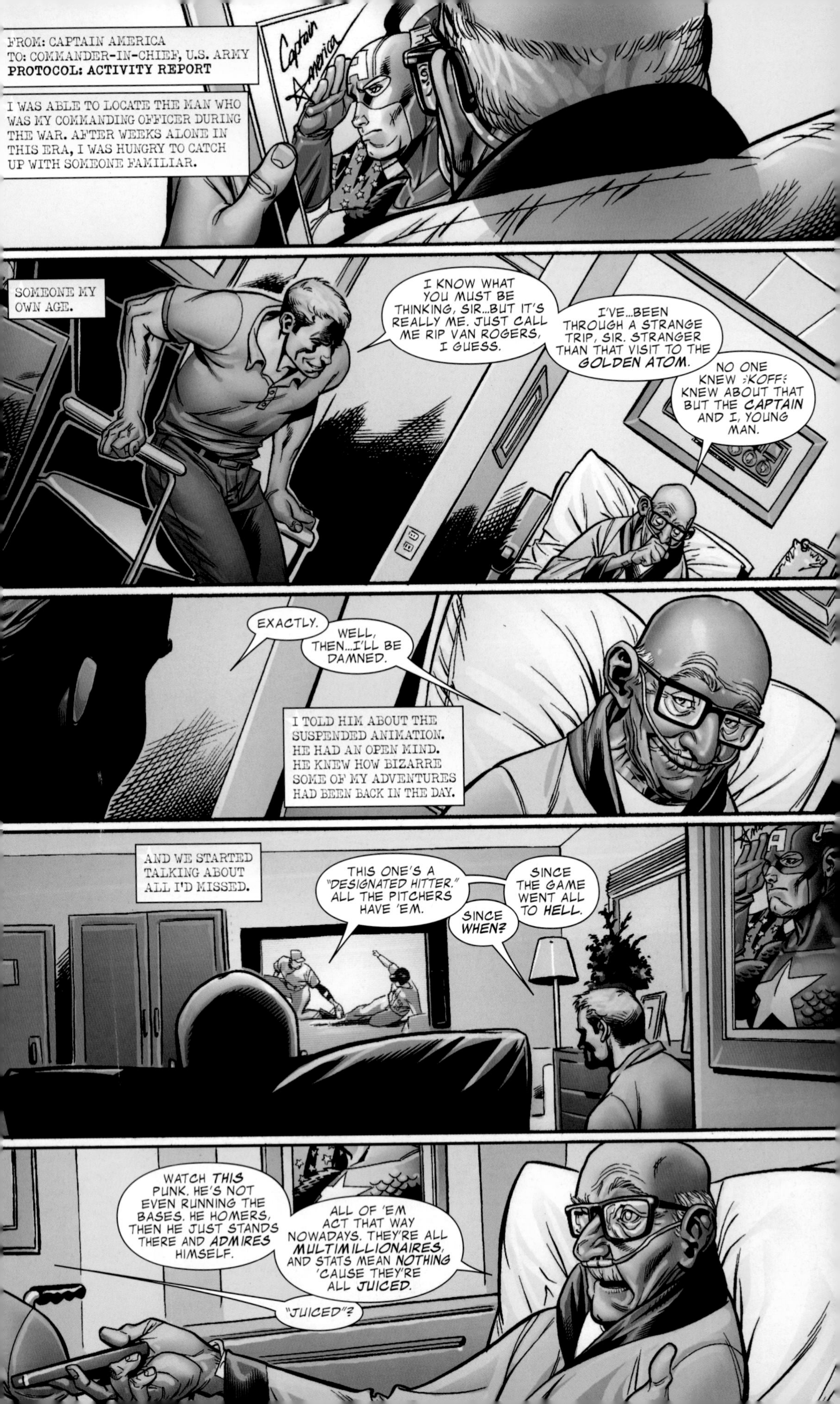

FROM: CAPTAIN AMERICA
TO: COMMANDER-IN-CHIEF, U.S. ARMY
PROTOCOL: ACTIVITY REPORT
I WAS ABLE TO LOCATE THE MAN WHO WAS MY COMMANDING OFFICER DURING THE WAR. AFTER WEEKS ALONE IN THIS ERA, I WAS HUNGRY TO CATCH UP WITH SOMEONE FAMILIAR.
Captain America
SOMEONE MY OWN AGE.
I KNOW WHAT YOU MUST BE THINKING, SIR...BUT IT'S REALLY ME. JUST CALL ME RIP VAN ROGERS, I GUESS.
I'VE...BEEN THROUGH A STRANGE TRIP, SIR. STRANGER THAN THAT VISIT TO THE GOLDEN ATOM.
NO ONE KNEW :KOFF: KNEW ABOUT THAT BUT THE CAPTAIN AND I, YOUNG MAN.
EXACTLY.
WELL, THEN...I'LL BE DAMNED.
I TOLD HIM ABOUT THE SUSPENDED ANIMATION. HE HAD AN OPEN MIND. HE KNEW HOW BIZARRE SOME OF MY ADVENTURES HAD BEEN BACK IN THE DAY.
AND WE STARTED TALKING ABOUT ALL I'D MISSED.
THIS ONE'S A "DESIGNATED HITTER." ALL THE PITCHERS HAVE 'EM.
SINCE WHEN?
SINCE THE GAME WENT ALL TO HELL.
WATCH THIS PUNK. HE'S NOT EVEN RUNNING THE BASES. HE HOMERS, THEN HE JUST STANDS THERE AND ADMIRES HIMSELF.
ALL OF 'EM ACT THAT WAY NOWADAYS. THEY'RE ALL MULTIMILLIONAIRES, AND STATS MEAN NOTHING 'CAUSE THEY'RE ALL JUICED.
"JUICED"?

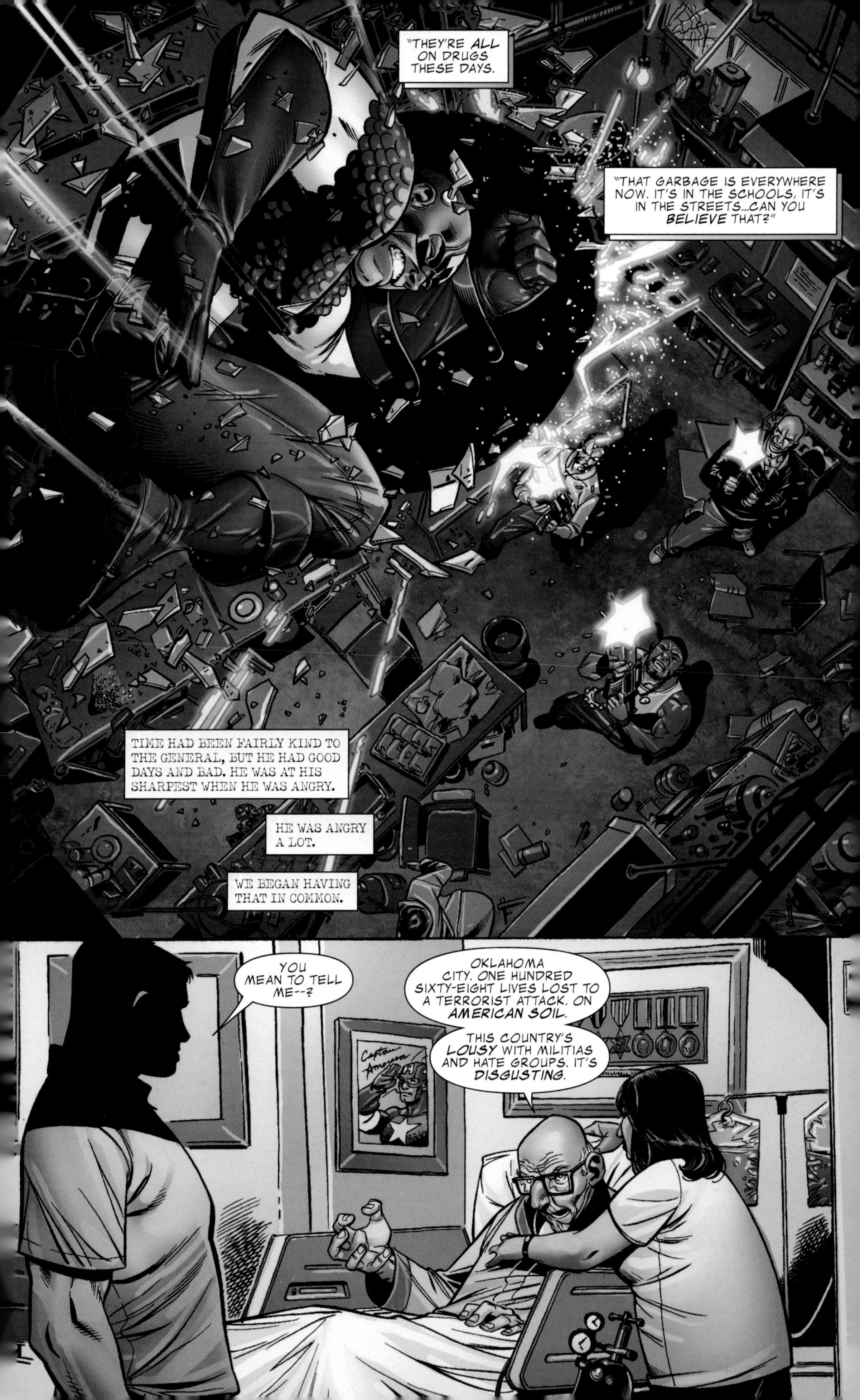
"THEY'RE ALL ON DRUGS THESE DAYS.
"THAT GARBAGE IS EVERYWHERE NOW. IT'S IN THE SCHOOLS, IT'S IN THE STREETS...CAN YOU BELIEVE THAT?"
TIME HAD BEEN FAIRLY KIND TO THE GENERAL, BUT HE HAD GOOD DAYS AND BAD. HE WAS AT HIS SHARPEST WHEN HE WAS ANGRY.
HE WAS ANGRY A LOT.
WE BEGAN HAVING THAT IN COMMON.
YOU MEAN TO TELL ME--?
OKLAHOMA CITY. ONE HUNDRED SIXTY-EIGHT LIVES LOST TO A TERRORIST ATTACK. ON AMERICAN SOIL.
THIS COUNTRY'S LOUSY WITH MILITIAS AND HATE GROUPS. IT'S DISGUSTING.

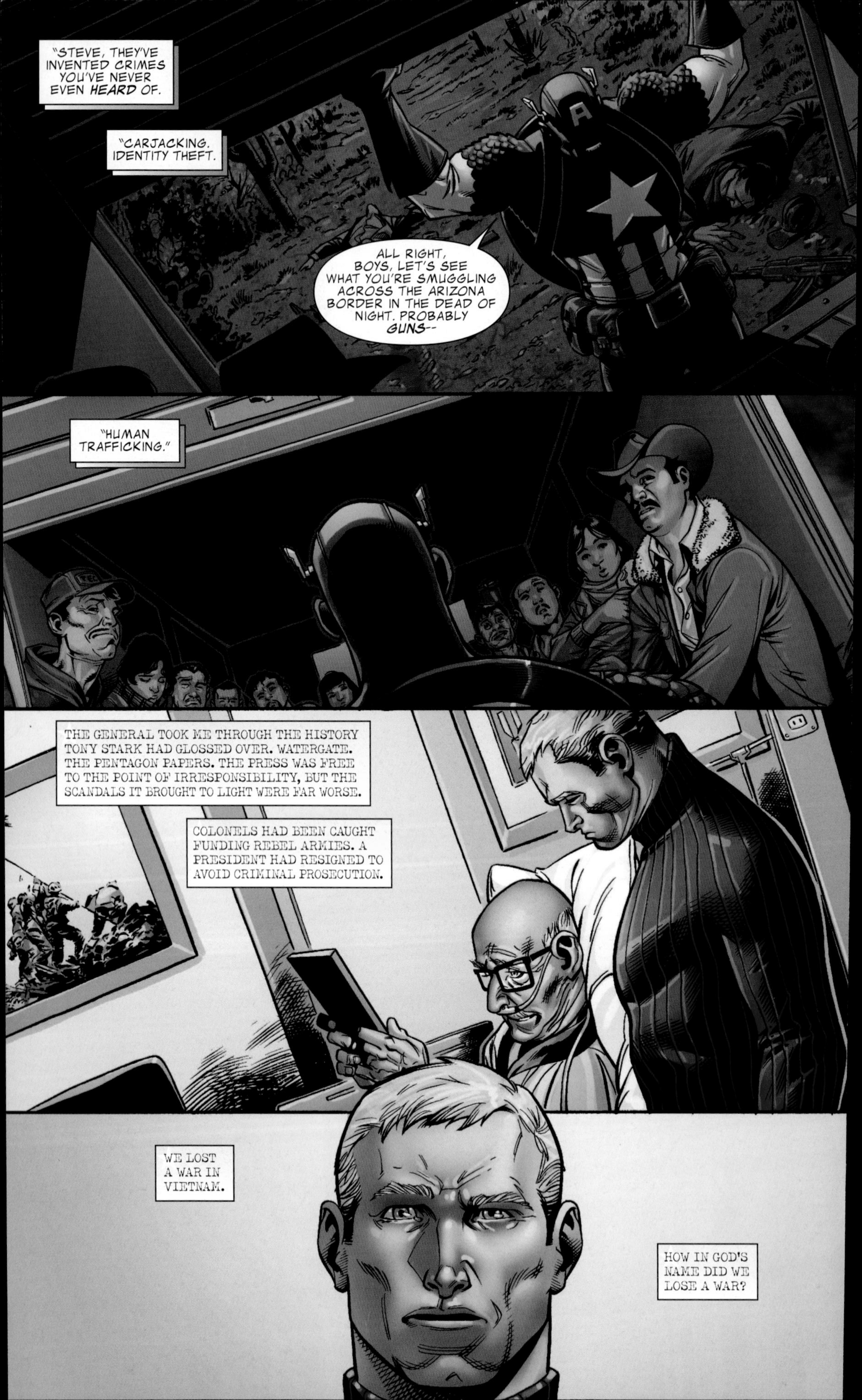
"STEVE, THEY'VE INVENTED CRIMES YOU'VE NEVER EVEN HEARD OF.
"CARJACKING. IDENTITY THEFT.
ALL RIGHT, BOYS, LET'S SEE WHAT YOU'RE SMUGGLING ACROSS THE ARIZONA BORDER IN THE DEAD OF NIGHT. PROBABLY GUNS--
"HUMAN TRAFFICKING."
THE GENERAL TOOK ME THROUGH THE HISTORY TONY STARK HAD GLOSSED OVER. WATERGATE. THE PENTAGON PAPERS. THE PRESS WAS FREE TO THE POINT OF IRRESPONSIBILITY, BUT THE SCANDALS IT BROUGHT TO LIGHT WERE FAR WORSE.
COLONELS HAD BEEN CAUGHT FUNDING REBEL ARMIES. A PRESIDENT HAD RESIGNED TO AVOID CRIMINAL PROSECUTION.
WE LOST A WAR IN VIETNAM.
HOW IN GOD'S NAME DID WE LOSE A WAR?

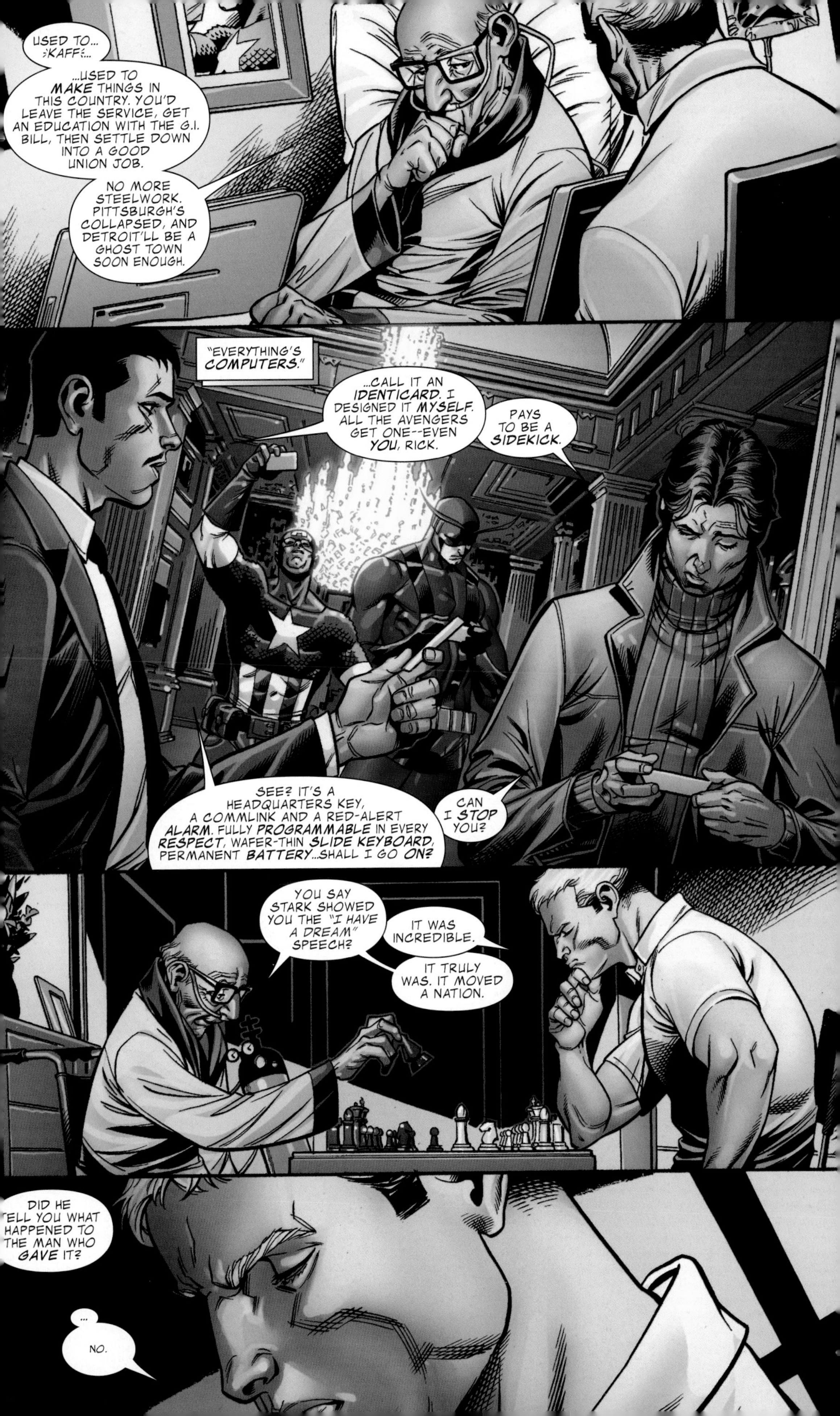
USED TO... ⁂KAFF⁂...
...USED TO MAKE THINGS IN THIS COUNTRY. YOU'D LEAVE THE SERVICE, GET AN EDUCATION WITH THE G.I. BILL, THEN SETTLE DOWN INTO A GOOD UNION JOB.
NO MORE STEELWORK. PITTSBURGH'S COLLAPSED, AND DETROIT'LL BE A GHOST TOWN SOON ENOUGH.
"EVERYTHING'S COMPUTERS."
...CALL IT AN IDENTICARD. I DESIGNED IT MYSELF. ALL THE AVENGERS GET ONE--EVEN YOU, RICK.
PAYS TO BE A SIDEKICK.
SEE? IT'S A HEADQUARTERS KEY, A COMMLINK AND A RED-ALERT ALARM. FULLY PROGRAMMABLE IN EVERY RESPECT, WAFER-THIN SLIDE KEYBOARD, PERMANENT BATTERY...SHALL I GO ON?
CAN I STOP YOU?
YOU SAY STARK SHOWED YOU THE "I HAVE A DREAM" SPEECH?
IT WAS INCREDIBLE.
IT TRULY WAS. IT MOVED A NATION.
DID HE TELL YOU WHAT HAPPENED TO THE MAN WHO GAVE IT?
...
NO.

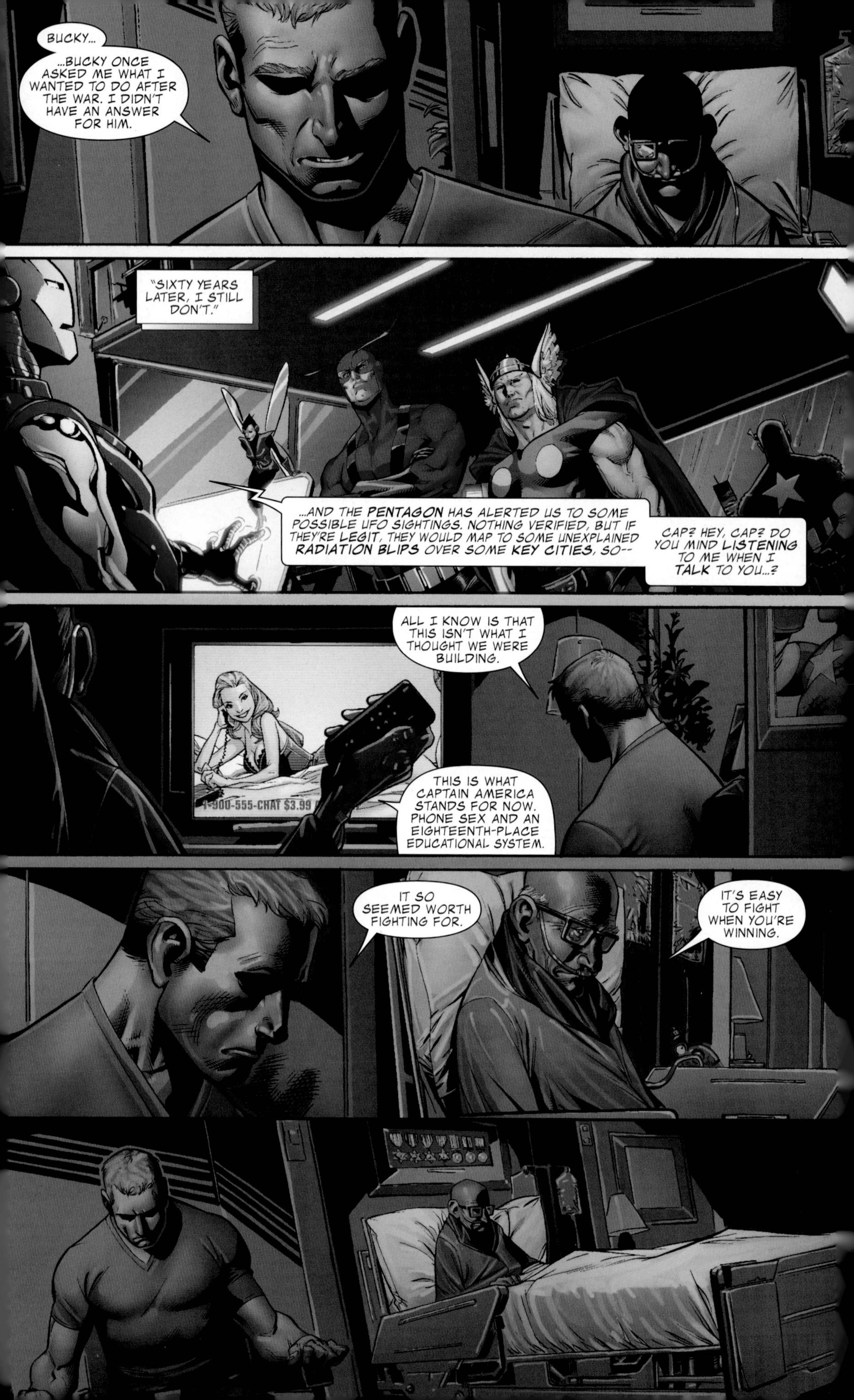
BUCKY...
...BUCKY ONCE ASKED ME WHAT I WANTED TO DO AFTER THE WAR. I DIDN'T HAVE AN ANSWER FOR HIM.
"SIXTY YEARS LATER, I STILL DON'T."
...AND THE PENTAGON HAS ALERTED US TO SOME POSSIBLE UFO SIGHTINGS. NOTHING VERIFIED, BUT IF THEY'RE LEGIT, THEY WOULD MAP TO SOME UNEXPLAINED RADIATION BLIPS OVER SOME KEY CITIES, SO--
CAP? HEY, CAP? DO YOU MIND LISTENING TO ME WHEN I TALK TO YOU...?
ALL I KNOW IS THAT THIS ISN'T WHAT I THOUGHT WE WERE BUILDING.
1-900-555-CHAT $3.99
THIS IS WHAT CAPTAIN AMERICA STANDS FOR NOW. PHONE SEX AND AN EIGHTEENTH-PLACE EDUCATIONAL SYSTEM.
IT SO SEEMED WORTH FIGHTING FOR.
IT'S EASY TO FIGHT WHEN YOU'RE WINNING.

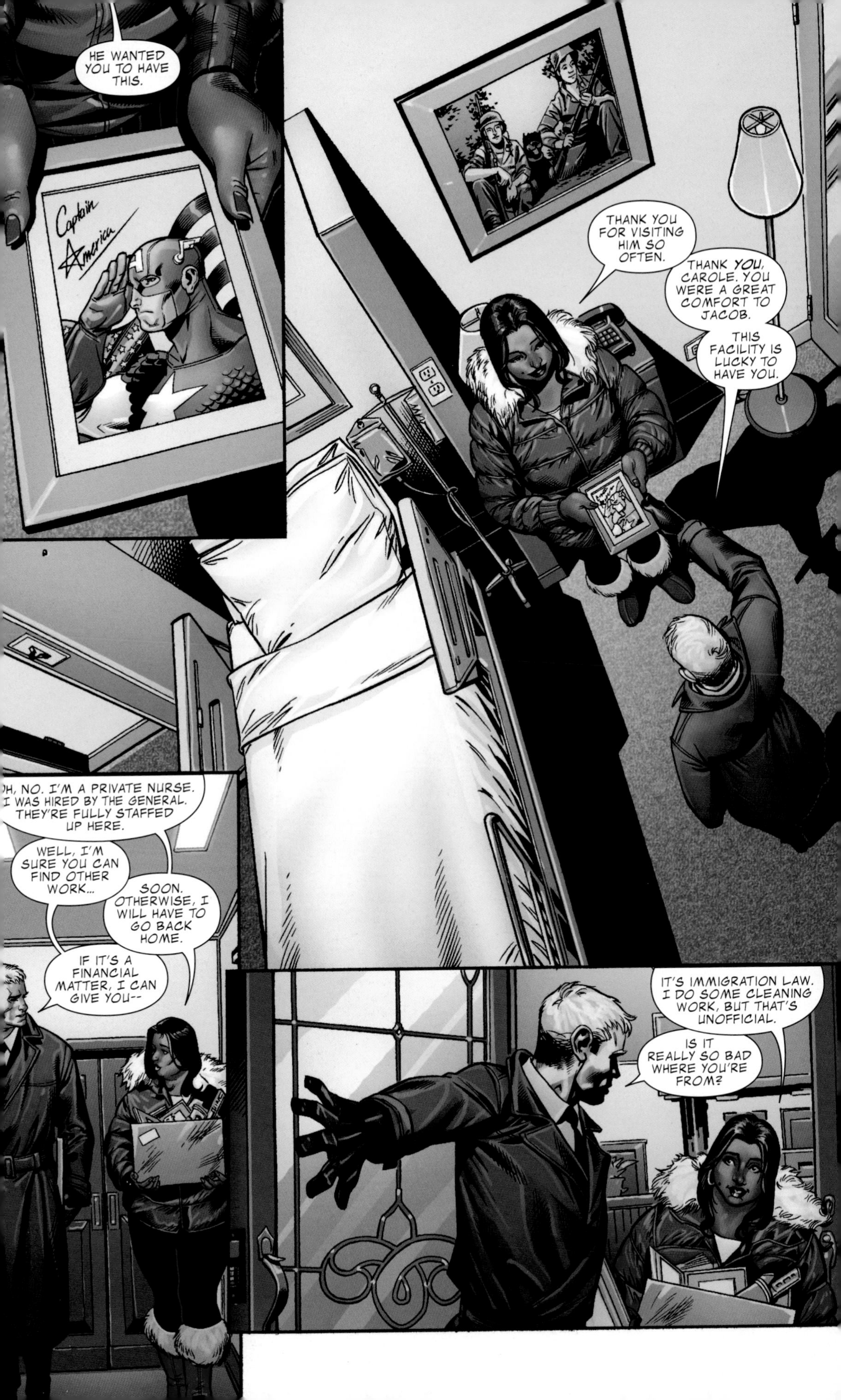
HE WANTED YOU TO HAVE THIS.
Captain America
THANK YOU FOR VISITING HIM SO OFTEN.
THANK YOU, CAROLE. YOU WERE A GREAT COMFORT TO JACOB.
THIS FACILITY IS LUCKY TO HAVE YOU.
OH, NO. I'M A PRIVATE NURSE. I WAS HIRED BY THE GENERAL. THEY'RE FULLY STAFFED UP HERE.
WELL, I'M SURE YOU CAN FIND OTHER WORK...
SOON. OTHERWISE, I WILL HAVE TO GO BACK HOME.
IF IT'S A FINANCIAL MATTER, I CAN GIVE YOU--
IT'S IMMIGRATION LAW. I DO SOME CLEANING WORK, BUT THAT'S UNOFFICIAL.
IS IT REALLY SO BAD WHERE YOU'RE FROM?

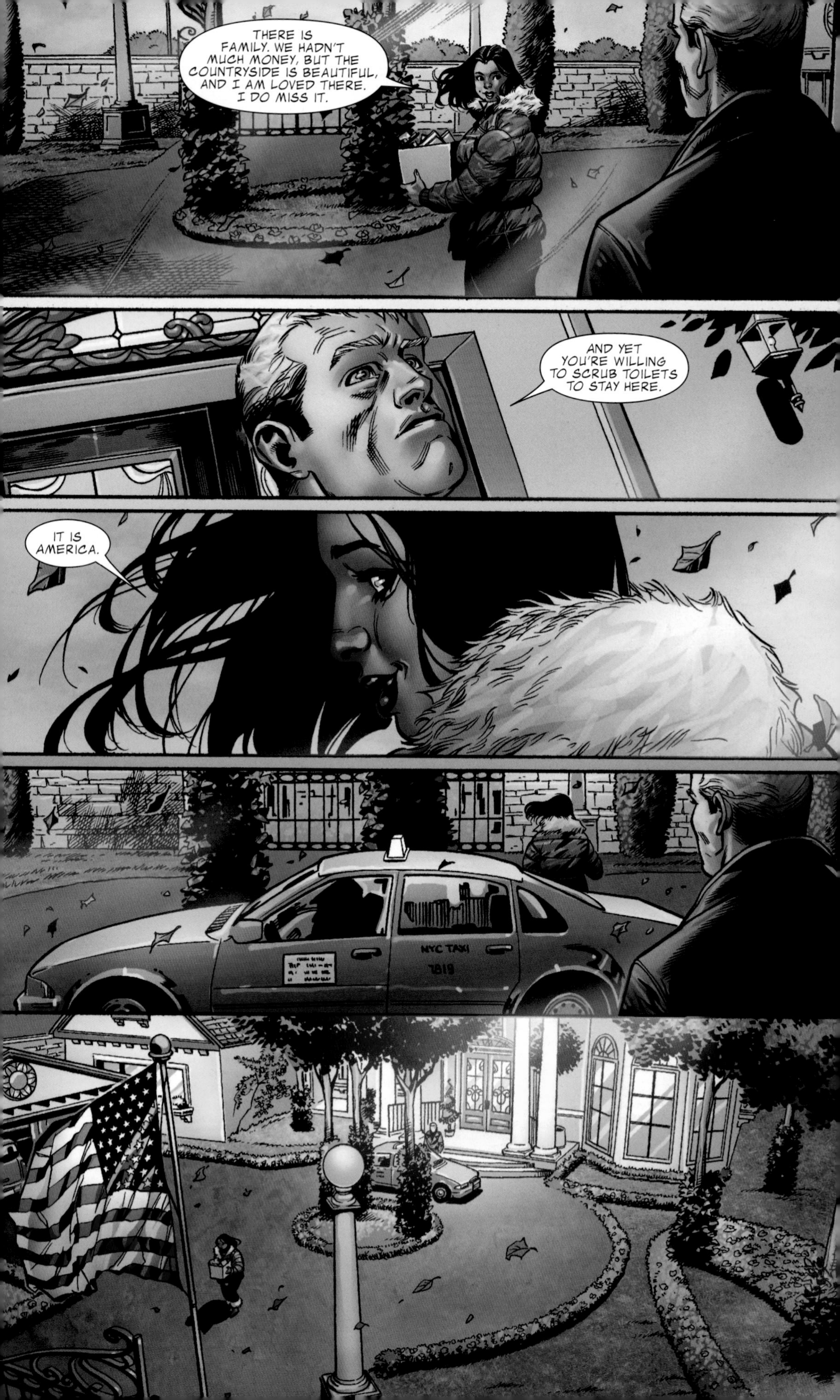
THERE IS FAMILY. WE HADN'T MUCH MONEY, BUT THE COUNTRYSIDE IS BEAUTIFUL, AND I AM LOVED THERE. I DO MISS IT.
AND YET YOU'RE WILLING TO SCRUB TOILETS TO STAY HERE.
IT IS AMERICA.
NYC TAXI
7818

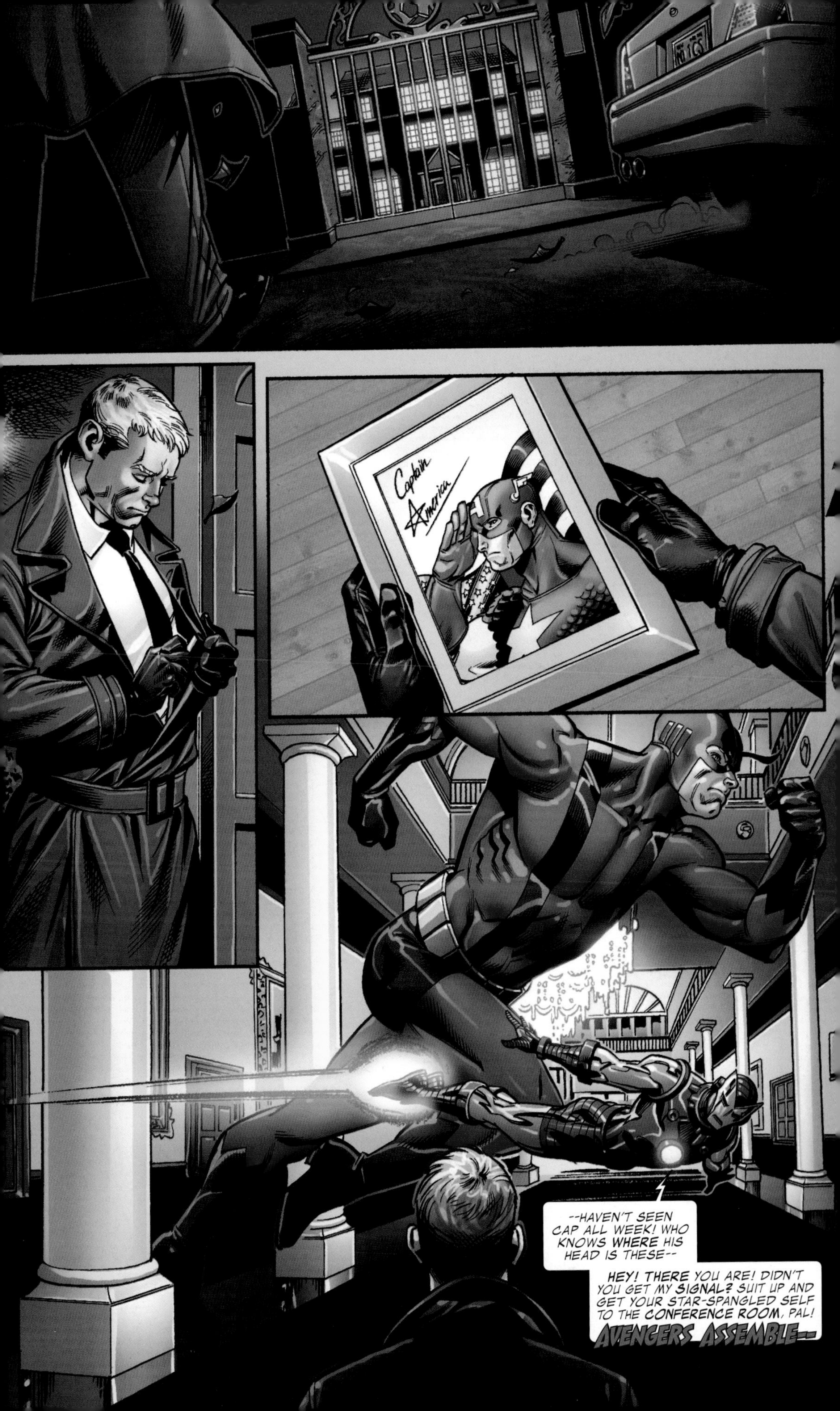
Captain America
--HAVEN'T SEEN CAP ALL WEEK! WHO KNOWS WHERE HIS HEAD IS THESE--
HEY! THERE YOU ARE! DIDN'T YOU GET MY SIGNAL? SUIT UP AND GET YOUR STAR-SPANGLED SELF TO THE CONFERENCE ROOM, PAL!
AVENGERS ASSEMBLE--

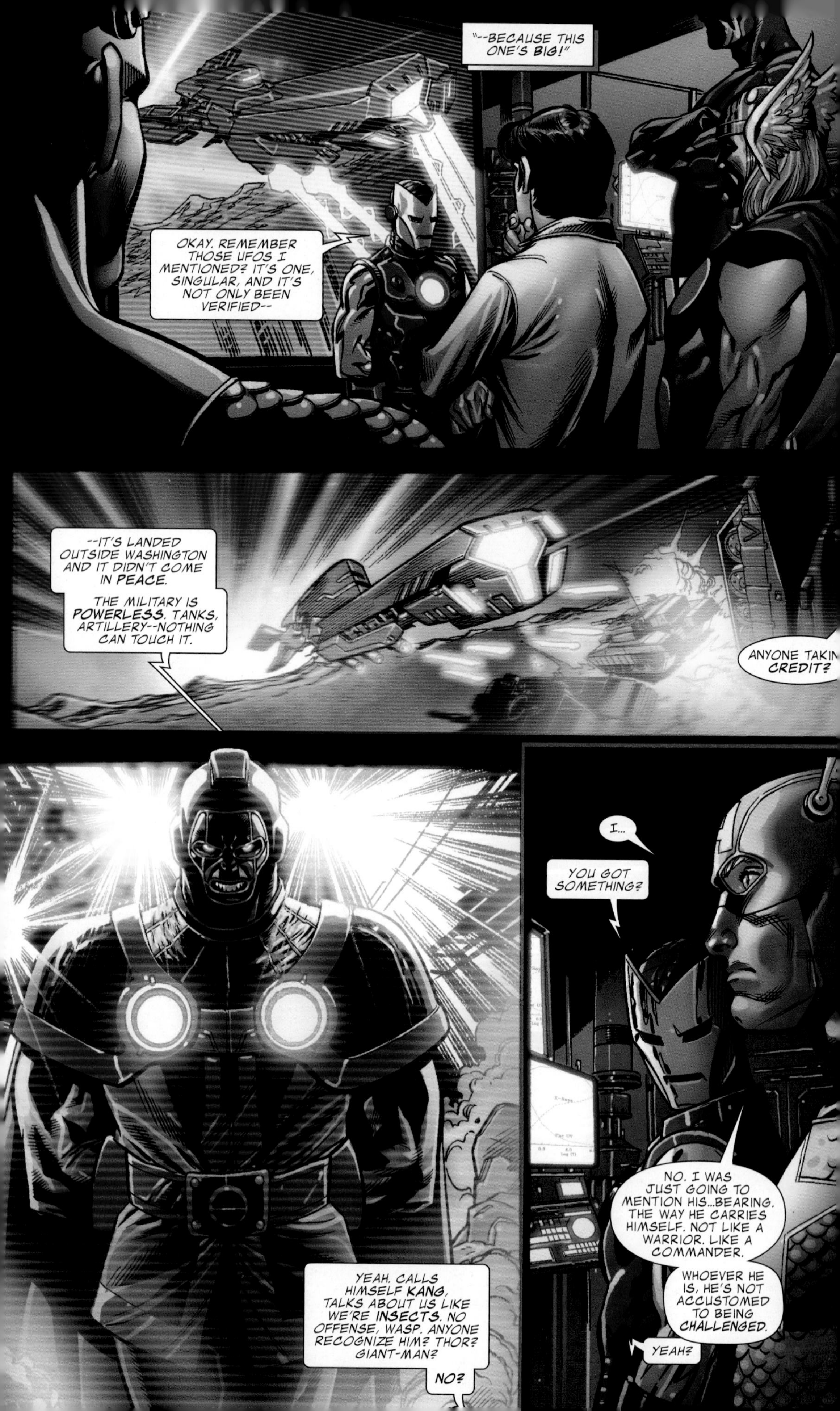
"--BECAUSE THIS ONE'S BIG!"
OKAY. REMEMBER THOSE UFOS I MENTIONED? IT'S ONE, SINGULAR, AND IT'S NOT ONLY BEEN VERIFIED--
--IT'S LANDED OUTSIDE WASHINGTON AND IT DIDN'T COME IN PEACE.
THE MILITARY IS POWERLESS. TANKS, ARTILLERY--NOTHING CAN TOUCH IT.
ANYONE TAKIN CREDIT?
YEAH. CALLS HIMSELF KANG, TALKS ABOUT US LIKE WE'RE INSECTS. NO OFFENSE, WASP. ANYONE RECOGNIZE HIM? THOR? GIANT-MAN?
NO?
I...
YOU GOT SOMETHING?
NO. I WAS JUST GOING TO MENTION HIS...BEARING. THE WAY HE CARRIES HIMSELF. NOT LIKE A WARRIOR. LIKE A COMMANDER.
WHOEVER HE IS, HE'S NOT ACCUSTOMED TO BEING CHALLENGED.
YEAH?

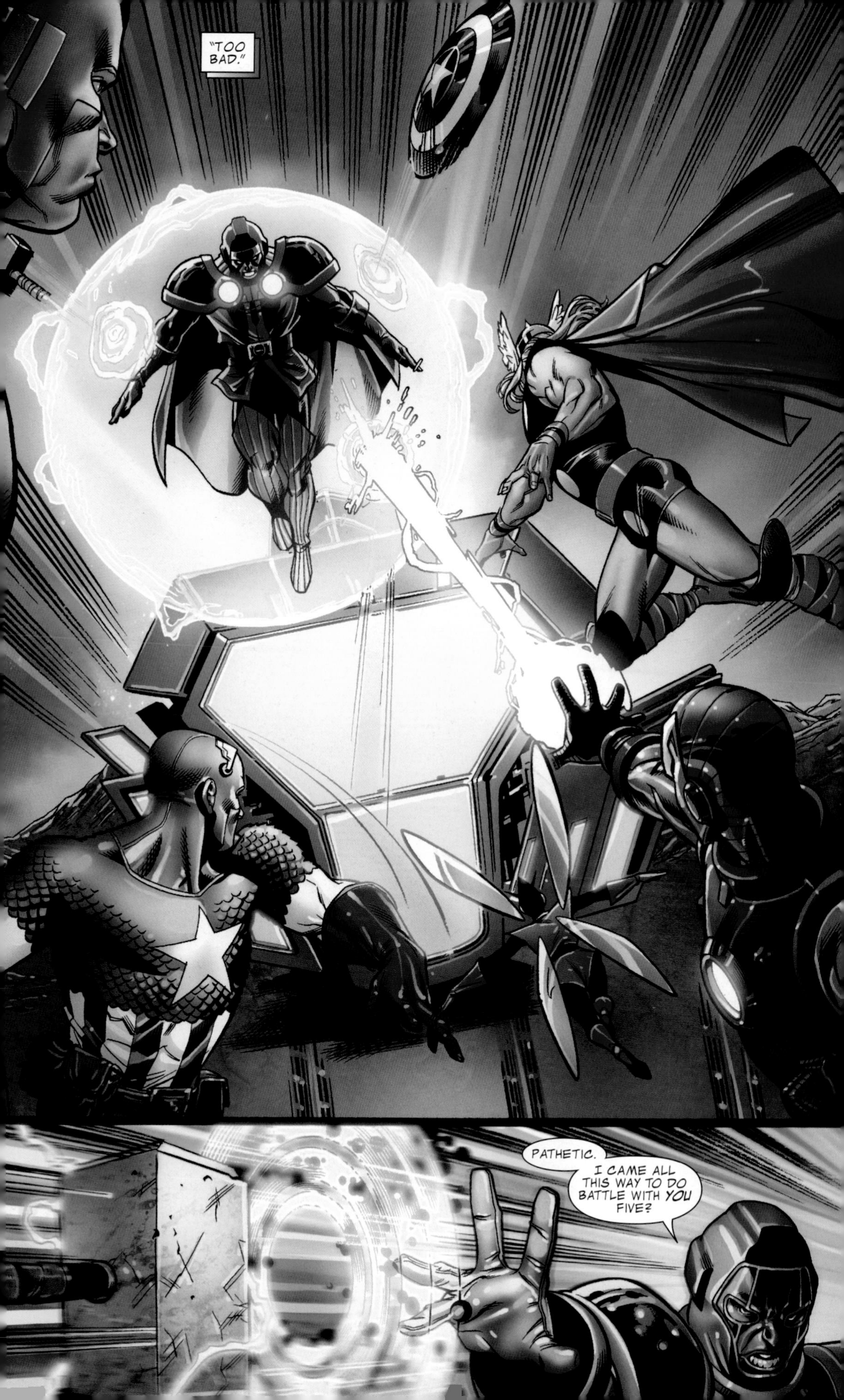
"TOO BAD."
PATHETIC.
I CAME ALL THIS WAY TO DO BATTLE WITH YOU FIVE?

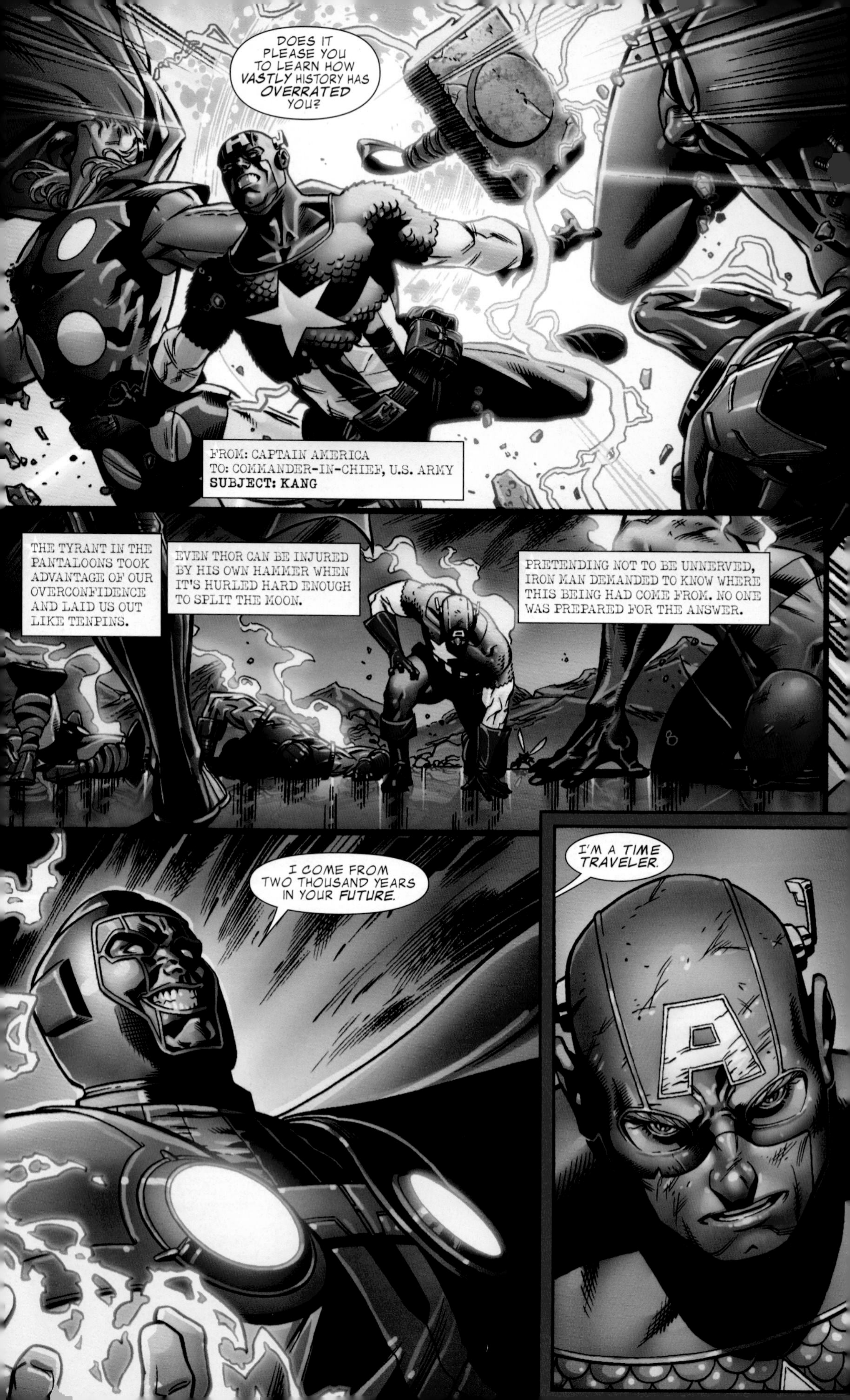
DOES IT PLEASE YOU TO LEARN HOW VASTLY HISTORY HAS OVERRATED YOU?
FROM: CAPTAIN AMERICA
TO: COMMANDER-IN-CHIEF, U.S. ARMY
SUBJECT: KANG
THE TYRANT IN THE PANTALOONS TOOK ADVANTAGE OF OUR OVERCONFIDENCE AND LAID US OUT LIKE TENPINS.
EVEN THOR CAN BE INJURED BY HIS OWN HAMMER WHEN IT'S HURLED HARD ENOUGH TO SPLIT THE MOON.
PRETENDING NOT TO BE UNNERVED, IRON MAN DEMANDED TO KNOW WHERE THIS BEING HAD COME FROM. NO ONE WAS PREPARED FOR THE ANSWER.
I COME FROM TWO THOUSAND YEARS IN YOUR FUTURE.
I'M A TIME TRAVELER.

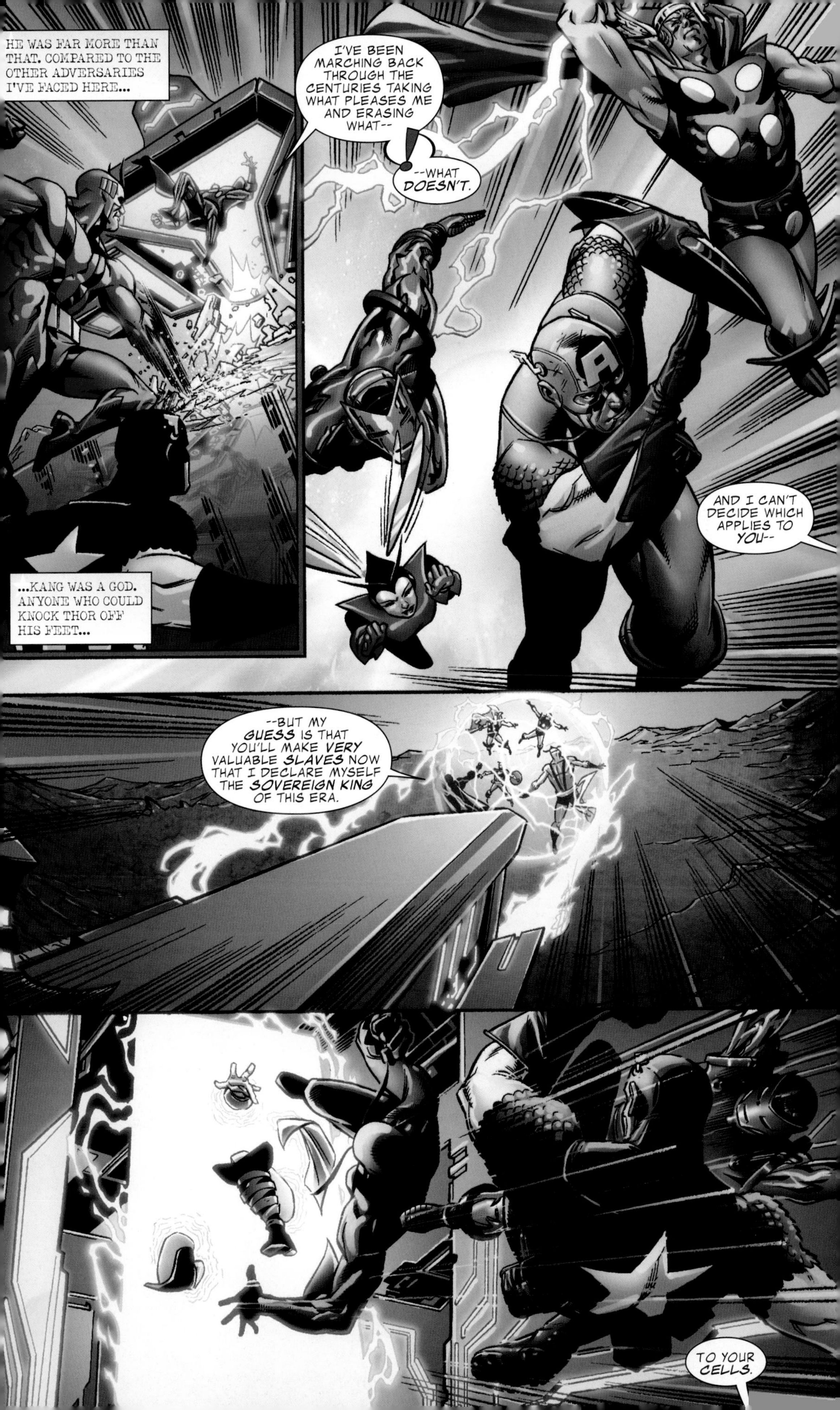
HE WAS FAR MORE THAN THAT. COMPARED TO THE OTHER ADVERSARIES I'VE FACED HERE...
I'VE BEEN MARCHING BACK THROUGH THE CENTURIES TAKING WHAT PLEASES ME AND ERASING WHAT--
!
--WHAT DOESN'T.
...KANG WAS A GOD. ANYONE WHO COULD KNOCK THOR OFF HIS FEET...
AND I CAN'T DECIDE WHICH APPLIES TO YOU--
--BUT MY GUESS IS THAT YOU'LL MAKE VERY VALUABLE SLAVES NOW THAT I DECLARE MYSELF THE SOVEREIGN KING OF THIS ERA.
TO YOUR CELLS.

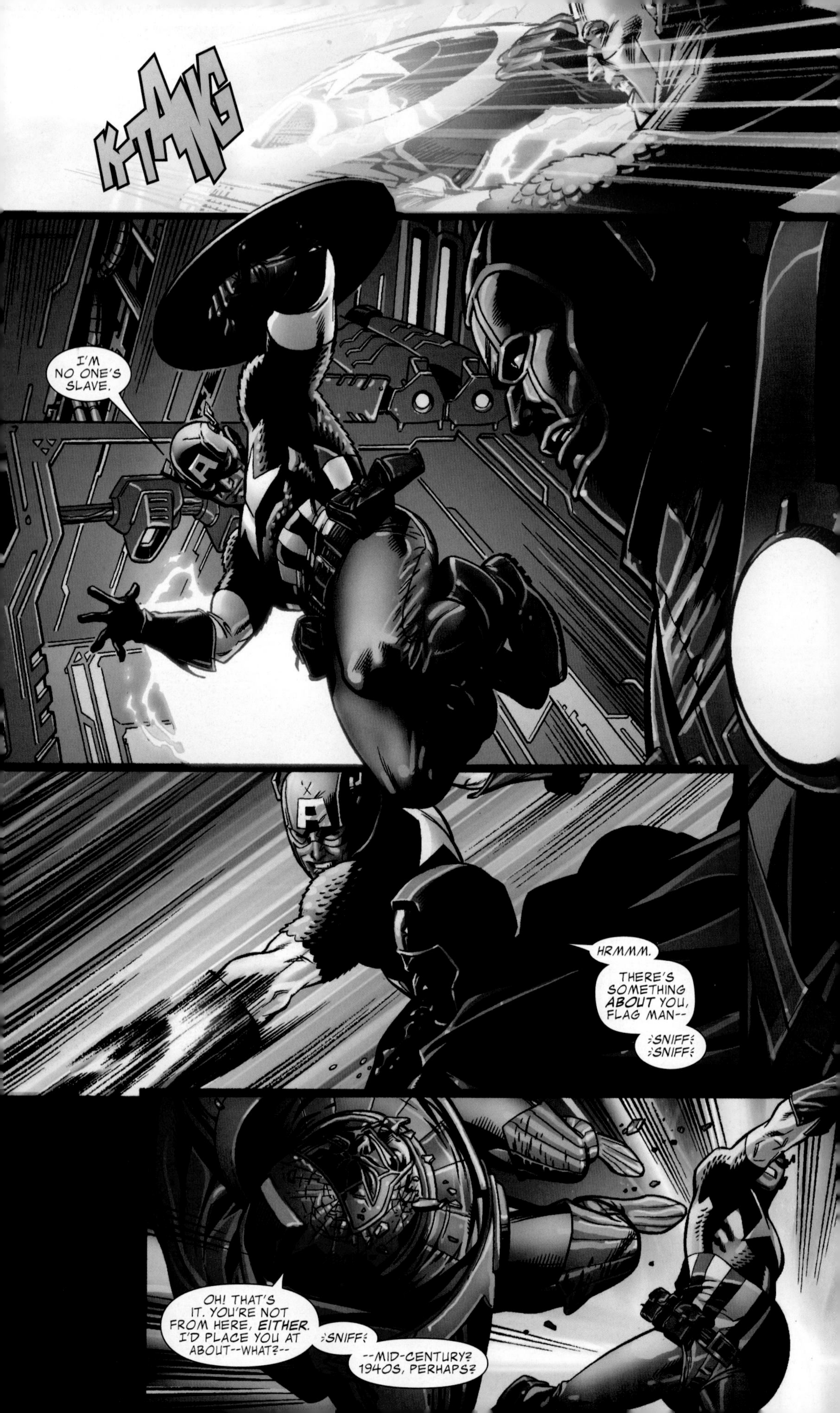
K-TANG
I'M NO ONE'S SLAVE.
HRMMM.
THERE'S SOMETHING *ABOUT* YOU, FLAG MAN--
<SNIFF> <SNIFF>
OH! THAT'S IT. YOU'RE NOT FROM HERE, *EITHER*. I'D PLACE YOU AT ABOUT--WHAT?--
<SNIFF>
--MID-CENTURY? 1940S, PERHAPS?

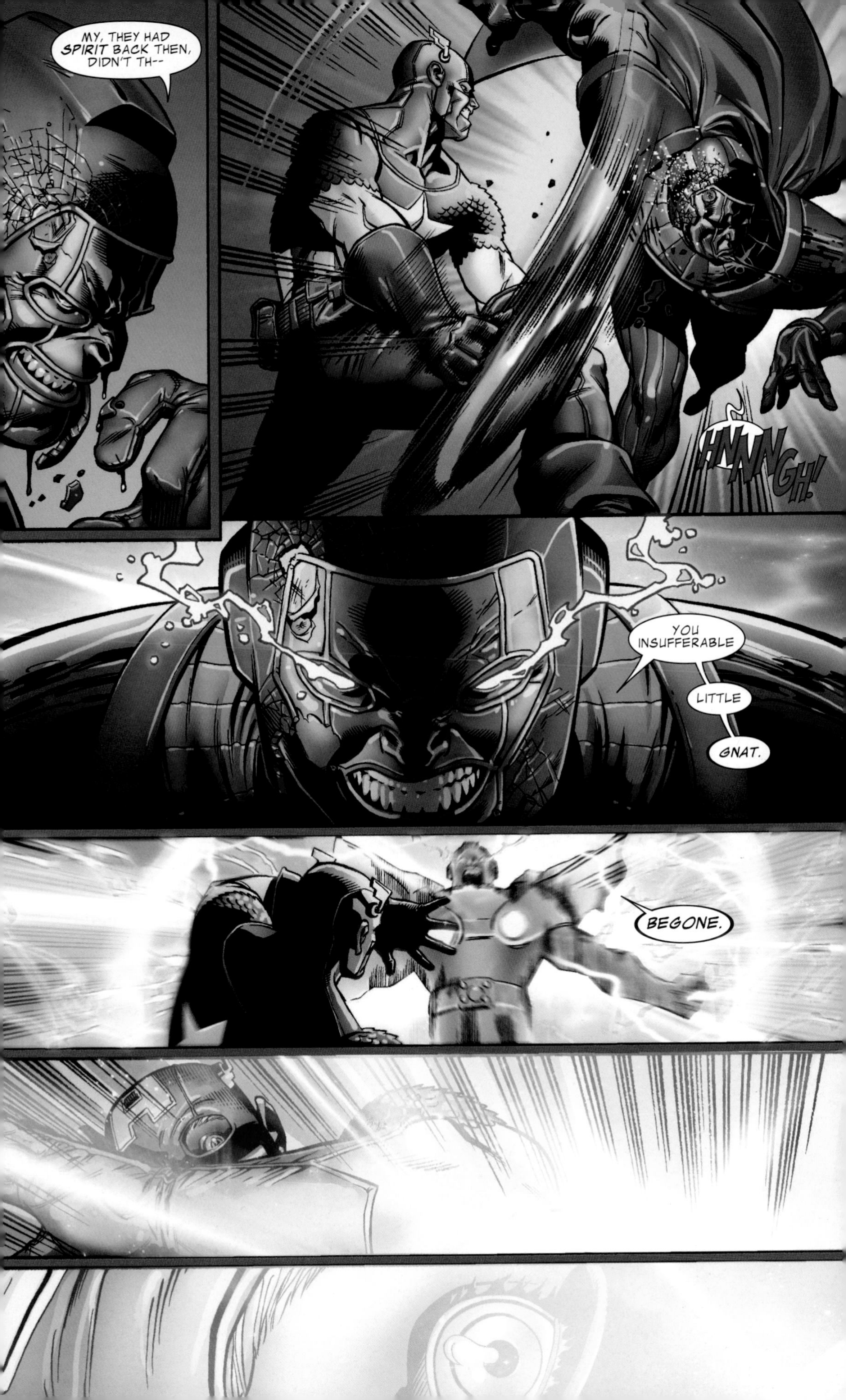
MY, THEY HAD SPIRIT BACK THEN, DIDN'T TH--
HNNNGH!
YOU INSUFFERABLE
LITTLE
GNAT.
BEGONE.

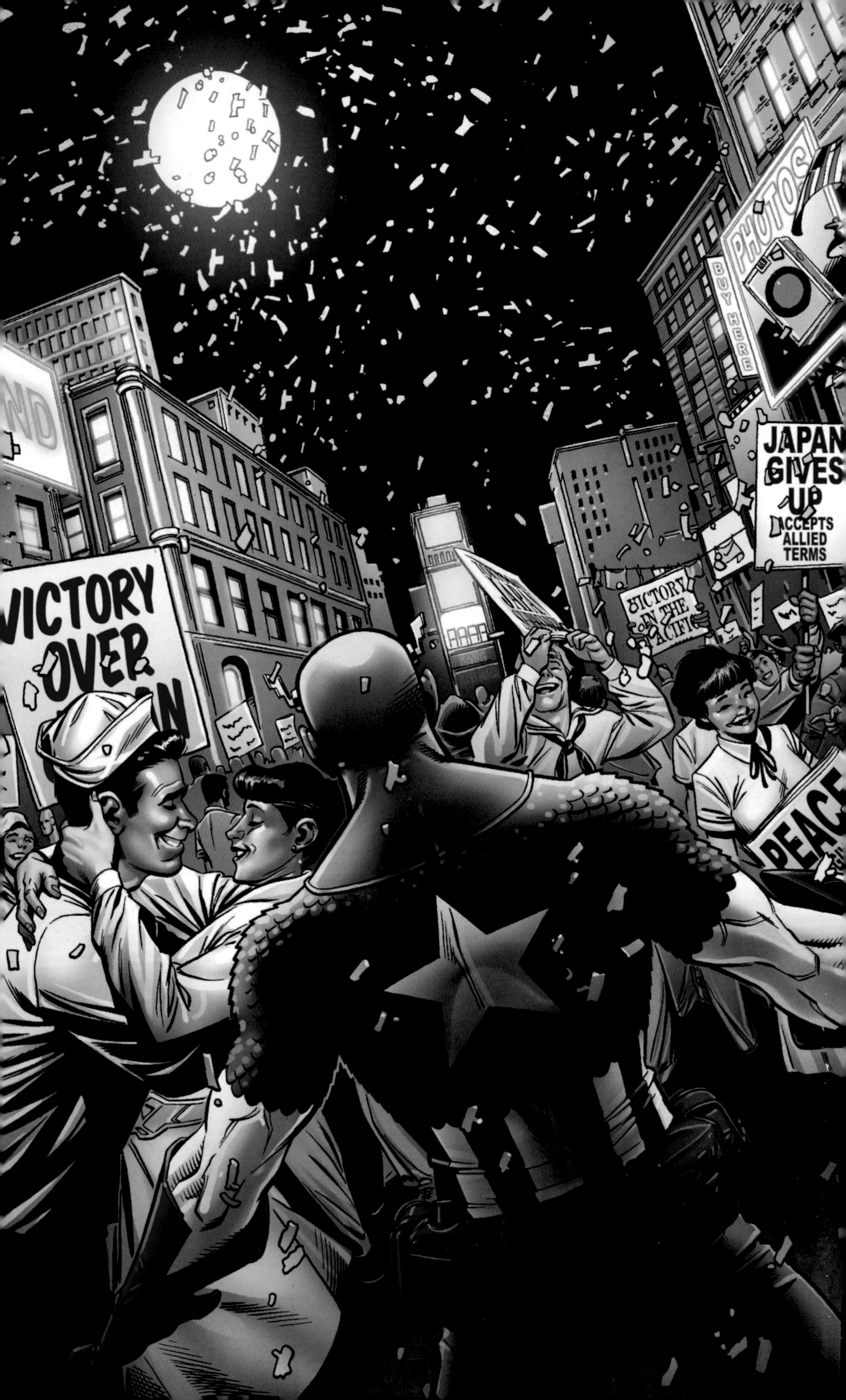
PHOTOS
BUY HERE
JAPAN GIVES UP ACCEPTS ALLIED TERMS
VICTORY OVER
VICTORY IN THE PACIFIC
PEACE

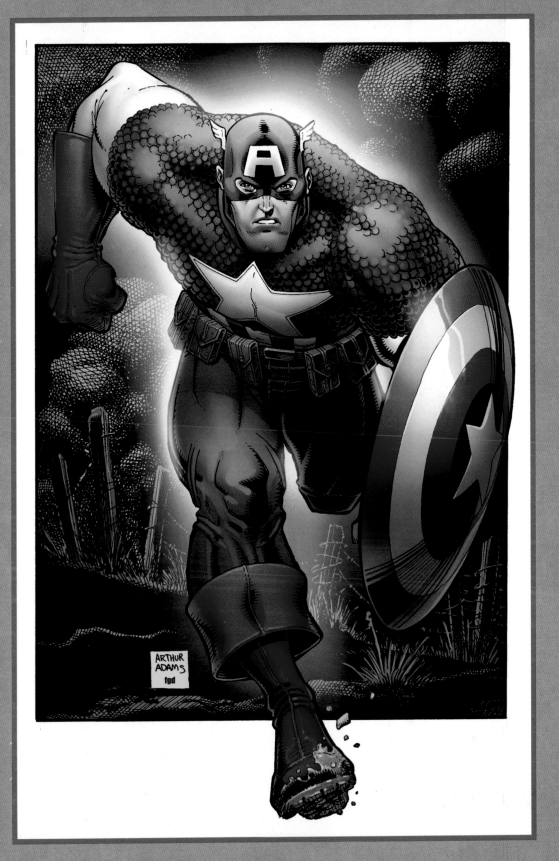

[1]
Variant by Artur Adams & Frank D'Armata

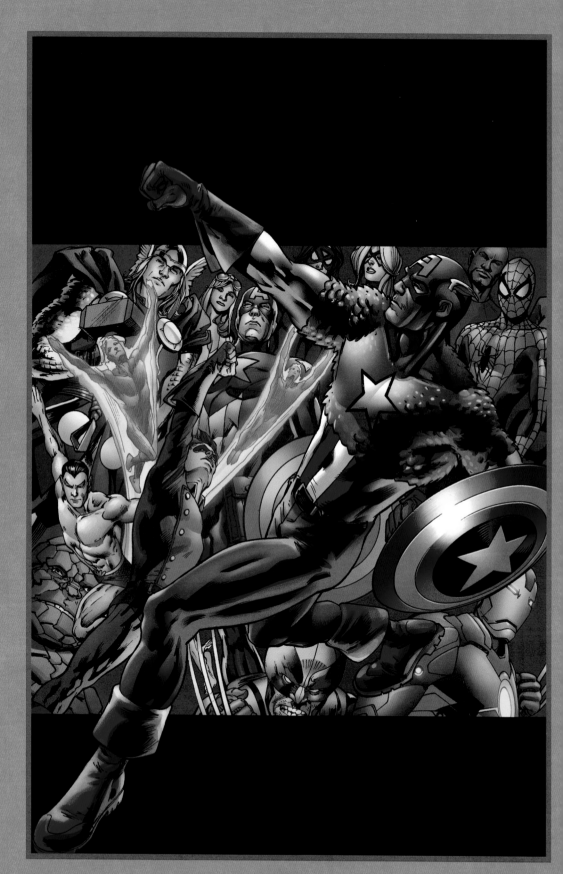

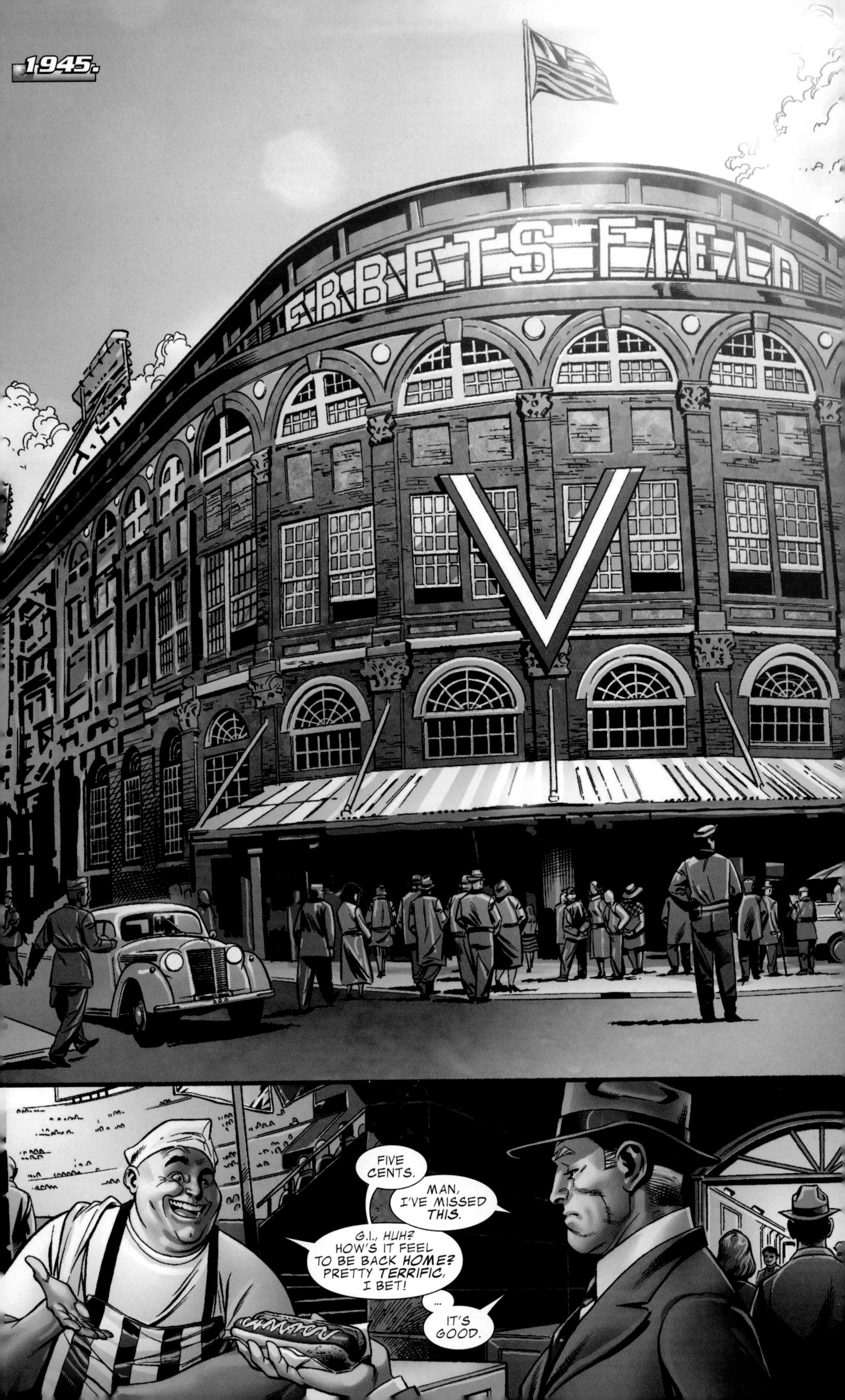
1945.
FIVE CENTS.
MAN, I'VE MISSED *THIS*.
G.I., HUH? HOW'S IT FEEL TO BE BACK *HOME*? PRETTY *TERRIFIC*, I BET!
... IT'S GOOD.

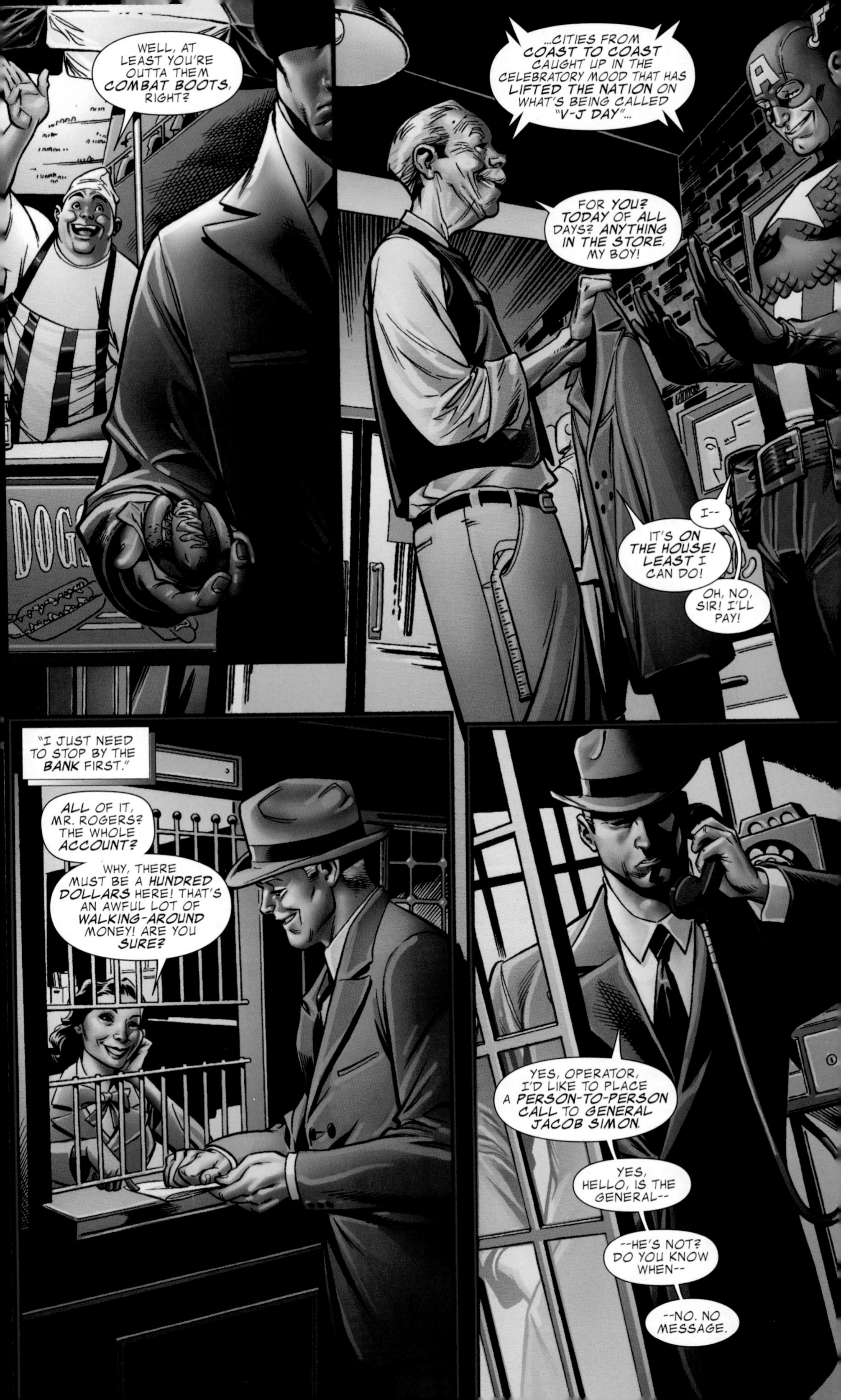
WELL, AT LEAST YOU'RE OUTTA THEM COMBAT BOOTS, RIGHT?
DOGS
...CITIES FROM COAST TO COAST CAUGHT UP IN THE CELEBRATORY MOOD THAT HAS LIFTED THE NATION ON WHAT'S BEING CALLED "V-J DAY"...
FOR YOU? TODAY OF ALL DAYS? ANYTHING IN THE STORE, MY BOY!
I--
IT'S ON THE HOUSE! LEAST I CAN DO!
OH, NO, SIR! I'LL PAY!
"I JUST NEED TO STOP BY THE BANK FIRST."
ALL OF IT, MR. ROGERS? THE WHOLE ACCOUNT?
WHY, THERE MUST BE A HUNDRED DOLLARS HERE! THAT'S AN AWFUL LOT OF WALKING-AROUND MONEY! ARE YOU SURE?
YES, OPERATOR, I'D LIKE TO PLACE A PERSON-TO-PERSON CALL TO GENERAL JACOB SIMON.
YES, HELLO, IS THE GENERAL--
--HE'S NOT? DO YOU KNOW WHEN--
--NO. NO MESSAGE.

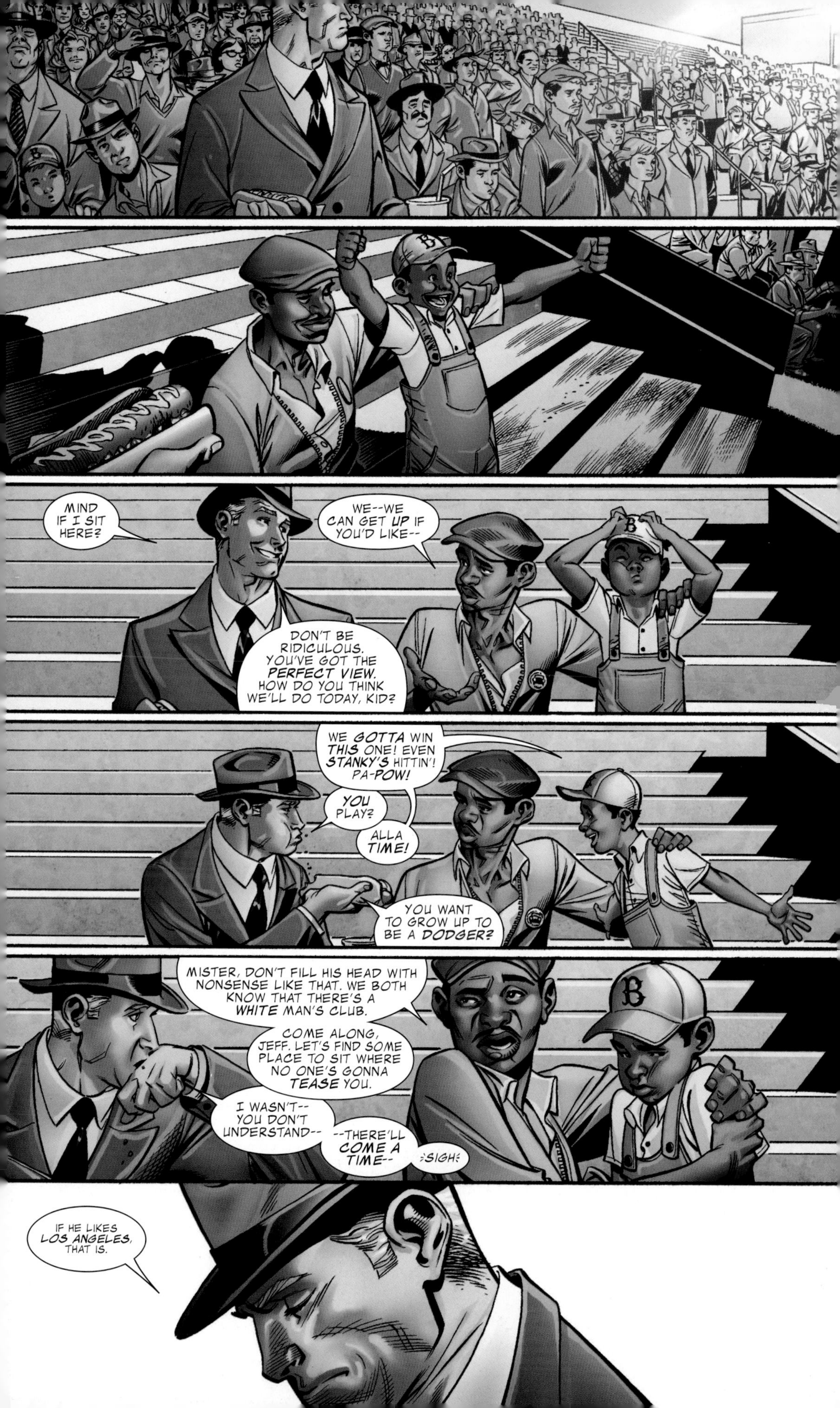
MIND IF I SIT HERE?
WE--WE CAN GET UP IF YOU'D LIKE--
DON'T BE RIDICULOUS. YOU'VE GOT THE PERFECT VIEW. HOW DO YOU THINK WE'LL DO TODAY, KID?
WE GOTTA WIN THIS ONE! EVEN STANKY'S HITTIN'! PA-POW!
YOU PLAY?
ALLA TIME!
YOU WANT TO GROW UP TO BE A DODGER?
MISTER, DON'T FILL HIS HEAD WITH NONSENSE LIKE THAT. WE BOTH KNOW THAT THERE'S A WHITE MAN'S CLUB.
COME ALONG, JEFF. LET'S FIND SOME PLACE TO SIT WHERE NO ONE'S GONNA TEASE YOU.
I WASN'T-- YOU DON'T UNDERSTAND--
--THERE'LL COME A TIME--
SIGH
IF HE LIKES LOS ANGELES, THAT IS.

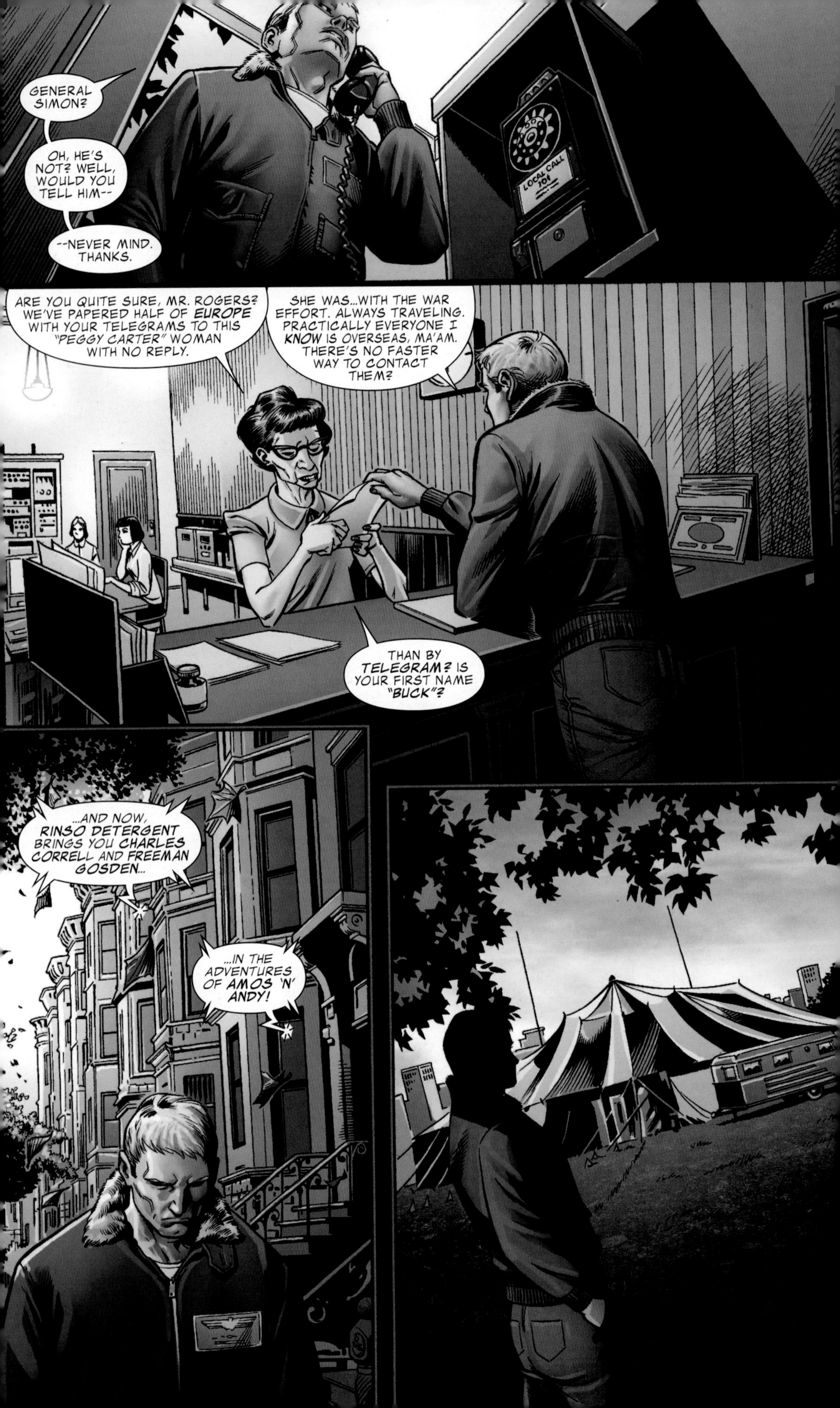
GENERAL SIMON?
OH, HE'S NOT? WELL, WOULD YOU TELL HIM--
--NEVER MIND. THANKS.
LOCAL CALL 10¢
ARE YOU QUITE SURE, MR. ROGERS? WE'VE PAPERED HALF OF EUROPE WITH YOUR TELEGRAMS TO THIS "PEGGY CARTER" WOMAN WITH NO REPLY.
SHE WAS...WITH THE WAR EFFORT. ALWAYS TRAVELING. PRACTICALLY EVERYONE I KNOW IS OVERSEAS, MA'AM. THERE'S NO FASTER WAY TO CONTACT THEM?
THAN BY TELEGRAM? IS YOUR FIRST NAME "BUCK"?
...AND NOW, RINSO DETERGENT BRINGS YOU CHARLES CORRELL AND FREEMAN GOSDEN...
...IN THE ADVENTURES OF AMOS 'N' ANDY!

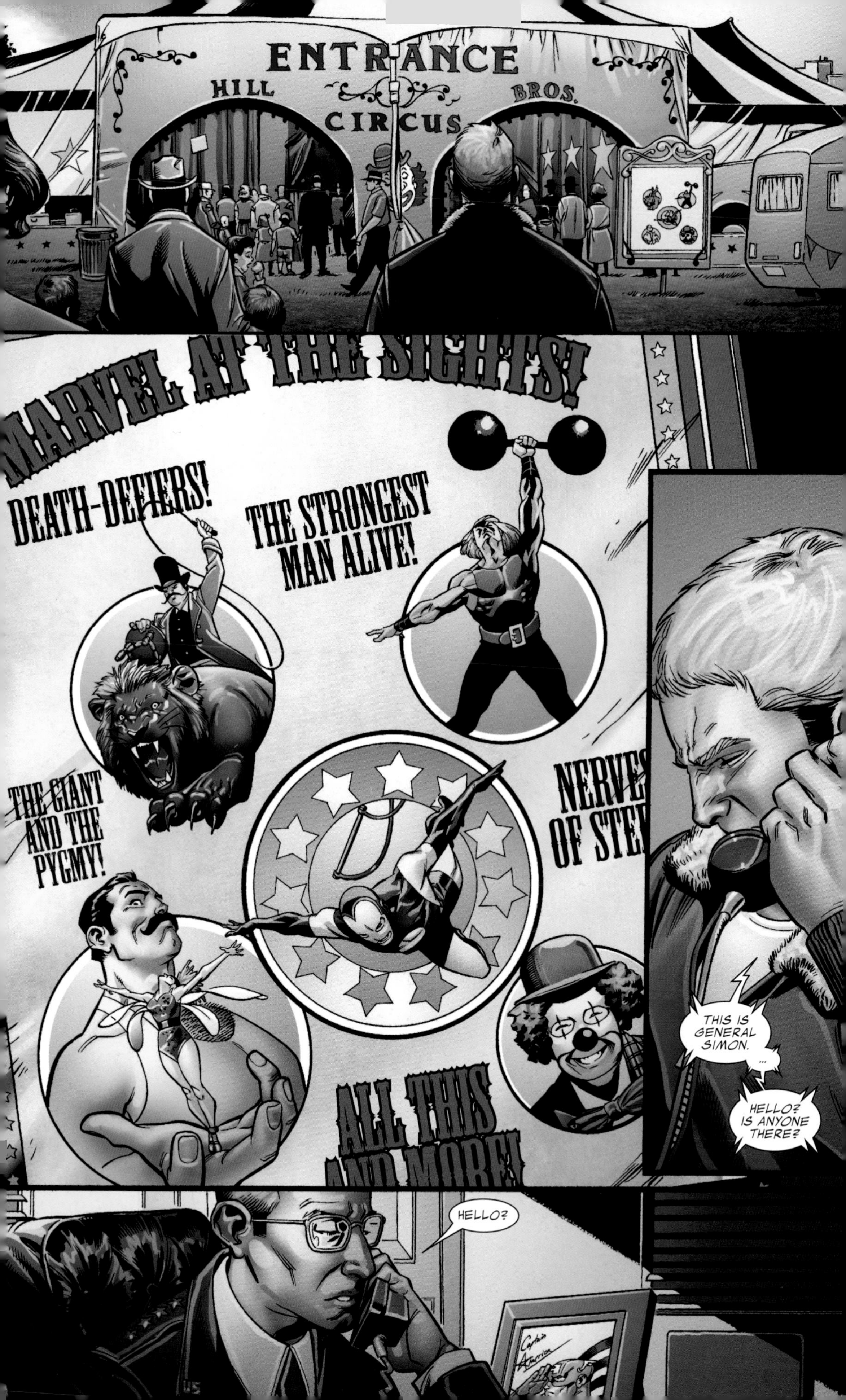
ENTRANCE
HILL BROS. CIRCUS
MARVEL AT THE SIGHTS!
DEATH-DEFIERS!
THE STRONGEST MAN ALIVE!
THE GIANT AND THE PYGMY!
NERVES
ALL THIS AND MORE!
THIS IS GENERAL SIMON.
...
HELLO? IS ANYONE THERE?
HELLO?

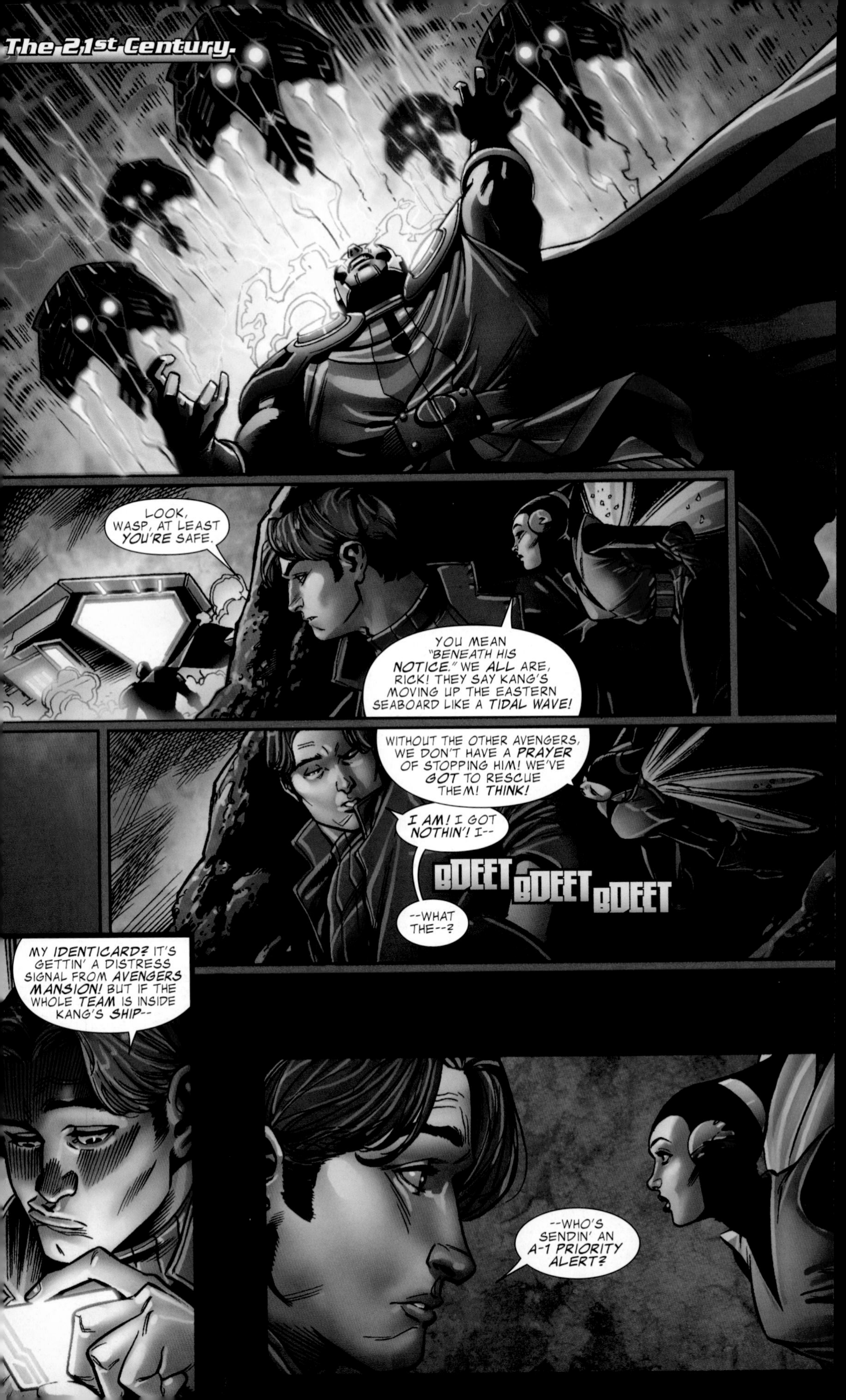
The 21st Century.
LOOK, WASP, AT LEAST YOU'RE SAFE.
YOU MEAN "BENEATH HIS NOTICE." WE ALL ARE, RICK! THEY SAY KANG'S MOVING UP THE EASTERN SEABOARD LIKE A TIDAL WAVE!
WITHOUT THE OTHER AVENGERS, WE DON'T HAVE A PRAYER OF STOPPING HIM! WE'VE GOT TO RESCUE THEM! THINK!
I AM! I GOT NOTHIN'! I--
BDEET BDEET BDEET
--WHAT THE--?
MY IDENTICARD? IT'S GETTIN' A DISTRESS SIGNAL FROM AVENGERS MANSION! BUT IF THE WHOLE TEAM IS INSIDE KANG'S SHIP--
--WHO'S SENDIN' AN A-1 PRIORITY ALERT?

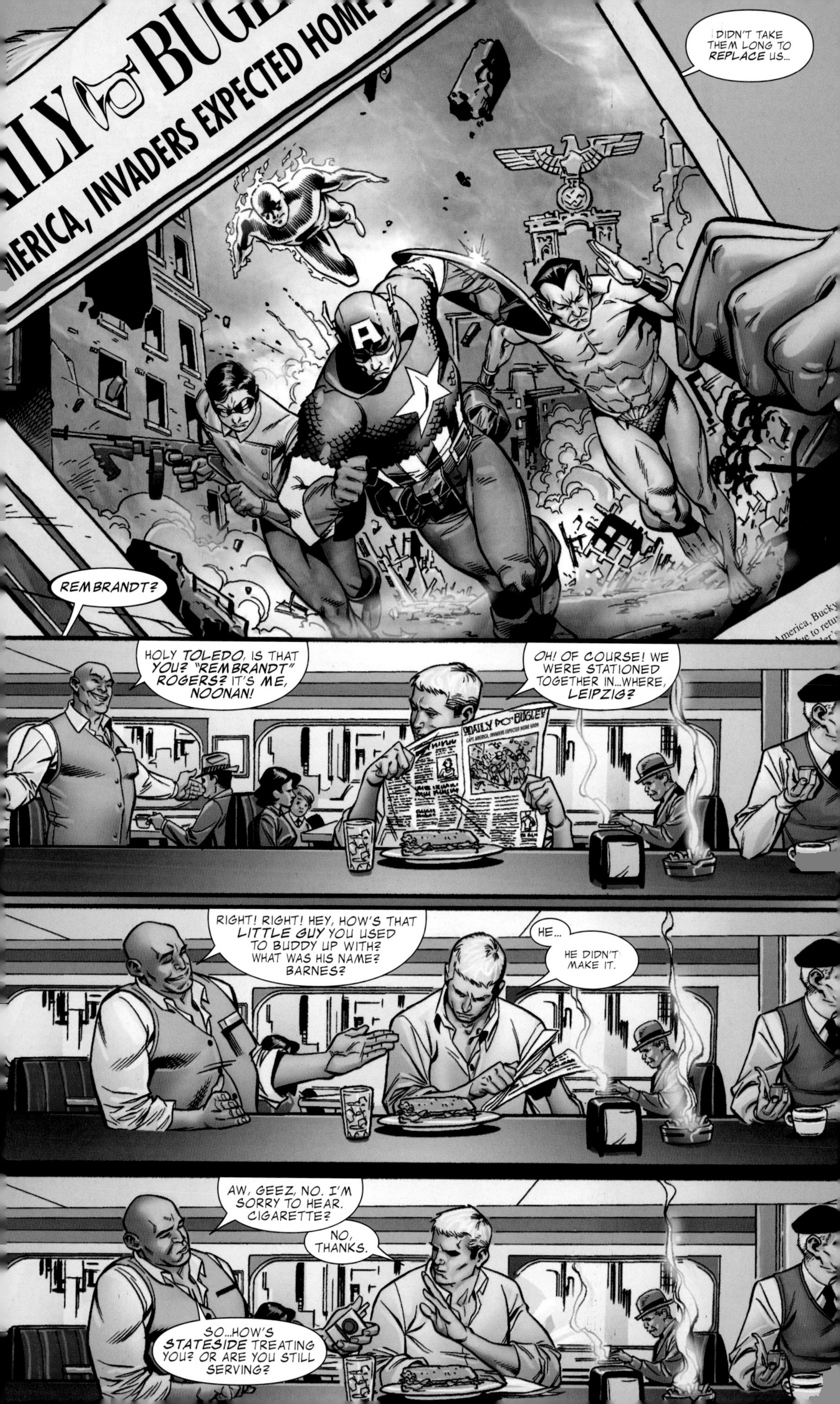
AILY BUGLE
ERICA, INVADERS EXPECTED HOME
DIDN'T TAKE THEM LONG TO REPLACE US...
REMBRANDT?
HOLY TOLEDO, IS THAT YOU? "REMBRANDT" ROGERS? IT'S ME, NOONAN!
OH! OF COURSE! WE WERE STATIONED TOGETHER IN...WHERE, LEIPZIG?
RIGHT! RIGHT! HEY, HOW'S THAT LITTLE GUY YOU USED TO BUDDY UP WITH? WHAT WAS HIS NAME? BARNES?
HE...
HE DIDN'T MAKE IT.
AW, GEEZ, NO. I'M SORRY TO HEAR. CIGARETTE?
NO, THANKS.
SO...HOW'S STATESIDE TREATING YOU? OR ARE YOU STILL SERVING?

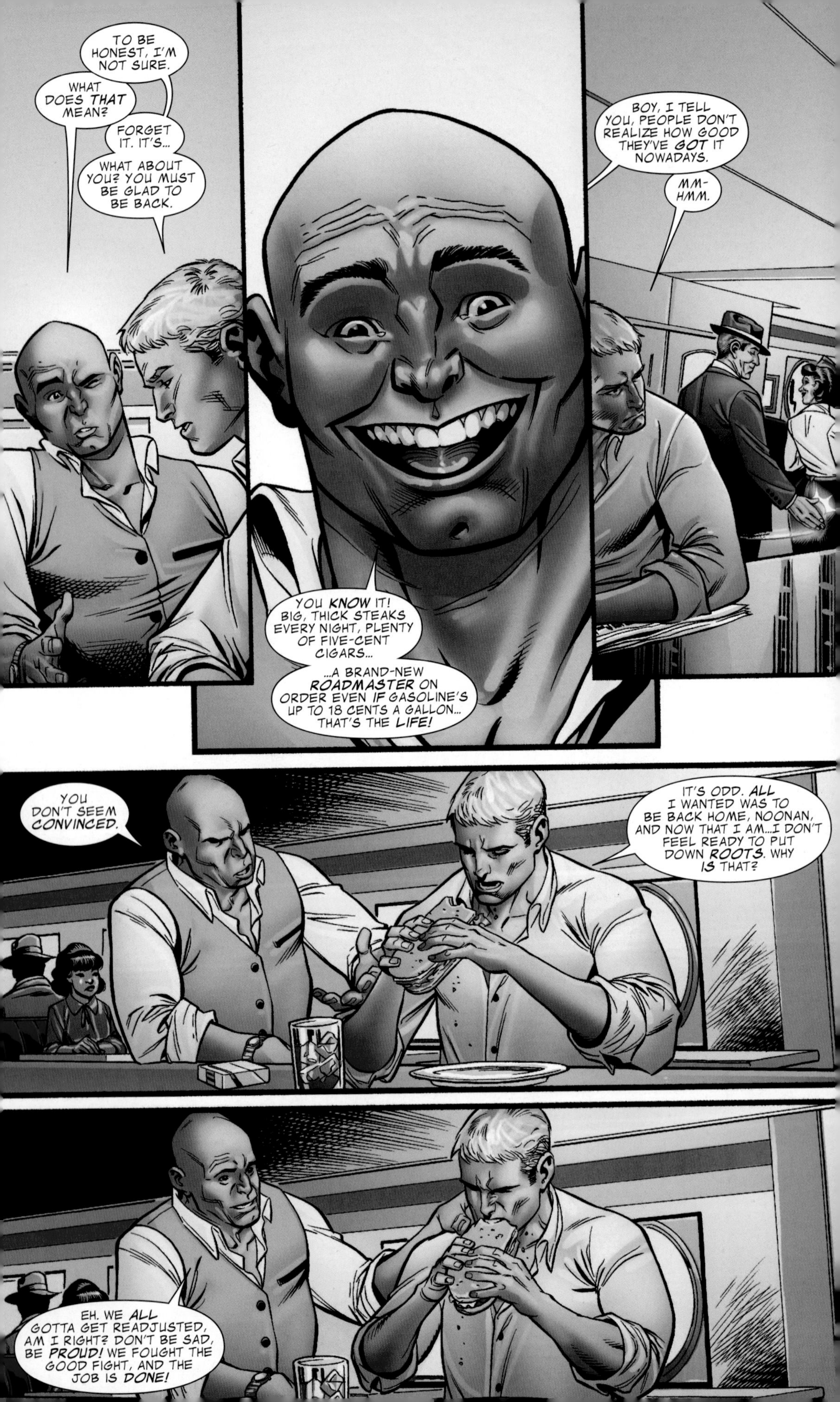

TO BE HONEST, I'M NOT SURE.
WHAT DOES THAT MEAN?
FORGET IT. IT'S...
WHAT ABOUT YOU? YOU MUST BE GLAD TO BE BACK.
YOU KNOW IT! BIG, THICK STEAKS EVERY NIGHT, PLENTY OF FIVE-CENT CIGARS...
...A BRAND-NEW ROADMASTER ON ORDER EVEN IF GASOLINE'S UP TO 18 CENTS A GALLON... THAT'S THE LIFE!
BOY, I TELL YOU, PEOPLE DON'T REALIZE HOW GOOD THEY'VE GOT IT NOWADAYS.
MM-HMM.
YOU DON'T SEEM CONVINCED.
IT'S ODD. ALL I WANTED WAS TO BE BACK HOME, NOONAN, AND NOW THAT I AM...I DON'T FEEL READY TO PUT DOWN ROOTS. WHY IS THAT?
EH. WE ALL GOTTA GET READJUSTED, AM I RIGHT? DON'T BE SAD, BE PROUD! WE FOUGHT THE GOOD FIGHT, AND THE JOB IS DONE!

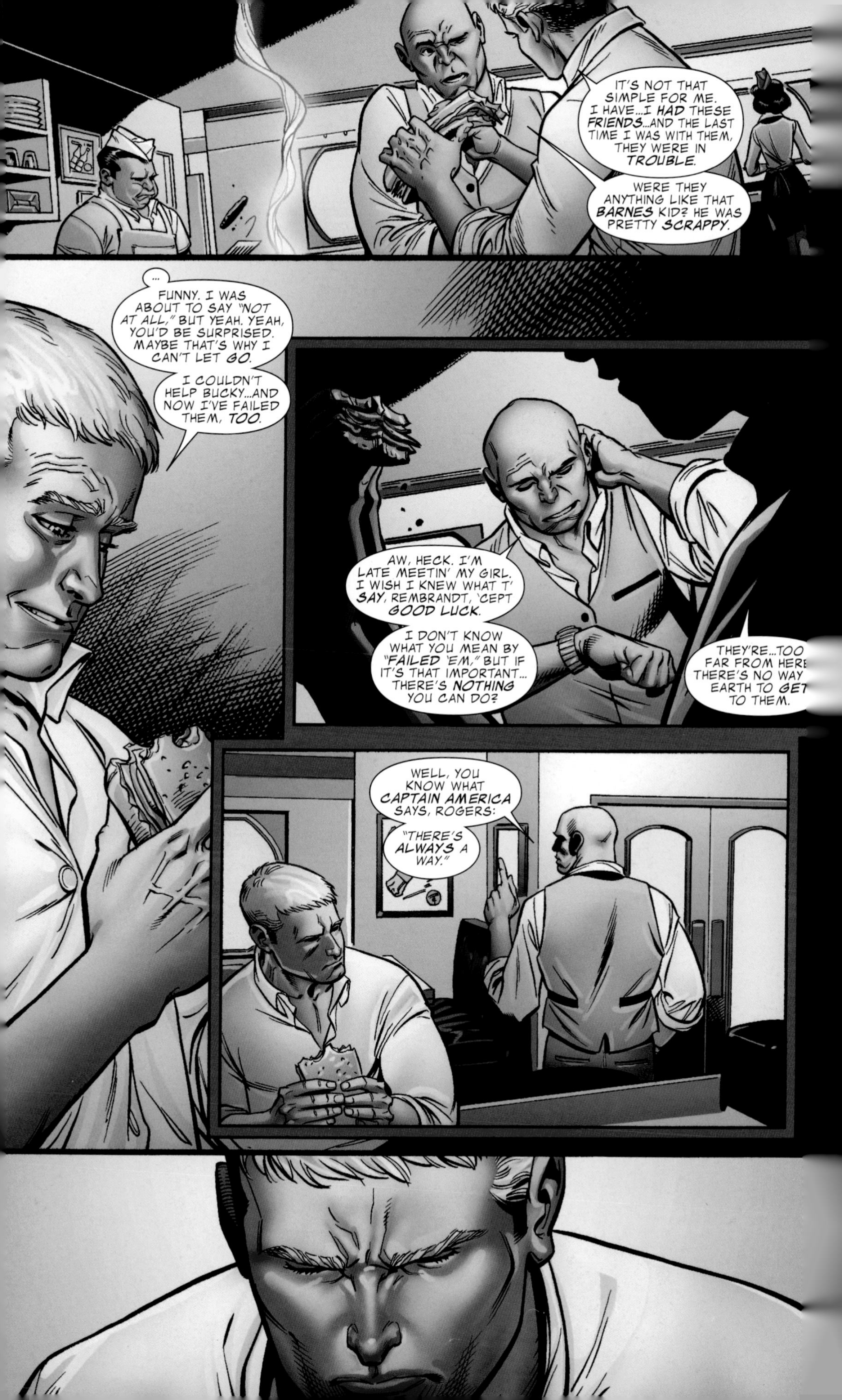

IT'S NOT THAT SIMPLE FOR ME. I HAVE...I HAD THESE FRIENDS...AND THE LAST TIME I WAS WITH THEM, THEY WERE IN TROUBLE.
WERE THEY ANYTHING LIKE THAT BARNES KID? HE WAS PRETTY SCRAPPY.
...
FUNNY. I WAS ABOUT TO SAY "NOT AT ALL," BUT YEAH. YEAH, YOU'D BE SURPRISED. MAYBE THAT'S WHY I CAN'T LET GO.
I COULDN'T HELP BUCKY...AND NOW I'VE FAILED THEM, TOO.
AW, HECK. I'M LATE MEETIN' MY GIRL. I WISH I KNEW WHAT T' SAY, REMBRANDT, 'CEPT GOOD LUCK.
I DON'T KNOW WHAT YOU MEAN BY "FAILED 'EM," BUT IF IT'S THAT IMPORTANT... THERE'S NOTHING YOU CAN DO?
WELL, YOU KNOW WHAT CAPTAIN AMERICA SAYS, ROGERS:
"THERE'S ALWAYS A WAY."

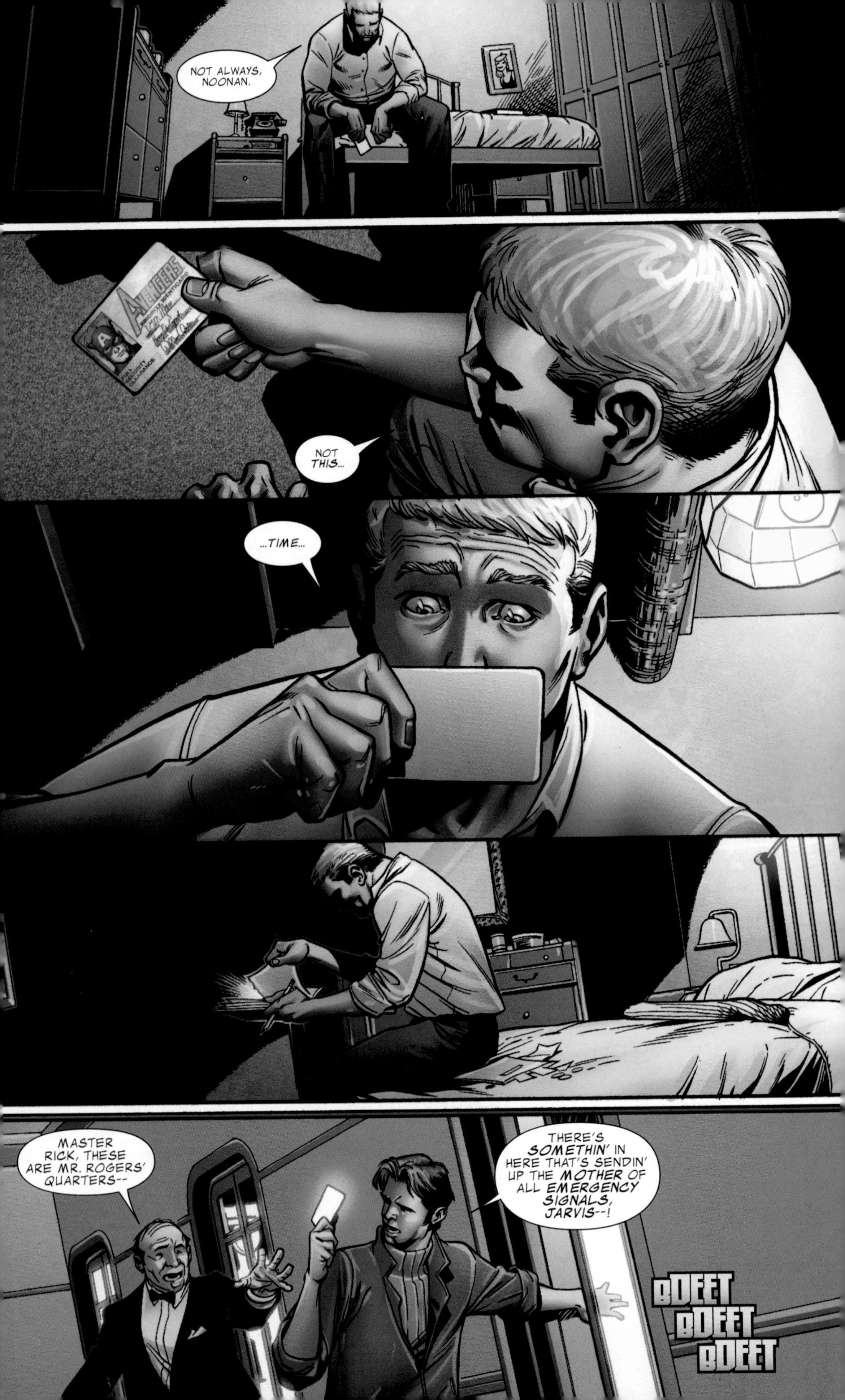
NOT ALWAYS, NOONAN.
NOT THIS...
...TIME...
MASTER RICK, THESE ARE MR. ROGERS' QUARTERS--
THERE'S SOMETHIN' IN HERE THAT'S SENDIN' UP THE MOTHER OF ALL EMERGENCY SIGNALS, JARVIS--!
BDEET
BDEET
BDEET

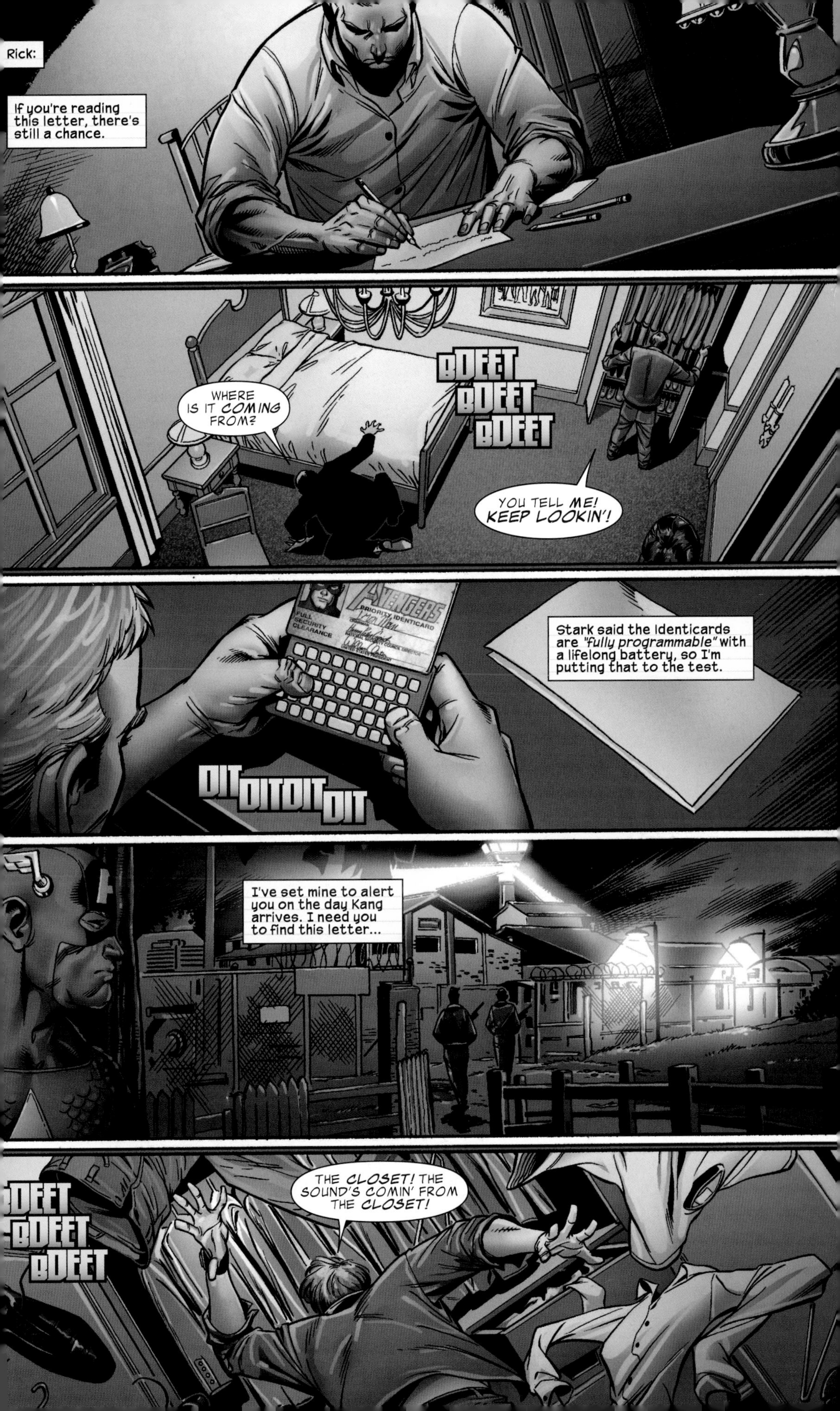

Rick:
If you're reading this letter, there's still a chance.
WHERE IS IT COMING FROM?
BDEET BDEET BDEET
YOU TELL ME! KEEP LOOKIN'!
AVENGERS
PRIORITY IDENTICARD
FULL SECURITY CLEARANCE
Stark said the Identicards are "fully programmable" with a lifelong battery, so I'm putting that to the test.
DIT DIT DIT DIT
I've set mine to alert you on the day Kang arrives. I need you to find this letter...
BDEET BDEET BDEET
THE CLOSET! THE SOUND'S COMIN' FROM THE CLOSET!

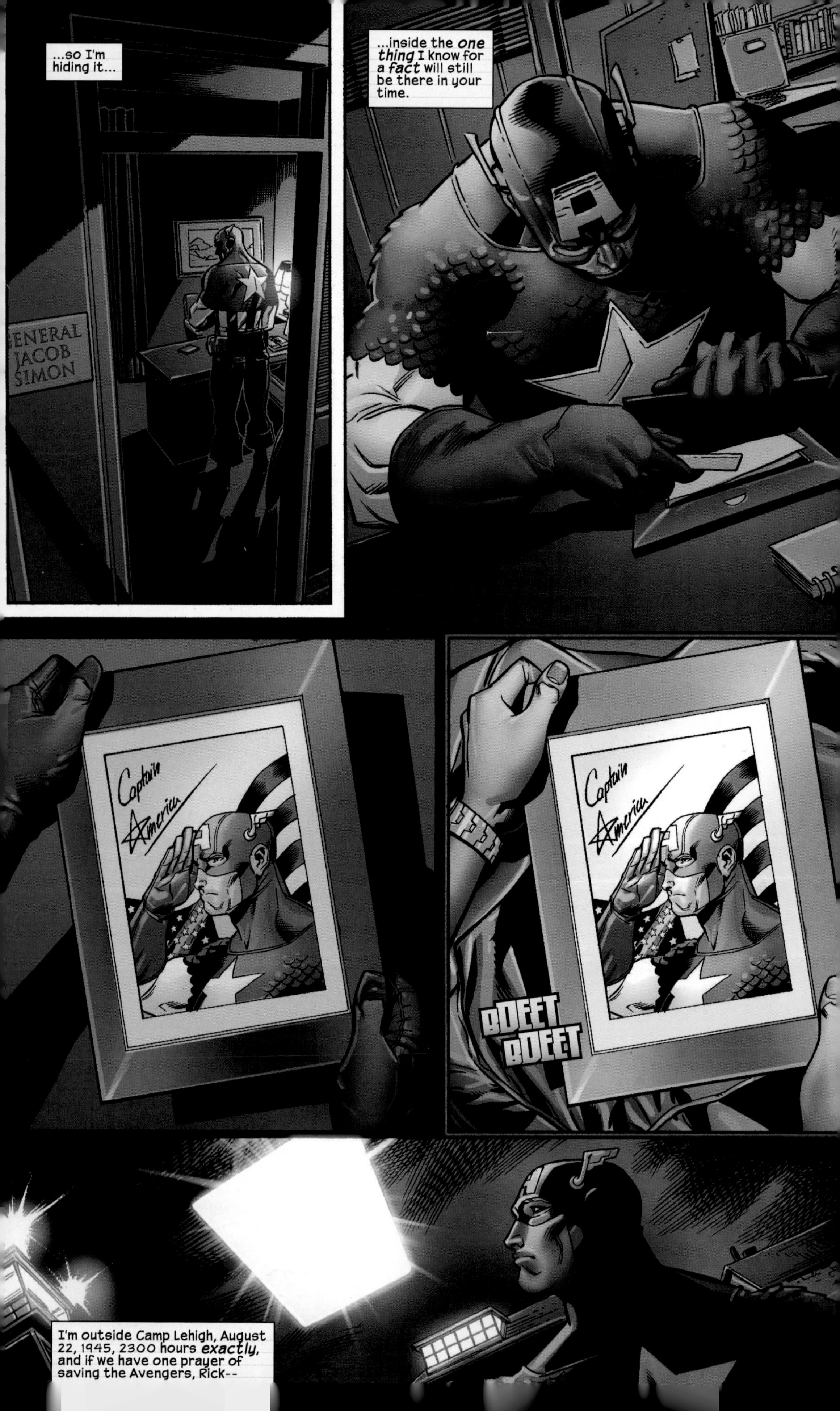
...so I'm hiding it...
GENERAL JACOB SIMON
...inside the one thing I know for a fact will still be there in your time.
Captain America
Captain America
BDEET BDEET
I'm outside Camp Lehigh, August 22, 1945, 2300 hours exactly, and if we have one prayer of saving the Avengers, Rick--

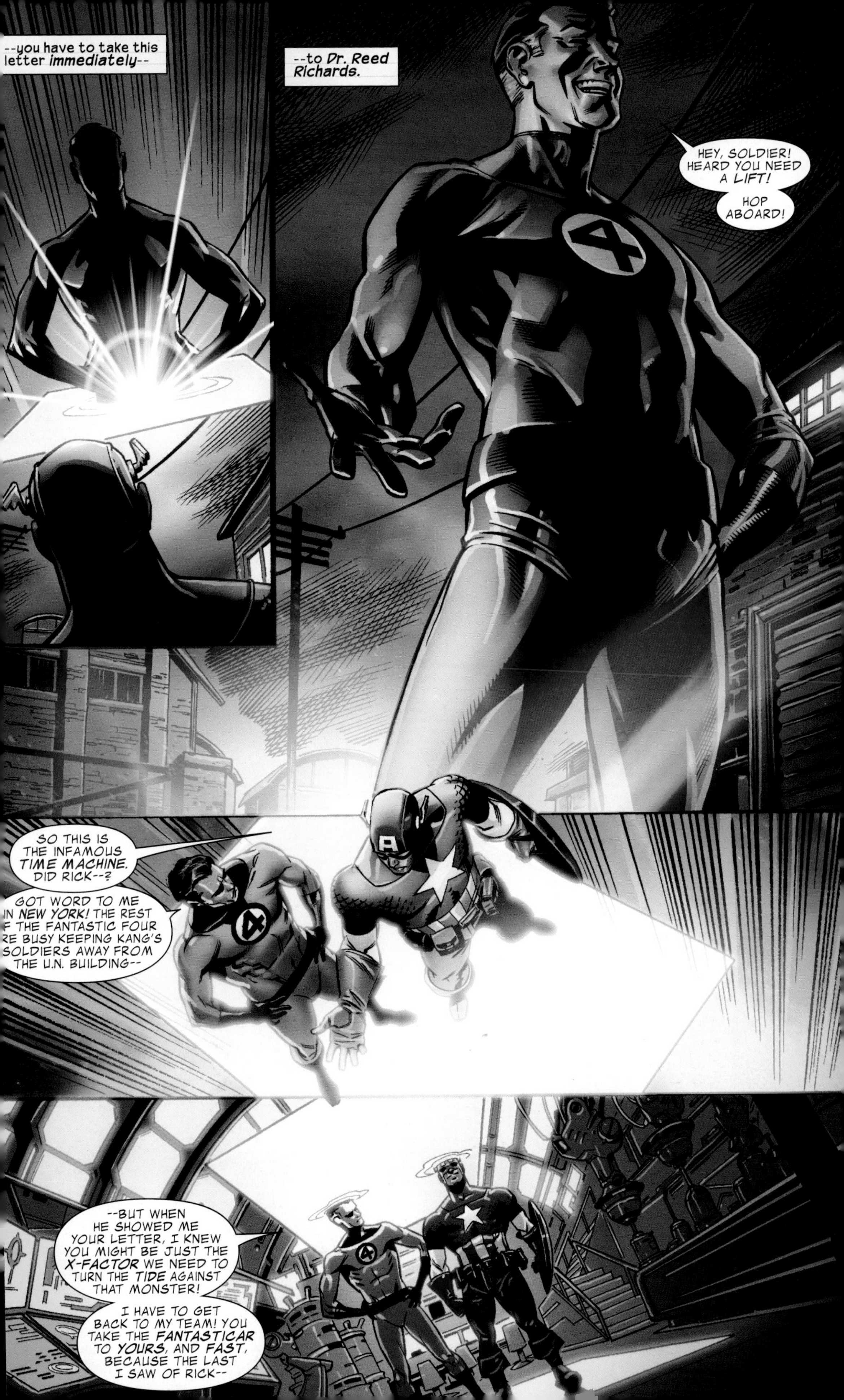
--you have to take this letter *immediately*--
--to *Dr. Reed Richards.*
HEY, SOLDIER! HEARD YOU NEED A *LIFT!*
HOP ABOARD!
SO THIS IS THE INFAMOUS *TIME MACHINE.* DID RICK--?
GOT WORD TO ME IN *NEW YORK!* THE REST F THE FANTASTIC FOUR RE BUSY KEEPING KANG'S SOLDIERS AWAY FROM THE U.N. BUILDING--
--BUT WHEN HE SHOWED ME YOUR LETTER, I KNEW YOU MIGHT BE JUST THE *X-FACTOR* WE NEED TO TURN THE *TIDE* AGAINST THAT MONSTER!
I HAVE TO GET BACK TO MY TEAM! YOU TAKE THE *FANTASTICAR* TO *YOURS,* AND *FAST,* BECAUSE THE LAST I SAW OF RICK--

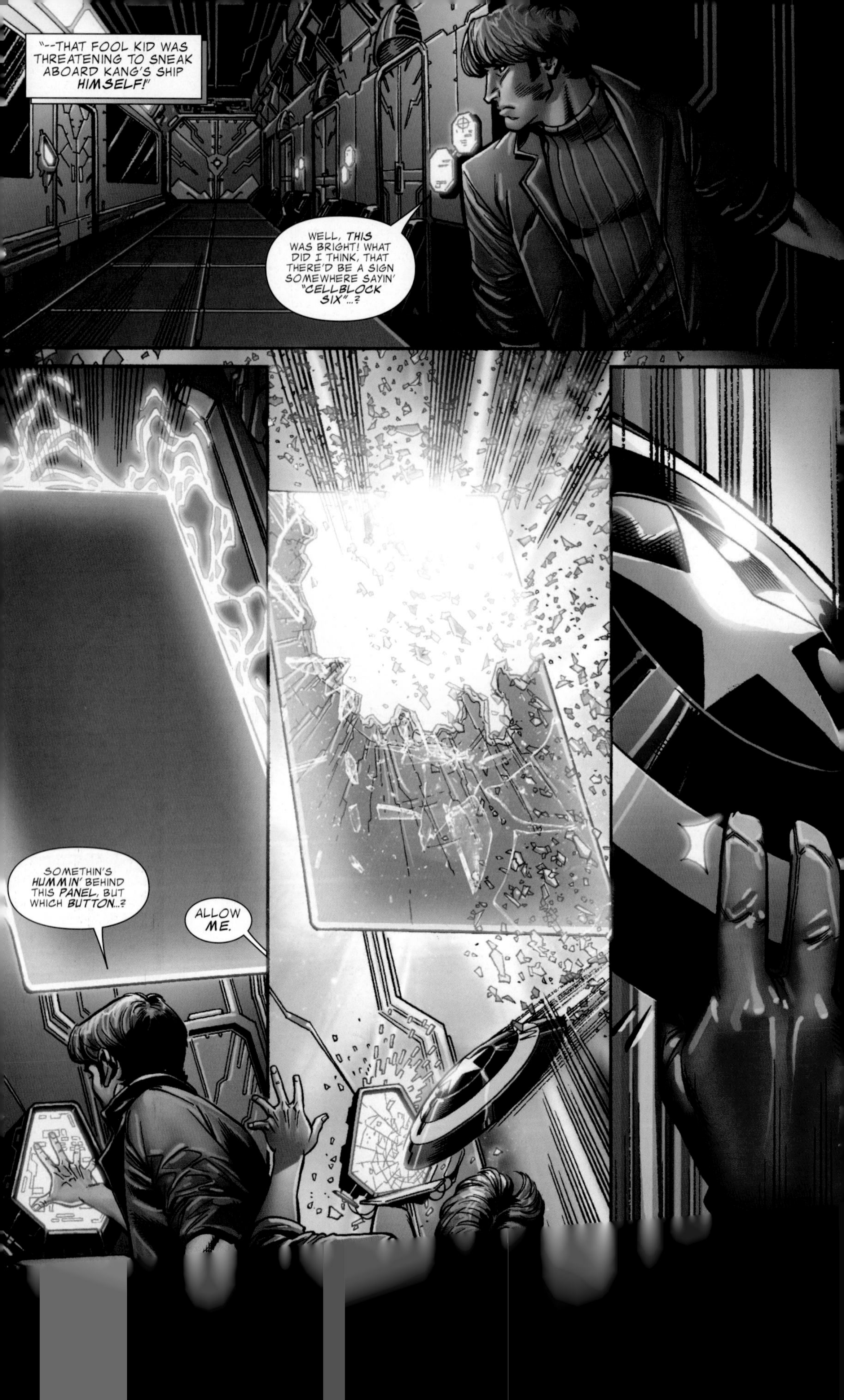
"--THAT FOOL KID WAS THREATENING TO SNEAK ABOARD KANG'S SHIP HIMSELF!"
WELL, THIS WAS BRIGHT! WHAT DID I THINK, THAT THERE'D BE A SIGN SOMEWHERE SAYIN' "CELLBLOCK SIX"...?
SOMETHIN'S HUMMIN' BEHIND THIS PANEL, BUT WHICH BUTTON...?
ALLOW ME.

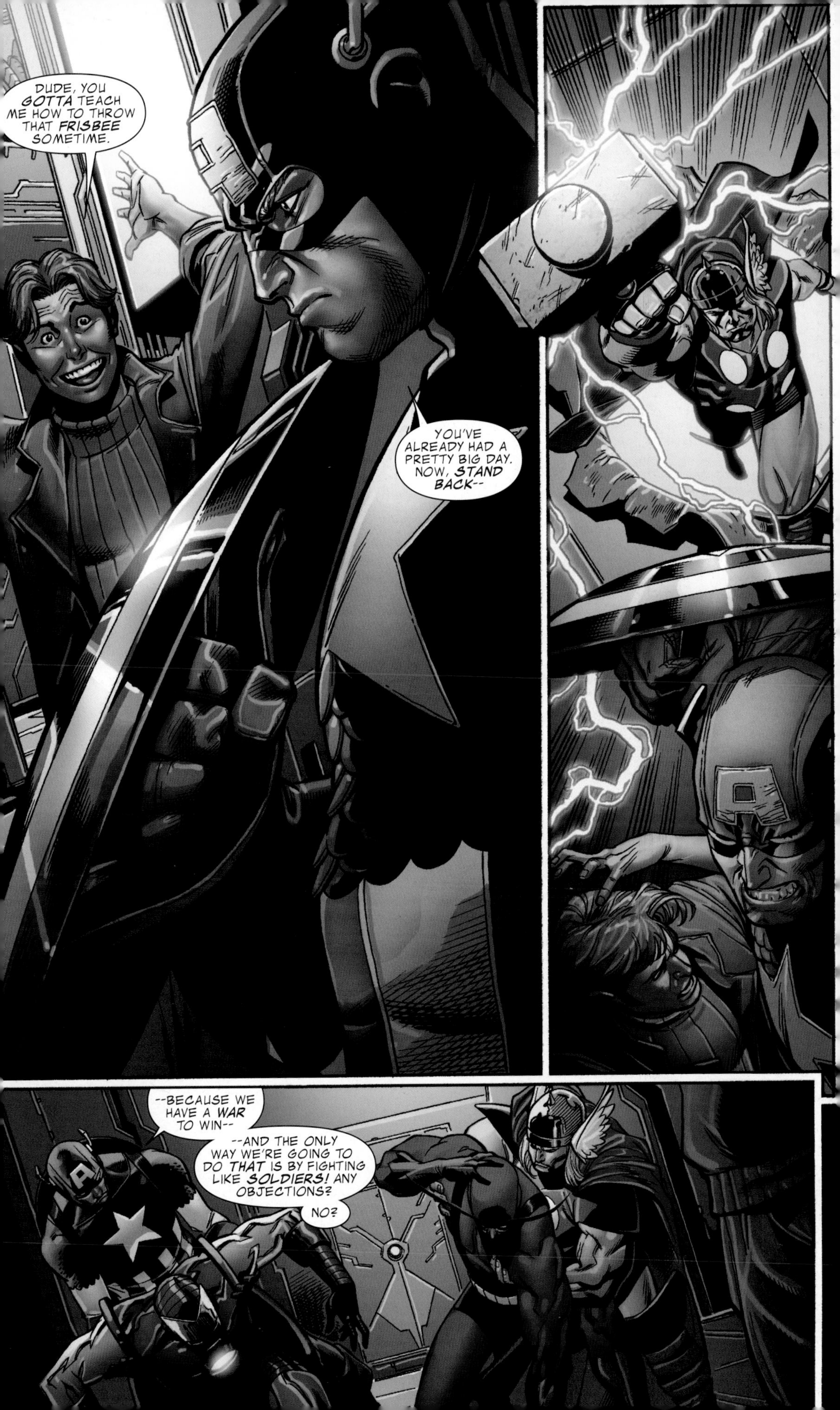
DUDE, YOU GOTTA TEACH ME HOW TO THROW THAT FRISBEE SOMETIME.
YOU'VE ALREADY HAD A PRETTY BIG DAY. NOW, STAND BACK--
--BECAUSE WE HAVE A WAR TO WIN--
--AND THE ONLY WAY WE'RE GOING TO DO THAT IS BY FIGHTING LIKE SOLDIERS! ANY OBJECTIONS?
NO?

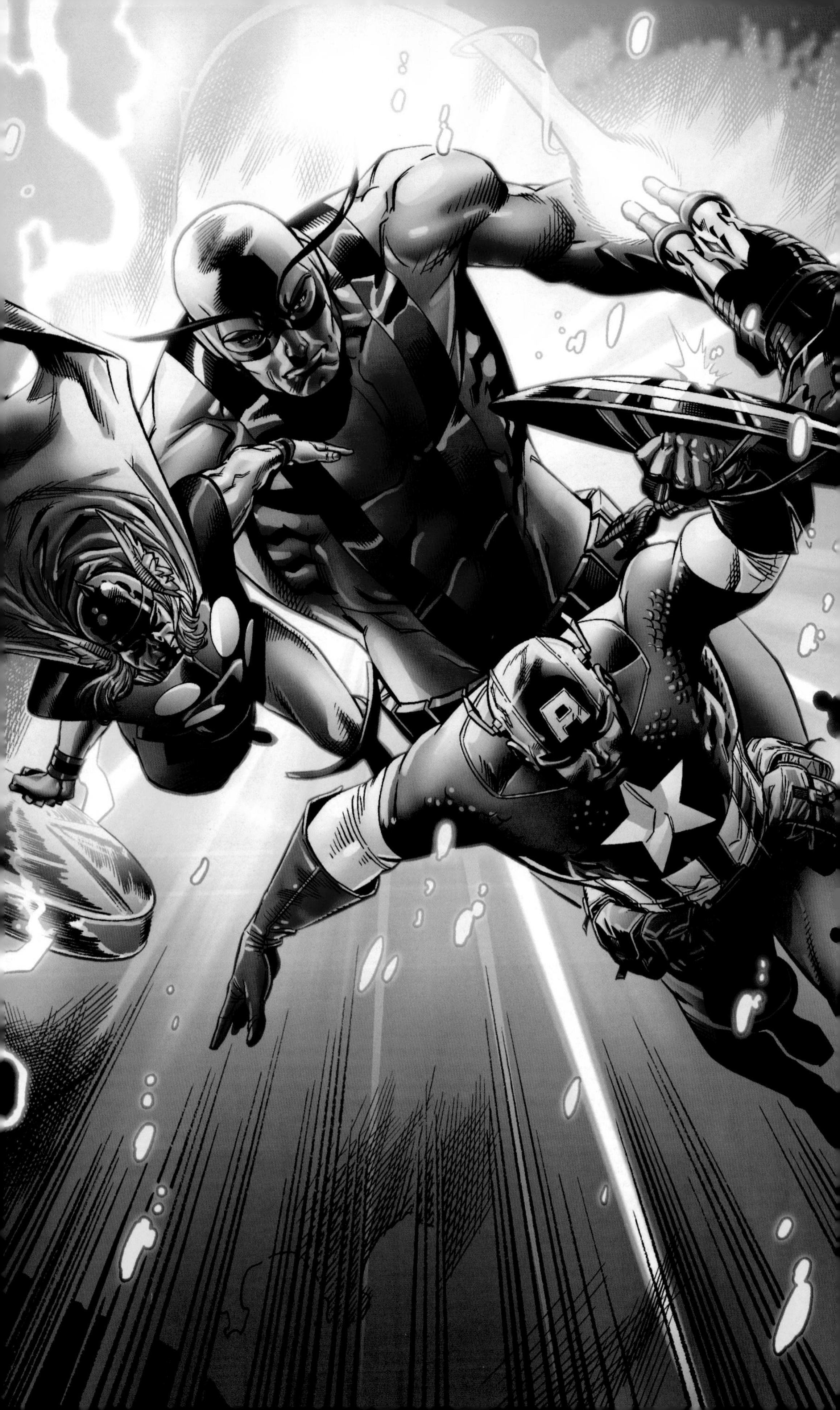

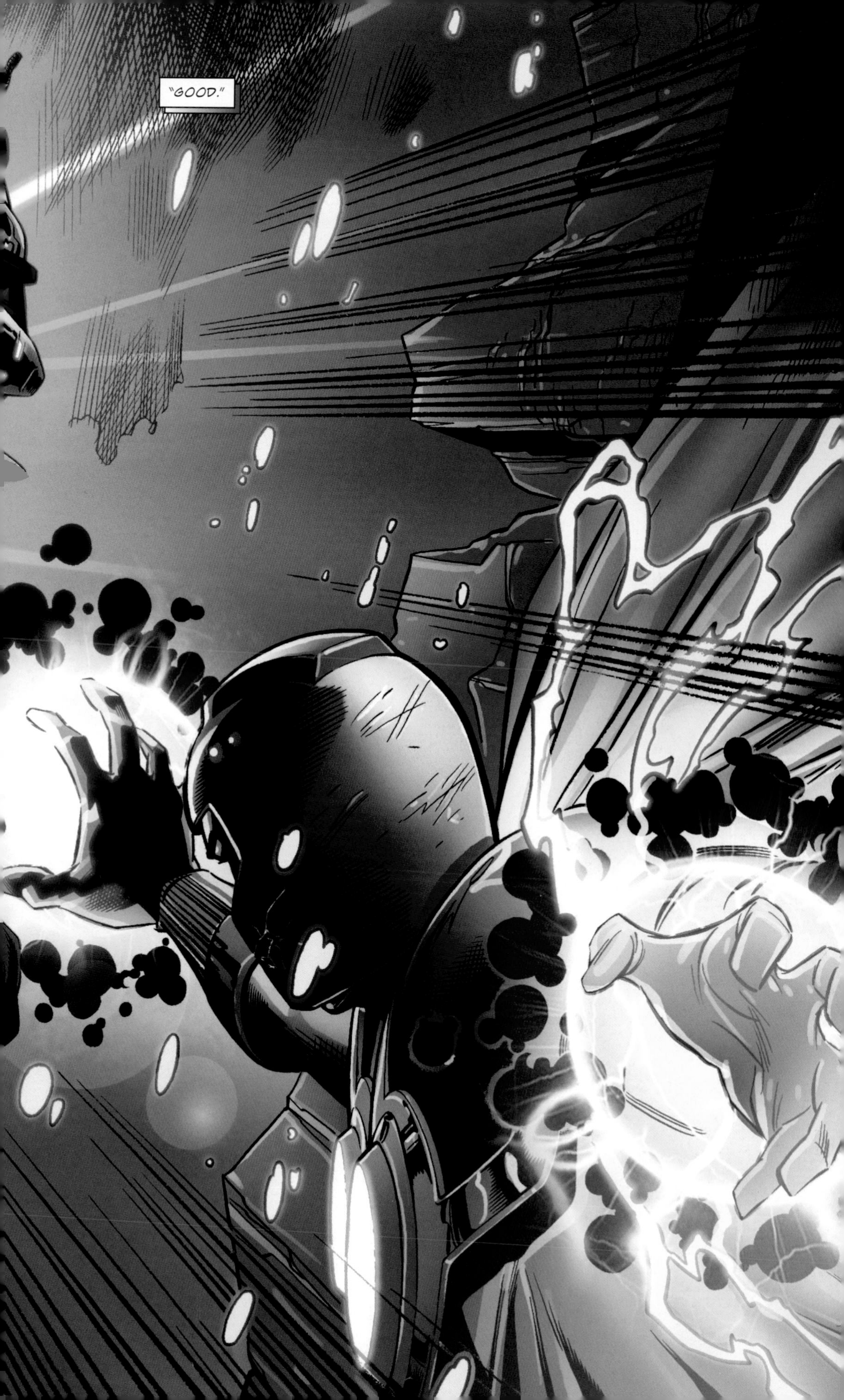
"GOOD."

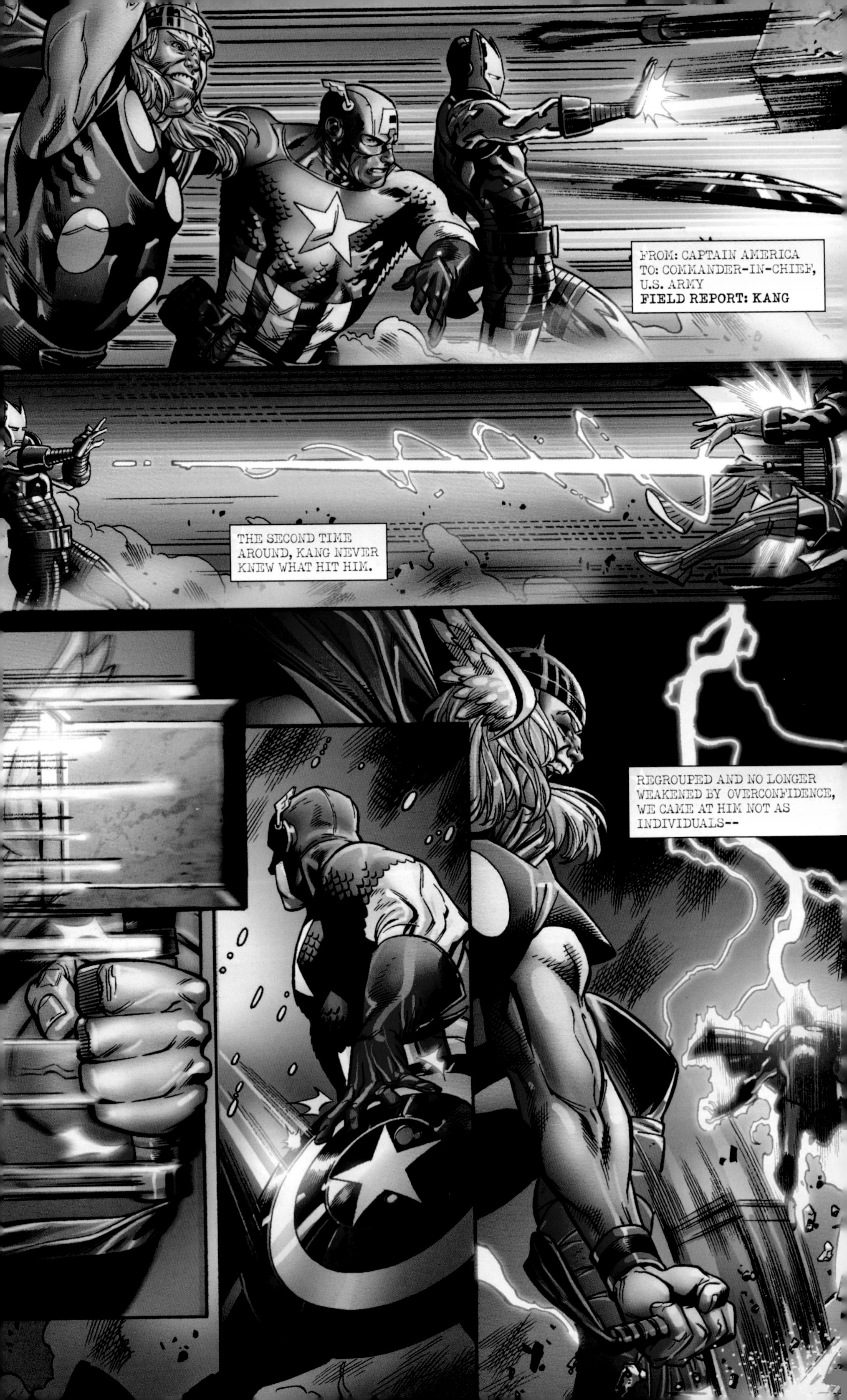
FROM: CAPTAIN AMERICA
TO: COMMANDER-IN-CHIEF, U.S. ARMY
FIELD REPORT: KANG
THE SECOND TIME AROUND, KANG NEVER KNEW WHAT HIT HIM.
REGROUPED AND NO LONGER WEAKENED BY OVERCONFIDENCE, WE CAME AT HIM NOT AS INDIVIDUALS--

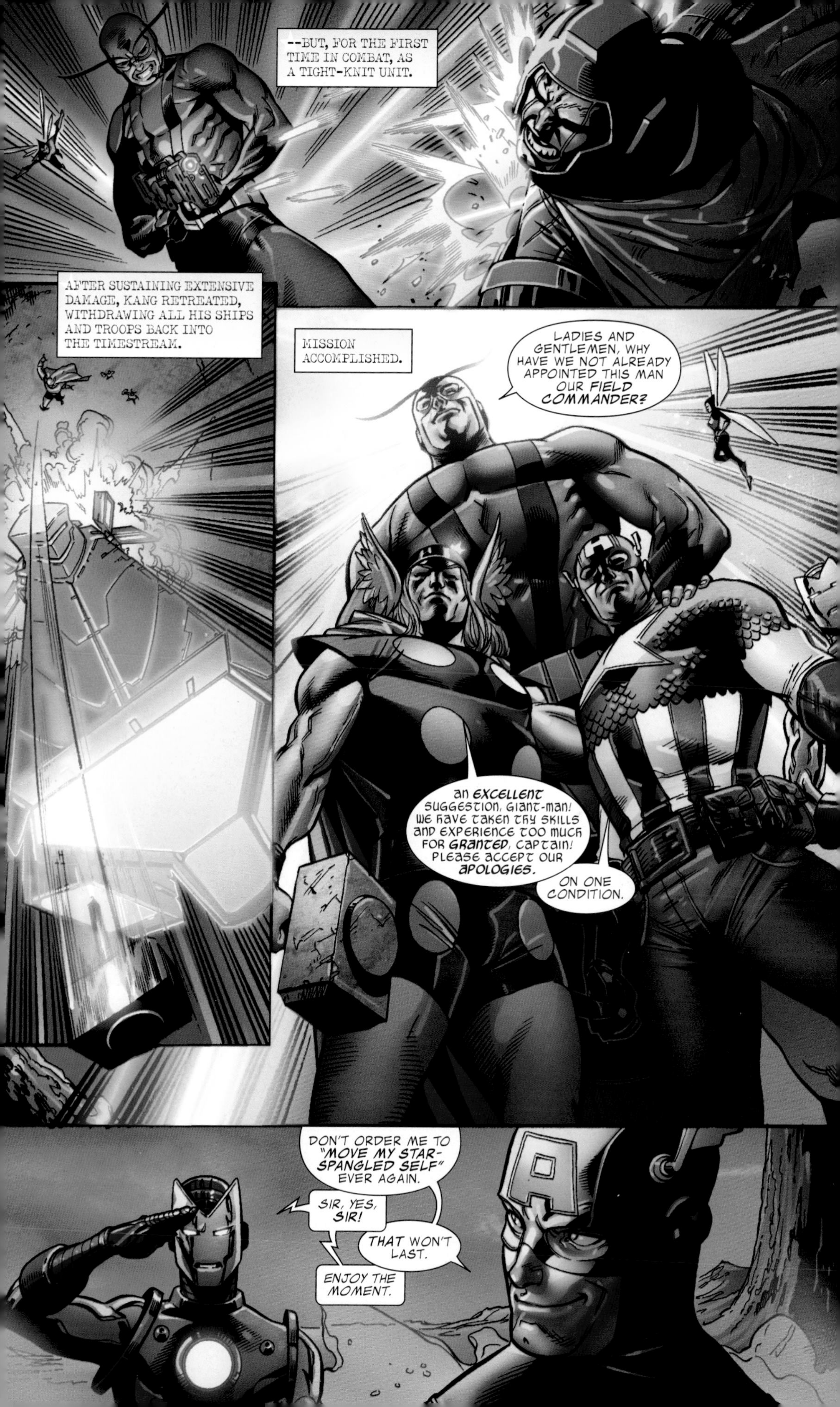
--BUT, FOR THE FIRST TIME IN COMBAT, AS A TIGHT-KNIT UNIT.
AFTER SUSTAINING EXTENSIVE DAMAGE, KANG RETREATED, WITHDRAWING ALL HIS SHIPS AND TROOPS BACK INTO THE TIMESTREAM.
MISSION ACCOMPLISHED.
LADIES AND GENTLEMEN, WHY HAVE WE NOT ALREADY APPOINTED THIS MAN OUR FIELD COMMANDER?
AN EXCELLENT SUGGESTION, GIANT-MAN! WE HAVE TAKEN THY SKILLS AND EXPERIENCE TOO MUCH FOR GRANTED, CAPTAIN! PLEASE ACCEPT OUR APOLOGIES.
ON ONE CONDITION.
DON'T ORDER ME TO "MOVE MY STAR-SPANGLED SELF" EVER AGAIN.
SIR, YES, SIR!
THAT WON'T LAST.
ENJOY THE MOMENT.

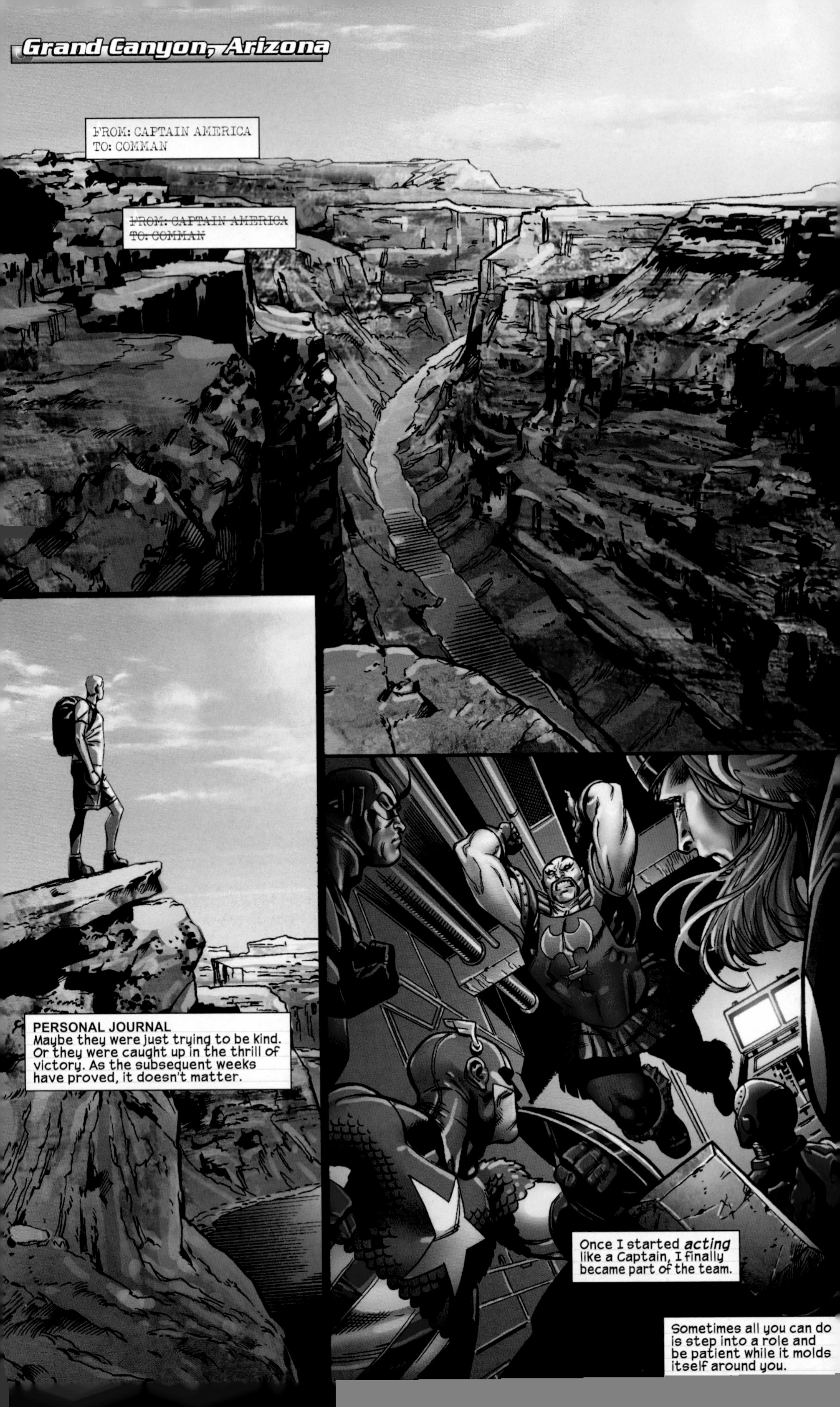
Grand Canyon, Arizona
FROM: CAPTAIN AMERICA
TO: COMMAN
FROM: CAPTAIN AMERICA
TO: COMMAN
PERSONAL JOURNAL
Maybe they were just trying to be kind. Or they were caught up in the thrill of victory. As the subsequent weeks have proved, it doesn't matter.
Once I started *acting* like a Captain, I finally became part of the team.
Sometimes all you can do is step into a role and be patient while it molds itself around you.

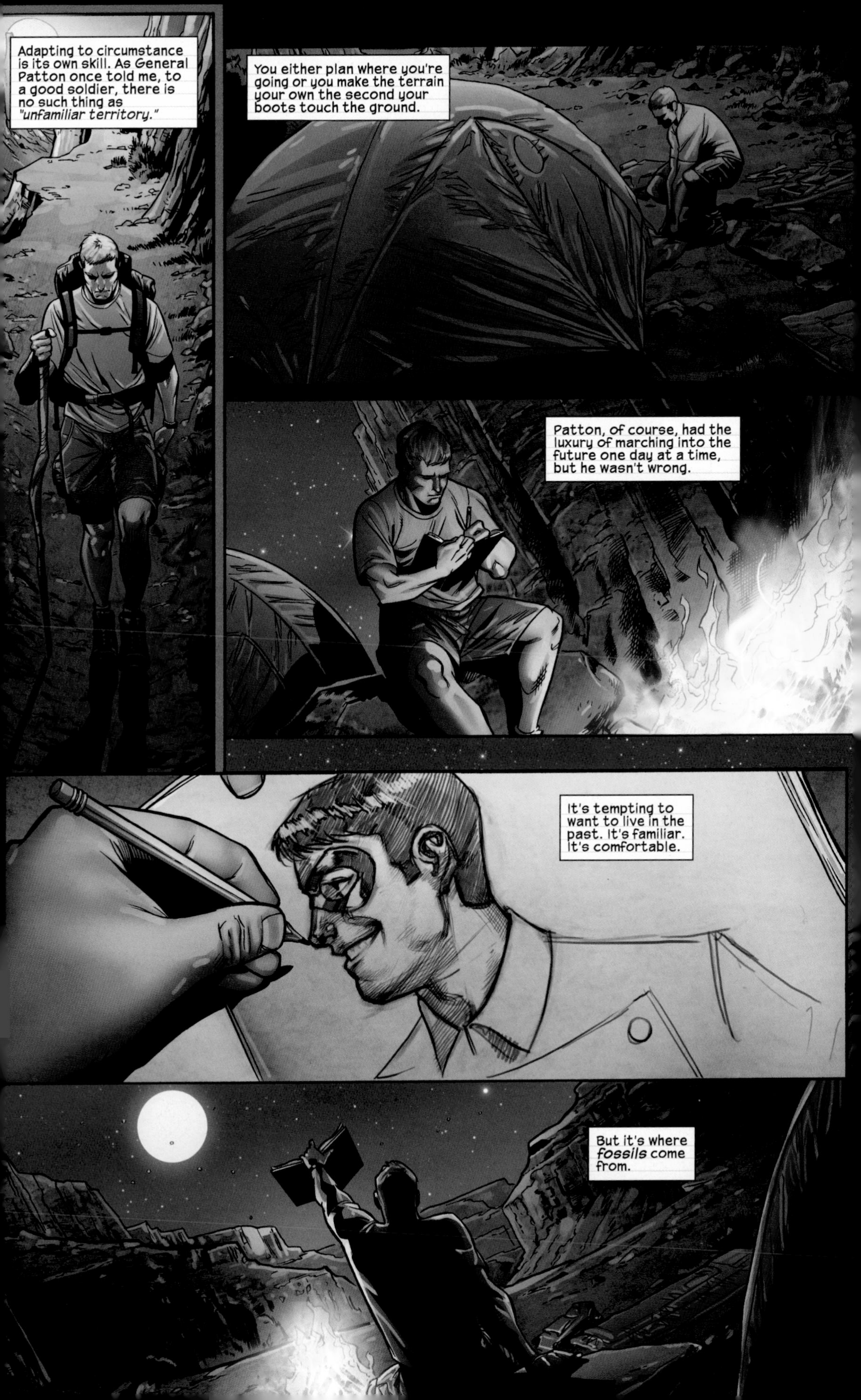
Adapting to circumstance is its own skill. As General Patton once told me, to a good soldier, there is no such thing as *"unfamiliar territory."*
You either plan where you're going or you make the terrain your own the second your boots touch the ground.
Patton, of course, had the luxury of marching into the future one day at a time, but he wasn't wrong.
It's tempting to want to live in the past. It's familiar. It's comfortable.
But it's where *fossils* come from.

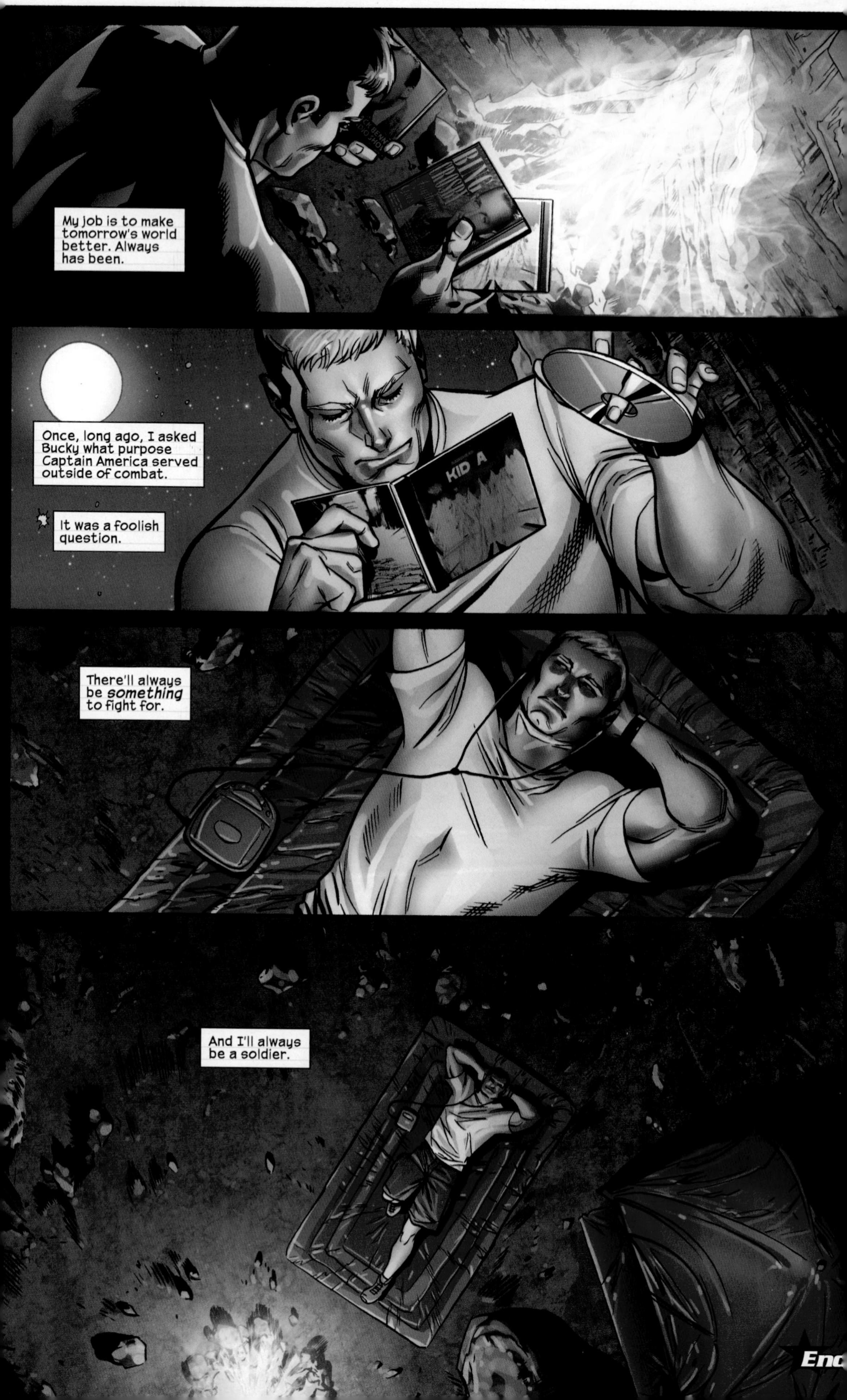
My job is to make tomorrow's world better. Always has been.
Once, long ago, I asked Bucky what purpose Captain America served outside of combat.
It was a foolish question.
KID A
There'll always be *something* to fight for.
And I'll always be a soldier.
End

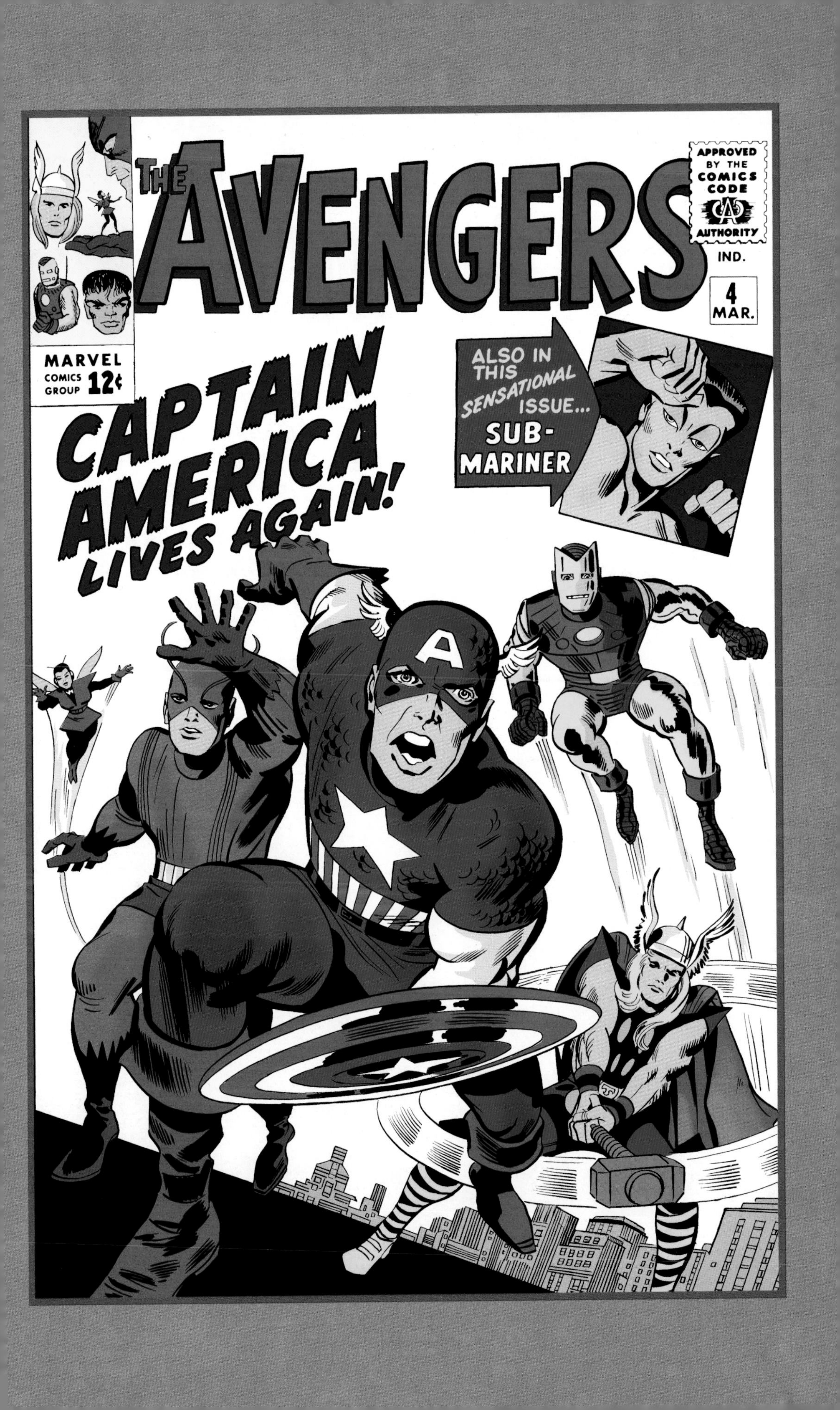
THE AVENGERS
APPROVED BY THE COMICS CODE AUTHORITY
IND.
4
MAR.
MARVEL COMICS GROUP 12¢
CAPTAIN AMERICA LIVES AGAIN!
ALSO IN THIS SENSATIONAL ISSUE... SUB-MARINER

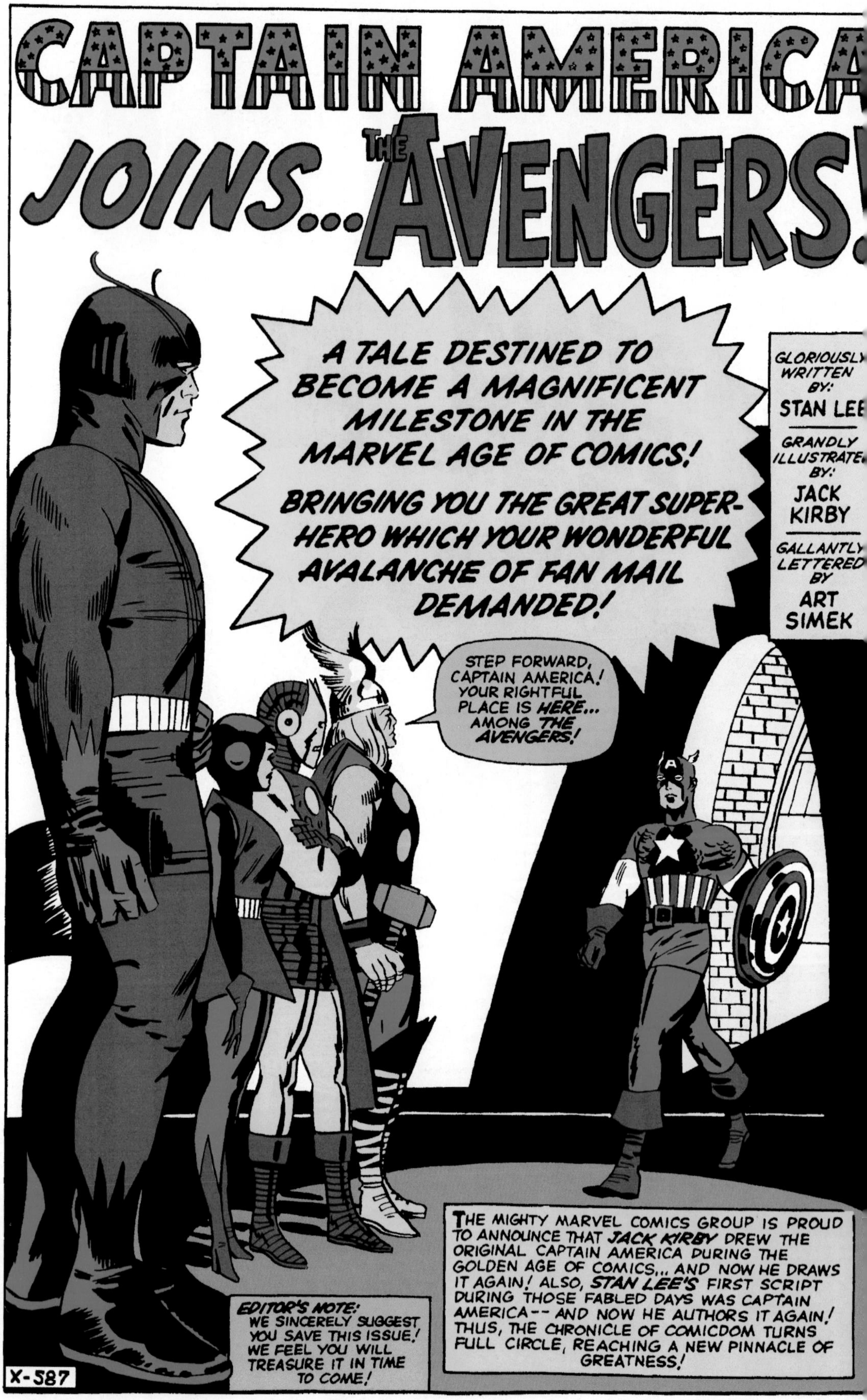

CAPTAIN AMERICA JOINS... THE AVENGERS!
A TALE DESTINED TO BECOME A MAGNIFICENT MILESTONE IN THE MARVEL AGE OF COMICS!
BRINGING YOU THE GREAT SUPER-HERO WHICH YOUR WONDERFUL AVALANCHE OF FAN MAIL DEMANDED!
GLORIOUSLY WRITTEN BY: STAN LEE
GRANDLY ILLUSTRATED BY: JACK KIRBY
GALLANTLY LETTERED BY ART SIMEK
STEP FORWARD, CAPTAIN AMERICA! YOUR RIGHTFUL PLACE IS HERE... AMONG THE AVENGERS!
THE MIGHTY MARVEL COMICS GROUP IS PROUD TO ANNOUNCE THAT JACK KIRBY DREW THE ORIGINAL CAPTAIN AMERICA DURING THE GOLDEN AGE OF COMICS... AND NOW HE DRAWS IT AGAIN! ALSO, STAN LEE'S FIRST SCRIPT DURING THOSE FABLED DAYS WAS CAPTAIN AMERICA -- AND NOW HE AUTHORS IT AGAIN! THUS, THE CHRONICLE OF COMICDOM TURNS FULL CIRCLE, REACHING A NEW PINNACLE OF GREATNESS!
EDITOR'S NOTE: WE SINCERELY SUGGEST YOU SAVE THIS ISSUE! WE FEEL YOU WILL TREASURE IT IN TIME TO COME!
X-587

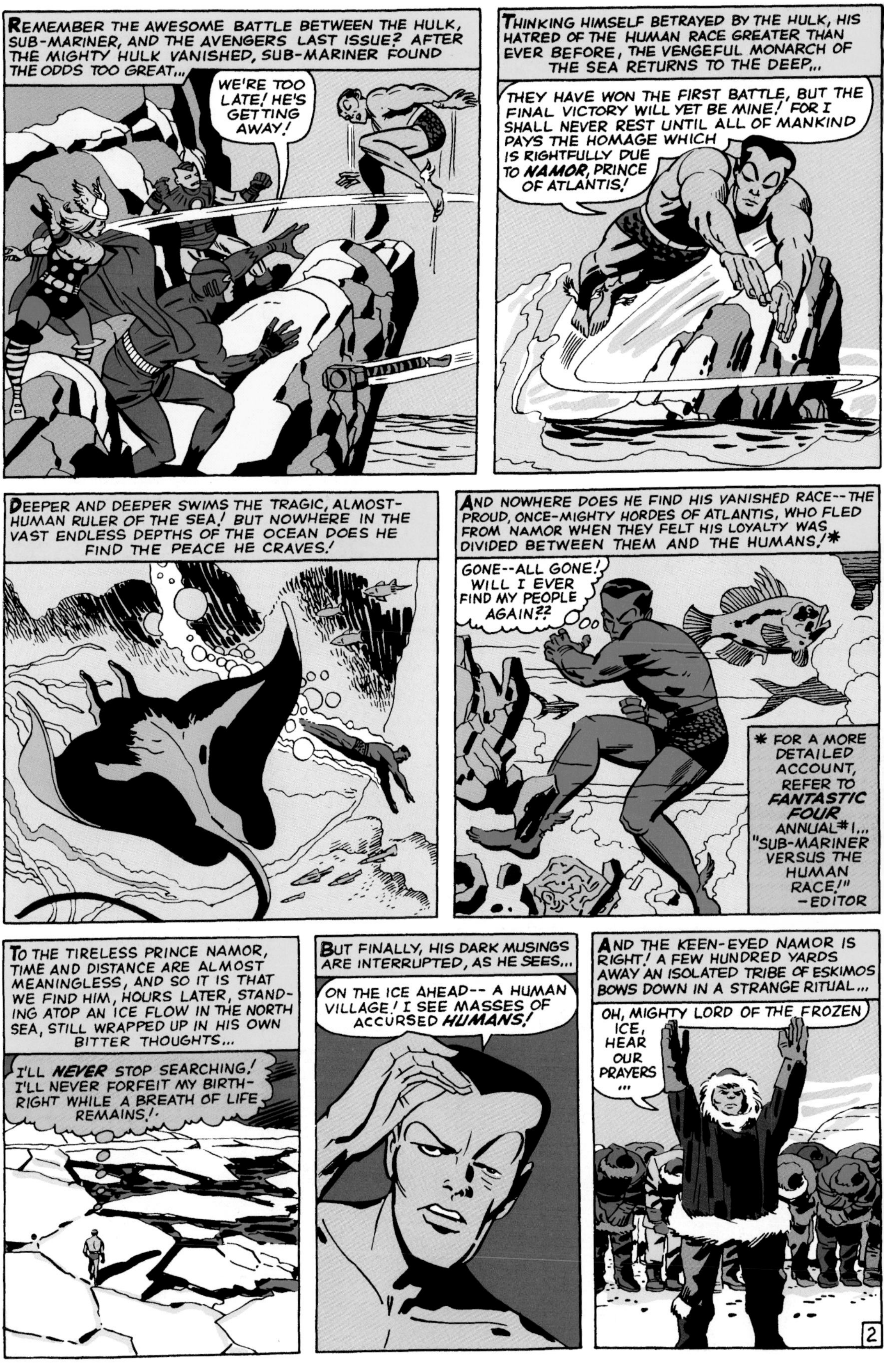

REMEMBER THE AWESOME BATTLE BETWEEN THE HULK, SUB-MARINER, AND THE AVENGERS LAST ISSUE? AFTER THE MIGHTY HULK VANISHED, SUB-MARINER FOUND THE ODDS TOO GREAT...
WE'RE TOO LATE! HE'S GETTING AWAY!
THINKING HIMSELF BETRAYED BY THE HULK, HIS HATRED OF THE HUMAN RACE GREATER THAN EVER BEFORE, THE VENGEFUL MONARCH OF THE SEA RETURNS TO THE DEEP...
THEY HAVE WON THE FIRST BATTLE, BUT THE FINAL VICTORY WILL YET BE MINE! FOR I SHALL NEVER REST UNTIL ALL OF MANKIND PAYS THE HOMAGE WHICH IS RIGHTFULLY DUE TO NAMOR, PRINCE OF ATLANTIS!
DEEPER AND DEEPER SWIMS THE TRAGIC, ALMOST-HUMAN RULER OF THE SEA! BUT NOWHERE IN THE VAST ENDLESS DEPTHS OF THE OCEAN DOES HE FIND THE PEACE HE CRAVES!
AND NOWHERE DOES HE FIND HIS VANISHED RACE--THE PROUD, ONCE-MIGHTY HORDES OF ATLANTIS, WHO FLED FROM NAMOR WHEN THEY FELT HIS LOYALTY WAS DIVIDED BETWEEN THEM AND THE HUMANS!*
GONE--ALL GONE! WILL I EVER FIND MY PEOPLE AGAIN??
* FOR A MORE DETAILED ACCOUNT, REFER TO FANTASTIC FOUR ANNUAL #1... "SUB-MARINER VERSUS THE HUMAN RACE!" -EDITOR
TO THE TIRELESS PRINCE NAMOR, TIME AND DISTANCE ARE ALMOST MEANINGLESS, AND SO IT IS THAT WE FIND HIM, HOURS LATER, STANDING ATOP AN ICE FLOW IN THE NORTH SEA, STILL WRAPPED UP IN HIS OWN BITTER THOUGHTS...
I'LL NEVER STOP SEARCHING! I'LL NEVER FORFEIT MY BIRTHRIGHT WHILE A BREATH OF LIFE REMAINS!
BUT FINALLY, HIS DARK MUSINGS ARE INTERRUPTED, AS HE SEES...
ON THE ICE AHEAD-- A HUMAN VILLAGE! I SEE MASSES OF ACCURSED HUMANS!
AND THE KEEN-EYED NAMOR IS RIGHT! A FEW HUNDRED YARDS AWAY AN ISOLATED TRIBE OF ESKIMOS BOWS DOWN IN A STRANGE RITUAL...
OH, MIGHTY LORD OF THE FROZEN ICE, HEAR OUR PRAYERS ...
2

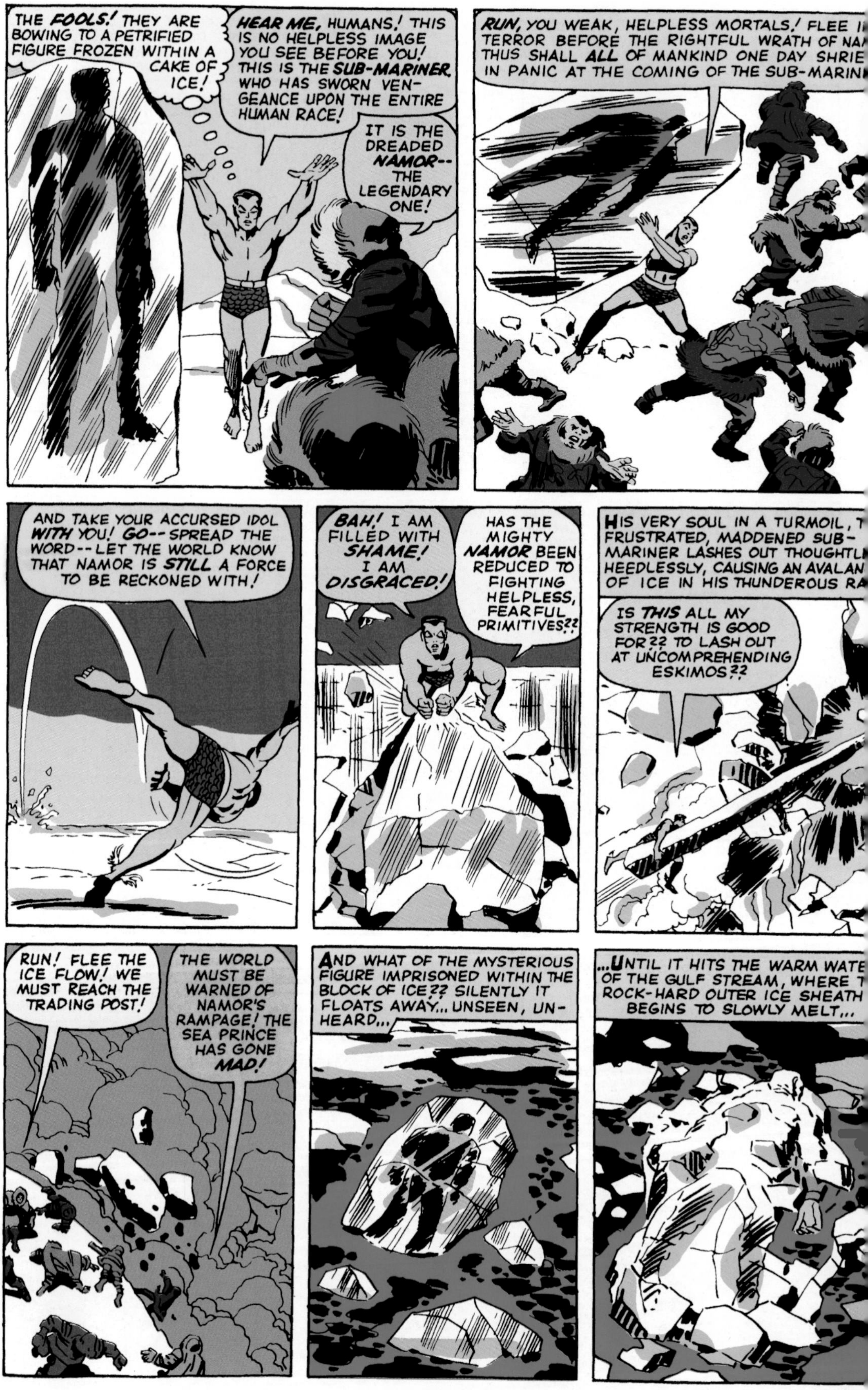
THE *FOOLS!* THEY ARE BOWING TO A PETRIFIED FIGURE FROZEN WITHIN A CAKE OF ICE!
HEAR ME, HUMANS! THIS IS NO HELPLESS IMAGE YOU SEE BEFORE YOU! THIS IS THE *SUB-MARINER,* WHO HAS SWORN VENGEANCE UPON THE ENTIRE HUMAN RACE!
IT IS THE DREADED *NAMOR--* THE LEGENDARY ONE!
RUN, YOU WEAK, HELPLESS MORTALS! FLEE I
TERROR BEFORE THE RIGHTFUL WRATH OF NA
THUS SHALL *ALL* OF MANKIND ONE DAY SHRIE
IN PANIC AT THE COMING OF THE SUB-MARIN
AND TAKE YOUR ACCURSED IDOL *WITH YOU! GO--* SPREAD THE WORD--LET THE WORLD KNOW THAT NAMOR IS *STILL* A FORCE TO BE RECKONED WITH!
BAH! I AM FILLED WITH *SHAME!* I AM *DISGRACED!*
HAS THE MIGHTY *NAMOR* BEEN REDUCED TO FIGHTING HELPLESS, FEARFUL PRIMITIVES??
HIS VERY SOUL IN A TURMOIL, T
FRUSTRATED, MADDENED SUB-
MARINER LASHES OUT THOUGHTL
HEEDLESSLY, CAUSING AN AVALAN
OF ICE IN HIS THUNDEROUS RA
IS *THIS* ALL MY STRENGTH IS GOOD FOR?? TO LASH OUT AT UNCOMPREHENDING ESKIMOS??
RUN! FLEE THE ICE FLOW! WE MUST REACH THE TRADING POST!
THE WORLD MUST BE WARNED OF NAMOR'S RAMPAGE! THE SEA PRINCE HAS GONE *MAD!*
AND WHAT OF THE MYSTERIOUS FIGURE IMPRISONED WITHIN THE BLOCK OF ICE?? SILENTLY IT FLOATS AWAY... UNSEEN, UNHEARD...
...UNTIL IT HITS THE WARM WATE
OF THE GULF STREAM, WHERE T
ROCK-HARD OUTER ICE SHEATH
BEGINS TO SLOWLY MELT...

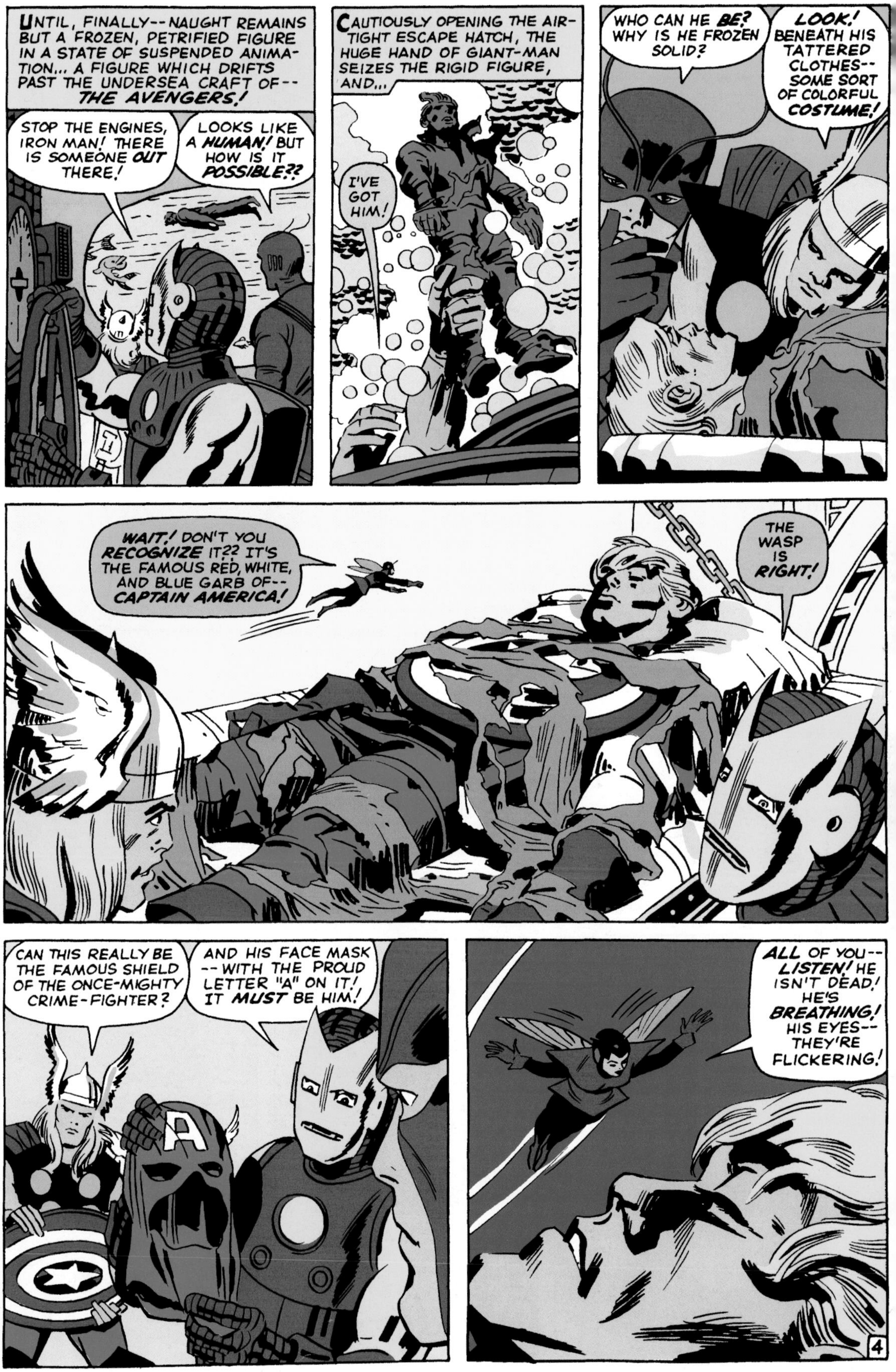
UNTIL, FINALLY--NAUGHT REMAINS BUT A FROZEN, PETRIFIED FIGURE IN A STATE OF SUSPENDED ANIMATION... A FIGURE WHICH DRIFTS PAST THE UNDERSEA CRAFT OF-- THE AVENGERS!
STOP THE ENGINES, IRON MAN! THERE IS SOMEONE OUT THERE!
LOOKS LIKE A HUMAN! BUT HOW IS IT POSSIBLE??
CAUTIOUSLY OPENING THE AIR-TIGHT ESCAPE HATCH, THE HUGE HAND OF GIANT-MAN SEIZES THE RIGID FIGURE, AND...
I'VE GOT HIM!
WHO CAN HE BE? WHY IS HE FROZEN SOLID?
LOOK! BENEATH HIS TATTERED CLOTHES-- SOME SORT OF COLORFUL COSTUME!
WAIT! DON'T YOU RECOGNIZE IT?? IT'S THE FAMOUS RED, WHITE, AND BLUE GARB OF-- CAPTAIN AMERICA!
THE WASP IS RIGHT!
CAN THIS REALLY BE THE FAMOUS SHIELD OF THE ONCE-MIGHTY CRIME-FIGHTER?
AND HIS FACE MASK --WITH THE PROUD LETTER "A" ON IT! IT MUST BE HIM!
ALL OF YOU-- LISTEN! HE ISN'T DEAD! HE'S BREATHING! HIS EYES-- THEY'RE FLICKERING!

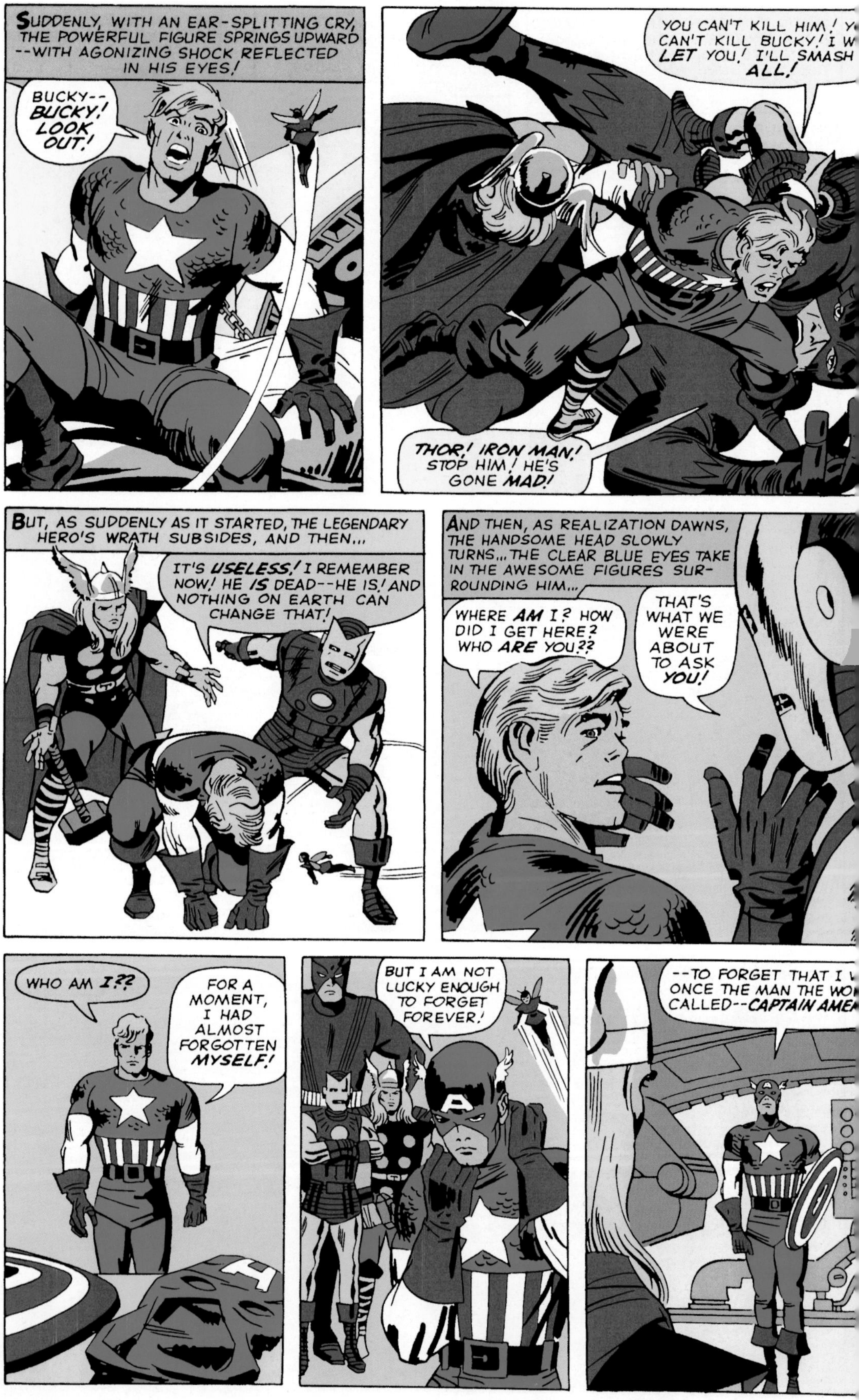

SUDDENLY, WITH AN EAR-SPLITTING CRY, THE POWERFUL FIGURE SPRINGS UPWARD --WITH AGONIZING SHOCK REFLECTED IN HIS EYES!
BUCKY-- BUCKY! LOOK OUT!
YOU CAN'T KILL HIM! Y CAN'T KILL BUCKY! I W LET YOU! I'LL SMASH ALL!
THOR! IRON MAN! STOP HIM! HE'S GONE MAD!
BUT, AS SUDDENLY AS IT STARTED, THE LEGENDARY HERO'S WRATH SUBSIDES, AND THEN...
IT'S USELESS! I REMEMBER NOW! HE IS DEAD--HE IS! AND NOTHING ON EARTH CAN CHANGE THAT!
AND THEN, AS REALIZATION DAWNS, THE HANDSOME HEAD SLOWLY TURNS... THE CLEAR BLUE EYES TAKE IN THE AWESOME FIGURES SURROUNDING HIM...
WHERE AM I? HOW DID I GET HERE? WHO ARE YOU??
THAT'S WHAT WE WERE ABOUT TO ASK YOU!
WHO AM I??
FOR A MOMENT, I HAD ALMOST FORGOTTEN MYSELF!
BUT I AM NOT LUCKY ENOUGH TO FORGET FOREVER!
--TO FORGET THAT I ONCE THE MAN THE WO CALLED--CAPTAIN AME

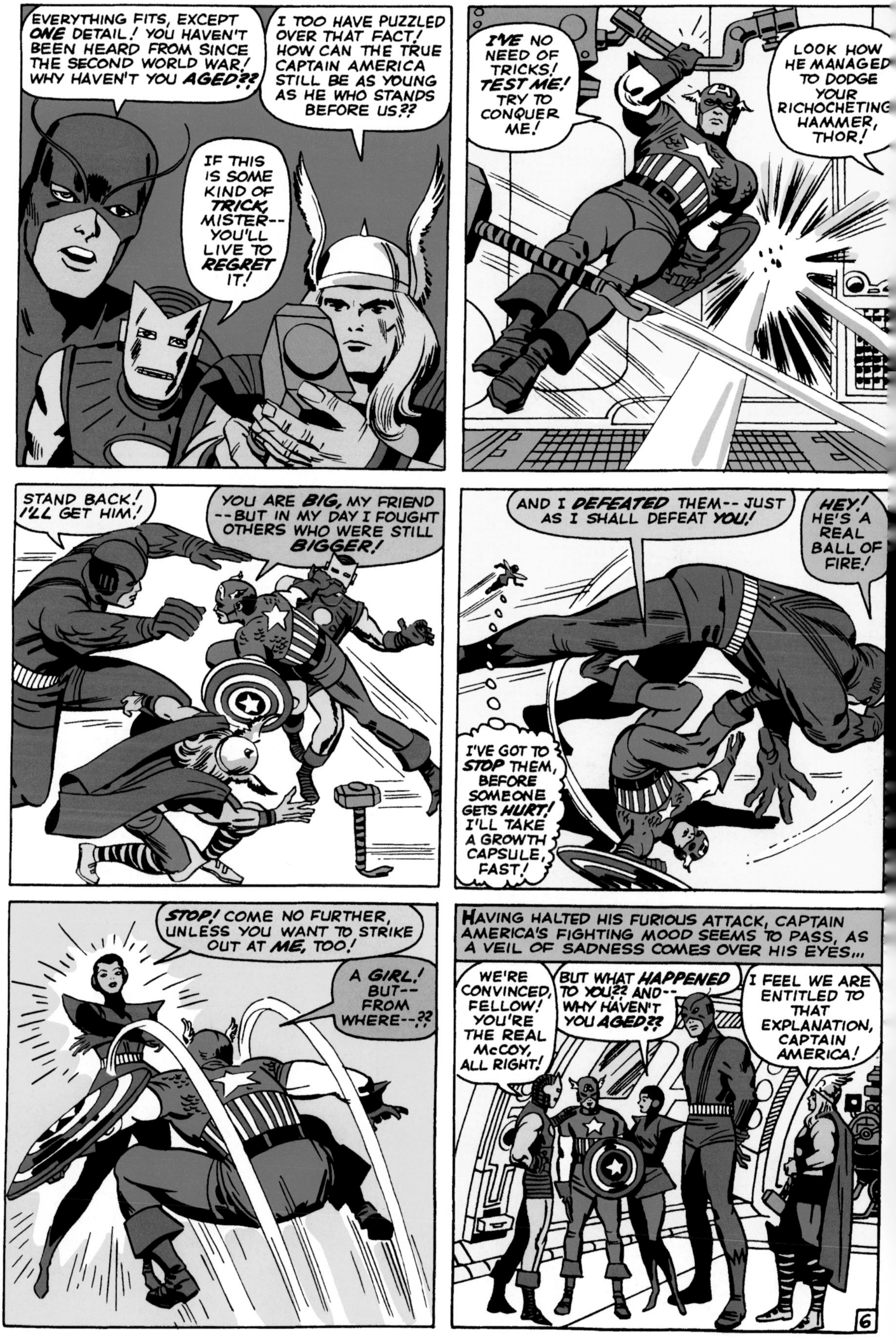
EVERYTHING FITS, EXCEPT ONE DETAIL! YOU HAVEN'T BEEN HEARD FROM SINCE THE SECOND WORLD WAR! WHY HAVEN'T YOU AGED??
I TOO HAVE PUZZLED OVER THAT FACT! HOW CAN THE TRUE CAPTAIN AMERICA STILL BE AS YOUNG AS HE WHO STANDS BEFORE US??
IF THIS IS SOME KIND OF TRICK, MISTER-- YOU'LL LIVE TO REGRET IT!
I'VE NO NEED OF TRICKS! TEST ME! TRY TO CONQUER ME!
LOOK HOW HE MANAGED TO DODGE YOUR RICHOCHETING HAMMER, THOR!
STAND BACK! I'LL GET HIM!
YOU ARE BIG, MY FRIEND --BUT IN MY DAY I FOUGHT OTHERS WHO WERE STILL BIGGER!
AND I DEFEATED THEM-- JUST AS I SHALL DEFEAT YOU!
HEY! HE'S A REAL BALL OF FIRE!
I'VE GOT TO STOP THEM, BEFORE SOMEONE GETS HURT! I'LL TAKE A GROWTH CAPSULE, FAST!
STOP! COME NO FURTHER, UNLESS YOU WANT TO STRIKE OUT AT ME, TOO!
A GIRL! BUT-- FROM WHERE--??
HAVING HALTED HIS FURIOUS ATTACK, CAPTAIN AMERICA'S FIGHTING MOOD SEEMS TO PASS, AS A VEIL OF SADNESS COMES OVER HIS EYES...
WE'RE CONVINCED, FELLOW! YOU'RE THE REAL McCOY, ALL RIGHT!
BUT WHAT HAPPENED TO YOU?? AND-- WHY HAVEN'T YOU AGED??
I FEEL WE ARE ENTITLED TO THAT EXPLANATION, CAPTAIN AMERICA!
6

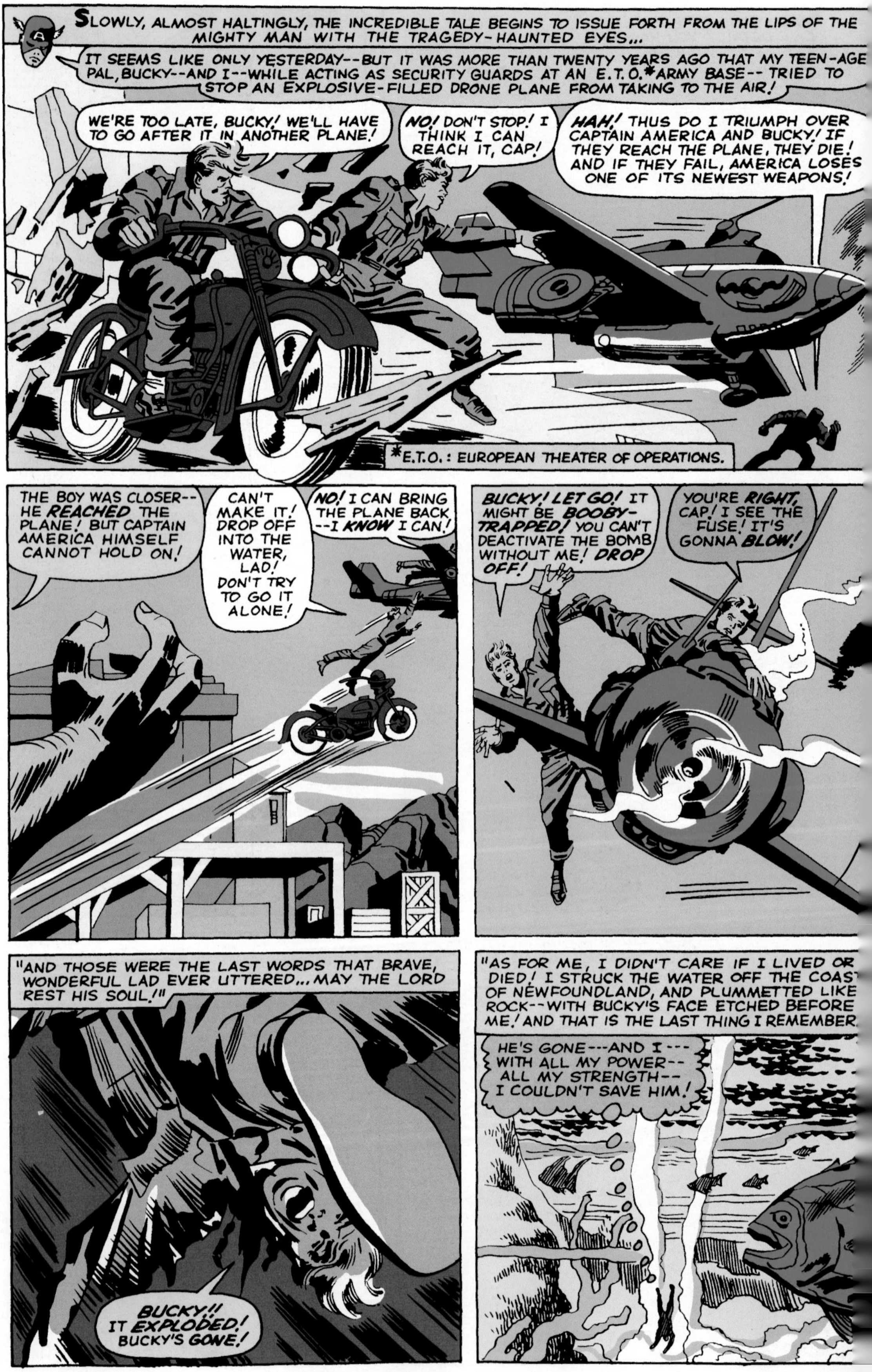
SLOWLY, ALMOST HALTINGLY, THE INCREDIBLE TALE BEGINS TO ISSUE FORTH FROM THE LIPS OF THE MIGHTY MAN WITH THE TRAGEDY-HAUNTED EYES...
IT SEEMS LIKE ONLY YESTERDAY--BUT IT WAS MORE THAN TWENTY YEARS AGO THAT MY TEEN-AGE PAL, BUCKY--AND I--WHILE ACTING AS SECURITY GUARDS AT AN E.T.O.* ARMY BASE--TRIED TO STOP AN EXPLOSIVE-FILLED DRONE PLANE FROM TAKING TO THE AIR!
WE'RE TOO LATE, BUCKY! WE'LL HAVE TO GO AFTER IT IN ANOTHER PLANE!
NO! DON'T STOP! I THINK I CAN REACH IT, CAP!
HAH! THUS DO I TRIUMPH OVER CAPTAIN AMERICA AND BUCKY! IF THEY REACH THE PLANE, THEY DIE! AND IF THEY FAIL, AMERICA LOSES ONE OF ITS NEWEST WEAPONS!
*E.T.O.: EUROPEAN THEATER OF OPERATIONS.
THE BOY WAS CLOSER--HE REACHED THE PLANE! BUT CAPTAIN AMERICA HIMSELF CANNOT HOLD ON!
CAN'T MAKE IT! DROP OFF INTO THE WATER, LAD! DON'T TRY TO GO IT ALONE!
NO! I CAN BRING THE PLANE BACK --I KNOW I CAN!
BUCKY! LET GO! IT MIGHT BE BOOBY-TRAPPED! YOU CAN'T DEACTIVATE THE BOMB WITHOUT ME! DROP OFF!
YOU'RE RIGHT, CAP! I SEE THE FUSE! IT'S GONNA BLOW!
"AND THOSE WERE THE LAST WORDS THAT BRAVE, WONDERFUL LAD EVER UTTERED... MAY THE LORD REST HIS SOUL!"
BUCKY!! IT EXPLODED! BUCKY'S GONE!
"AS FOR ME, I DIDN'T CARE IF I LIVED OR DIED! I STRUCK THE WATER OFF THE COAST OF NEWFOUNDLAND, AND PLUMMETTED LIKE ROCK--WITH BUCKY'S FACE ETCHED BEFORE ME! AND THAT IS THE LAST THING I REMEMBER.
HE'S GONE---AND I---WITH ALL MY POWER--ALL MY STRENGTH--I COULDN'T SAVE HIM!

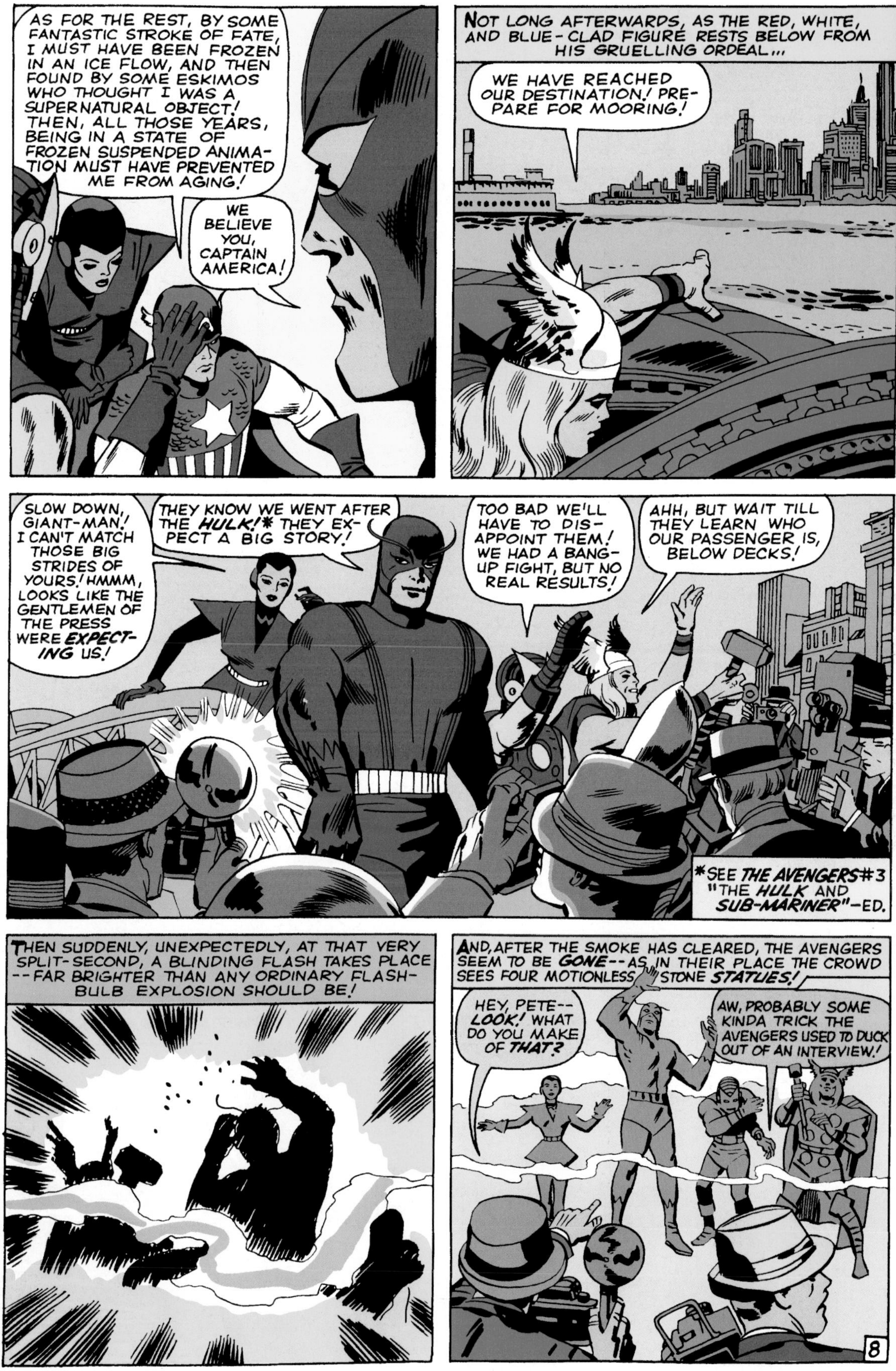

AS FOR THE REST, BY SOME FANTASTIC STROKE OF FATE, I MUST HAVE BEEN FROZEN IN AN ICE FLOW, AND THEN FOUND BY SOME ESKIMOS WHO THOUGHT I WAS A SUPERNATURAL OBJECT! THEN, ALL THOSE YEARS, BEING IN A STATE OF FROZEN SUSPENDED ANIMATION MUST HAVE PREVENTED ME FROM AGING!
WE BELIEVE YOU, CAPTAIN AMERICA!
NOT LONG AFTERWARDS, AS THE RED, WHITE, AND BLUE-CLAD FIGURE RESTS BELOW FROM HIS GRUELLING ORDEAL...
WE HAVE REACHED OUR DESTINATION! PREPARE FOR MOORING!
SLOW DOWN, GIANT-MAN! I CAN'T MATCH THOSE BIG STRIDES OF YOURS! HMMM, LOOKS LIKE THE GENTLEMEN OF THE PRESS WERE EXPECTING US!
THEY KNOW WE WENT AFTER THE HULK!* THEY EXPECT A BIG STORY!
TOO BAD WE'LL HAVE TO DISAPPOINT THEM! WE HAD A BANG-UP FIGHT, BUT NO REAL RESULTS!
AHH, BUT WAIT TILL THEY LEARN WHO OUR PASSENGER IS, BELOW DECKS!
*SEE THE AVENGERS #3 "THE HULK AND SUB-MARINER" -ED.
THEN SUDDENLY, UNEXPECTEDLY, AT THAT VERY SPLIT-SECOND, A BLINDING FLASH TAKES PLACE --FAR BRIGHTER THAN ANY ORDINARY FLASHBULB EXPLOSION SHOULD BE!
AND, AFTER THE SMOKE HAS CLEARED, THE AVENGERS SEEM TO BE GONE--AS IN THEIR PLACE THE CROWD SEES FOUR MOTIONLESS STONE STATUES!
HEY, PETE-- LOOK! WHAT DO YOU MAKE OF THAT?
AW, PROBABLY SOME KINDA TRICK THE AVENGERS USED TO DUCK OUT OF AN INTERVIEW!
8

BITTERLY DISAPPOINTED, THE REPORTERS AND PHOTOGRAPHERS RUSH OFF, TRYING TO FIND THE AVENGERS... AS THE CROWD DRIFTS AWAY TO NOTHINGNESS...

THAT'S A PRETTY CRUMMY TRICK TO PULL ON US, AFTER US WAITING ALL DAY FOR THIS INTERVIEW!

LET'S GO FIND 'EM! THEY COULDN'T HAVE GOTTEN FAR!

MINUTES LATER, THE LAST OCCUPANT OF THE UNDERSEA CRAFT SLOWLY CLIMBS UP THE HATCHWAY, HAVING BEEN AWAKENED BY THE COMMOTION ABOVE...

BUT, UPON REACHING THE SURFACE, HE FINDS...

EVERYONE'S GONE! THE PIER IS DESERTED! BUT-- WHY WOULD THEY DASH OFF WITHOUT ME ??

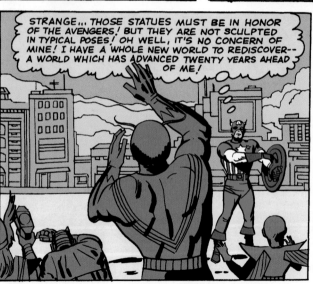

STRANGE... THOSE STATUES MUST BE IN HONOR OF THE AVENGERS! BUT THEY ARE NOT SCULPTED IN TYPICAL POSES! OH WELL, IT'S NO CONCERN OF MINE! I HAVE A WHOLE NEW WORLD TO REDISCOVER-- A WORLD WHICH HAS ADVANCED TWENTY YEARS AHEAD OF ME!

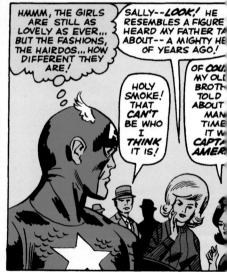

HMMM, THE GIRLS ARE STILL AS LOVELY AS EVER... BUT THE FASHIONS, THE HAIRDOS... HOW DIFFERENT THEY ARE!

SALLY-- LOOK! HE RESEMBLES A FIGURE I HEARD MY FATHER TA[LK] ABOUT-- A MIGHTY HE[RO] OF YEARS AGO!

HOLY SMOKE! THAT CAN'T BE WHO I THINK IT IS!

OF COU[RSE!] MY OL[D] BROTH[ER] TOLD [ME] ABOUT [THE] MAN[Y] TIME[S] IT W[AS] CAPT[AIN] AMER[ICA]

AND THE NEW YORK SKY-LINE-- EVER IMPRESSIVE-- EVER CHANGING! WHAT CAN THIS MAGNIFICENT STRUCTURE BE-- WITH ALL THE WORLD'S FLAGS ARRAYED AROUND IT ??

HEY! WATCH THE LIGHTS CROSSING THE STREET, MAC!

THE CARS HAVE CHANGED MOST OF ALL-- AS THEY ALWAYS DO! WE NEVER HAD SO MAN[Y] SMALL ONES IN THE THIRTIES AND FORTIES.

WAIT! I KNOW YOU! YOU'RE-- AWW, NO! IT CAN'T BE! IT'S IMPOSSIBLE!

BUT I CAN'T BE WRONG! I SAW YOU ONCE, WHEN I WAS A KID! NEVER FORGOT IT!

NO, OFFICER-- YOU'RE NOT MISTAKEN! I AM CAPTAIN AMERICA!

AND ALL THESE YEARS--ALL OF US--YOUR FANS--ALL YOUR ADMIRERS--WE THOUGHT YOU WERE DEAD! BUT YOU'VE COME BACK--JUST WHEN THE WORLD HAS NEED OF SUCH A MAN-- JUST LIKE FATE PLANNED IT THIS WAY!

FORGIVE ME, CAP, WILLYA? I--I SEEM TO HAVE SOMETHING IN MY EYE!

LATER, AFTER THE OFFICER HAS DIRECTED CAPTAIN AMERICA TO A NEARBY HOTEL...

I WONDER IF THE YOUNGSTER OF TODAY, WHO'VE GROWN UP WITH IT, REALIZE WHAT A TRULY WONDERFUL THING TELEVISION IS-- TO ONE WHO HAD NEVER SEEN IT!

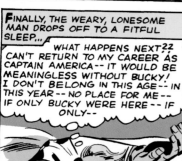

FINALLY, THE WEARY, LONESOME MAN DROPS OFF TO A FITFUL SLEEP...

WHAT HAPPENS NEXT?? CAN'T RETURN TO MY CAREER AS CAPTAIN AMERICA-- IT WOULD BE MEANINGLESS WITHOUT BUCKY! I DON'T BELONG IN THIS AGE-- IN THIS YEAR-- NO PLACE FOR ME-- IF ONLY BUCKY WERE HERE-- IF ONLY--

THEN, SUDDENLY, HIS SUPER-KEEN SENSES DETECTING A SOFT TREAD IN THE DOORWAY, THE STARTLED BLUE EYES OPEN WIDE, AND...

BUCKY!! IT'S YOU!!

YOU'VE COME BACK!! BUCKY, YOU'VE COME BACK!!

I DON'T KNOW WHAT YOU'RE YAPPIN' ABOUT, MISTER! MY NAME'S RICK JONES, AND I'VE FOLLOWED YOUR TRAIL HALFWAY ACROSS TOWN!

THEY TELL ME YOU WERE THE LAST TO SEE THE AVENGERS--AND I GOTTA FIND THEM! SO HOW ABOUT DOIN' A LITTLE TALKIN', HUH?

IT'S UNBELIEVABLE! YOU'RE LIKE HIS TWIN BROTHER! YOUR VOICE-- YOUR FACE--EVERYTHING!! YOU COULD BE BUCKY'S DOUBLE!

LOOK, FELLA, YOU'RE NOT READIN' ME! ARE YOU GONNA TELL ME WHAT YOU KNOW ABOUT THE AVENGERS' DISAPPEARANCE, OR DO YOU WANT ME TO MENTION YOUR NAME TO MY PAL, THE HULK, WHEN I RUN INTO HIM AGAIN??

I DON'T KNOW WHO THE HULK IS, LAD-- BUT IF THE AVENGERS ARE MISSING, I'LL BE GLAD TO HELP YOU FIND THEM!

10

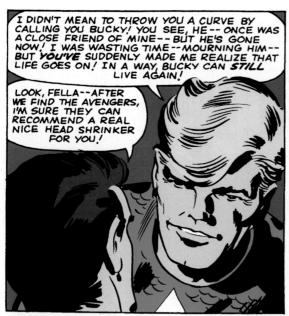

I DIDN'T MEAN TO THROW YOU A CURVE BY CALLING YOU BUCKY! YOU SEE, HE-- ONCE WAS A CLOSE FRIEND OF MINE-- BUT HE'S GONE NOW! I WAS WASTING TIME-- MOURNING HIM-- BUT *YOU'VE* SUDDENLY MADE ME REALIZE THAT LIFE GOES ON! IN A WAY, BUCKY CAN *STILL* LIVE AGAIN!

LOOK, FELLA-- AFTER WE FIND THE AVENGERS, I'M SURE THEY CAN RECOMMEND A REAL NICE HEAD SHRINKER FOR YOU!

HE THINKS I'M SOME SORT OF *MADMAN!* WELL, I'LL PROVE TO HIM THAT I'M *NOT!*

PICTURES WERE TAKEN OF THE AVENGERS AT THE DOCK! *GET GOING!* I WANT TO STUDY THEM!

SURE CAP, RIGH AWAY

ALL SUD HE CHAN HE A LIK GUY W USE BE OBEY --A FA

MINUTES LATER, IN A DARKROOM BELONGING TO ONE OF RICK'S *TEEN-BRIGADE* MEMBERS...

THESE NEWS PICTURES *SEEM* ALRIGHT, BUT I'M NOT SATISFIED! CAN YOU MAKE *ENLARGEMENTS?*

SURE! THERE'S AN ENLARGER AROUND HERE SOMEWHERE!

AND SO...

IT'LL BE READY IN A MINUTE!

AH! THAT'S MORE LIKE IT! THAT'S WHAT I WANTED!

WAIT-- IT'S GETTING CLEARER! *NOW* LOOK!

WHAT *IS* I DON'T ANYTHIN

NO PRESS PHOTOG'S CAMERA EVER LOOKED LIKE *THAT*-- NOT EVEN TWENTY YEARS LATER!

IT-- IT LOOKS LIKE SOME KINDA *GUN!*

IT'S UP TO *YOU* NOW, SON! IF YOU WANT T LEARN WHAT HAPPENED TO THE AVENGERS YOU'VE GOT TO FIND THAT MAN THE PICTURE!

NOW YOU'RE TALKIN' MY LANGUAGE, CAP! JUST SIT TIGHT AND WATCH MY SMOK I'LL ALERT MY TEEN-BRIGADE, ALL OVER T CITY...

WITHIN AN HOUR, THE SEARCH IS ON, AS SHARP EYED TEEN-AGERS COVER THE CITY, SEEKING A PASTY-FACED MAN, WEARING OVAL SUNGLASSES, WITH JET BLACK HAIR! NOT MUCH TO GO ON, PERHAPS, BUT STILL A STARTING POINT FOR THE EAGER BRIGADERS...

THAT'S NOT HIM! HAIR'S NOT BLACK ENOUGH!

THOUGHT I HAD HIM-- BUT HE'S MUCH TOO OLD!

WORKING AROUND THE CLOCK THE ALERT TEEN-BRIGADE TAKES CANDID CAMERA SNAPSHOTS OF ALL POSSIBLE SUSPECTS, SENDING THEM IMMEDIATELY TO RICK JONES.

THAT GUY'S ANOTHER FALSE ALARM, BUT I'VE GOT A HALF-DOZEN SNAPS TO SEND RICK ANYWAY!

THEN, RACING THRU THE VAST CITY LIKE AN AVENGING STREAK, THE NIMBLE, SEEMINGLY TIRELESS CAPTAIN AMERICA FOLLOWS UP EACH LEAD, NO MATTER WHERE IT MAY TAKE HIM...

IT'S LIKE OLD TIMES AGAIN, BEING IN COSTUME--ON THE TRAIL OF SOME STRANGE, UNKNOWN MENACE!

THIS IS WHAT I WAS MEANT TO DO! THIS IS THE DESTINY I CAN NEVER ESCAPE!

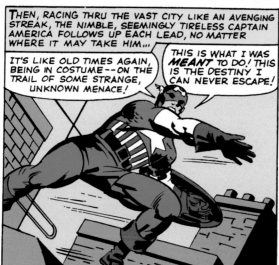

AND THEN, FINALLY...

IT'S HIM! THE ONE WE'RE AFTER!

WITHOUT A MOMENT'S HESITATION, TWO HUNDRED POUNDS OF FIGHTING FURY CRASH THRU THE SHATTERING WINDOW...

BUT, IN HIS EAGERNESS, THE ATTACKING CRIME-FIGHTER HAS FAILED TO NOTICE THE GUNMEN IN THE ADJOINING ROOM--GUNMEN WHO HEAR THE CRASH AND RACE TO THE SCENE, THEIR WEAPONS THUNDERING,!!

GET THAT COSTUMED CLOWN, WHO-EVER HE IS!

IT'LL BE A CINCH!

12

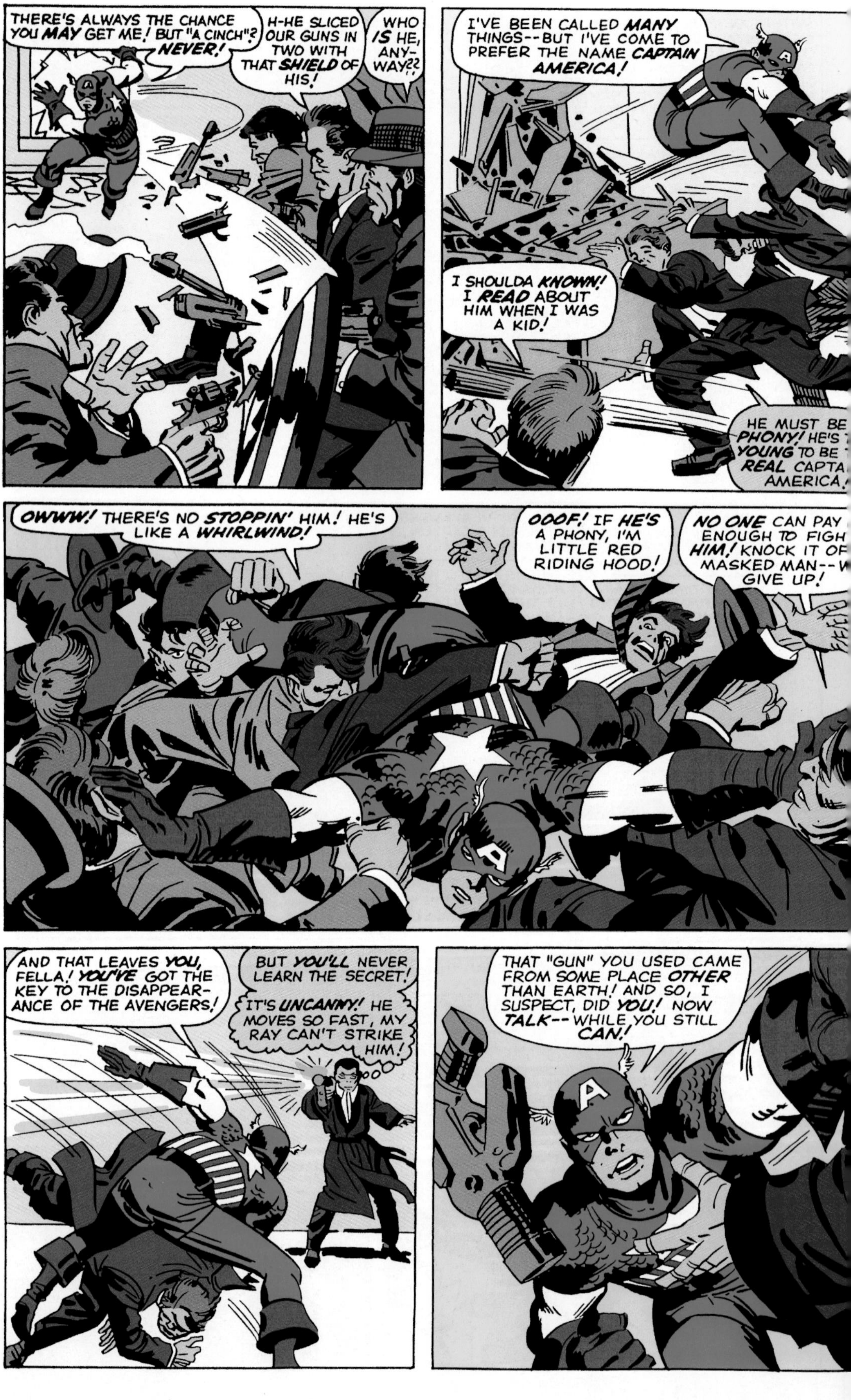

THERE'S ALWAYS THE CHANCE YOU MAY GET ME! BUT "A CINCH"? NEVER!
H-HE SLICED OUR GUNS IN TWO WITH THAT SHIELD OF HIS!
WHO IS HE, ANYWAY??
I'VE BEEN CALLED MANY THINGS--BUT I'VE COME TO PREFER THE NAME CAPTAIN AMERICA!
I SHOULDA KNOWN! I READ ABOUT HIM WHEN I WAS A KID!
HE MUST BE PHONY! HE'S YOUNG TO BE REAL CAPTA AMERICA!
OWWW! THERE'S NO STOPPIN' HIM! HE'S LIKE A WHIRLWIND!
OOOF! IF HE'S A PHONY, I'M LITTLE RED RIDING HOOD!
NO ONE CAN PAY ENOUGH TO FIGH HIM! KNOCK IT OF MASKED MAN-- GIVE UP!
AND THAT LEAVES YOU, FELLA! YOU'VE GOT THE KEY TO THE DISAPPEARANCE OF THE AVENGERS!
BUT YOU'LL NEVER LEARN THE SECRET!
IT'S UNCANNY! HE MOVES SO FAST, MY RAY CAN'T STRIKE HIM!
THAT "GUN" YOU USED CAME FROM SOME PLACE OTHER THAN EARTH! AND SO, I SUSPECT, DID YOU! NOW TALK-- WHILE YOU STILL CAN!

VERY WELL! I SEE THAT FURTHER RESISTANCE IS USELESS!

AFTER YOU HAVE HEARD MY STORY, YOU MAY FEEL *PITY* FOR ME, INSTEAD OF THAT RAW HATRED WHICH I SEE MIRRORED IN YOUR EYES!

I WAS *RIGHT!* YOU'RE *NOT* A HUMAN!

HOLY COW! LOOK WHAT WE'VE BEEN *WORKIN'* FOR! LEMME *OUT* OF HERE!

I'VE *HAD* IT! ME FOR THE STRAIGHT AND *NARROW* FROM NOW ON!

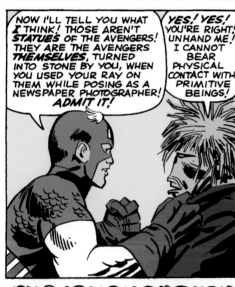

NOW I'LL TELL YOU WHAT *I* THINK! THOSE AREN'T *STATUES* OF THE AVENGERS! THEY ARE THE AVENGERS *THEMSELVES,* TURNED INTO STONE BY YOU, WHEN YOU USED YOUR RAY ON THEM WHILE POSING AS A NEWSPAPER PHOTOGRAPHER! *ADMIT IT!*

YES! YES! YOU'RE *RIGHT!* UNHAND ME! I CANNOT BEAR PHYSICAL CONTACT WITH PRIMITIVE BEINGS!

"I COME FROM A FAR DISTANT GALAXY! MY NAME WOULD BE MEANING-LESS TO YOU AS EARTH TONGUES CANNOT EVEN PRONOUNCE IT!"

"CENTURIES AGO, DUE TO EN-GINE FAILURE, MY SPACE SHIP CRASHED ON EARTH, IMBEDDING ITSELF DEEP INTO THE BOTTOM OF THE SEA!"

"I MEANT EARTHLINGS NO HARM! I ROAMED YOUR PLANET, SEEKING SOMEONE TO HELP ME FREE MY SHIP! BUT THOSE I SAW *FEARED* ME--ATTACKED ME! IN SELF-DEFENSE I USED MY RAY GUN ON THEM, TURNING THEM TO STONE FOR ONE HUNDRED OF YOUR EARTH HOURS!"

BEHOLD! IT IS A MONSTER FROM THE *NETHERWORLD!* IT MUST BE *SLAIN!*

NO! I NEED HELP! STAY BACK --PLEASE--DON'T MAKE ME *DO* THIS! *NO!*

IT IS BE-WITCHED! ONE *LOOK* AT IT TURNS MEN TO STONE!

YOUR HAIR-- IN THE DARK, YOU MUST HAVE LOOKED LIKE A *WOMAN* TO THEM -- AND TURNING MEN TO STONE-- *THAT* MUST BE THE ORIGIN OF THE LEGEND OF *MEDUSA!* BUT-- WHY DID YOU USE YOUR POWER ON THE *AVENGERS??*

BECAUSE OF THE ONE WHO CALLS HIMSELF *SUB-MARINER!* HE FOUND ME SOME DAYS AGO--TOLD ME *HE* WOULD FREE MY SHIP FROM THE OCEAN'S DEPTHS IF I WOULD TURN THE AVENGERS TO STONE! I--I *HAD* TO DO IT!

14

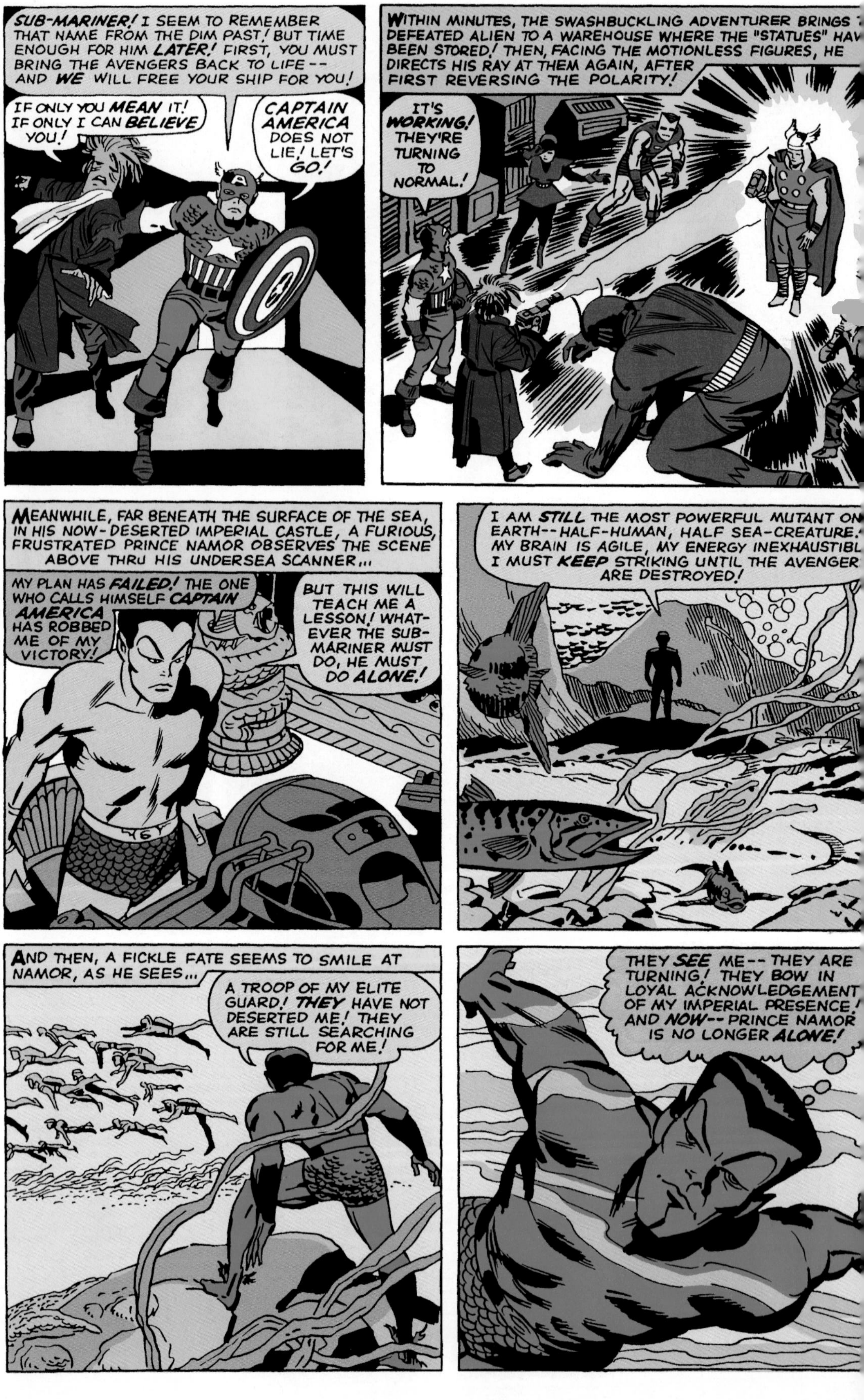
SUB-MARINER! I SEEM TO REMEMBER THAT NAME FROM THE DIM PAST! BUT TIME ENOUGH FOR HIM LATER! FIRST, YOU MUST BRING THE AVENGERS BACK TO LIFE -- AND WE WILL FREE YOUR SHIP FOR YOU!
IF ONLY YOU MEAN IT! IF ONLY I CAN BELIEVE YOU!
CAPTAIN AMERICA DOES NOT LIE! LET'S GO!
WITHIN MINUTES, THE SWASHBUCKLING ADVENTURER BRINGS THE DEFEATED ALIEN TO A WAREHOUSE WHERE THE "STATUES" HAVE BEEN STORED! THEN, FACING THE MOTIONLESS FIGURES, HE DIRECTS HIS RAY AT THEM AGAIN, AFTER FIRST REVERSING THE POLARITY!
IT'S WORKING! THEY'RE TURNING TO NORMAL!
MEANWHILE, FAR BENEATH THE SURFACE OF THE SEA, IN HIS NOW-DESERTED IMPERIAL CASTLE, A FURIOUS, FRUSTRATED PRINCE NAMOR OBSERVES THE SCENE ABOVE THRU HIS UNDERSEA SCANNER...
MY PLAN HAS FAILED! THE ONE WHO CALLS HIMSELF CAPTAIN AMERICA HAS ROBBED ME OF MY VICTORY!
BUT THIS WILL TEACH ME A LESSON! WHATEVER THE SUB-MARINER MUST DO, HE MUST DO ALONE!
I AM STILL THE MOST POWERFUL MUTANT ON EARTH--HALF-HUMAN, HALF SEA-CREATURE! MY BRAIN IS AGILE, MY ENERGY INEXHAUSTIBLE! I MUST KEEP STRIKING UNTIL THE AVENGERS ARE DESTROYED!
AND THEN, A FICKLE FATE SEEMS TO SMILE AT NAMOR, AS HE SEES...
A TROOP OF MY ELITE GUARD! THEY HAVE NOT DESERTED ME! THEY ARE STILL SEARCHING FOR ME!
THEY SEE ME -- THEY ARE TURNING! THEY BOW IN LOYAL ACKNOWLEDGEMENT OF MY IMPERIAL PRESENCE! AND NOW-- PRINCE NAMOR IS NO LONGER ALONE!

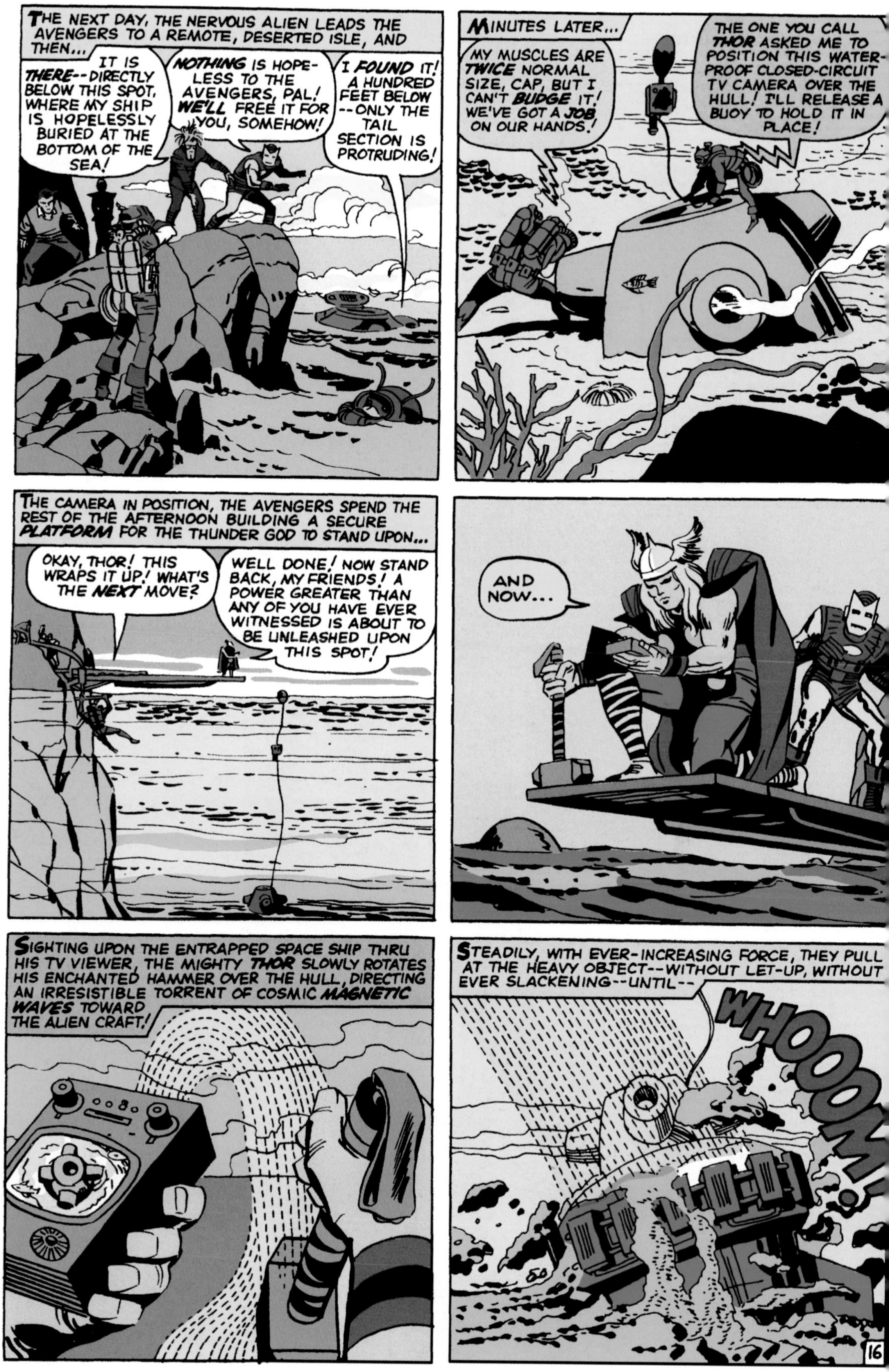
THE NEXT DAY, THE NERVOUS ALIEN LEADS THE AVENGERS TO A REMOTE, DESERTED ISLE, AND THEN...
IT IS THERE--DIRECTLY BELOW THIS SPOT, WHERE MY SHIP IS HOPELESSLY BURIED AT THE BOTTOM OF THE SEA!
NOTHING IS HOPELESS TO THE AVENGERS, PAL! WE'LL FREE IT FOR YOU, SOMEHOW!
I FOUND IT! A HUNDRED FEET BELOW --ONLY THE TAIL SECTION IS PROTRUDING!
MINUTES LATER...
MY MUSCLES ARE TWICE NORMAL SIZE, CAP, BUT I CAN'T BUDGE IT! WE'VE GOT A JOB ON OUR HANDS!
THE ONE YOU CALL THOR ASKED ME TO POSITION THIS WATER-PROOF CLOSED-CIRCUIT TV CAMERA OVER THE HULL! I'LL RELEASE A BUOY TO HOLD IT IN PLACE!
THE CAMERA IN POSITION, THE AVENGERS SPEND THE REST OF THE AFTERNOON BUILDING A SECURE PLATFORM FOR THE THUNDER GOD TO STAND UPON...
OKAY, THOR! THIS WRAPS IT UP! WHAT'S THE NEXT MOVE?
WELL DONE! NOW STAND BACK, MY FRIENDS! A POWER GREATER THAN ANY OF YOU HAVE EVER WITNESSED IS ABOUT TO BE UNLEASHED UPON THIS SPOT!
AND NOW...
SIGHTING UPON THE ENTRAPPED SPACE SHIP THRU HIS TV VIEWER, THE MIGHTY THOR SLOWLY ROTATES HIS ENCHANTED HAMMER OVER THE HULL, DIRECTING AN IRRESISTIBLE TORRENT OF COSMIC MAGNETIC WAVES TOWARD THE ALIEN CRAFT!
STEADILY, WITH EVER-INCREASING FORCE, THEY PULL AT THE HEAVY OBJECT--WITHOUT LET-UP, WITHOUT EVER SLACKENING--UNTIL--
WHOOOOM!
16

IT **WORKED!** YOU FREED THE SHIP, THOR!

WHY DO YOU SOUND SURPRISED? WAS THAT NOT MY **INTENTION??**

YOU KEPT YOUR WORD! NOW I CAN REPAIR MY SHIP IN MINUTES, AND DEPART FROM THIS WRETCHED PLANET!

NOW THAT IT'S FLOATING FREE, THE WATER MAKES IT ALMOST WEIGHTLESS!

LEAVE IT HERE! I'LL MAKE MY REPAIRS UNDER WATER, SAFE FROM ANY PRYING EYES!

SUIT YOURSELF, TER! AS LONG A HIT THE ROAD, DON'T CARE H YOU DO

AND THAT'S THAT! I WONDER WHAT THE A.A.A. WOULD HAVE SAID IF THE ALIEN HAD CALLED **THEM** FOR EMERGENCY REPAIRS.!??

Y'KNOW, GIANT-MAN, I LIKE YOUR STYLE! YOU **AVENGERS** MAKE A GREAT TEAM! IN FACT, I WAS WON-DERING...

BUT CAPTAIN AMERICA'S SEN-TENCE IS CUT SHORT BY A THUNDEROUS EXPLOSION WHICH ROCKS THE LITTLE ISLE AT THAT SPLIT-SECOND!

AND, WHEN THE STARTLED AVENG RECOVER THEIR EQUILIBRIUM, T ARE AMAZED TO SEE...

NAMOR! AND A SQUAD OF UND SEA WARRIO

YOU SEE BEFORE YOU THE ACCURSED **ENEMY,** MY BRAVE FOLLOWERS! **ATTACK!** FIGHT SHOULDER TO SHOULDER WITH YOUR PRINCE!

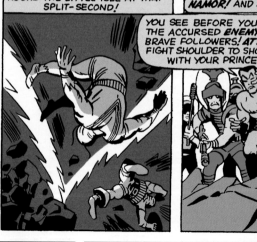

THOUGH THE FIRST ONSLAUGHT IS UNEX-PECTED AND DEVESTATING, THE AVENGERS' BATTLE-TRAINED REFLEXES ARE EQUAL TO THE CHALLENGE!

YOU'LL HAVE TO DO BETTER THAN **THAT,** LAUGH-ING BOY!

YOU'LL **GET** YOUR WISH, IRON MAN! **NAMOR** WILL DO BETTER! YOUR IRON ARMOR CANNOT SAVE YOU FROM THE SEA MONARCH'S ATTACK!!

I'LL HAVE TO ACT **FAST** HIS FISTS ARE LIKE LIV SLEDGE-HAMMERS! MY ARMOR CAN'T TAKE IT MU LONGER

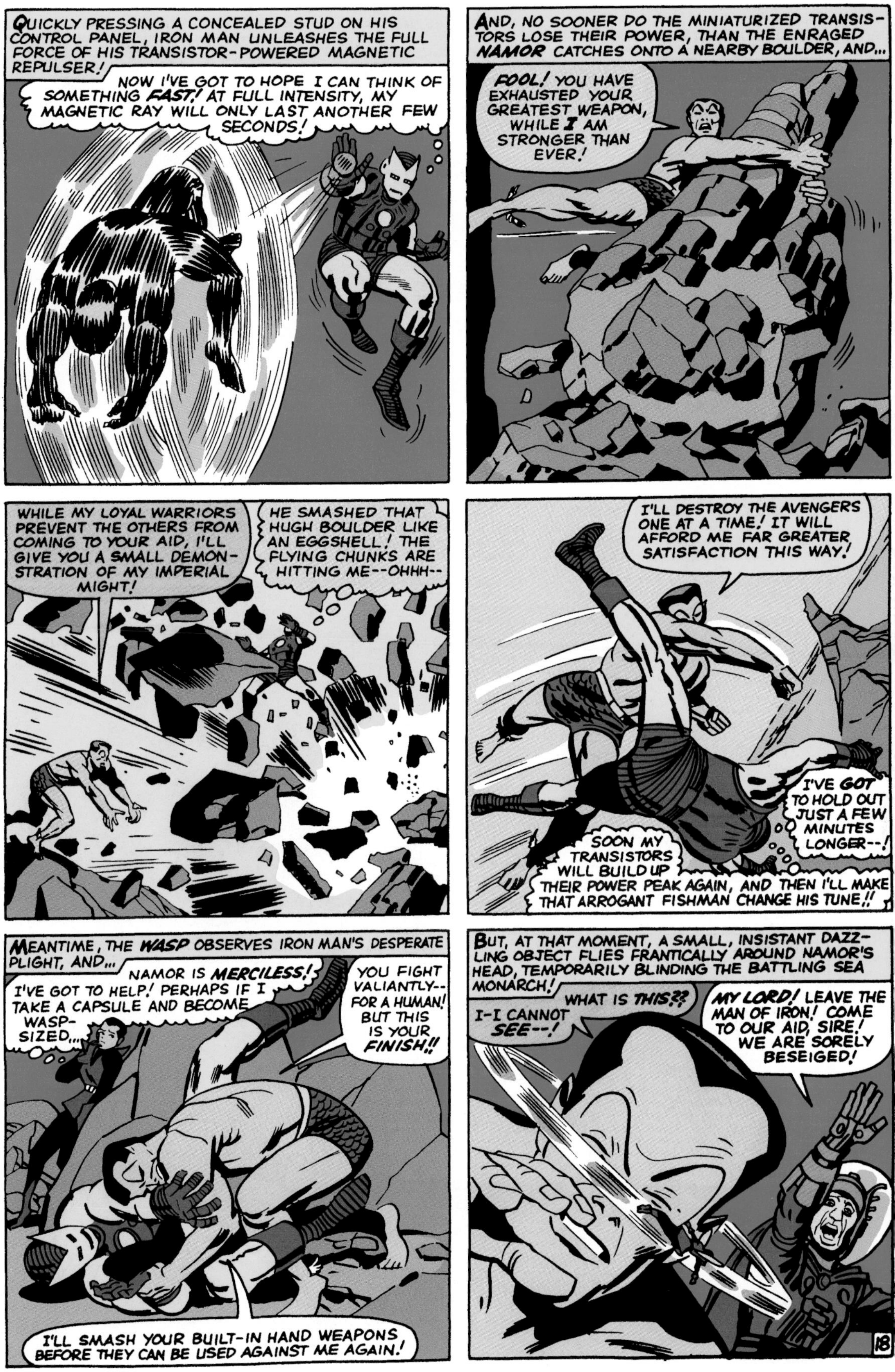
QUICKLY PRESSING A CONCEALED STUD ON HIS CONTROL PANEL, IRON MAN UNLEASHES THE FULL FORCE OF HIS TRANSISTOR-POWERED MAGNETIC REPULSER!
NOW I'VE GOT TO HOPE I CAN THINK OF SOMETHING FAST! AT FULL INTENSITY, MY MAGNETIC RAY WILL ONLY LAST ANOTHER FEW SECONDS!
AND, NO SOONER DO THE MINIATURIZED TRANSISTORS LOSE THEIR POWER, THAN THE ENRAGED NAMOR CATCHES ONTO A NEARBY BOULDER, AND...
FOOL! YOU HAVE EXHAUSTED YOUR GREATEST WEAPON, WHILE I AM STRONGER THAN EVER!
WHILE MY LOYAL WARRIORS PREVENT THE OTHERS FROM COMING TO YOUR AID, I'LL GIVE YOU A SMALL DEMONSTRATION OF MY IMPERIAL MIGHT!
HE SMASHED THAT HUGH BOULDER LIKE AN EGGSHELL! THE FLYING CHUNKS ARE HITTING ME--OHHH--
I'LL DESTROY THE AVENGERS ONE AT A TIME! IT WILL AFFORD ME FAR GREATER SATISFACTION THIS WAY!
I'VE GOT TO HOLD OUT JUST A FEW MINUTES LONGER--!
SOON MY TRANSISTORS WILL BUILD UP THEIR POWER PEAK AGAIN, AND THEN I'LL MAKE THAT ARROGANT FISHMAN CHANGE HIS TUNE!!
MEANTIME, THE WASP OBSERVES IRON MAN'S DESPERATE PLIGHT, AND...
NAMOR IS MERCILESS!
I'VE GOT TO HELP! PERHAPS IF I TAKE A CAPSULE AND BECOME WASP-SIZED...
YOU FIGHT VALIANTLY--FOR A HUMAN! BUT THIS IS YOUR FINISH!!
I'LL SMASH YOUR BUILT-IN HAND WEAPONS BEFORE THEY CAN BE USED AGAINST ME AGAIN!
BUT, AT THAT MOMENT, A SMALL, INSISTANT DAZZLING OBJECT FLIES FRANTICALLY AROUND NAMOR'S HEAD, TEMPORARILY BLINDING THE BATTLING SEA MONARCH!
WHAT IS THIS??
I-I CANNOT SEE--!
MY LORD! LEAVE THE MAN OF IRON! COME TO OUR AID, SIRE! WE ARE SORELY BESEIGED!
18

DIZZY AND EXHAUSTED, THE WASP FLIES OFF, AS NAMOR TURNS FROM IRON MAN AND RUSHES TO ANSWE[R] HIS LIEUTENANT'S CALL FOR HELP!

IT'S *THOR!* HE'S HOLDING MY MEN AT BAY WITH THAT WRETCHED *HAMMER* OF HIS!

SHOW YOURSELF, NAMOR! I TIRE OF WASTING MY STRENGTH ON THESE LOWLY MINIONS OF YOURS! I CRAVE A FOE MORE WORTHY OF MY METTLE!

FALL BACK! WAIT FOR THE COMMAND OF OUR LORD NAMOR!

QUICKLY! BEFORE THE *OTHERS* REACH US, CONCENTRATE ALL YOUR FIRE POWER ON *THOR--* FROM THIS SAFE DISTANCE!

KEEP HIM REELING WHILE I ATTACK HIM WITH MY BARE HANDS!

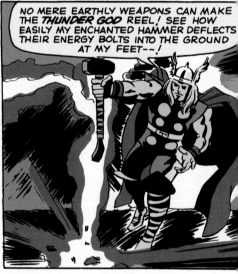

NO MERE EARTHLY WEAPONS CAN MAKE THE *THUNDER GOD* REEL! SEE HOW EASILY MY ENCHANTED HAMMER DEFLECTS THEIR ENERGY BOLTS INTO THE GROUND AT MY FEET--!

THE ENERGY FROM OUR RAY GUNS IS TRAVELING *BACK* TO US ALONG THE GROUND! *DISPERSE!!*

WE ARE NO MATCH FOR *THOR!* THE SUB-MARINER MUST CONQUER HIM *ALONE!*

AND THEN, WITH THE FORCE AND FURY OF T[HE] RAGING SEAS, NAMOR STRIKES!

WHEN YOU SWING THAT HAMMER, YOU'RE INVINCIBLE! BUT I'LL SEE TO IT THAT YOU NEVER SWING IT *AGAIN!*

WITLESS MUTA[NT,] THIS IS NO *HUMAN* Y[OU] ATTACK! THIS IS THE MIGHTY *THO[R!]*

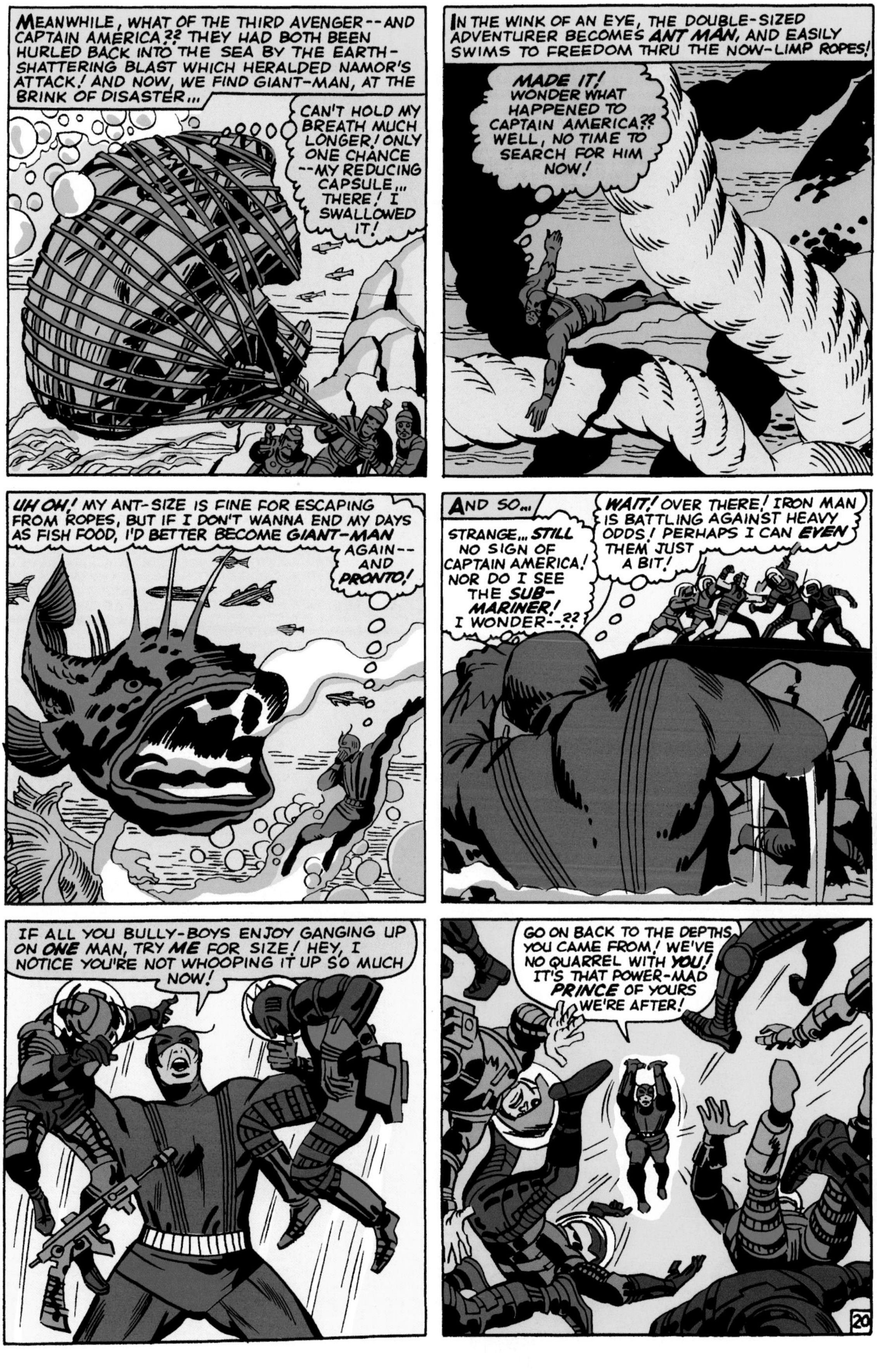
MEANWHILE, WHAT OF THE THIRD AVENGER--AND CAPTAIN AMERICA?? THEY HAD BOTH BEEN HURLED BACK INTO THE SEA BY THE EARTH-SHATTERING BLAST WHICH HERALDED NAMOR'S ATTACK! AND NOW, WE FIND GIANT-MAN, AT THE BRINK OF DISASTER...
CAN'T HOLD MY BREATH MUCH LONGER! ONLY ONE CHANCE --MY REDUCING CAPSULE... THERE! I SWALLOWED IT!
IN THE WINK OF AN EYE, THE DOUBLE-SIZED ADVENTURER BECOMES ANT MAN, AND EASILY SWIMS TO FREEDOM THRU THE NOW-LIMP ROPES!
MADE IT! WONDER WHAT HAPPENED TO CAPTAIN AMERICA?? WELL, NO TIME TO SEARCH FOR HIM NOW!
UH OH! MY ANT-SIZE IS FINE FOR ESCAPING FROM ROPES, BUT IF I DON'T WANNA END MY DAYS AS FISH FOOD, I'D BETTER BECOME GIANT-MAN AGAIN--AND PRONTO!
AND SO...
STRANGE... STILL NO SIGN OF CAPTAIN AMERICA! NOR DO I SEE THE SUB-MARINER! I WONDER--??
WAIT! OVER THERE! IRON MAN IS BATTLING AGAINST HEAVY ODDS! PERHAPS I CAN EVEN THEM JUST A BIT!
IF ALL YOU BULLY-BOYS ENJOY GANGING UP ON ONE MAN, TRY ME FOR SIZE! HEY, I NOTICE YOU'RE NOT WHOOPING IT UP SO MUCH NOW!
GO ON BACK TO THE DEPTHS YOU CAME FROM! WE'VE NO QUARREL WITH YOU! IT'S THAT POWER-MAD PRINCE OF YOURS WE'RE AFTER!
20

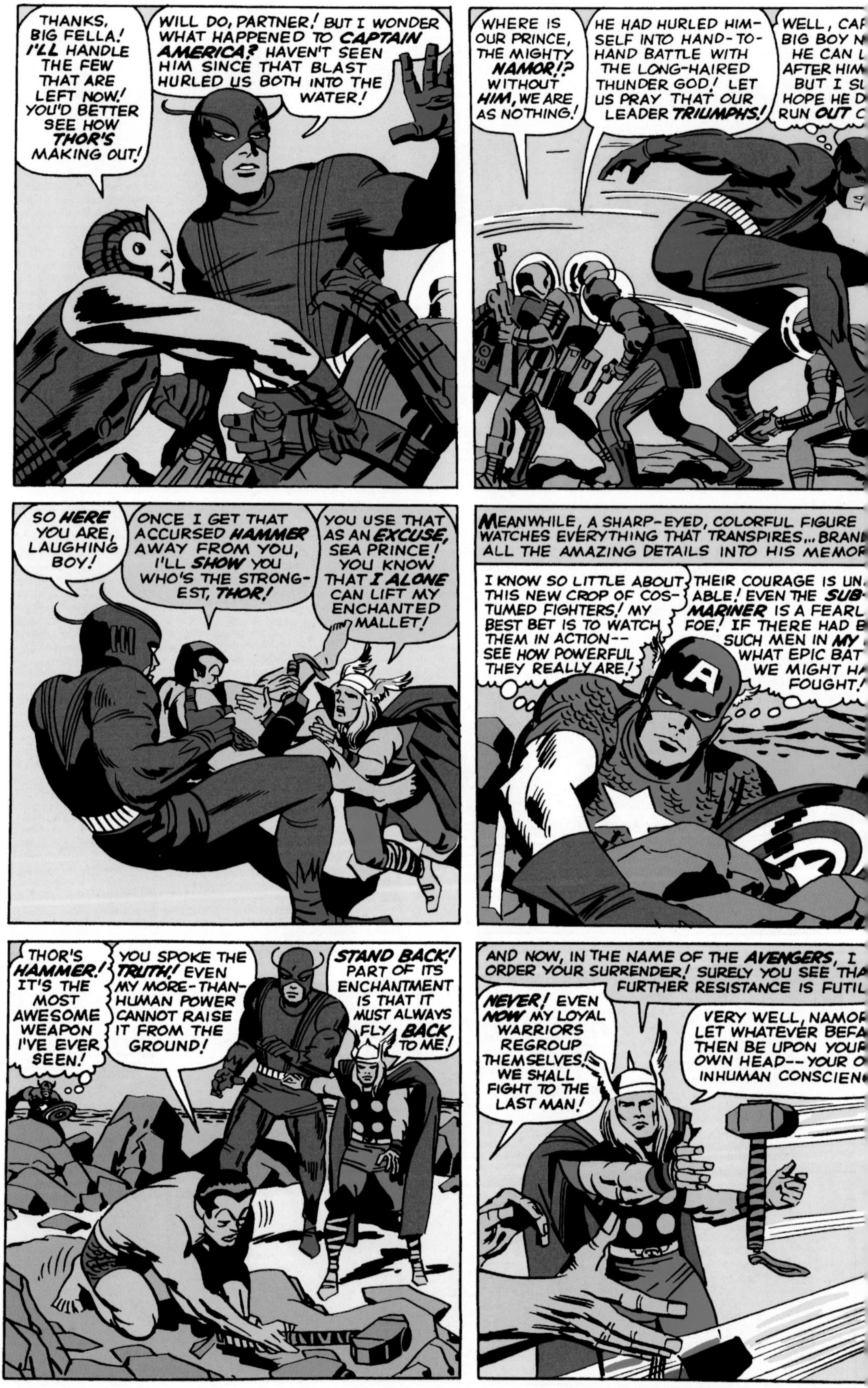

THANKS, BIG FELLA! I'LL HANDLE THE FEW THAT ARE LEFT NOW! YOU'D BETTER SEE HOW THOR'S MAKING OUT!
WILL DO, PARTNER! BUT I WONDER WHAT HAPPENED TO CAPTAIN AMERICA? HAVEN'T SEEN HIM SINCE THAT BLAST HURLED US BOTH INTO THE WATER!
WHERE IS OUR PRINCE, THE MIGHTY NAMOR!? WITHOUT HIM, WE ARE AS NOTHING!
HE HAD HURLED HIMSELF INTO HAND-TO-HAND BATTLE WITH THE LONG-HAIRED THUNDER GOD! LET US PRAY THAT OUR LEADER TRIUMPHS!
WELL, CA
BIG BOY N
HE CAN L
AFTER HIM
BUT I S
HOPE HE D
RUN OUT
SO HERE YOU ARE, LAUGHING BOY!
ONCE I GET THAT ACCURSED HAMMER AWAY FROM YOU, I'LL SHOW YOU WHO'S THE STRONGEST, THOR!
YOU USE THAT AS AN EXCUSE, SEA PRINCE! YOU KNOW THAT I ALONE CAN LIFT MY ENCHANTED MALLET!
MEANWHILE, A SHARP-EYED, COLORFUL FIGURE WATCHES EVERYTHING THAT TRANSPIRES... BRAN
ALL THE AMAZING DETAILS INTO HIS MEMO
I KNOW SO LITTLE ABOUT THIS NEW CROP OF COSTUMED FIGHTERS! MY BEST BET IS TO WATCH THEM IN ACTION-- SEE HOW POWERFUL THEY REALLY ARE!
THEIR COURAGE IS UN
ABLE! EVEN THE SUB-
MARINER IS A FEARL
FOE! IF THERE HAD B
SUCH MEN IN MY
WHAT EPIC BAT
WE MIGHT HA
FOUGHT!
THOR'S HAMMER! IT'S THE MOST AWESOME WEAPON I'VE EVER SEEN!
YOU SPOKE THE TRUTH! EVEN MY MORE-THAN-HUMAN POWER CANNOT RAISE IT FROM THE GROUND!
STAND BACK! PART OF ITS ENCHANTMENT IS THAT IT MUST ALWAYS FLY BACK TO ME!
AND NOW, IN THE NAME OF THE AVENGERS, I ORDER YOUR SURRENDER! SURELY YOU SEE THA
FURTHER RESISTANCE IS FUTIL
NEVER! EVEN NOW MY LOYAL WARRIORS REGROUP THEMSELVES! WE SHALL FIGHT TO THE LAST MAN!
VERY WELL, NAMOR
LET WHATEVER BEFA
THEN BE UPON YOUR
OWN HEAD-- YOUR O
INHUMAN CONSCIEN

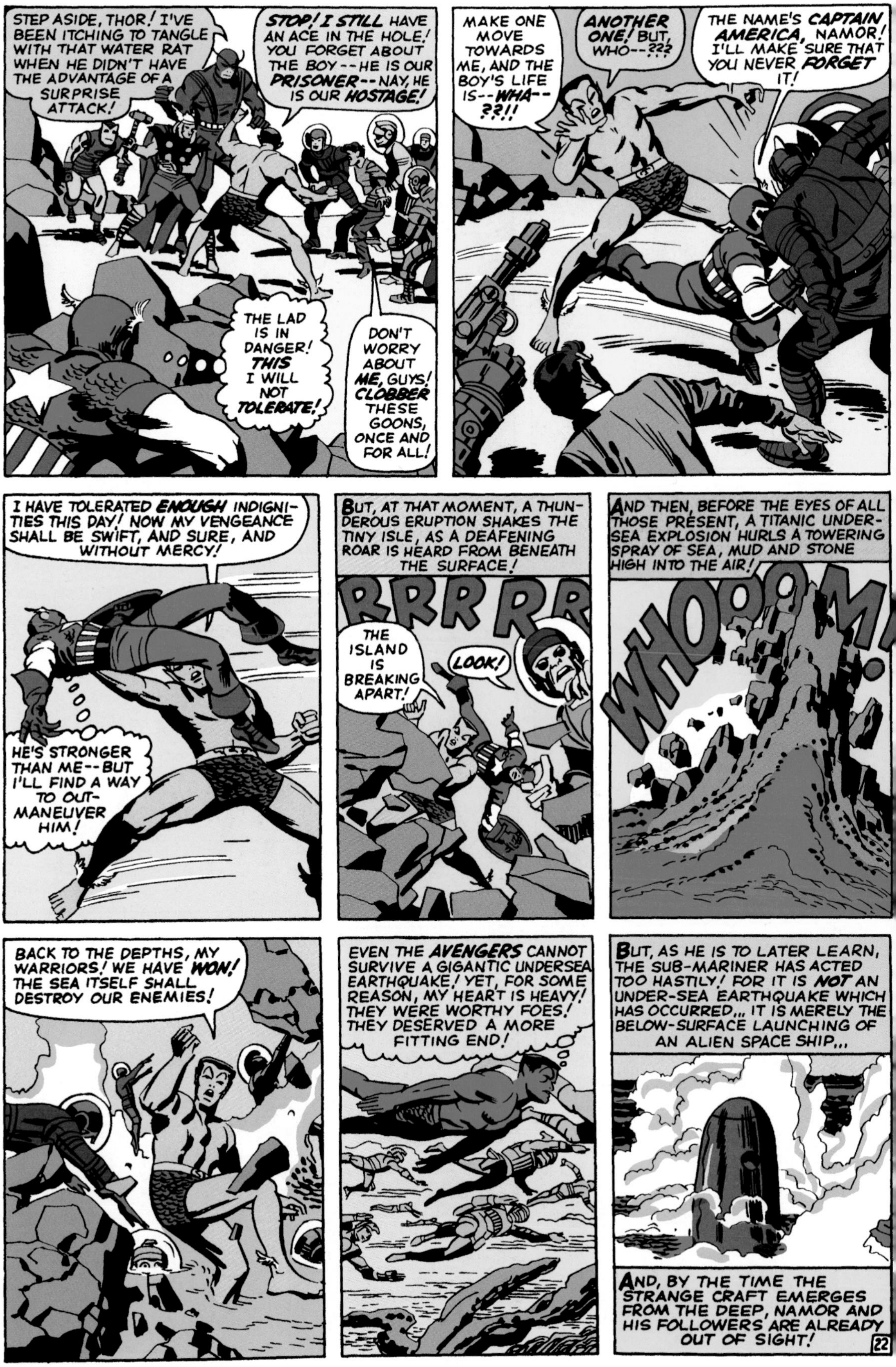
STEP ASIDE, THOR! I'VE BEEN ITCHING TO TANGLE WITH THAT WATER RAT WHEN HE DIDN'T HAVE THE ADVANTAGE OF A SURPRISE ATTACK!
STOP! I STILL HAVE AN ACE IN THE HOLE! YOU FORGET ABOUT THE BOY--HE IS OUR PRISONER--NAY, HE IS OUR HOSTAGE!
THE LAD IS IN DANGER! THIS I WILL NOT TOLERATE!
DON'T WORRY ABOUT ME, GUYS! CLOBBER THESE GOONS, ONCE AND FOR ALL!
MAKE ONE MOVE TOWARDS ME, AND THE BOY'S LIFE IS--WHA--??!!
ANOTHER ONE! BUT, WHO--???
THE NAME'S CAPTAIN AMERICA, NAMOR! I'LL MAKE SURE THAT YOU NEVER FORGET IT!
I HAVE TOLERATED ENOUGH INDIGNITIES THIS DAY! NOW MY VENGEANCE SHALL BE SWIFT, AND SURE, AND WITHOUT MERCY!
HE'S STRONGER THAN ME--BUT I'LL FIND A WAY TO OUT-MANEUVER HIM!
BUT, AT THAT MOMENT, A THUNDEROUS ERUPTION SHAKES THE TINY ISLE, AS A DEAFENING ROAR IS HEARD FROM BENEATH THE SURFACE!
RRRRR
THE ISLAND IS BREAKING APART!
LOOK!
AND THEN, BEFORE THE EYES OF ALL THOSE PRESENT, A TITANIC UNDER-SEA EXPLOSION HURLS A TOWERING SPRAY OF SEA, MUD AND STONE HIGH INTO THE AIR!
WHOOOM!
BACK TO THE DEPTHS, MY WARRIORS! WE HAVE WON! THE SEA ITSELF SHALL DESTROY OUR ENEMIES!
EVEN THE AVENGERS CANNOT SURVIVE A GIGANTIC UNDERSEA EARTHQUAKE! YET, FOR SOME REASON, MY HEART IS HEAVY! THEY WERE WORTHY FOES! THEY DESERVED A MORE FITTING END!
BUT, AS HE IS TO LATER LEARN, THE SUB-MARINER HAS ACTED TOO HASTILY! FOR IT IS NOT AN UNDER-SEA EARTHQUAKE WHICH HAS OCCURRED... IT IS MERELY THE BELOW-SURFACE LAUNCHING OF AN ALIEN SPACE SHIP...
AND, BY THE TIME THE STRANGE CRAFT EMERGES FROM THE DEEP, NAMOR AND HIS FOLLOWERS ARE ALREADY OUT OF SIGHT!
22

NOT UNTIL LATER WILL THE IRONY OF THE SITUATION DAWN UPON THE FRUSTRATED SEA PRINCE! FOR, THE VERY ALIEN HE HAD HOPED WOULD *DESTROY* THE AVENGERS, HAS UNWITTINGLY *RESCUED* THEM AT THE CRUCIAL MOMENT!

IT'S THE *ALIEN!* HE'S RETURNING TO THE STARS!

THE WATERS HAVE SUBSIDED! THE ISLAND IS STILL INTACT!

BUT NAMOR IS GONE--AND SO IS OUR CHANCE TO DEFEAT HIM!

EASY, LAD! IT'S ALL OVER! YOU'RE SAFE NOW!

I NOTICE IT TOOK A THREAT TO THE *BOY* TO BRING YOU INTO ACTION, FELLA!

THOUG NAMOR GONE, I WE SHA MEET AGAIN MORTAL BAT! BU OF US IS NOT PRES

I THOUGHT YOU'D *NEVER* NOTICE, BLUE-EYES!

I WAS DOING WHAT *ANY* GIRL WOULD DO IN A MOMENT OF CRISES--POWDERING MY NOSE, OF COURSE!

ONLY *ONE* THING PUZZLES ME --WHEN I WRITE THIS DOWN IN MY DIARY, DO I CALL IT A *VICTORY*-- OR A *DEFEAT??*

THAT'S FOR *HISTORY* TO DECIDE, HON! RIGHT NOW, WE'VE *ANOTHER* DE- CISION TO AWAIT...

RIGHT! WE HAVE AN *OFFER* TO PROPOSE TO CAPTAIN AMERICA!

I HAVE SEEN YOU IN --AND THERE ARE N BRAVER! IF YOUR O IS WHAT I *HOPE* I' MY ANSWER IS Y

SPOKEN WITH HONOR, AND WITH DIGNITY, LIKE A *MAN!*

THUS, WE ARE PRIVILEGED TO WIT- NESS A MOMENTOUS MOMENT IN THE ANNALS OF HIGH ADVENTURE...

WE WELCOME YOU, CAPTAIN AMERICA, TO THE RANKS OF-- *THE AVENGERS!*

23

BUT, THERE IS ONE WHOSE HEART IS STILL HEAVY-- STILL FILLED WITH A DREAD FEAR--

HE'S THE GREATEST GUY I EVER MET-- AND I CAN TELL HE WANTS ME TO BE HIS PARTNER! BUT WHAT ABOUT--THE *HULK??*

HE'S SURE TO RETURN *SOME DAY*... AND WHEN HE FINDS OUT THAT *CAPTAIN AMERICA* HAS REPLACED HIM-- WILL *ANYTHING* BE ABLE TO STOP HIM THEN??!

BUT, NOTHING IN LIFE IS CERTAIN! WE MUST TAKE THE GOOD AND THE AS FATE DEALS THEM OUT! *ONE* THIN CERTAIN, THOUGH--EACH ISSUE OF *THE AVENGERS* FEATURES PLENT SUPER-HEROES, SUPER-VILLAINS AND SUPER-THRILLS-- JUST AS Y WANT THEM!

THE E